KASHMĪR UNDER THE SULTĀNS

KASHMĪR UNDER THE SULTĀNS

MOHIBBUL HASAN

Kashmīr Under the Sultāns
Mohibbul Hasan

First Published 1959
Reprinted 2005
Reprinted 2018
Reprinted 2023
Reprinted 2026

ISBN 978-81-87879-49-7

Published by
AAKAR BOOKS
28 E Pocket IV, Mayur Vihar Phase I
Delhi 110 091, India
www.aakarbooks.com

Typeset at
Arpit Printographers, Delhi

Printed at
D.K. Fine Art Press, Delhi

To
The Memory of My Father

Preface

Adequate attention has been paid by scholars to ancient and early medieval Kashmīr. But the period from the fourteenth century onwards has not yet been the subject of any comprehensive study. The contributions of Newall, Kaul, and Kāk are very sketchy, and are based on slender evidence. The chapter on Kashmīr in the *Cambridge History of India* has more detail, but is based mainly on the Mughal sources, and concentrates only on political events. A more recent work is Ṣufī's *Kashmīr*, a history of Kashmīr from the ancient times to the present day. The scope of his work is so wide that it was not possible for him to utilise all original authorities. The few chapters that he has devoted to Kashmīr under the Sultans are brief, uncritical, and lacking in historical perspective.

In the present study I have attempted to reconstruct the history of Kashmīr from the foundation of the Sultanate till its conquest by Akbar. I have described not only the political events, but also the administrative institutions, the social and economic life, and the cultural activities of the period. I have based the account on the original sources; but unfortunately, in the case of Kashmīr of this period, shrewd observers like Abū'l Faẓl, Ibn Baṭṭūṭa, and Hiuen Tsiang are sadly wanting; and consequently there is a great paucity of details concerning the administrative system and the social and economic conditions. The extant Kashmīr chronicles are not only unconcerned with social and economic problems, they sometimes even ignore important political happenings. Such of the Ṣūfī works as exist are largely naive tales of miracles performed by the saint and his disciples; and it is with difficulty that one can pick out from them some telling fact relevant to historical investigation.

It remains for me to express my gratitude to Mr. M.K. Kidwāi, formerly Chief Secretary to the Jammu and Kashmīr Government, who not only provided me with research facilities, but also played host to me during my visit to Kashmīr in 1952. I am also greatly obliged to Mr. Asadu'llāh Kāẓmī, formerly Director of Research and Publication, Jammu and Kashmīr Government, and to Professor Hasan Shāh of Srīnagar for their constant and helpful interest in this work.

I am under deep obligation to various scholars who assisted me in a number of ways: to Dr. B.C. Sen and Dr. K.M. Ashraf for reading the manuscript and giving valuable suggestions; to Dr. A. B. M. Ḥabību'llāh for directing my attention to the need for a monograph on this period and for offering useful advice; to Dr. P.B. Chakravartī for translating the Sanskrit chronicles of Jonarāja, Śrīvara, Prājyabhaṭṭa, and Śuka into English for me; to Dr. Munību'r-Raḥmān who, in spite of his manifold activities, undertook the painful task of reading my proofs; to Dr. Maqbūl Aḥmad for drawing my attention to the Arab geographical works which contain brief references to Kashmīr; to Father V. Courtois for placing the valuable Gottwald Collection, St. Xavier's College, Calcutta, at my disposal; to Professors A. Rashīd and Nūru'l Ḥasan for obtaining for my use photostat copies of manuscripts from England; to Dr. Tāhir Riẓvī for his help in the preparation of the maps; to Mr. Arshad 'Alī Bēg for assisting me in the compilation of the index; and to Mr. Robert Vincent for seeing the book through the press.

I should also like to thank Messrs. B.S. Kesavan and Y.M. Mulay of the National Library, Calcutta; P.C. Bose of the Calcutta University Library; S. Chaudhri of the Asiatic Society Library, Calcutta; S. Bashīru'd-Dīn and Maẓaffar 'Alī of the Lytton Library, Aligarh Muslim University; and John Irwin of the Victoria and Albert Museum, London, for their unfailing help and kindness. Finally, I am much indebted to the Council of the Iran Society and its Secretary, Dr. M. Isḥāque, for undertaking the publication of this work; and to the authorities of the University of Calcutta for a generous grant which enabled me to obtain photostat copies of manuscripts from libraries abroad, and to visit Kashmīr in order to collect materials for this work.

Contents

List of Illustrations

MAPS

Abbreviations Used in Citing References to Sources[1]

A.A. : Abū'l Fazl, *Ā'īn-i-Akbarī.*

A.N. : ____ *Akbar-nāma.*

B.S. : *Bahāristān-i-Shāhī* Author not known. Quoted from the India Office and British Museum MSS.

B.N. : Bibliotheque Nationale, Paris.

Briggs : Brigs, J., *History of the rise of the Mahomedan power in India, till the year* 1612.

B.M. : British Museum.

Elliot : Elliot & Dawson, *History of India as told by its own Historians.*

Firishta : Firishta, *Ta'rīkh-i-Firishta.*

F.K. : 'Abdu'l Wahhāb. *Futūḥāt-i-Kubravīya.*

Ḥasan : Ḥasan b. 'Alī, *Ta'rīkh-i-Ḥasan.*

H.M. : Haidar Malik, *Ta'rīkh-i-Kashmir.*

I.A. : Indian Antiquary.

I.O. : India Office.

J.A.S.B. : Journal of the Asiatic Society, Calcutta.

J.I.H. : Journal of Indian History.

Jonar : Jonarāja, *Rājataraṅgiṇī,* tr. by J.C. Dutt into English as *Kings of Kashmīra.* Also quoted from the Calcutta and Bombay editions of the Sanskrit texts.

J.P.H.S. : Journal of the Punjab Historical Society.

J.R.A.S. : Journal of the Royal Asiatic Society. London.

Munich MS. : *Ta'rīkh-i-Kashmīr.* Author not known. K. Hof-Und Staatsbibliothek, Muenchen.

M.T. : Badā'unī, *Muntakhabu't-Tawārīkh.*

Nasīb : Baba Nasīb, *Tazkira-i-Mashā'ikh-i-Kashmīr.*

N.A. : Abā Raffī'u'd-Dīn Aḥmad, *Nawādiru'l-Akhbār.*
P.I.H.C. : Proceedings of the Indian History Congress.
Prāj. : Prājyabhaṭṭa, *Rājavalipatākā,* tr. by J. C. Dutt into English as *Kings of Kashmīra*. Also quoted from the Calcutta and Bombay editions of the Sanskrit texts.
R.P.D. : Research and Publication Department Library, Srīnagar.
S.A. : Sayyid 'Alī, *Ta'rīkh-i-Kashmīr.*
S.O.S. (Bulletin) : *Bulletin of the School of Oriental and African Studies,* University of London.
Śriv. : Śrīvara, *Jaina Rājataraṅgiṇī,* tr. by J.C. Dutt into English as *Kings of Kashmīra.* Also quoted from the Calcutta and Bombay editions of the Sanskrit texts.
Śuka : Śuka, *Rājataraṅgiṇī,* tr. by J.C. Dutt into English as *Kings of Kashmīra.* Also quoted from the Calcutta and Bombay editions of the Sanskrit texts.
Stein: Kalhaṇa, *Rājataraṅiṇī,* tr. by M.A. Stein.
T.A. : Niẓāmu'd-Dīn, *Tabaqāt-i-Akbarī.*
T.H. : Pīr Ḥasan Shāh, *Ta'rīkh-i-Hasan.*
T.R. : Mīrzā Haidar, *Ta'rīkh-i-Rashīdī,* tr. by Ross and Elias. Also quoted from the A.S.B. manuscript.
W.K. : Muḥammad'A'ẕam, *Wāqi'āt-i-Kashmīr.*

1. For details see the chapter on Sources and Appendix D containing the Bibliography.

Note on Transliteration

The system of transliteration followed is, with slight modifications, that adopted by the Royal Asiatic Society.

Arabic letter	Latin equivalent
ت	*t*
ث	*s̤*
ج	*ch* as in *church*
ح	*ḥ*
خ	*kh*
ج	*z̤*
ز	*z*
ظ	*s*
ش	*sh*
ص	*ṣ*
ض	*ẓ*
ظ	*ṭ*
ظ	*z̤*
ع	ʻ
غ	*gh*
ه	*h* where *h* in a final position represents the 'silent *h*', it is not transliterated, and the preceding vowel is written *a*.

Names of places are transliterated in their Persian form. Muslims bearing Hindu names are generally transliterated in the same manner. But *ṭ* in Baṭ should be pronounced as in the English word *talk*.

Tiles from the Tomb of Madanī
Dated 848/1444. Srī Partāp Museum, Srīnagar.

Introduction

For several reasons, the Sultanate period (1320–1586) is the most formative period in the history of Kashmir. First, the independent Muslim kingdom of Kashmir rested essentially on secular foundations as is evident from the sultans' exemplary respect for Hinduism and Buddhism. When it was suggested to Shihabuddin (1354–73) by his Hindu minister to melt the brass image of Buddha for coining it into money, the Sultan, according to Pandit Jonaraja, angrily remarked: "Past generations have set up images to obtain fame and even merit, and you propose to demolish them. Some have obtained renown by setting up images of gods, others by worshipping them, some by duly maintaining them, and some by demolishing them. How great is the enormity of such a deed?" Second, the sultans' matrimonial alliances with the neighbouring rajas did help create a general impression about their ability to win the confidence and good-will of non-Muslims for the stability of their kingdom. Third, the sultans placed great trust and confidence in the Brahmans by giving them key positions in the government. Conscious of their social position, they made them equal partners in government. What further fostered close ties between the government and the Brahmans was the sultans' attempt at understanding their religion not only empathetically but also through participation in their rituals and ceremonies. One more significant aspect of the Sultanate was the patronage extended by the Kashmiri rulers to Sufis, 'ulama, artisans and traders from Central Asia and Persia who brought about the Persian and Central Asian orientation of Islam and Islamic culture in the Valley. With Kashmir's gradual transition to Islam, the concept of Kashmiriyat emerged and flourished as a result of the social role of the Muslim Rishis. The Rishis had much in common with certain practices of ancient Buddhist and Saivite sages. Yet by adapting local traditions to Islam, the Rishis gave a unique orientation to Islam without distorting its essential requirement of adhering oneself to the Qur'an and the Sunnah in everyday life.

Viewed against the foregoing perspective, Professor Mohibbul Hasan's *Kashmir Under the Sultans* has an intrinsic merit of lucidly introducing a reader to a subject that begins with the foundation of the Sultanate and ends with the conquest of Kashmir by Akbar. True, the focus of the book is on political history. But its chief merit lies in encapsulating such political, social, economic and cultural activities of the period that exercised an indelible influence on Kashmir. During the Sultanate period, as Professor Hasan observes, Kashmir had achieved a high standard of culture, but with the disappearance of her independence, her culture gradually declined. Srinagar was denuded of poets, painters, and scholars, who had once adorned the courts of the Sultans, because, owing to the absence of local patronge, they were compelled to leave the Valley and seek their livelihood elsewhere. They entered the service of the Mughal emperors, and added to the brilliance of the court, thereby precipitating the cultural impoverishment of Kashmir.

Nothing indeed is more central to Kashmir's contemporary history than the question of historical identity and culture personality. Kashmiriyat may appear to be a vague appellation in linguistic terms as well as in several other respects. However, it needs to be understood in its historical perspective and also within the broader framework of the rich and unique cultural heritage of Kashmir. Both Lal Ded and her spiritual progeny, Shaikh Nuruddin Rishi, contributed a great deal to the evolution of the idea of Kashmiriyat. In fact, the Kashmiri mind began to develop and grow healthy with the birth of Kashmiri poetry during the Sultanate period. There is little doubt that the diffusion of the teachings of Islam at the grass root level took place through the medium of Kashmiri Sufi poetry and the folk songs.

Considering the useful insights of Prof. Mohibbul Hasan

into the political and cultural currents and cross-currents of Kashmir history, it is worthy of note that the Kashmiri mind of the present day is prepared to modify, even to reject much of the old, but in no case it is, prepared to repudiate totally the rich inheritance of the Sultanate period.

Therefore, the historical influences that have moulded the Kashmiris are apt to show amply the relevance of their unique individuality and that of the need for the statesmen of the subcontinent to recognize and understand the same with empathy.

October 20, 2004

Muhammad Ishaq Khan
Professor and Head
Department of History
Kashmir University

Chapter 1

Sources

Before attempting a survey of the extant sources for the Sultanate period of Kashmīr history, it is necessary to mention those contemporary authorities which have perished, for they were utilised by the later writers. The early Shāh Mīr period appears to have been devoid of all historical writings; and it was only from the reign of Sulṭān Zainu'l-'Ābidīn, which was characterised by great literary and artistic activity, that chronicles both in Sanskrit and in Persian began to be composed. Thus, Notthosoma Pandit described the life and achievements of Zainu'l-'Ābidīn in Kashmīrī and called his work *Jainacarita,* and Bodhabhaṭṭ wrote a play in Kashmīrī on the same theme.[1] Similarly Mullā Aḥmad and Mullā Nādirī, the Sulṭān's court poets, completed their histories of Kashmīr in Persian.[2] But unfortunately none of these chronicles is extant. Nor is there any trace of the histories composed by Qāzī Ibrāhīm in the second reign of Sulṭān Fatḥ Shāh and by Mullā Ḥasan Qārī in the time of the Chaks.[3] However, these accounts and those by Mullā Aḥmad and Nādirī were utilised extensively by Ḥaidar Malik, Ḥasan b. 'Alī, Muḥammad A'ẓam and other chroniclers.

We may divide the extant sources into five classes :

1. Contemporary Sanskrit. These consist of the four chronicles of Jonarāja. Śrīvara, Prājyabhaṭṭa and Śuka and another work commonly known as Kṣemendra's *Lokaprakāśa.* 2. Contemporary Persian. These may be further sub-divided into *(a)* Kashmīr Chronicles *(b)* General Histories of India *(c)* Mughal Histories *(d)* Central Asian Histories *(e)* Histories

of the Delhi Sultanate *(f)* Biographies of Saints. (3) Later Persian Works (4) Kashmīrī Literature and Folklore (5) European Accounts (6) Archaeological Evidence.

1. CONTEMPORARY SANSKRIT AUTHORITIES

Kalhaṇa, in his *Rājataraṅgiṇī* described the history of Kashmīr from the earliest times to 1149-50. Janarāja, two hundred years after him, continued the narrative down to the reign of Zainu'l-'Ābidīn and called it, like Kalhaṇa, *Rājataraṅgiṇī.* He was a scholar of Sanskrit and was attached to the court of Zainu'l-'Ābidīn, but he wrote his work under the orders of Siryabhaṭṭa, the superintendent of the courts of justice.[4] He was, according to Stein, a man of "considerable attainments though apparently without much originality".[5]

Jonarāja's *Rājataraṅgiṇī* is the earliest extant and most important source for the history of Kashmīr from 1150 to about 1459. It gives a brief but useful account of the social and political condition of Kashmīr from 1150 to the accession of Shāh Mīr, and thus helps us to understand the circumstances which led to the establishment of the Sultanate. It describes the reigns of the early Sulṭāns in a rather sketchy manner, passing over some of the important events like Riñchana's conversion to Islām and the arrival of Sayyid 'Alī Hamadānī in Kashmīr. However, the period from 1389 to 1459, during most of which the author himself lived, is treated in some detail. But being a courtier of Sulṭān Zainu'l-'Ābidīn, Jonarāja is inclined to exaggerate the virtues of his master and gloss over his failings. For the same reason he is prejudiced in favour of Sikandar, the Sultān's father, and places all the blame for the misfortunes of the latter's reign upon his minister Sūhabhaṭṭa, whose faults he greatly magnifies. His topography is on the whole reliable. He also records the dates of the accession and death of each ruler correctly though he rarely mentions the dates of important events within each reign, a defect that is common to all the chronicles of Kashmīr.

Jonarāja died in 1459; but after him his pupil Śrīvara continued the narrative from where he had left off, and called it *Jaina-Rājataraṅgiṇī*. Śrīvara was, like Jonarāja, attached to the court of Zainu'l-'Ābidīn, and after the latter's death served Ḥasan Shāh and Muḥammad Shāh. Besides being the author of this chronicle, he translated *Yūsuf u Zulaikhā* from Persian into Sanskrit and named it *Kathā-Kautaka*.[6] In addition to being a scholar, a poet and a historian, he was also a musician, and was in charge of a section of the music department in the reign of Hasan Shāh.[7]

Śrīvara's *Rājataraṅgṇī* gives a detailed account of the remaining years of Zainu'l-'Ābidīn's reign from 1459 to 1470 and of the reigns of his successors till the accession of Fatḥ Shāh in 1486. His work is, however, inferior to that of Jonarāja; and, as Stein observes, he "is a slavish imitator of Kalhaṇa, not above reproducing whole verses from his predecessor. His text looks, in great portion, more like a cento from the *Rājataraṅgiṇī*, than an original composition".[8] At the same time, since he wrote his chronicle partly, as he himself says, "to free myself from my endless obligations to him (Zainu'l-'Ābidīn), and partly because I am attracted by his merits,"[9] he is, like Jonarāja, inclined to exalt the virtues of Zainu'l-'Ābidīn and minimize his failings. But in spite of these defects, his work is very valuable, for it is the only contemporary source for the period it covers, and has, therefore, been drawn upon liberally by the later Persian chroniclers.

After the death of Śrīvara, Prājyabhaṭṭa composed his *Rājāvalipatākā*, describing the history of the period from 1486 to 1512. This work is much inferior to Śrīvara's. Its topography is very defective, and the chronology is incomplete. The history of the twenty-six years is described only in sixty-four *ślokas* and in a confused manner. The important events connected with the struggle for the throne between Muḥammad Shāh and Fatḥ Shāh are left out.

The last chronicle was written by Śuka Pandit, a pupil of Prājyabhaṭṭa, who named his work *Rājataraṅgīṇī* after that of Kalhaṇa, and dealt with the period from 1517 to 1596. His work is not as useful as those of Jonarāja and Śrīvara. His topography is incorrect; he supplies few dates, and the sequence of events is sometimes wrongly given. The second invasion and conquest of Kashmīr by Mīrzā Ḥaidar are barely mentioned. The struggle for power between 'Idī Raina and Daulat Chak is not referred to, while the history of the Chaks and the Mughal conquest of Kashmīr is described very briefly.

The *Lokaprakāśa* seems to have been written by a number of persons including Kṣemendra (d. 1066), who wrote only a portion of it.[10] The mention of Shāh Jahān in Book ii suggests that some parts were written as late as the seventeenth century.[11] It has been suggested by Buhler that it is a Kośa;[12] but actually it is a kind of a note-book in which all kinds of things have been collected together.[13] The work appears to be both a Kośa and a practical handbook dealing with the various aspects of life and administration in Kashmīr.[14] The language of the book is corrupt; its Sanskrit being mixed up with Persian and Kashmīrī words.

The *Lokaprakāśa* consists of four parts. In the first part the author gives the names of the four principal castes along with those of sixty sub-castes, and the titles of government officers and ministers.[15] The second part, which contains bills of exchange, bonds, commercial contracts, official orders and so forth, is the biggest and most important of all.[16] It has, however, no connection with Kṣemendra, and appears to have been written in the time of the Sulṭāns and in the seventeenth century. The third part does not deal with any single subject as is the case with the first and second parts, but consists of a hotchpotch of things. It gives a list of synonyms of different varieties of fishes, birds and mice, and of salt, gold ornaments and gold coins. It also contains verses from the *Mahābhārata* and satires on prostitutes and monks.[17] The fourth part begins with a satire on the Kāyasthas, that is writers and physicians and on Brahmans who had become Muslims. It also gives a list of the districts of Kashmīr.[18]

Thus the *Lokaprakāśa* contains useful material for the study of the social life and administration of Kashmīr. Its only drawback is that it is difficult to know exactly when the different sections were written. Professor A. Weber has published the extracts of the work in *Indische Studien*, XVIII, pp. 89–412, and it is this that I have utilised.

2. CONTEMPORARY PERSIAN AUTHORITIES

(a) Kashmīr Chronicles

With the exception of Sayyid 'Alī's *Ta'rīkh-i Kashmīr,* which was written in the reign of Yūsuf Shāh,[19] all the extant Persian chronicles of Kashmīr were composed after the Mughal conquest of the country. In spite of this they are very important and must be regarded as original sources, because their authors had passed their childhood and youth in the times of the later Shāh Mīrs and the Chaks, and wrote either from personal observation or utilised the accounts of earlier authorities which are not known to exist.

The *Ta'rīkh-i-Kashmīr* by Sayyid 'Alī is a history of Kashmīr to the time of Yūsuf Shāh. The author was a Baihaqī Sayyid, and was related to the Shāh Mīr family through his mother who was the sister of Sulṭān Nāzuk Shāh. His father's name was Sayyid Muḥammad, who served Mīrzā Ḥaidar in his wars in Kashmīr. Sayyid 'Alī also appears to have been in the service of Mīrzā Ḥaidar, and took part in the last campaign which led to the latter's death.

The manuscripts of Sayyid 'Alī's *Ta'rīkh* are very rare, but I have utilised the copy which has recently been acquired by the Research and Publication Department, Srīnagar. Unhappily, however, the manuscript is defective at the beginning, and so it is difficult to say from which period the work began with the history of Kashmīr. The existing manuscript abruptly commences with the arrival in Srīnagar in the reign of Shihābu'd-Dīn of Sayyid Tāju'd-Dīn, who was sent by Sayyid 'Alī Hamadānī to find out if the conditions were favourable for him to visit Kashmīr. It then gives the most fantastic account of the exploits of Sayyid Ḥasan, the son of Sayyid Tāju'd-Dīn, who had entered the service of Shihābu'd-Dīn. He is said to have conquered not only Delhi, Āgra, and Lahore, but also Persia, Badakhshān, Kābul, and many other places outside India. The work next describes the part played by Sayyid 'Alī Hamadānī and his son Sayyid Muḥammad in spreading Islām in the Valley, and their relations with Quṭbu'd-Dīn and Sikandar respectively. It also throws light on the policy of Sikandar towards his non-Muslim subjects, but it does not refer to the political events of his reign. However, the history of Zainu'l-'Ābidīn and Ḥasan Shāh is described in some detail, although Ḥaidar Shāh's reign and the civil war between Muḥammad Shāh and Fatḥ Shāh is dismissed only in a few lines. But perhaps the most valuable portion of the book is that which deals with Mīrzā Ḥaidar's career in Kashmīr, for the author relates the events on the basis of personal observation. As regards the Chak period, with the exception of the controversy over the execution of Yūsuf Aindar which is briefly given, it is practically passed over. The remaining part, covering over one-third of the book, contains biographical sketches of the Sūfīs and Rishīs who flourished during the Sultanate period. The work is thus valuable for the religious history of the period. For the political history it is important because it is the earliest Persian chronicle of Kashmīr known to exist, and is based on Qāẓī Ibrāhīm's *Ta'rīkh-i-Kashmīr* and other works which are lost. But its chief merit is due to the fact that it contains an eye-witness account of Mīrzā Ḥaidar's rule in Kashmīr and the manner of his death. The work is not of much value from the point of view of chronology and topography.

The *Ta'rīkh-i-Kashmīr* by an anonymous writer is a history of Kashmīr from the earliest times to the reign of Shamsu'd-Dīn II. Based on the Sanskrit chronicles and earlier Persian accounts, it is one of the earliest extant histories of Kashmīr in Persian, being written in 1590 and not in 1629 as mentioned in the catalogue by Aumer. The work does not give any chronology except for the reigns of Muḥammad Shāh and Fatḥ Shāh, and for Mīrzā Ḥaidar's first invasion of Kashmīr. It also does not mention the arrival of Sayyid 'Alī Hamadānī in the Valley, although it was such an important event in the country's social and religious history. Moreover, the account of the period following Ḥaidar Shāh's death is very confused and unreliable. Nevertheless, the work is a useful source, for it describes those events in detail which have been omitted by the *Bahāristān-i Shāhī,* Ḥaidar Malik's *Ta'rīkh,* and other Persian chronicles. I have consulted the MS. belonging to the K. Hof—und

Staatsbibliothek in Muenchen. No other copy of the work, so far as I know, is extant.

The *Bahāristān-i-Shāhī* by an unknown writer is really a history of Kashmīr from the accession of Riñchana to 1614, the pre-Islamic period being dismissed only in a few pages. Nothing is known of the author except that he was a Shī'ite, and was probably in the service of the Baihaqī Sayyids for he describes their careers in greater detail than other chroniclers do, and is almost fulsome in his adulation of their piety, courage, and generosity. The sources for his history are the Sanskrit chronicles of Jonarāja and Śrīvara as well as the Persian accounts of Mullā Aḥmad, Mullā Nādirī, Qāẓī Ibrāhīm, and Ḥasan Qārī. For the later Shāh Mīr and the Chak periods he wrote from personal experience or on the basis of information he gathered from the older people.

The *Bahāristān-i-Shāhī* is written in an ornate and verbose style. It gives occasionally the *Laukika* dates along with the *Hijra* dates. The history of the Shāh Mīrs up to the reign of Ḥasan Shāh is briefly narrated, and important events like the revolt in Lohara against Quṭbu'd-Dīn, the Regency of Queen Sūra and the civil war during the reign of Zainu'l-'Ābidīn are omitted. Sulṭān Ḥaidar Shāh is dismissed in a few lines, while there is no mention of the political events of Ḥasan Shāh's reign. The period from Muḥammad Shāh onwards is, however, treated in detail. The history of the Mughal conquest of Kashmīr is also exhaustively given, and is a useful supplement to and check upon the Mughal accounts. Moreover, this is the only work which relates in detail the life of Yūsuf Shāh and Ya'qūb Shāh in exile and the manner of their death. Thus, in spite of its defects, the *Bahāristān-i-Shāhī* is a very important source.

The *Ta'rīkh-i-Kashmīr* by Ḥasan b. 'Alī Kashmīrī is a short history of Kashmīr from the earliest times to 1616, written at the request of Jalālu'd-Dīn Malik Muḥammad Nājī[20], who was anxious to preserve a record of the achievements of his ancestors. Ḥasan b. 'Alī's sources are the same as those of the author of the *Bahāristān*. His account also suffers from the same limitations as does the *Bahāristān*. In addition he omits altogether the history of the later Shāh Mīrs and the Chaks, and makes only a casual reference to Ya'qūb Shāh's submission to Akbar. He, however, gives a detailed history of the Sultanate period up to the end of Ḥasan Shāh's reign; and it is for this period that his history is valuable.

The most well-known Persian history of Kashmīr is that of Ḥaidar Malik, the son of Ḥasan Malik of Chādura, which was the family's hereditary seat. He descended from Rāmachandra, the commander-in-chief of Sūhadeva, and his family played an important part during the Sultanate period. He himself served Yūsuf Khān Chak, the son of Ḥusain Shāh, for twenty-four years, and accompanied him in his exile to India after the Mughal conquest of Kashmīr. He fought side by side with Yūsuf Khān, who was employed by Akbar to crush the refractory chiefs. When Jahāngīr became emperor he granted Yūsuf Khān a jāgīr in Bengal and sent him with Quṭbu'd-Dīn to suppress Shēr Afgan. After the latter was killed, Ḥaidar Malik gave protection in his own house to Shēr Afgan's wife Mihru'n-Nisa', the future Nūr Jahān. When Yūsuf Khān died Ḥaidar Malik entered the service of Jahāngīr, who conferred upon him the titles of *Chaghatāy* and *Ra'īsu'l-Mulk*.

Ḥaidar Malik began writing his *Ta'rīkh-i-Kashmīr* in 1618 and completed it in 1030/1620–21. A study of this work, of the *Bahāristān-i-Shāhī,* and of Ḥasan b. 'Alī's chronicle shows that their authors obtained information from the same sources. But in addition, Ḥaidar Malik records many of the old traditions preserved in this own family. So far as the Chak period is concerned Ḥaidar Malik was himself a witness to many events, being a young man at the time, though he does not mention the part he played in them. He writes in a simple lucid style; his topography is correct, though his chronology is not reliable. Just as the author of the *Bahāristān* exalts the achievements of the Baihaqī Sayyids, so does Ḥaidar Malik eulogise the wisdom and courage of his grandfather, Malik Muḥammad Nājī. He was a Shī'ite, but he writes dispassionately and freely criticises Ya'qūb Shāh for his intolerant policy towards the Sunnīs. His account of the reign of the Chak Sulṭāns, particularly of their attempts to repel the Mughal invasion, is detailed and valuable. Unfortunately he does not describe the life of Yūsuf Shāh and

Ya'qūb Shān in captivity or of their last days.

Of the three manuscripts of Ḥaidar Malik's *Ta'rīkh* that I have consulted, the India Office copy gives the most detailed account of the Shāh Mīr and Chak dynasties. The copy in the Research and Publication Department, Srīnagar, is only an abridgement, while the copy in the Bibliotheque Nationale, Paris, is an abridged redaction, and sometimes differs in chronology and factual details from the other manuscripts.

(b) General Histories of India

The *Ṭabaqāt-i-Akbarī* by Niẓāmu'd-Din[21] contains a section dealing with the history of Kashmīr from the earliest times to its conquest by Akbar. Niẓāmu'd-Dīn based his account on two sources: The *Ta'rīkh-i-Rashīdī* by Mīrzā Ḥaidar and the *Ta'rikh-i-Kashmīr*. But who is the author of the latter work, he does not say. Moreover, since his account of Kashmīr forms part of his general history of the provinces of the Mughal Empire, it is not detailed. His chronology is also defective and it is not always possible to identify the names of persons and places mentioned in his work.

The *Ta'rīkh-i-Firishta* by Muḥammad Qāsim Hindu Shāh Astrabādī known as Firishta also contains a chapter on Kashmīr. But it mostly follows the *Ṭabaqāt-i-Akbarī,* and has little new information to offer. The description of the agriculture, religion and buildings of Kashmīr is based on the *Ta'rīkh-i-Rashidi.*

The *Muntakhabu't-Tawārīkh* by 'Abdu'l-Qādir Badā'ūnī does not deal separately with Kashmīr, but refers to it in connection with the account of Akbar's reign. The work furnishes useful information about Akbar's relations with the Chak rulers. There are also occasional references to eminent saints and literary figures of Kashmīr.

The *Ma'āṣir-i-Raḥīmī* by Khwāja 'Abdu'l-Bāqī Nihāwandi completed in 1616 is a life of 'Abdu'r-Raḥīm Khān-i-Khānān, but it also contains a section on the history of Kashmīr. It is, however, based on the *Ṭabaqāt-i-Akbarī* and does not add to our knowledge.

The *Majālisu'l-Salāṭīn* by Muḥammad Sharīf an-Najafī completed in 1628-29 is a brief history of India. A portion of the work gives a detailed account of Riñchana's conversion to Islām. I have consulted Br. Mus Add. 30,779 which is an English translation of the extracts relating to Kashmīr.

The *Haft Iqlīm* by Amīn Aḥmad Rāzī is a geographical encyclopaedia completed in 1594. It gives a brief account of Mīrzā Ḥaidar's conquest of Kashmīr, and makes short notices of some Kashmīrī poets, saints and rulers. There is also a reference to the shawl industry of the Valley.

(c) Mughal Histories

The *Akbar-nāma* by Abū'l-Faẓl makes a brief but useful reference to Mīrzā Ḥaidar's rule in Kashmīr. He, however, describes in detail the invasions of Kashmīr by Abū'l-Ma'ālī and Qarā Bahādur, the relations of the Mughals with the Chaks, and the final conquest of the Valley by Akbar. His chronology and topography are correct, and, barring a few lapses, his account is generally truthful. His *Ā'īn-i-Akbarī* is an important authority because of the light it throws on the topography of the Valley and the life of the inhabitants.

The *Tuzuk-i-Jahāngīrī* by the emperor Jahāngīr contains useful references to the history, habits and customs of the people of Kashmīr.

(d) Central Asian Histories

The *Ẓafar-nāma* by Sharafu'd-Dīn 'Alī Yazdī is a history of Tīmūr and Khalīl Sulṭān completed in 1424-25. It throws light on Sikandar's relations with Tīmūr when the latter invaded India. It also gives a brief description of the geography and people of Kashmīr. Similarly in the *Malfūẓāt-i-Tīmūrī,* which is said to have been written by Tīmūr himself, there are references to his relations with Sulṭān Sikandar and to the topography of the Valley.

The *Ta'rīkh-i-Rashīdī* by Mīrzā Ḥaidar Dughlat, a cousin of Bābur from his mother's side, is a history of the Mongol rulers of Mughalistān and Kāshghar, completed in 1546. Mīrzā Ḥaidar twice invaded Kashmīr : once from Kāshghar in the early part of 1533, and again from Lahore in November 1540 when he conquered the Valley and ruled for ten years. He describes his first invasion in detail, but the account of the second invasion and of his administration of Kashmīr is very meagre. He, however, gives an interesting picture of the buildings, agriculture, religion and arts and crafts of Kashmīr as he found them. It was unfortunate that his life was cut short by the rebellion of the Kashmīrī nobles, otherwise he might have left us a more valuable account of Kashmīr.

(e) Histories of the Delhi Sultanate

Although Kashmīr had cultural, commercial and political relations with India during medieval times, yet the chronicles of the Delhi Sultanate very rarely make any reference to them. The *Ta'rikhi-i-Mubārak Shāhī* by Yaḥyā b. Aḥmad b. 'Abdu'llāh Sirhindī only mentions the conflict between 'Alī Shāh of Kashmīr and Jasrat Khokar. *Ta'rīkh-i-Dā'ūdī* and *Ta'rīkh-i-Khān-i-Jahānī* describe A'ẓam Humāyūn's relations with Mīrzā Ḥaidar and the Kashmīr nobles at the time of his revolt against Islām Shāh. But they wrongly state that A'ẓam Humāyūn was killed in an engagement with the Kashmīrī forces while Mīrzā Ḥaidar was still alive. Moreover, they do not throw any light on the relations between the Kashmīrī nobles and Shēr Shāh.

(f) Biographies of Saints

The *Khulāṣatu'l-Manāqib*[22] is a life of Sayyid 'Alī Hamadānī by Nūru'd-Din Ja'far Badakhshī, one of his disciples. But the work does not refer to any of the activities of the Sayyid in Kashmīr. The MS. of the work I have consulted was originally in the Berlin Library, but since the last World War it has been in the Tubingen University Library, the Librarian of which very kindly sent me a photostat copy. Another work by Ja'far Badakhshī, which contains a life of Sayyid 'Alī Hamadānī, is *Manqabatu'l-Jawāhir* written in about 1378.

Tuḥfatu'l-Aḥbāb, written about the middle of the fifteenth century, is a life of Mīr Shamsu'd-Dīn who introduced the Nūrbakhshīya teachings into Kashmīr. The author's name is not known but his father was an important disciple of Shamsu'd-Dīn and he himself was a fanatical Nūrbakhshīya. He was a child when Shamsu'd-Dīn arrived in the Valley, but he grew up in close association with him. He gives a detailed account of how Shamsu'd-Dīn came to the Valley, the obstacles he encountered in propagating his faith, and the success that attended him in Kashmīr and Baltistān. However, in his zeal to represent the saint as the champion of Islām he is in the habit of indulging in imaginary accounts of his iconoclastic activities. Nevertheless, his work is valuable because it contains the history of Islām's progress in Kashmīr, brief notices of Kashmīr's political history, and of the social life and beliefs of its inhabitants. The copy of the MS. I have consulted is in the private collection of Āghā Sayyid Muḥammad Yūsuf, the Shī'ite *Mujtahid* of Kashmīr, who is a descendant of Mīr Shamsu'd-Dīn. He very kindly placed the work at my disposal during my visit to Kashmīr in the summer of 1952. I was told by the Āghā Sāheb that there is another copy of the MS. in the possession of his relations who are at Skārdu.

The *Hilyatu'l-'Ārifin* is a biography of Shaikh Ḥamza Makhdūm by Khwāja Isḥāq Qārī, his disciple. Although the work is mostly concerned with the miracles performed by the Shaikh, it throws some light on the social conditions in the Valley. The *Tazkiratu'l-'Ārifīn* by Mullā 'Alī Raina completed in 1587 is another biography of Shaikh Ḥamza which is useful for the study of the social and religious life of the period.

The *Majālisu'l-Mū'minīn* by Sayyid Nūru'llāh Shushtarī, which contains biographical notes on eminent Shī'ites, gives a short account of the lives of Sayyid 'Alī Hamadānī and Muḥammad Nūrbakhsh, and briefly mentions how the teachings of the latter were introduced into Kashmīr and Baltistān.

3. LATER PERSIAN WORKS

(a) Kashmīr Chronicles

The *Ta'rīkh-i-Kashmīr* by Nārāyan Kaul 'Ājiz, a Kashmīrī Brahman, is a history of Kashmīr from the earliest times to 1710, the year it was completed. As it is only an abridgement of Ḥaidar Malik's chronicle, it does not contain any new information.

The *Nawādiru'l-Akhbār* by Abā Rafī'u'd-Dīn Aḥmad is a history of Kashmīr completed at Shāhjahānābād in 1723. The author's ancestors came from Balkh but he was himself a Kashmīrī by birth. His work deals with the Hindu period very briefly, but describes the history of the Sulṭāns in detail. It closely agrees with the *Bahāristān-i-Shāhī* and Ḥaidar Malik's history, but supplies additional information regarding the improvements effected by Mīrzā Ḥaidar in Kashmīr, and also contains more details, though not always correct, regarding the attitude of the Sulṭāns towards the non-Muslims. Its chronology is however incorrect; it confuses Yūsuf Shāh Chak with Yūsuf Khān, the son of Ḥusain Shāh, and its account of the life of Yūsuf Shāh and Ya'qūb Shāh, whom it always calls Ya'qūb Khān, is not reliable. The importance of the work is that it preserves the Sunnī traditions of the Valley, though it makes the mistake of over-estimating the influence of the religious factor in the civil wars.

The *Wāqi'at-i-Kashmīr* by Muḥammad A'ẓam was completed in 1747. It is an abridgement of the earlier works. But in addition to the political history it contains a useful account of the saints and scholars who flourished in Kashmīr during the Sultanate period.

The *Gauhar-i-Ālam* by a Badī'u'-d-Dīn Abu'l-Qāsim is a history of Kashmīr from the earliest times to 1789. The author claims to have consulted the *Nūr-nāma* and the accounts by Ḥasan Qārī and Muḥammad A'ẓam. But he does not bring to light any new facts. His style is cumbersome and ornate, and he occasionally makes statements which are not supported by any authority.

The *Ḥashmat-i-Kashmīr* by 'Abdu'l-Qādir Khān completed at Banaras in 1850 is a history of Kashmīr based mainly on the *Gauhar-i-'Ālam.* It also contains brief notices on Tibet, Badakhshān, and the neighbouring countries. Besides the *Ḥashmat-i-Kashmīr* there were many other works written in the nineteenth century.[23] But with the exception of the *Ta'rīkh-i-Ḥasan* by Pīr Ḥasan Shāh (d. 1898) none of them is important, all being abridgements of Ḥaidar Malik's history. The *Ta'rikh-i-Ḥasan* consists of four parts. The first deals with the geography of Kashmīr, its Muslim monuments, its castes, tribes and religious sects. The second describes the history of Kashmīr from the earliest times to the author's own days. The Hindu period is based upon Kalhaṇa's *Rājataraṅgiṇī,* the section on the Sulṭāns has been drawn mainly from the *Bahāristān-i-Shahī,* though works of Ḥaidar Malik, Niẕāmu'd-Dīn, Abū'l-Faẓl and others have been consulted. The third part contains the biographies of saints based on *Taẕkiras* and local traditions. The last part is chiefly concerned with Persian poetry as it flourished under the Sulṭāns and the Mughal Emperors. All the volumes are useful, and are written in a clear, simple, lucid style.

(b) Mughal and Provincial Histories

Among the later Mughal histories none is important for our study except the *Ma'āṣiru'l-Umarā'* by Ṣamṣāmu'd-Daula, which contains brief notices of the invasions of Kashmīr by Mīrzā Ḥaidar and Abū'l-Ma'ālī, and of its final conquest by Akbar. Of the provincial histories mention may be made only of three; the *Aḥwāl-i-Kishtwār* written in 1882-83; the *Ta'rīkh-i-Rājgān-i-Jammu* or *Rājdarshanī* composed in 1847; and *Ta'rīkh-i-Rājgān-i-Rajaurī* published in 1907. All these works make occasional references to the Valley; but since most of their accounts are legendary, they are not of much historical importance. It is strange that although Jammu, Kishtwār and Rajaurī were for long periods subject to the authority of the Sulṭāns of Kashmīr, these chronicles completely ignore this fact.

(c) Biographies of Saints

The *Taẕkira-i-Mashā'ikh-i-Kashmir* by Bābā Nasīb relates the part played by Nūru'd-Dīn Rishī and his disciples in spreading Islām in the Valley, and gives interesting accounts of religious discussions between the Brahman priests and Muslim saints. Another work known as the *Majmū'a dar Ansāb Mashā'ikh-i-Kashmīr* gives a short account of how Islām spread in the Valley from the time of Riñchana to that of Mūsā Raina, with useful sidelights on the political events of this period. The *Futūḥāt-i-Kubravīya* written by 'Abdu'l-Wahhāb in 1749 describes the progress of Islām in Kashmīr from the time of Riñchana to that of Akbar. In addition it contains a brief history of the Sulṭāns of Kashmīr and short sketches of the lives of Sayyid 'Alī Hamadānī, his son Muḥammad Hamadānī, and other saints of the Valley. Other *Tazkiras* which contain occasional historical notes and references to social life are the *Asrāru'l-Abrār* by Dā'ūd Mishkātī written in 1653; the *Khawāriqu'l-Sālikīn* known as *Ta'rīkh-i-Hādi* written in 1667-98; *Nūr-nāma*, a life of Nūru'd-Dīn Rishī by Bābā Nasību'd-Dīn Ghāzī composed in 1630-31; and the *Ta'rīkh-i-Kabīr* by Mu'īnu'd-Dīn Miskīn published in 1904.

4. KASHMIRI LITERATURE AND FOLKLORE

Medieval Kashmīr was rich in Kashmīrī poetic literature, but unfortunately only a small portion of it has come down to us. The songs of Lallā Ded have been collected and translated by Barnett and Grierson; a few mystical verses of Nūru'd-Dīn Rishī and the lyrics of Habba Khātūn have been edited by J.L. Kaul. They throw some light on the social and cultural life of medieval Kashmīr. The folklores and traditions of the Valley collected by Lawrence, Knowles, Grierson and many European travellers also give us a glimpse of the manners and customs of the inhabitants.

5. EUROPEAN ACCOUNTS

No European ever visited Kashmīr during the time of the Shāh Mīr and Chak rulers. The first Europeans to set foot on Kashmīr soil were Father Jerome Xavier and Benedict de Goes who arrived in the company of Akbar in 1597. They have left an account of their impressions which, though useful, are very sketchy. The description of Kashmīr by Francisco Pelsaert is also very brief. But Bernier, who visited the Valley with Aurangzēb, relates in detail the social and economic life of the people. The description of Father Desideri is useful as it furnishes information about the trade of Kashmīr, while the account of Father Fryre is important for the light it throws on the social life of the people. The accounts of European travellers, who visited Kashmīr in the eighteenth and nineteenth centuries, are valuable because they contain earlier traditions of the country, and help us in identifying some of the old localities which have either disappeared or changed their names.

6. ARCHAEOLOGICAL EVIDENCE

The archaeological evidence for this period is very scanty. The coins which have been found furnish us only with the names and titles of the Sulṭāns, but they are not of much chronological importance. On the other hand, the architectural remains are too few; most of the palaces, mosques, and *khānqāhs* erected by the Sulṭāns having been destroyed in the course of civil wars and foreign invasions. With the exception of the Mazār-i-Salāṭīn and the tomb and mosque of Madanī, which are in a very bad state of preservation, the other monuments that we see today have either been rebuilt or renovated in later times. The few inscriptions that have been discovered do not substantially add to our historical knowledge.

NOTES

1. Śrīv., Bk. i, chap, v, Nos. 37 sq.; Munich, f. 72b.
2. These works have been referred to in all the Persian histories of Kashmīr. T.H., i, f. 152a, also refers to other works like the *Ta'rīkh-i-Qāẓī Ḥamīd* and *Muntakhabu't-Iawārīkh* by Ḥasan Bēg.
3. Qārī's chronicle is no longer extant. Crawford, *Bibliotheca Lindesiana,* wrongly considers MS. No. 518 to be Qārī's work. Actually it is A'ẓam's *Wāqi'āt-i-Kashmīr,* and Qārī's name has been mentioned in the MS. (f. 4b) only as an authority. Storey, on the other hand, makes the mistake of regarding it as Hasan b. 'Alī's chronicle.
4. Jonar., (Bo, ed.), No. 11.
5. Stein, ii, 373.
6. Ṣūfī, *Kashīr,* i, 167.
7. Śrīv., p. 231.
8. Stein, ii, 373.
9. Śrīv., p. 99.
10. *Indische Studien,* xviii, 298, 300.

11. *Ibid.*, 337, 341.
12. *Ibid.*, 292.
13. *Ibid.*, 292–3.
14. Stein, ii, 376.
15. *Indische Studien*, xviii, 302 sqq.
16. *Ibid.*, 342 sqq.
17. *Ibid.*, 348 sqq.
18. *Ibid.*, 369 sqq.
19. Ṣūfī, i, p. x1, says that the work was written in Muḥammad Shāh's first reign, but this is incorrect, for it gives the names of Muḥammad Shāh's successors and of all the Chak rulers up to Yūsuf Shāh. The MS. does not bear any date of its composition, but from the absence of the names of Sayyid Mubārak and Lohar Shāh it appears that it was completed early in 1579 during Yūsuf Shāh's first reign, which lasted for about two months.
20. He is evidently Ḥaidar Malik's grandfather. In Ḥaidar Malik's chronicle he is styled as Kamālu'd-Dīn. But in the present work (f. 3a) he is called Jalālu'd-Dīn. This is probably due to a mistake of the copyist.
21. Baini Prasad says in his translation of T.A., iii, p. XXX, that the *Ta'rīkh-i-Kashmīr* which Niẓāmu'd-Dīn consulted was the Persian translation of the *Rājataraṅgiṇi.* But this is only half the truth. Niẓāmu'd-Dīn must have also consulted, in addition, the Persian chronicles, for his chronology and some of his details do not agree with the Sanskrit chronicles. Moreover, for the period of the later Shāh Mīrs and the Chaks some Persian chronicle was necessary, because Śuka wrote in 1596, and the author of T.A. could not have utilised his work. From a close study of both T.A. and the Munich MS., it appears that Niẓāmu'd-Dīn drew extensively from the later chronicle.
22. There are other works besides which throw light on 'Alī Hamadānī's life. Some of them have been discussed in this chapter, while others have been mentioned in the Bibliography. For more details see *Yaghmā*, iv, No. 8, pp. 337 sqq; and *Journal Asiatique,* ccxl, pp. 53.
23. Storey, *Bibliographical Survey of Persian Literature,* section ii, Fasc. 3, pp. 684–7, gives the names of many such works. But all of them are mere summaries of Ḥaidar Malik's *Ta'rīkh.*

Chapter 2

The Geography of Kashmīr

The influence of geography on the social and political history of Kashmīr has been very profound. The rivers and springs, soil and climate of the Valley have all played an important part in shaping the character and life of its people throughout the centuries. But none of the natural features have exerted a more direct influence on the history of the country than the great mountain ramparts that encircle it.[1] It is to these mountains that the Valley owes its rivers and its streams, its rains and the fertility of its soil, and even its floods and famines. It is also to them that it owed not only immunity from foreign invasions for long periods, but also "a historical existence of marked individuality".[2]

Extent and Boundary

Kashmīr is situated in the Western Himālayas at an average height of 6,000 ft. above the sea. It resembles a great irregular oval consisting of a similarly shaped level value in the centre with a ring of mountains around it. The flat part of the country measures about eighty-four miles in length from the south-west to north-east, while its width varies from twenty to twenty-five miles. Its area has been estimated at 1,800 or 1,900 sq. miles. It is surrounded by an unbroken ring of high mountains, and, reckoned from the summit lines of these ranges, the length of the irregular oval enclosed by them is 116 miles, with a width varying from forty-five to seventy-five miles. The whole area within the mountains has been estimated at about 3,900 sq. miles.

The mountains surrounding Kashmīr consist of three main ranges. The most important of these is the Pīr Panjāl Range which, with a width of fifty to sixty miles, forms the southern and south-western boundary of the Valley. It begins from the southernmost part of the country where the Bānihāl Pass, 9,200 ft. above the sea, marks the lowest depression in the chain of mountains. After running for about thirty miles from east to west, the range turns to the north-northwest. In this direction it continues for about fifty miles more, and, after attaining its greatest elevation in the Tatakūtī Peak (15,524 ft.) it gradually descends towards the Jehlam Valley.

The boundary of the Valley in the north-east is formed by the main Central Himālayan range, which separates the Jehlam and the Indus drainage. The eastern boundary is formed by a high spur of this range which branches at about ten miles east-south-west from the Zōjī-Lā Pass, and runs due south, its peaks maintaining an elevation of from 12,000 to 14,000 ft. It thus forms the watershed between the Jehlam and the Chināb, and separates Kashmīr from the Maru-Wardwan Valley. The range then turns to the north-west, and joins the Pīr Panjāl Range at the Bānihāl Pass.

The mountains which enclose the Kashmīr Valley in the north and north-west, may be looked upon as one great range. A few miles west of the spot from which the eastern boundary spur branches near the Zōjī-Lā, another minor range branches off. This runs due west for about 100 miles at an elevation of from 1,200 to 1,300 ft. with a breadth varying from twelve to twenty-four miles, and forms the northern boundary of the Valley, separating the Jehlam on the south from its important tributary, the Kishangangā on the north. After reaching 75° 15' E, the ridge gradually curves round to the south until it joins the Kājnāg Peak, north-west of Bārāmūla[3], thus forming the north-western boundary of the Valley. The mountain-ring, which surrounds the Valley, has only one gap. This is the narrow gorge at Bārāmūla through which the Jehlam escapes to the plains of the Punjāb, and thence to the sea.

The natural boundaries of the Valley agree closely with its frontiers. But to have a more precise idea about the extent of the country, it will be useful if we take a brief notice of the territories that surround it.

To the south-east lies the Valley of Kishtwār on the upper Chināb. Its rulers had matrimonial relations with the Sulṭāns of Kashmīr, and were usually subject to them. Lower down on the Chināb is the district of Bhadravāh. South of the Pīr Panjāl Range there were small hill-states, which were inhabited by the "unruly Khaśas" and were tributary to Kashmīr. To the south-west was the important hill-state of Rajaurī, comprising the valleys drained by the Tohī and its tributaries. On the north-west of Rajaurī lay the kingdom of Pūnch, and to the north-west of Pūnch was the Jehlam Valley. This was held in olden times as an outlying frontier district of Kashmīr, as far as Buliāsa. Further to the west lay the district of Pakhlī.[4] To the north-west of the Kashmīr Valley was situated the tract known as Karnāv. Its inhabitants were Kaśas, and their chiefs acknowledged the suzerainty of strong Kashmīr rulers. To the north lies the valley of Kishangangā inhabited by the Dard tribes.[5] To the east lies Baltistān and Ladākh inhabited by the people of Tibetan race. Further south along the range on the east of the Valley in situated a long narrow valley known as Maru-Wardwan.

Topography

The Kashmīr Valley is divided into two parts. One comprises the plain formed by the alluvium of the Jehlam and its main tributaries; the other consists of the plateaus or *karēwas* elevated above the plain.

The Jehlam, which forms the main arterial drainage system for the Valley's lakes and rivers and of the inner slopes of the mountains, is first formed by the meeting of several streams like the Sāndran, the Bring, the Ārapath and the Lidar which drain the south-eastern portion of the Valley. This meeting takes place in the plain close to Anantnāg.[6] At Khanabal[7] the Jehlam becomes navigable and continues so up to Bārāmūla, a distance of 102 miles, thus forming the most important highway of Kashmīr. At Khanabal also begins the great plain which stretches on both sides of the river as far as Bārāmūla. In its winding course the Jehlam receives many streams. But just before reaching Srīnagar, it is formed by a stream which drains the lake called Dal to the east of the city. The surplus waters of the lake flow out towards the Jehlam by a canal which is now called Chūnth Kul but which in ancient times bore the name of Mahāsarit.[8]

A large stream called Dūdgangā, made up by the waters of several streams that drain the south-western mountains, joins the Jehlam on the left bank at the city of Srīnagar. Immediately below Srīnagar, we come to the marshes which stretch along both sides of the river for a considerable distance. The marshes to the north of the river are more extensive and belong to the delta of the Sind river, the greatest tributary of the Jehlam within the Valley, which originates near the Zōjī-Lā and Amburnāth Peak. It has a course of over sixty miles and drains the mountain range in the north. The valley of the Sind, called after its name, forms the district of Lār, one of the main sub-divisions of the Valley in the north. The Sind river joins the Jehlam near the village of Shādipur.[9] The Jehlam continues on in a north-westerly direction until it joins the Volur lake. It then flows out from the lake at the south-west corner. It receives many streams in its course up to Bārāmūla, but the chief one among them being the Pohur stream which drains the Lōlāb Valley, and enters the main river at Dubgām, about four miles below the town of Sōpūr.[10] The river goes on winding through a flat country like that above Srīnagar until it reaches Bārāmūla, where the gorge begins. After this there is no further possibility of navigation. In its course from Khanabal to the Volur lake the fall of the river is 165 ft., in the first thirty miles, and 55 ft. in the next twenty-four miles. But from the Volur to Bārāmūla the fall is very slight.

In ordinary times the Jehlam flows gently between its high banks, but in times of flood, it not only overflows its natural banks, it even overtops the artificial embankments constructed on either side of the river. As a result crops are damaged, houses are destroyed, lives are lost. The loss caused by the floods is always considerable below Srīnagar as the fall of the country is slight, and the flood water remains on the land rotting the crops.

But above Srīnagar, owing to the slope of the country, the flood water escapes quickly, and so the crops are often damaged.

Kashmīr abounds in lovely lakes and springs. Of the latter the Volur and the Dal are the most important. The Volur is the largest fresh water lake in India, being about twelve and a half miles by five in extent. It is fed by several streams, while from the south the Jehlam seeks a passage through it. Its shores are ill-defined, and it consists of miles of marshlands with reeds growing, and when the floods come its water spreads over many miles of the country. The boatmen of Kashmīr look upon it with apprehension even in normal times, for the quiet surface of the lake changes into a sea of rolling waves, most dangerous to the flat-bottomed crafts of the country. However, it performs a very useful service by retaining the valuable loamy rich deposits of the Jehlam which, otherwise, would escape to the Punjāb.

The Dal lake, measuring about four miles by two and a half, lies close to Srīnagar in the east. Its water which is clear and soft as silk is said to be specially suited to the fabrics of the *pashmīna*, and at the same time renders the colours fast whilst bringing out their brightness.[11] The Dal is also like the Volur rich in natural products. Kashmīr possesses many other lakes too, like the Mansabal and the Anchar Dal, but they do not possess the same importance as the Volur and the Dal.

The springs in Kashmīr are as useful for irrigation as the mountain streams and rivers. One of the springs, the Maliknāg, is sulphurous, and its water is highly prized for garden cultivation; while the Kokarnāg is given the first place as a source of drinking water. The town of Anantnāg possesses a large number of springs which send out numerous streams. Perhaps the most beautiful of all the springs is the Achabal which gushes out of the Soṣanwar hill. Vērnāg on the way to Jammu is another spring of great importance. People in Kashmīr regard the springs as sacred, because their water is cold in summer and warm in winter.

Besides the central plain surrounded by the mountains, there are also many side valleys which are drained by the tributaries of the Jehlam, and which add much ground to the total cultivated area of the country. The slope of the mountain where cultivation is not possible are rich in forests, and above this are rich alpine pastures. These side valleys have been the sites of important battles in medieval times.

The second division of the Valley consists of high ground called *udar* in Kashmīrī, and *karēwa* and *uddara* in the Persian and Sanskrit chronicles respectively.[12] The *karēwas* are considered by the geologists to be due to alluvial deposits, and they occur either isolated, or are connected by slopes with the mountains that surround the Valley. They rise generally from 100 to 300 ft. above the level of the Valley. Most of them are found on the south-western side, stretching from Shupiyan[13] to Bārāmūla. Beyond Sōpūr again the north-western and end of the Valley most *karēwa* ground. The *karēwas* also occur in the north-east and south-east side of the country. Those *karēwas* which are attached to the mountains are cultivated with the help of the water-courses brought from the higher ground, but owing to the inferiority of the soil they are much less fertile than the plain. Those however which are isolated, are either entire wastes, covered with low jungle, or, if cultivated, yield only poor crops because of the uncertainty of rainfall and the difficulty of irrigation. Some of these *karēwas*, owing to their elevation and commanding position, have been the sites of severe fighting in the past.

Passes

The mountain walls which surround the Valley, are pierced by a number of openings through which it maintains contact with the outside world. Here mention will be made only of those passes which had commercial or strategic importance in the past. The routes towards the Punjāb which crossed the Pīr Panjāl barrier have exercised great influence on the history of Kashmīr. The route leading over the Zōjī-Lā in the east has also always been an important thoroughfare, connecting Kashmīr with Ladākh and thence with Tibet, Turkistān, and China. But the routes leading over the mountains in the north and north-west have not been of much significance for the history of the country.

The Bānihāl Pass (9,200 ft.) is situated at the eastern extremity of the Pīr Panjāl Range. Owing to its small elevation it has always been a convenient route of communication with the upper Chināb valley and the eastern Punjāb hill-states. This pass is the only route across the Pīr Panjāl Range on which communication is never completely stopped by snow-fall. It is by this route that the State of Jammu was, as it is today, connected with Kashmīr.[14] It is closed for horses and vehicles from the end of December onwards for two months. The distance between Jammu and Srīnagar is reckoned at 177 miles.[15]

Sidau or Būdil Pass (14,000 ft.) connects Srīnagar with Akhnūr and Siālkōt in an almost straight line. Owing to its high ridges it can be used only for foot-traffic, but owing to its shortness it was formerly a favourite route with the Kashmīrīs. The name Sidau is given to the pass from the first village reached by it on the Kashmīr side. Śrīvara refers to it as Siddhādeśa, an adaptation of Kalhaṇa's Siddhapatha.[16] By this route Jammu is only 129 miles from Srīnagar.[17]

From the point close to the west of the pass of Sidau where the main range changes its direction towards north-north-west, there branches off in a westerly direction the lower Ratan Range. Beyond this lie the passes of Rūprī and Darhāl (13,000 ft.). They give most direct access to Rajaurī, and are crossed without much trouble during the summer months. In the past, therefore, they must have been used very frequently.

The Pīr Panjāl Pass[18] (11,400 ft.) gives access to the valleys of the two Tohīs of Rajaurī and Pūnch, from which direct routes of communication led to the central and western Punjāb. Hirapūr[19] was the entrance station for those reaching Kashmīr from Rajaurī and the neighbouring places, and a point of departure for those leaving Kashmīr for Rajaurī. The starting point from the Punjab side was Bhimbhar.[20] This route played an important part in the time of the Sulṭāns.[21] Influenced by the consideration of its natural advantages, Akbar also, after the conquest of the Valley, chose it for the construction of his Imperial Road which was to connect Lahore with Kashmīr. The route was open for seven months in the year.

The old Imperial Road, constructed by the Mughals across the Pīr Panjāl Pass, on ascending the narrow valley kept on its left side high above the Pīr Panjāl stream. But from a point close to the 'Āliābād Sarāi, a high mountain ridge slopes down from the south and falls off towards the valley in a wall of precipitous cliff. This ridge is known as Hastivanj. Before the construction of the Imperial Road, the old route to the pass crossed the Hastivanj route and followed throughout the right bank of the Pīr Panjāl stream.[22] This route was used for the march of troops before the construction of the Pīr Panjāl route.[23] It was by this route that Qāsim Khān, Akbar's commander, entered Kashmīr.

The route via the Tōshamaidān Pass was very important owing to its natural advantages. It was the shortest route leading into the valley of Pūnch, and hence to that portion of the western Punjāb which lies between the Jehlam and the Indus. This route was followed by Hiuen Tsiang on his way to Pūnch, and by Mahmūd of Ghaznī when he attempted an invasion of Kashmīr. It remained a popular trade route until the construction of the Jehlam Valley cart-road. However, owing to the elevation of the pass, this route was always closed by snow longer than the Pīr Panjāl route. During the winter months, therefore, the road from Pūnch to Kashmīr lay by the lower passes in the west, leading into the Valley below Bārāmūla.

The Jehlam Valley beyond Bārāmūla is confined between two ranges of mountains. The one to the south is a branch of the Pīr Panjāl Range; the range to the north belongs to a mountain system which culminates in the Kājnāg Peak (14,400 ft.). These two ranges accompany the course of the river for eighty miles westwards to Muẓaffarābād. Owing to the confined nature of this defile, and steep and rugged cross ridges the use of the route was difficult; and so its military and commercial importance was in the past less than that of Pīr Panjāl or Tōshamaidān routes. It is only from the time of the Afghān occupation of Kashmīr that this western route attained real prominence. The route was important as leading to the Hazāra district and the North-West Frontier Province, which are now in West Pakistan. It is continued towards Kashmīr on the right bank of the Jehlam, the crossing of the latter being entirely avoided. Since this route does not pass through much high ground, it is the only one that is almost free from snow in winter, and was, until the Partition, the easiest route from the Punjāb to Kashmīr. It was also convenient for those who wished to proceed towards Attock and Peshāwar from Kashmīr. It must have also been used for Kashmīr's trade with Persia and western Turkistān. Hiuen Tsiang and Ou-K'ong entered Kashmīr from the west by this route, and it is by this route that many learned scholars and Ṣufis from Persia and Turkistān came to the valley.

It must be remembered that there was no line of communication along the left side of the Jehlam Valley corresponding to the present Murree-Bārāmūla road. But for two marches down the valley, as far as Urī, a convenient route leads over the easy Ḥāji Pīr Pass (8,500 ft.) to Pūnch. It is never closed by snow owing to its small elevation. It was hence much used during winter months when the more direct routes to Kashmīr via Pīr Panjāl, the Tōshamaidān, and other passes were rendered impassable.

The Marbal Pass (11,570 ft.) connects Kashmīr with Kishtwār. After crossing the pass, the Wardwan and Chināb rivers are crossed by rope bridges. The route is closed in winter.[24]

The Zōjī-Lā Pass (11,300 ft.) has always been an important thoroughfare. It connects Kashmīr with Ladākh and thence with Tibet and China. From Ladākh also routes led to Baltistān and, across the Karakoram Mountains, to Chinese Turkistān.[25] It was through the Zōjī-Lā Pass that Riñchana entered Kashmīr, and Mīrzā Ḥaidar Dughlat first invaded the country. It was also through this pass that Kashmīr maintained commercial and cultural relations with China and Turkistān.

The mountains which enclose the Kashmīr Valley in the north-west and north, have a number of passes connecting it with the Kishangangā Valley, which was at times subject to the authority of Kashmīr rulers. But the routes leading over these passes were not as important as those already described.

The route, however, which leads from the Kashmīr Valley into that part of the upper Kishangangā Valley known as Gurēz and is connected with those leading to Astōr and Baltistān, is an important one. The road made in recent years is called the "Gilgit Transport Road", and crosses the range by the Trāgabal or the Rāzdiangan Pass, nearly 12,000 ft. high. But the route frequented in ancient times lay some eight miles further to the east. This was via Dudakhut Pass. An easy track over the ridge leads down to Gurēz. This route, being direct and comparatively easy during the summer, was much frequented by the Dard traders until the construction of the Gilgit Road. From Gurēz the route leads across the Kamrī Pass (13,000 ft.) to Astōr and Gilgit.[26] At Burzil, the last halting place on this side of the watershed, two roads part: one leads north-eastwards across the Deosai Plateau to Skārdu;[27] the other goes north to Astōr. Following the latter, the Dorikun Pass (13,000 ft.) is crossed, and then the Indus basin is reached. The next spur that has to be crossed is known as Hatū Pīr, and then Gilgit is reached. The road to Skārdu has to cross difficult passes, the highest of them being the Burjī Pass, 15,700 ft. high.

NOTES

1. Stein, Kalhaṇa's *Rājat.*, ii, 390.
2. *Ibid.*, intro., i, 30.
3. It is a town situated on the Jehlam in Lat. 34° 13′, Long. 84° 23′, 34′ miles west of Srīnagar.
4. This comprised the whole of the hill territory between Kashmīr in the east and the Indus in the west, including the lower valley of the Kishangangā and the valleys of the streams which flow into the latter. (See for more details, Stein, ii, 434).
5. The Dard tribes inhabit the territories of Chitrāl, Yasīn, Gilgit, Chilās, Bunjī, and Kishangangā valley. (See for more details, Stein, i, Intro., p. 91; Drew, *Jummo and Kashmīr*, pp. 7, 422sq.).
6. It is the second largest town in the Valley situated in Lat. 33° 44′, Long. 75° 12′. It is also called Islāmabād.
7. It is near Anantnāg and is its port on the Jehlam.
8. Stein, ii, 416.
9. It is situated in Lat. 34° 11′, Long. 74° 43′. It is a contraction of the

original name of Shihābu'd-Dīnpūr given to it by Sultān Shihābu'd-Dīn who founded the town. (See Munich MS., f. 56b; and Stein, ii, 329 n. 1.).

10. It is a town on both sides of the Jehlam situated in Lat . 34° 17′, Long. 74° 31′. Its ancient name was Suyyapura and was founded by Avantivarman's minister Suyya. (Stein, v, No. 118n.).
11. Pearce Gervis, *This is Kashmīr*, p. 138.
12. Stein, ii, 425.
13. A town on the south-east side of the Valley situated in Lat. 33° 44′, Long. 74° 53′, 29 miles from Srīnagar.
14. It is by this route that Ya'qūb Sarfī and other Kashmīrīs proceeded to the court of Akbar to seek his help against Ya'qūb Shāh (F.K., ff. 211a-b.).
15. Drew, *Jummo and Kashmīr*, 524.
16. Stein, ii, 473-4, 393 n. 27.
17. Drew, *Jummo and Kashmīr*, 524.
18. Srīv, p. 251, calls it Pañchāladeva. It corresponds to Pīr Panjāl; Pīr being the nearest Muslim equivalent for Deva. (See Stein, ii. 397-8).
19. It is a village 7 miles south-west of Shupiyan, situated in Lat. 33° 41′ Long. 74° 46′. It is called Shūrapura by Śrīvara.
20. It is a small town in Lat. 32° 58′ Long. 74° 8′. It is 150 miles from Srīnagar by the Pīr Panjāl route.
21. J.A.S.B., lxiv, 376.
22. Stein, ii, 395.
23. A.A., ii, 347 sqq.
24. Drew, *Jummo and Kashmīr*, 532-3.
25. See for these routes Chapter XII under the section of Trade.
26. From Gilgit routes lead to Transoxiana. See Chapter XII.
27. This is the most frequented route between Kashmīr and Skārdu. The distance is 158 miles. The other route by Drās to Skārdu is 242 miles. Up to Tashgām the route to Leh and Skārdu is common. (Drew, *Jummo and Kashmīr*, 377, 531).

Chapter 3

The Foundation of the Sultanate

During the eight century Kashmīr was several times subjected to the attacks of the Arabs. Two centuries later, Maḥmud of Ghaznī twice led his armies for its conquest. But although both the Arab and Turkish invasions ended in failure, it will be useful to take a brief notice of them, for it is to these that Kashmīr owed its earliest contact with political Islām.

The Arab Invasions

The conquest of Kābul and Turkistān by Qutaiba b. Muslim during the caliphate of Walīd, brought the Arabs to the borders of the kingdom of Kashmīr. But within six years from the death of Qutaiba much of his work was undone.[1] However, under the Caliph Hishām (724-43), Naṣr b. Sayyār, the first Arab governor of Transoxiana, not only reconquered most of the territories overrun earlier by Qutaiba, but even reached as far as Kāshghar.[2] Under the early 'Abbāsids these conquests were further extended and consolidated. In 751 the Arabs gained a victory over the Chinese and compelled them to abandon Gilgit as well as their other possessions in the extreme west.[3] The kingdom of Kābul over which the hold of the Umayyads had been precarious was reduced while Ma'mūn ar-Rashīd was governor of Khurāsān, and its ruler accepted Islām.[4] Later, when Ma'mūn became Caliph (813–33), he entered into relations with the rulers of Tibet and its neighbours.[5] The news of these Arab advances must have been a source of anxiety to the kings of Kashmīr, although there is no evidence to suggest that the Arabs ever contemplated the invasion of the Valley from the north, either from Kābul of Kāshghar. The real threat to the Valley came from the Arabs who had established themselves in Sindh.

Muḥammad Qāsim occupied Sindh and the lower Punjāb between the years 711 and 713. He then marched from Multān and carried his arms to the borders of the kingdom of Kashmīr.[6] Threatened by the Arab advance, Rājā Candrāpīda of Kashmīr sent an envoy to the Chinese emperor asking for help against the Arabs.[7] However, no aid was received; but fortunately Muḥammad b. Qāsim was recalled by the Caliph Sulaimān to Damascus, and so the Arab danger was for the time being removed. In the reign of the Caliph Hishām (724–43) the Arabs of Sindh under their energetic and ambitious governor Junaid again threatened Kashmīr. But Lalitāditya (724–60), who was the ruler of Kashmīr at this time, defeated him and overran his kingdom.[8] His victory was, however, not decisive for the Arab aggression did not cease. That is why the Kashmīrī ruler, pressed by them from the south and by the Turkish tribes and the Tibetans from the north, had to invoke the help of the Chinese emperor and to place himself under his protection.[9] But, although he did not receive any aid, he was able to stem the tide of Arab advance by his own efforts.[10]

When Hishām b. Amr at-Taghlībī was appointed governor of Sindh by the Caliph Manṣūr (754-75), he also attempted an invasion of the valley, and reached as far as the southern slopes of the Himālayas, which were subject to Kashmir. He, however, failed to enter the Valley, and occupy it as has been claimed by the Arab historians.[11] This was the last attempt of the Arabs to invade Kashmīr; and when again a Muslim invasion of the Valley took place it was undertaken not by an Arab chief but by a Turkish Sulṭān.

Maḥmūd of Ghaznī's Invasions

In 1002 Maḥmūd of Ghaznī routed the forces of Jaipāl, Raja of Waihand, who, affected by the humiliation of defeat, burnt himself to death. Jaipāl's son and successor Anandpāl also suffered a crushing defeat at the hands of Maḥmūd (1009), and died after a few years. Anandpāl's son Trilocanpāl, whose power was now confined only to the Salt Range, appealed to

Saṁgrāmarāja (1003-28), the king of Kashmīr, for help against Maḥmūd. Saṁgrāmarāja sent a large army under his commander-in-chief Tuṅga. Maḥmūd met the forces of Trilocanpāl, supported by the Kashmīr contingent, one of the valleys which leads towards Kashmīr from the neighbourhood of Jehlam.[12] Tuṅga, having won a victory over a reconnaissance party of the Sulṭān, began to think too lightly of the invader. The result was that when Maḥmūd personally advanced to attack the enemy, Tuṅga, in spite of the advice of Trilocanpāl to take shelter behind a rock, advanced to face him. But Maḥmūd put him to flight. Trilocanpāl tried to retrieve the situation, but he too was defeated (1014).[13]

Provoked by Saṁgrāmarāja's conduct, Maḥmūd decided to invade Kashmīr and punish him. He marched to Jehlam and then, proceeding along the valley of the river Tohī, tried to enter Kashmīr by the Tōshamaidān Pass. But his further progress was checked by the strong fort of Loharkōt which guarded the pass.[14] Maḥmūd besieged the fort for a month, but without any success; and owing to heavy snowfall, which cut off his communications, he was compelled to raise the siege. While retreating he lost his way. Many of his troops perished, and he himself escaped with difficulty. This was his first serious reverse in India.[15]

In September-October, 1021, Maḥmūd again set out from Ghaznī to invade Kashmīr in order to retrieve his prestige. He followed the same route as before, but once again the fort of Loharkōt stopped his advance. He besieged it for a month, but failed to reduce it. Meanwhile as severe winter had set in, he was compelled to withdraw. After these two failures Maḥmūd abandoned the idea of invading Kashmīr again.[16]

When two centuries later the storm of Turkish invasion again burst on the plains of Hindustān, it did not affect Kashmīr, for Shihābu'd-Dīn Ghūrī, and after him the Turkish Sulṭāns of Delhi, remained pre-occupied with the extension and consolidation of their territories in Hindustān. Even when, by the end of the thirteenth century, they had succeeded in subduing the whole of Northern India, they did not undertake the hazardous adventure of invading Kashmīr, but directed their arms to the conquest of the Deccan and South India which was easier to achieve. And when in the second quarter of the fourteenth century Muslim rule came to be established in the Valley, it was not the result of foreign invasion but was due to internal conditions obtaining there.

Decline of Hindu Rule

Signs of internal decay began to manifest themselves with the establishment of the Lohara dynasty in 1003. Henceforth the Hindu rule in Kashmīr started on its downward course until it met its overthrow in about 1320 under Sūhadeva. The kings who, during this period, occupied the throne were for the most part weak and worthless, and allowed themselves to be dominated by low favourites and corrupt ministers. The people were subjected to the hated corvée, and to all kinds of oppressive taxes in addition to the illegal exactions of the officials. The Ḍāmaras or feudal chiefs grew powerful, defied royal authority, and by their constant revolts plunged the country into confusion. Life and property were not safe, agriculture declined, and there were periods when trade came to a standstill. Socially and morally too the court and the country had sunk to the depths of degradations.[17]

Saṁgrāmarāja (1003-28), the first ruler of the Lohara dynasty, neglected the administration and allowed his greedy officers and vile favourites to plunder the people.[18] On his death his son Harirāja ascended the throne, but he died after a reign of twenty-two days. Ananta (1028-63), Saṁgrāmarāja's younger son, then became king. His expensive habits involved him in heavy debt, so that he had to pawn even the royal diadem and throne to a foreign trader.[19] Luckily, however, at this time his queen Sūryamatī, intervened and took charge of the affairs. She paid off the debts from her own savings, and secured the services of able ministers who governed the country well.[20] But during the reign of Kalaśa (1063-89) the valley was once again plunged into chaos. He neglected public business and lived in the society of immoral and vicious courtiers who completely dominated him.[21] He became so depraved as to violate his own daughter.[22]

The next ruler Harṣa (1089-1101) was in many ways a remarkable man. He was handsome, courageous and of a powerful frame.[23] He loved music, and patronised art and learning. In the beginning he ruled wisely and made his subjects happy,[24] but later his character degenerated under the influence of his evil counsellors,[25] and he became cruel, licentious and perverse. His sensualities led him to commit acts of incest.[26] His foreign campaigns were nowhere successful.[27] Inside the Valley the pretenders and feudal chiefs were a constant source of trouble; and although he suppressed them with revolting cruelties, they again raised their heads.[28] His reckless expenditure on troops and costly pleasures involved him in financial difficulties. To meet the crisis he began looting the wealth of the temples[29] and exploiting his subjects by imposing upon them new and oppressive taxes. He even went to the extent of taxing the night soil.[30] The result of his misgovernment and tyranny was that the nobles rose against him, and put him to a miserable death.

The Second Lohara Dynasty

Uccala (1101-11) was generous, capable and energetic. But "with robbers as ministers and feudatories, a brother ready to become a pretender, a land without treasure", he found it impossible to establish law and order in the country.[31] Sussala (1112-28) ruled for sixteen years with a brief interval of one year when Bhikṣācara, Harṣa's grandson, occupied the throne. Sussala oppressed his subjects to fill the treasury, and failed to subdue the chiefs who were in a state of constant rebellion.[32] It was in the midst of an open revolt that Jayasiṁha (1128-55) succeeded to the throne of his father. He lacked a strong will, did not display any acts of personal bravery during his reign and failed to crush the Ḍāmaras. Yet by cunning diplomacy and unscrupulous intrigue he succeeded in giving peace to the country. As Kalhaṇa observes: "He restored to this land, which owing to the baseness of the time was like a decayed forest, wealth, population and habitation."[33]

Jayasiṁha was the last great Hindu ruler of Kashmīr. After his death the country again lapsed into chaos. The political and economic decline, which had set in since the beginning of the eleventh century and which Jayasiṁha had in vain tried to arrest, became more rapid after him. His successor were weak and incompetent. They neglected their duty of protecting their subjects and instead robbed them with the help of their favourites. Their misrule was taken advantage of by the nobles who became strong and defied the royal authority. In 1198, however, Jagadeva became king, and he endeavoured to establish peace and prosperity in the Valley. But his efforts were not successful, for the corrupt officials drove him out of the country. Although he later recovered the throne, he was soon poisoned and died in 1212-3. He was succeeded by his son Rājadeva (1212-13 to 1235) whose power was limited by aggressive nobles.[34] His son Saṁgrāmadeva (1235-52) was a strong man, but was helpless when the chiefs compelled him to leave the country. Although he later succeeded in recovering the throne, he was shortly afterwards slain. The reign of Rāmadeva (1252-73), Rājadeva's son, was uneventful. As he had no child, he adopted Lakṣmaṇadeva, the son of a Brahman, as his heir-apparent. Lakṣmaṇadeva (1273-86), who succeeded him, was incompetent, and was constantly harassed by the Turks and his turbulent nobles. His son Siṁhadeva (1286-1301) ruled over a kingdom considerably reduced in size. He was dominated by evil counsellors, and was in the end assassinated by Darya, the husband of his nurse's daughter with whom he had illicit relations.[35]

Siṁhadeva's brother Sūhadeva (1301-20) succeeded in bringing the whole of Kashmir under his rule. But the heavy fines and taxes which he exacted, made him unpopular. He did not exempt even the Brahmans from taxation.[36] He was a bad ruler, "the Rākṣas of a king who, under the plea of protecting the country, devoured it for nineteen years and twenty-five days".[37] Moreover, like his predecessors, he neglected the defences of the country by leaving the passes unguarded. As a result, adventurers and spies entered the Valley without any difficulty.[38] Socially and morally the people of Kashmīr had sunk to the lowest depths, for old and young alike had taken to falsehood, intrigue, dishonesty and discord.[39] Such was the state of Kashmīr when the storm of foreign invasion by Zuljū burst upon the country.

Zuljū's Origin

Who was this Zuljū[40] that overwhelmed Kashmīr? Jonarāja calls him the commander of the great king Karmasena.[41] But it is not possible to identify the latter. Abū'l-Fazl, who based himself entirely on the Sanskrit chronicles for this period of Kashmīr history, refers to Zuljū as chief commander of the king of Qandahār.[42] Niẓāmu'd-Dīn and Firishta say that he was Mīr Bakhshī of the ruler of Qandahār.[43] But these statements are apocryphal. Qandahār did not have at this time any chief of its own, but was a possession of Ghiyāṣu'd-Dīn, the Kurt ruler of Herāt, who was tributary to the Īl-Khāns of Persia.[44] Ghiyāṣu'd-Dīn himself was not powerful enough to send an army for the conquest of Kashmīr; and besides he was confronted with internal rebellions and intrigues, and with an invasion of Prince Yasūr, the Nikūdarī.[45] It is, therefore, wrong to say that Zuljū came from Qandahār. Zuljū was in reality a Mongol who came from Turkistān[46] which was at this time ruled by descendants of Chaghatāy, the son of Chingīz Khān,[47] and his army consisted of both Turks and Mongols.[48] As regards his religion he does not seem to have been a Muslim. By this time only a few of the Chaghatāy chiefs had embraced Islām. Most of the them had remained attached to the pagan beliefs of their forefathers.[49]

Mongol Invasions

In the thirteenth century the Mongols, emerging from their Mongolian steppes, overran considerable parts of Asia and Europe. Kashmīr too was subjected to a series of invasions. Thus Ogatāy, Chingīz Khān's third son, despatched Mugatu towards India and Kashmīr, and he returned after ravaging parts of these countries.[50] Again in 1253 Tair was sent with an army to Kashmīr and India.[51] After Tair's death his troops came under the command of Sali who is said to have conquered Kashmīr and sent several thousand prisoners to Hūlāgū Khān.[52] Details of these Mongol invasions are not available, but they appear to have been in the nature of raids and affected only the outer hills of Kashmīr. The invasion of Zuljū in the spring of 1320 was a continuation of these previous attempts to conquer the Valley.

Zuljū's Invasion

Zuljū entered Kashmīr by the Jehlam Valley route, and as the passes were not properly defended, he did not meet with any resistance. Hearing of the invasion, Sūhadeva tried to persuade Zuljū to withdraw by paying him a large sum of money, which he raised by taxing all classes of people, including the Brahmans.[53] But the effect of this was that, while it increased Sūhadeva's unpopularity among his subjects, it only served to whet Zuljū's appetite for loot. And the Mongol chief, instead of withdrawing, continued to advance. Sūhadeva tried to organise resistance, but did not succeed, for the people of Kashmīr, owing to the financial exactions and injustices to which they had been subjected by him and his predecessors, remained apathetic to his appeals.[54] He, therefore, fled to Kishtwār, leaving his people to the mercy of the invaders who perpetrated all kinds of atrocities upon them. They set fire to the dwellings, massacred the men and made women and children slaves. For many years afterwards the blackened remains of ruined homesteads told the tale of the conquerors' cruelties. The only place which remained partially safe from the fury of the Mongols was the district of Lār,[55] where Rāmacandra, Sūhadeva's commander-in-chief, shut himself up in the fort, and endeavoured to protect his family, his followers, and inhabitants of the town and the neighbourhood. In fact, he was the only person who tried to maintain some semblance of authority in the Valley;[56] and, after Zuljū's departure, he moved down to Andarkōt and drove out the Gaddis who had come from Kishtwār on a raid.[57]

The Mongols continued their ravages in the Valley for eight months, until the commencement of winter.[58] During the period fields had been for the most part left uncultivated, for the inhabitants had either been killed or escaped to the mountains. And as the Mongols had consumed or burnt the existing stocks of grain in the country, they were now threatened by an acute shortage of supplies. It was owing to this reason, and not because of the cold weather, that Zuljū decided to depart from the Valley.[59] His officers advised him to leave by the same route of Bārāmūla and Pakhlī by which he had entered, because it was shorter and passable even in winter.[60] But he ignored their advice, and asked the prisoners to point out the shortest route to India where he expected to find provisions for his army. To revenge themselves on the Mongols for their sufferings, they directed them to the most hazardous route via Brinal.[61] When the Mongol army reached the top of the hill in the Divasar pargana, there was a severe snowfall which destroyed the whole army of Zuljū, including the prisoners.

Condition of the Valley after the Mongol Withdrawal

After the withdrawal of the Mongols the inhabitants resturned to the Valley from the mountains whither they had fled to escape massacre or enslavement. They witnessed the havoc which the invaders had caused. Many found themselves without houses, without relations, and without friends. In addition to these sufferings, they were subjected to the harassments of the neighbouring hill tribes, who raided the Valley and plundered them of whatever they still possessed, and then carried them away as slaves. Moreover, to crown it all, famine started them in the face.[62]

As there was no organised government in the country, the local chiefs made themselves independent. In some cases the inhabitants themselves organised their defence against the depredations of robbers and the hill tribes by taking possession of a fort and choosing some strong person as their leader.[63] Among those who took advantage of the prevailing anarchy, the most prominent person was Rinchana.

Rinchana : Sultan Sadru'd-Dīn (1320-23)

Rinchana whose full name was Lha-chen-rgyal-bu-rin-chen (Lhachen rGyalbu Rinchana), was the son of the Ladākhi chief, Lha-chen-dNgos-grub (Lhachen dNgos-grub), who ruled Ladākh from 1290 to 1320.[64] The wars between the Ladākhīs and Baltīs had been very frequent in the past. However, owing to the Pax-Mongolica which covered both Ladākh and Baltistān, these wars had for the time being ceased. But after the death of Kublāy Khān (1260-94), which plunged his empire into confusion, they were renewed. In a campaign the Baltīs were victorious over the Ladākhīs, and "they avenged their fathers and their forefathers."[65] As a result Rinchana's father lost his life. Rinchana succeeded in avenging his father by killing a number of Baltī chiefs.[66] But realising his position to be precarious, he left his country for Kashmīr, which he entered by the Zōjī-Lā Pass. On reaching the village of Gagangīr, he decided to settle there with the permission of Rāmacandra to whom the place belonged.[67]

During Zuljū's invasion, Rinchana remained in the district of Lār, and was employed by Rāmacandra to establish law and order, and protect the inhabitants from robbers. Bu performing his duties with energy and efficiency, he grew influential and won the confidence of the people.[68] But so long as Zuljū was in Kashmīr, Rinchana lay low; it was only after the Mongol chief's withdrawal that he, like many others in the Valley, asserted his independence, and began to aspire to the throne of Kashmīr.[69] But although he had secured a following in the Lār district in the course of, and after Zuljū's invasion, he knew he was not strong enough to Rāmacandra in the open. He therefore decided upon a ruse. He sent his Ladākhī followers in the guise of merchants, selling woollen clothes, to the town of Lār.[70] They carried on business for some time so that no suspicion might be aroused. Then, one day, they entered the fort under the pretext of trade, with their weapons concealed, and took Rāmacandra's men by surprise. Meanwhile, Rinchana also, at the appointed time, attacked the fort. Rāmacandra's troops were routed and he was killed. His son Rāwancandra with his whole family was taken prisoner.[71] As there was no one strong enough to challenge Rinchana, he occupied the throne at the end of the year 1320.

Rinchana and seized power with the support of his Ladākhī followers.[72] But he realized that, being a stranger in Kashmīr, his government would not be stable unless he won the goodwill of the people of the country. The first thing, therefore, which he did was to befriend Rāwancandra. After releasing him he conferred upon him the title of Raina (Lord or Master), made him his commander-in-chief, and gave him the pargana of Lār and the province of Ladākh as jāgīr.[73] He then married Rāwancandra's sister Koṭa Rānī. In this way Rin̆chana succeeded in gaining the loyalty of Rāwancandra, and in making him forget the murder of his father.

Rin̆chana was faced with two dangers at the outset of his reign. The first was due to the appearance of Sūhadeva, who returned from Kishtwār to claim his kingdom from which he had so ignominously fled. But Sūhadeva was repulsed, and retired in haste to Kishtwār.[74] The people of Kashmīr did not forget how he had betrayed them in the hour of their greatest need, and so no one came forward to welcome him, and none regretted his departure.

The other danger was from the Lavanyas[75] who during Zuljū's invasion had become independent and now refused to acknowledge Rin̆chana as ruler. Rin̆chana, however, succeeded in suppressing them by playing the different chiefs against each other. In this way he established his authority over the whole Valley.[76]

Rin̆chana's Conversion to Islam

Rin̆chana's mind was inquisitive and alert. He was fond of the society of learned men and Hindu and Buddhist priests, and used to discuss with them their respecitve religions in order to find a satisfactory answer to the question: "What is truth?" But the discussions failed to satisfy his spiritual cravings. Buddhism, the faith in which he was born, had become diluted with foreign elements and so could not offer him any solace. Hinduism also did not appeal to him because of its caste-ridden rules and the arrogance of the Brahmans who were its custodians. Owing to his inability to discover the truth, he felt a sense of frustration and a spiritual vacuum in his life. As a result, he was troubled and restless, and passed sleepless nights, weeping and praying to God to guide him to the right path.[77] It was in such a state of spiritual unrest that he came into contact with Sayyid Sharafu'd-Dīn, commonly known as Bulbul Shāh, who was a disciple of Shāh Ni'matu'llāh Fārsī belonging to the

Suhrawardīya Order of Ṣūfīs[78] and had to come to Kashmīr in the reign of Sūhadeva from Turkistān with one thousand fugitives from the Mongol invasion.[79] Rin̄chana learnt from him about Islām, and was so much impressed by its teachings, which were simple, free from ceremonies, caste and priesthood, that he became a Muslim[80] and adopted the name of Ṣadru'd-Dīn according to the saint's advice. The next person to embrace Islām after Rin̄chana was his brother-in-law, Rāwancandra. The royal patronage which Islām secured won for it new converts. Rin̄chana built for Bulbul Shāh a hospice on the bank of the Jehlam, near the palace, and endowed it with a number of villages, whose income was to be spent for supporting its servants and supplying food to the travellers and the poor. He also built near the hospice a mosque where he prayed in congregation five times a day. This was the first mosque ever to have been built in Kashmīr. Later on it was destroyed by fire, and a smaller mosque was built in its place.[81]

Meanwhile Rin̄chana was faced with a serious conspiracy headed by Ṭukka, his former prime minister. Ṭukka was angry with Rin̄chana for dismissing him from his office and appointing in his place Vyālarāja, and then inflicting the punishment of death upon his brother.[82] He therefore planned to destroy Rin̄chana; and while the latter was at Vimśaprastha, Ṭukka and his followers made a surprise attack on him. Although Vyālarāja came to his rescue, he received a serious wound, and as a result fainted. His enemies, thinking that Rin̄chana was dead, proceeded to occupy Srīnagar. They plundered the city, but began to quarrel among themselves for the spoils. Meanwhile the king had recovered from his swoon, and taking advantage of the disunity among his enemies, he took them surprise. He seized them, and ordered their execution. But his thirst for revenge not being satiated, he had the wombs of their wives ripped open by the sword.[83] The wound, however, which Rin̄chana had recieved on the head, proved to be mortal, and he died within a few months at the end of 1323, after a reign of over three years.[84] He was buried near the mosque he had built. His grave was discovered in 1909 by A.H. Francke, the well-known Tibetan scholar and archaeologist of the Moravian Mission.[85] Rinchana's rule, while harsh and stern, was firm and rested on law. He was able and energetic, and tried to give peace to the land which had been in a state of chaos for a long time. Unfortunately he was on the throne only for a short period; and the man who succeeded him was too weak and incompetent to continue his work.

Udayānadeva (1323-38)

Rinchana left behind a son named Ḥaidar who was under the guardianship of Shāh Mīr, his trusted counsellor.[86] As Ḥaidar was a minor, his mother Koṭa Rānī acted as Regent. But this arrangement was not regarded as satisfactory, for it was apprehended that without a sovereign the country might again lapse into anarchy. It was therefore decided to set up on the throne a senior and an experienced member of the former royal family of Kashmīr. Koṭa Rānī, Rinchana's widow, accordingly, on the advice of Shāh Mīr and other nobles of the land, recalled Udayānadeva, the brother of Sūhadeva, from Swat where he had been living since Zuljū's invasion, made him king, and married him.[87] Udayānadeva was, however, cowardly and incompetent, and it was really Koṭa Rānī who was the virtual ruler.[88]

Soon after Udayānadeva's accession to the throne, Kashmīr was faced with a great threat from an invasion of the Turks who entered the country via Hirapūr.[89] Udayānadeva became terror-stricken and fled to Ladākh. But Koṭā Rānī did not lose heart. She rose to the occasion, and with the help of her chief officers, like her brother Rāwancandra, Shāh Mīr, and Bhaṭṭa Bhikṣaṇa,[90] she resolved to organise resistance to the invaders. She wrote to the chiefs who, taking advantage of the foreign invasion, had declared themselves independent, to give up their refractory conduct and unite under her banner to repel the enemy, for disunity and selfishness would bring them nothing but disaster, as it had done during the invasion of Zuljū. She asked them to recall to memory the invasion of Zuljū when owing to the cowardice of the leaders and disunity in the country the people had suffered so much. She called upon them to gird up their loins, and fight the enemy, because it was a thousand times better to be killed in the defence of one's family and country than to run away to safety, leaving the women and children behind to be taken prisoners. Her appeal woke the chiefs from their lethargy and they rallied round her. As a result, the campaign against the Turks was conducted vigorously, and they were defeated and compelled to withdraw from the Valley.[91] After their withdrawal, Udayānadeva returned to Srīnagar. But due to his cowardly flight his prestige had greatly suffered, and so henceforth he began to lead a secluded life, taking very little interest in public affairs. The real power in the state was wielded by Koṭā Rānī.[92]

Udayānadeva died in the year 1338, but Koṭā Rānī, in order to get time to consolidate her position, concealed his death for four days.[93] She had two sons. One of them was by her first husband, Rin̄chana, and was in charge of Shāh Mīr; the other was by Udayānadeva, and was under the guardianship of Bhaṭṭa Bhikṣaṇa. She ignored the claims of both her sons, and herself ascended the throne.[94] But no sooner did she assume the reins of government in her hands, than her position was threatened by her eldest son's tutor, Shāh Mīr.

Shāh Mīr

Shāh Mīr's ancestry is shrouded in legend. According to some accounts he was descended from the Pāṇḍūs,[95] heroes of the *Mahābhārata*, while others trace his descent to the rulers of Swāt.[96] But from a study of character and achievements of Shāh Mīr and his successors, it is more than probable that the family was of Turkish origin. The name of Shāh Mīr's father was Ṭahir and his grandfather's Waqūr Shāh, who was a very devout and religious man.[97]

Turkish adventures began to enter Kashmīr from the end of the eleventh century onwards in search of employment. They were treated with respect by the Hindu kings, who employed them in their armies. Similarly, in 1313, came Shāh Mīr to Valley with his tribe in search of fame and fortune. Sūhadeva, who was then ruling Kashmīr, employed him and gave him a village near Bārāmūla as jāgīr.[98] We do not know what role he played during Zuljū's invasion and in the events leading to Rin̄chana's rise to power. But it is certain that a man of his restless nature and abundant energy could not have remained a mere passive spectator of the happenings around him. Besides, from the confidence which Rinchana placed in him, it appears that he must have helped him in his struggle against Rāmacandra. It was because of this, and also because he stood aloof from the conspiracy hatched by Ṭukka, that Rinchana appointed him his minister as well as guardian of his only son Ḥaidar.[99]

During the reign of Udayānadeva, Shāh Mīr, by his tact and ability, further strengthened his position. He co-operated with Koṭā Rānī in organising resistance to the Turkish invasion, and in the end succeeded in repelling it. This considerably increased his prestige and popularity in the country, for he had saved the people from the fate to which they had been subjected only a few years ago by Zuljū. To consolidate his position further he entered into matrimonial alliances with the important feudal chiefs of the Valley.[100] Those with whom such alliances could not be formed, he brought under his influence by playing one against the other. All this filled Udayānadeva with jealous hostility towards Shāh Mīr, and made him apprehensive lest the latter should use Prince Ḥaidar, Rinchana's lawful successor, to drive him out or to exclude his heirs from the succession. But Shāh Mīr, assured of his own position and strength, ignored Udayānadeva.[101]

On Udayānadeva's death Koṭā Rānī ascended the throne, but alarmed at the ambition and growing power of Shāh Mīr, she appointed Bhaṭṭa Bhikṣaṇa as her prime minister who, being one of the ablest and most powerful men in the kingdom, she hoped, would act as a counterpoise to him.[102] Moreover, in order to be safe from the danger of Shāh Mīr's proximity in Srīnagar, where he was very popular, she transferred her capital to Andarkōt.[103] Shāh Mīr was, however, angry with Koṭā Rānī for having ignored him and raised another person to the highest office in the state; and he therefore made up his mind to overthrow both Koṭā Rānī and her chief confidant. First he succeeded by means of a conspiracy in securing the assassination of Bhikṣaṇa,[104] and then asked Koṭā Rānī to marry him and to share power with him, threatening to make war on her if she refused. But Koṭā Rānī rejected his proposal, for she did not want to marry a person who had been in her service; and being ambitious and domineering, she was not prepared to share power with any one. Shāh Mīr, therefore, set out from Srīnagar with an army against Andarkōt; and having defeated the troops which were sent by Koṭā Rānī to check his advance, he laid siege to the fort. Meanwhile, as most of the important chiefs of the kingdom had been won over by Shāh Mīr, and her forces began to desert and join him, she decided to surrender, and accept his proposals.[105] But although Shāh Mīr married her, he did not trust her, because she had given her consent reluctantly and under duress. Moreover, as she still possessed some following in the country, he felt apprehensive and he therefore threw her into prison along with her two sons.[106] He then himself ascended the throne under the title of Sulṭān Shamsu'd-Dīn and thus laid the foundation of his dynasty which ruled Kashmīr for over two hundred years. Koṭā Rānī died in prison in the year 1339.[107] What happened to her sons is not recorded in the chronicles.

NOTES

1. Gibb, *The Arab Conquest in Central Asia*, Chap. iii, 29-55.
2. Hitti, *History of the Arabs*, p. 210.
3. Stein, *Ancient Khotan*, pp. 11-2.
4. Balāẕuri, *Futūḥu'l-Būldān*, p. 393; Reinaud, *Memoire sur l'Inde*, pp. 182, 196.
5. *Ibid.*, 197.
6. Elliot, i, 436; *Chāch-nāma*, 192.
7. Majumdar, *The Classical Age*, 134, 174.
8. *Ibid.*
9. *Ibid.*; Reinaud, *Memoire sur l'Inde*, 90.
10. Majumdar, *The Classical Age*, 173-4.
11. Balāẕuri, *Futūḥu'l-Būldān*, p. 131; Mas'ūdī, *Murūju'ẕ-'Ẕahab*, (Trans. de Meynard), i, 373, says that Kashmīr was part of the country of Sindh. See also Elliot, i, 444.
12. It is a town situated on the west bank of the river Jehlam, 100 miles to the north-west of Lahore.
13. Nāẓim, *Sultān Maḥmūd of Ghazna*, 92-3; Stein, i, BK. vii, Nos. 47-62 and n.

14. Loharakoṭṭa of Lōhkōt or the Castle of Lohara lay in the valley now called Loharin belonging to the territory of Pūnch. It was situated in Lat. 33°48′ Long. 74° 23′. An isolated ridge in Loharin towards the right bank of the river Loharin just above the village of Gēgivand was the site of the fort. (See for more details Stein, ii, 293-300). Persian chronicles of Kashmīr call it Loharkōt.
15. Nāẓim, *Maḥmūd of Ghazna*, pp. 104-5.
16. *Ibid.*, 105.
17. In BK. vii and viii Kalhaṇa gives numerous instances of the deterioration of morals in the valley.
18. Stein, i, BK. vii Nos. 107-19.
19. *Ibid.*, No. 195.
20. *Ibid.*, Nos. 197 sqq.
21. *Ibid.*, Nos. 285 sqq.
22. *Ibid.*, No. 278.
23. *Ibid.*, Nos. 874-8.
24. *Ibid.*, Nos. 932-56.
25. *Ibid.*, No. 960.
26. *Ibid.*, Nos. 1147-8.
27. *Ibid.*, Nos. 1152 sqq.
28. *Ibid.*, Nos. 1037 sqq.
29. *Ibid.*, Nos. 1089-95; 1115 sqq.
30. *Ibid.*, No. 1107.
31. *Ibid.*, viii, No. 7.
32. *Ibid.*, 481 sqq.
33. *Ibid.*, Nos. 2446.
34. Jonar., pp. 8-9.
35. *Ibid.*, 9-14.
36. *Ibid.*, 16.
37. *Ibid.*, 19.
38. G.A., f. 96b.
39. H.M. ff. 93b-94b.
40. Persian chroniclers call him Zuljū. Jonar (Cal. Ed.) calls him Zalacha or Zalcha. Jonar., (Bo. Ed., No. 152) calls him Duluch. Narāyan Kaul and A′ẓam have Islamised his name as Zulqadar Khān.
41. Jonar., 16.
42. A.A., ii, 381.
43. T.A., iii, Munich MS. f. 47a.
44. Khwāndamīr, *Ḥabību's-Siyar*, iii, part ii, p. 69; Ṣaif b. Muḥammad, *Ta'rīkh-namā-i-Harāt*, pp. 369 sqq.
45. Howorth, *History of the Mongols*, iii, 568-9, 590-1; Ṣaif b.

Muḥammad, *Ta'rīkh-namā-i-Harāt*, pp. 680 sqq.
46. H.M., 95b; Ḥasan, 91a.
47. Prawdin, *The Mongol Empire*, 404-5.
48. B.S., f. 10a; Jonar. (Bo. ed.), No. 170; says Zuljū's army consisted Turks, Tājiks, and *mlecchas.*
49. Prawdin, *The Mongol Empire*, pp. 141 sqq; Vambery, *Bukhārā*, pp. 406-7; also p. 157 n. where the names of Chaghatāy rulers of Transoxiana are given.
50. *Ṭabaqāt-i-Nāṣirī* (trans. Raverty), p. 1126 n. 6.
51. *Ibid.*, 1135 n. 5; Howorth, *History of the Mongols*, iii, 184.
52. *Ṭabaqāt-i-Nāṣirī* (trans. Raverty), 1191 n; Howorth, iii, 185. But Howorth gives 1263 as the year of these conquests. See also Bretschneider, *Medieval Researches*, 137-8, 305.
53. Jonar., 17.
54. Ḥasan, 92b; H.M., 96a-b.
55. The district known as Lār comprises the whole of the territory drained by the Sind and its tributaries. The Sanskrit chronicles call it Lahara (Jonar. 18), but the Persian chronicles call it Lār. The fort of Lār was situated in the village of Gagangīr, in Lat. 34° 18′ Long. 75° 15′, about 10 miles west of Sonamarg on the road to Drās. (N.A., f. 14a; W.K., f. 11b; T.H., ii, 82a).
56. B.S., 12a; Hasan, 92b; H.M., 96b.
57. Lawrence, *Valley*, 189. Andarkōt is a village situated in Lat. 34° 13′ Long. 75° 42′, on the Sambal Lake about 12 miles north-west of Srīnagar.
58. B.S., 10a-11a; H.M.,f. 96b.
59. B.S., f. 11a; Ḥasan, 93a-94a; H.M. Jonar., p. 17. The chronicles say that the Mongols made this decision owing to the dread of approaching winter. But this is wrong for the Mongols, coming as they did from colder regions, could have easily faced the cold weather of Kashmīr.
60. Ḥasan, 94a-b; According to N.A., 14a, Zuljū set out to conquer Kishtwār on his counsellors' advice.
61. Ḥasan, 94b; B.S., 11a; H.M., 98a. Brinal is now in Kulgām Tahṣīl situated S.E. of the Valley in the Brinal-Lāmar Mountains. The route via Brinal leads tot he Bānihāl Pass.
62. Ḥasan, 94b-95a; H.M., (B.N.), 31b-32a.
63. B.S., 12a; Ḥasan, 95 a; H.M., 98b.
64. Francke, *Antiquities of Indian Tibet*, Vol. ii, 98; also I.A., July 1908, p. 187.
65. I.A., 1909, p. 60. The Persian chronicles do not mention the struggle between the Baltīs and Ladākhīs. They merely say that

Rinchana's father and relations were killed by the rival party, and so he came away to Kashmīr.

66. Jonarājā's Kālamānyas and Vakatanyas are the Baltīs and Ladākhīs respectively (p. 16). See also Munich MS. 47b. Ladākhī folklores contain a song which relates to the departure of a "Prince Rinchen" from Ladākh. (I.A., 1908, p. 187). The song is given in I.A., 1909, p. 59.
67. Ḥasan, 87b; B.S., 10a; H.M., 92b. Jonarāja's statement that Rinchana was a joint invader with Zuljū is incorrect. Munich MS. is wrong in saying that Rinchana, like Zuljū, took prisoners and looted.
68. Ḥasan, 82b. Ḥasan also states that Rinchana appropriated some of the revenues which he collected on behalf of Rāmacandra.
69. B.S., f. 12b.
70. Jonar. (Bo. ed.), Nos. 199-200. G.A., f. 99a says that Rinchana secured help from his brother who was ruler of Dārdu. But this is absurd.
71. B.S., 12a-b; Ḥasan, 95b; H.M., 99a.
72. Jonar., 18.
73. B.S., 12b; Ḥasan, 96a-b; H.M., 99b. Munich M.S., 48a, wrongly says that Koṭā was the wife of Rāmacandra.
74. B.S., 13a; Ḥasan, 96b; H.M., 100a.
75. Lavanyas must have formed in medieval times an important tribal section of the rural population in Kashmīr. Many of them must have held positions of influence as landowners. (See for more details Stein, i, No. 1171n.; and Lawrence, *Valley*, 306.)
76. Jonar., 19.
77. B.S., 114a; Ḥasan, 98a; H.M. 101b-102a.
78. B.S., 114b; *Majmū'a dar Ansāb Mashā'ikh-i-Kashmīr*, f. 106a; see also T.H., i, f. 136b and ii, f. 84b.
79. Moslem World, iv (1914), p. 340.
80. Persian chronicles represent this event as the outcome of a miracle. They state that, unable to arrive at any decision, Rinchana made up his mind to adopt the religion of the person whom he saw first in the morning. The first person he saw from his palace early next morning was Bulbul Shāh who was engaged in prayers. He immediately went up to him and, after making inquiries about the main tenets of his religion decided to adopt it. (Ḥasan, 99b-100a; H.M., 102-103a). Jonarāja is wrong in saying that Rinchana wanted to become a Śaivite, but that the Brahmans refused to convert him. In ancient and medieval times conversions from Buddhism to Hinduism and vice versa were of common

occurrence. In reality the reason why Rin̄chana did not embrace Śaivism was that it could not satisfy his spiritual cravings. It is probably out of bitterness against Rin̄chana's rejection of Śaivism that Jonarāja wrote that the Brahmans refused to take him into the fold of Hinduism. It was also due to the bitterness he felt at Riñchana's acceptance of Islām that he did not even so much as refer to the event in his chronicle.

81. B.S., f. 15a-b; Ḥasan, 100b-101a; H.M., 103a--b.
82. Jonar., 19-20; Munich MS., 148b-49a; I.A., July 1908, p. 187. According to Munich MS. Ṭukka was incited by Udayānadeva, brother of Sūhadeva, who wanted to seize the throne.
83. Jonar., pp. 21-2.
84. Jonar., 23, Munich MS. 50a.
85. J.P.H.S., i, No. 2, pp. 175-6.
86. B.S., f. 15b; Ḥasan, 101a; H.M., 104a. T.A., iii, 425, calls Ḥaidar as Chandra.
87. Jonar., 24; B.S., 16a; Ḥasan, 101b.
88. B.S., f. 16a; Ḥasan, 101b.
89. This was probably an incursion. But who these Turks were, and if they were sent by the Delhi Sulṭāns, have not been recorded. The chronicles give different names to the leader of the invaders. Most of the Persian chronicles call him urdil. (H.M., (B.N.) 33b; Ḥasan 101b). But Jonar., 25 calls him Achala.
90. According to H.M. (B.N.), f. 33b, he was Koṭā's foster-brother and was not an able officer.
91. B.S., f. 16b; Ḥasan, ff. 101b-102b; H.M., 104a-5a. H.M., (B.N.) says that the Turks having been defeated made peace, and then withdrew. Nārāyan Kaul follows this account.
92. H.M., f. 104a.
93. Jonar., p. 28.
94. *Ibid.*, B.S., f. 17a, is wrong in saying that Koṭā Rānī had no son alive at this time.
95. T.A., iii, 424; Firishta, p. 647. Jonar is silent over the question of their ancestry.
96. B.S., f. 9a; H.M., f. 91b; Ḥasan, f. 86b.
97. *Ibid.*, Jonar., p. 15, wrongly calls him Qaur Shāh Ṣūfī, *Kashīr*, i. p. 130n. follows Jonar.
98. Jonar., p. 15; B.S.. f. 9b; T.A., iii 424. Jonar., p. 24, says he was the chief of his tribe. I cannot identify the village that was given to him as jāgīr.
99. Jonar., 23; Munich MS., f. 50a.
100. Jonar., pp. 26-7; B.S., 16a.

101. Jonar., 26.
102. *Ibid.*, 28.
103. B.S., 17a; Ḥasan, 102a; H.M. 105b.
104. *Ibid.*, Jonar., 29, says that Shāh Mīr feigned illness, and that when Kākāpurī went to see him he stabbed him to death. But this story appears spurious. Since their relations were inimical it seems unlikely that Kākāpurī would have visited Shāh Mīr.
105. B.S., f. 17a; Ḥasan, ff. 103a-b; H.M., f. 105b.
106. Jonar., p. 32; Munich MS., 53a. The story that on entering the bridal chamber after the marriage ceremony she stabbed herself, and bringing out her entrails offered them to Shāh Mīr, seems to be apocryphal. Jonaraja, who is the earliest authority for this period, does not mention the incident.
107. Jonar., 32.

Chapter 4

Sulṭān Shamsu'd-Dīn and His Successors

Sulṭān Shamsu'd-Dīn (1339-42)

Shamsu'd-Dīn, like Riñchana, tried to heal the wounds inflicted on the Valley by Zuljū's invasion and nearly two centuries of feudal anarchy and misrule. He abolished many of the extra taxes which had been imposed on the people in the previous reigns, and cancelled those laws and regulations which were of an oppressive nature.[1] He took from the peasants one-sixth of the produce as revenue, and protected them from greedy officials.[2] He kept the feudal chiefs under control;[3] and in order to counteract their influence, he raised to prominence two families: the Māgres, who were of indigenous origin, and the Chaks who had migrated to Kashmīr from Dardistān in the reign of Sūhadeva under their leader Lankar Chak. Shamsu'd-Dīn made the latter his commander-in-chief, and similarly appointed other officers from among the Māgres.[4] However, we do not hear much of the activities of these families during the early Shāh Mīr period. It was in reality not until after the reign of Zainu'l-Ābidīn that they began to play an important part in the history of Kashmīr.

Shamsu'd-Dīn introduced a new era called the Kashmīrī era in place of the *Laukika* era which had been in force hitherto. The new calendar began with Riñchana's accession and conversion to Islām which was fixed at 720 A.H., and was used in all state documents during the Sultanate period. Its official use, however, ended with the Mughal conquest, although it continued to be used in the rural parts of the Valley until very recently.[5]

Towards the end of his days he left the administration in the hands of his two sons, Jamshēd and 'Alī Shēr.[6] He died in the year 1342[7] and was buried in Sumbal near Andarkōt. Unknown and, probably, of humble origin, Shamsu'd-Dīn came to Kashmīr in search of fortune, but he took advantage of the political chaos that prevailed in the country, and by his great energy, resource, and perseverance he rose to power and founded his dynasty. Although he ruled only for three years, yet, even in such a short time, he was able to win the loyalty of his subjects who looked upon him as their saviour.[8]

Sulṭān Jamshēd (1342-43)

Shamsu'd-Dīn left two sons, Jamshēd and 'Alī Shēr. Jamshēd being the eldest succeeded to the throne. He had already gained experience in state affairs in the time of Udayānadeva, when he and his brother had acted as governors of Kamrāj and Marāj.[9] During the reign of his father also he had been closely associated in the government of the country. He proved to be a good ruler, and endeavoured to promote the welfare of the people. He founded the town of Jāmnagar in the pargana of Adavin,[10] and built a bridge over the Jehlam at Sōpūr, and inns for travellers at various places.[11] However, he was not shrewd enough to realise the danger which threatened him and adopt measures to overcome it.

Jamshēd treated his younger brother, 'Alī Shēr, with kindness, placed confidence in him, and consulted him on all matters relating to administration.[12] But Alī Shēr was ambitious, and having been incited by some courtiers, he raised the banner of revolt in Avantipūr[13] in order to seize the throne. Jamshēd tried to conciliate him, but without any success. Meanwhile the Sulṭān has despatched his son with an army to suppress a revolt in Divasar.[14] Alī Shēr marched against his nephew and defeated him. But during his absence Jamshēd, on the advice of his minister, Lakṣman Bhaṭṭ, decided to capture Avantipūr, the seat of his brother's power. He accordingly besieged it, and inflicted great loss on the garrison. But hearing of the approach of Alī Shēr, he withdrew, and signed a truce for two months with his brother. But while he was absent in Kamrāj, 'Alī Shēr broke the truce; and having bribed Sirāj, who was of charge in Srīnagar, he took possession of the capital and declared himself as Sulṭān.[15] Jamshēd, finding himself not strong enough to fight, fled; and after aimlessly wandering about in the Valley for a year and ten months, he died in 1345.[16]

Sulṭān 'Alā'u'd-Dīn (1343-54)

On ascending the throne 'Alī Shēr styled himself as 'Alā'u'd-Dīn. From the few facts that are known about his reign of about eleven years, he appears to have been an able, just, and strong ruler. He continued the work of consolidation and reform begun by his predecessors. He brought back the peasants to the lands from which they had fled during Zuljū's invasion, and he repeopled the towns which had been depopulated.[17] The same year that he became Sulṭān, the Valley, owing to the untimely rains which destroyed the crops, suffered from a severe famine. But he did all he could to alleviate the sufferings of his subjects.[18] He erected many beautiful buildings at Andarkōt, which he made his capital, and founded the town of 'Alā'u'd-Dīnpūr, now a part of Srīnagar, after his own name.[19] He promulgated a law by which a childless widow, if immoral, was not entitled to get a share of her husband's property from the father-in-law.[20] During his reign the Lavanayas rose in revolt and then fled to Kishtwār. But they were pursued and captured by him, and were brought back to Kashmīr where they were thrown into prison and their leaders. executed.[21] 'Alā'u'd-Dīn died in the year 1354,[22] and was buried in his new town of 'Alā'u'd-Dīnpur.[23]

Sulṭān Shihābu'd-Dīn (1354-73)

Nothing is known of the early life of 'Alā'u'd-Dīn's son and successor, Shīrāshāmak (the little milk-drinker),[24] except that he had been associated by his father in the government of the kingdom. On ascending the throne he assumed the title of Shihābu'd-Dīn. He was full of energy and vigour, and his ambition was to establish his sway over the neighbouring territories. But before undertaking any wars of aggression, he first directed his attention to consolidate his position in his own country. Taking advantage of Zuljū's invasion and the chaos that followed it, the feudal chiefs had made themselves independent, and had built strong forts. Shihābu'd-Dīn's predecessors had reduced many of them, but there were still some left who refused to pay tribute and defied the authority of the government. Shihābu'd-Dīn, therefore, undertook a campaign against the refractory chiefs. He put to death those who refused to surrender, but spared those who promised to remain loyal to him. It was after he had assured himself that there would be no trouble in the Valley during his absence, that he set out to conquer the neighbouring territories which had once formed part of the kingdom of Kashmīr.

According to the Kashmīr accounts Shihābu'd-Dīn marched *via* Bārāmūla, and occupied Pakhlī and Swāt. Next he invaded Multān, Nu'mān and Kābul, Ghaznī and Qandahār, all of which he occupied one by one.[25] He then crossed the Hindu Kush and invaded Badakhshān.[26] After conquering it, he retraced his steps towards Gilgit and Dārdu which also he annexed. He then advanced to conquer Baltistān and Ladākh. The ruler of Kāshghar to whom these provinces belonged at the time, on hearing of Shihābu'd-Dīn's invasion, set out with a large force and offered him battle in Ladākh. Although the Kashmīr army was numerically inferior to that Kāshghar, yet it was victorious, and Baltistān and Ladākh were occupied. Meanwhile, Shihābu'd-Dīn's commander Malik Candra reduced Kishtwār and Jammu.[27] Shihābu'd-Dīn himself, on the other hand, marched from Ladākh to Nagarkōt (Kāngra), and after occupying it, encamped on the plains of the Sutlej. Here in 1361 he was met by Udakpati, the Rājā Nagarkōt, who had just returned with the spoils from a raid into the territory of Fīrūz Shāh Tughlaq. Shihābu'd-Dīn defeated him, and compelled him to surrender his booty and acknowledge his sovereignty.[28] Then with 50,000 horse and 50,000 foot Shihābu'd-Dīn set out to conquer Delhi, but was opposed by Fīrūz Shāh Tughlaq on the banks of the Sutlej. Since the battle between the rulers of Delhi and Srīnagar was indecisive, peace was concluded. It was agreed that all the territory from Sirhind to Kashmīr was to belong to Shihābu'd-Dīn, while the rest lying to the east was to go to Fīrūz Shāh.[29] A marriage alliance was also contracted by which Fīrūz Shāh's two daughters were married to Shihābu'd-Dīn and his brother Quṭub'd-Dīn, while Shihābu'd-Dīn's daughter was married to Fīrūz Shāh.[30] This was Shihābu'd-Dīn's last campaign, after which he returned to Kashmīr and devoted the remaining nine years of his reign to the work of reform.

The Kashmīr chronicles, describing the conquests of Shihābu'd-Dīn, have indulged in wildly exaggerated claims which are not supported by the contemporary authorities. Just as Kalhaṇa had two centuries earlier exaggerated the military exploits of his hero Lalītaditya,[31] so Jonārāja, and after him other Kashmīr chroniclers, magnified the achievements of Shihābu'd-Dīn. There is, for example, no evidence to suggest that Shihābu'd-Dīn crossed the Hindu Kush and occupied the territories beyond it. In fact both Niẓamu'd-Dīn and Firishta say that, realising the difficulties of crossing that mountain, he retraced his steps.[32] Similarly the claim that the Sulṭān conquered Kābul, Ghaznī and Qandahār appears to be fantastic. In reality his conquests covered a much limited area. These comprised Gilgit, Dardistān and Baltistān to the north, Ladākh to the east, Kishtwār, Jammu, Chamba and other hill states to the south, and most of the northern and western Punjāb and the Peshawar district to the west. As regards Shihābu'd-Dīn's relations with Fīrūz Shāh it is possible that the two rulers met each other while the latter was carrying on a campaign against the Rājā of Nagarkōt, and also, perhaps, concluded a treaty.[33] But there is no reliable evidence to support the view that there was a conflict between the Sulṭāns of Kashmīr and Delhi, or that a marriage alliance was concluded.[34]

Shihābu'd-Dīn was not only a proved warrior but also an able administrator, and governed his kingdom with firmness and justice. But one of his regulations, which survived for a long time, that for seven days in every month the *hānjīs* (boatmen) would be required to serve the king without wages, was very oppressive.[35] His exaction of Bāj also weighed heavily upon the people.[36] He was, however, a patron of learned men and opened a number of schools where the Qur'ān, Hadīṣ, and Fiqh were taught.[37] He was tolerant towards his non-Muslim subjects, and the statement of Persian chroniclers[38] that, towards the end of his reign, he indulged in iconoclastic activities is incorrect. For Jonarāja, who is the earliest and most reliable authority, says that when, owing to the expenses caused by his campaigns his treasury became empty, and Udayaśrī, his minister, suggested to melt the brass image of Buddha and coin the metal into money, the Sulṭān replied in anger: "Past generations have set up images to obtain fame and earn merit, and you propose to demolish them. Some have obtained renown by setting up images of gods, others by worshipping them, some by duly maintaining them, and some by demolishing them. How great is the enormity of such a deed!"[39]

Like his father and uncle, Shihābu'd-Dīn also built a new town. It was situated on a delightful spot at the confluence of the rivers Jehlam and Sind, and was called Shihābu'd-Dīnpūr after his own name. He erected in it a mosque, and laid out gardens and parks for the benefit of the people.[40] Meanwhile, in 1360[41], Kashmīr suffered from a serious flood which engulfed the whole town of Srīnagar. There was a great loss of life and property; and the Sulṭān had to take refuge in a hill fort. When, therefore, the waters subsided he laid the foundations near Kōh-i-Mārān of a new town which would not be affected by floods and named it Lakṣmīnagar after his queen Lakṣmī.[42] One more town which the Sulṭan built was Shihābpūr, now called Shihāmpūr, and is a part of Srīnagar.[43] He is also said to have erected many mosques and monasteries.

Shihābu'd-Dīn was a good judge of men, and took into his service persons known for their ability and integrity. Udayaśri and Koṭā Bhaṭṭa were two of his ministers in whom he placed great confidence.[44] Udayaśri was both his chief and finance minister.[45] But Koṭā Bhaṭṭa after some time renounced the world and retired to a forest. His military commanders were Malik Candra, Śura Lolaka,[46] and Acal Raina, a descendant of Rāmacandra, whom the Sulṭān gave the village of Chādura as Jāgīr.[47]

The last years of Shihābu'd-Dīn's life were not happy. He became attached to his queen Lakṣmī's sister's daughter named Lāsā who had been brought up by her. She was beautiful and clever, and by her intrigues she contrived to alienate the Sulṭān from his queen, and then secured the exile of their two sons, Ḥasan Khān and 'Alī Khān.[48] Shihābu'd-Dīn was very unhappy on account of his separation from the princes, but owing to the great influence which Lāsā exercised over him, he could not rescind his order. However, just before his death in 1373, he wrote to his sons, who were in Delhi, to return to Srīnagar. Only Ḥasan obeyed the summons, but did not arrive in time to see his father.[49]

Sulṭān Quṭbu'd-Dīn (1373-89)

On the death of Shihābu'd-Dīn his younger brother Hindāl ascended the throne under the title of Quṭbu'd-Dīn. He was not only an able ruler, but a man of culture, a poet and a patron of learning.[50] After suppressing the conspiracy of Udayaśri he founded a new town and named it Quṭbu'd-Dīnpūr after himself.[51] Towards the end of his reign a severe famine took place, but the Sultan did his best to relieve the sufferings of the people by distributing among them food, grain and money.[52]

Soon after his accession he was called upon to deal with a serious revolt in Lohara. Towards the end of Shihābu'd-Dīn's reign, its chief had revolted against his authority, and had refused to pay tribute. The Sulṭān had sent troops against him, but they had fled ignominously. When Quṭb'd-Din became ruler he despatched Lolaka, who had also served his brother, to reduce Lohara. Its chief, realising that resistance was futile, decided to surrender, and sent his Brahman agents to negotiate the terms of capitulation with the Kashmīrī commander. But the latter, thinking that the chief was not serious in his advances, had the messengers seized and punished as spies. This filled the chief with great anger, and he decided not to surrender, but to die fighting like a Kṣatriya. He and his followers came out of the fort, and attacked the besiegers with arrows and stones. Lolaka was killed, and his forces were repulsed. Thus Lohara remained unsubdued.[53]

Soon after, Quṭbu'd-Dīn was faced with a conspiracy headed by his chief minister Udayaśrī. We have seen that Shihābu'd-Dīn before his death had summoned his two sons from exile in Delhi. Only Prince Ḥasan had set out towards Kashmīr; but on hearing at Jammu the news of his father's death, he decided not to proceed further.[54] Quṭbu'd-Dīn, however, pressed him to return to Srīnagar and become his heir-apparent as he had no son of his own.[55] Prince Ḥasan, thereupon, came, and was received with affection and cordiality by the Sulṭān. But soon after his arrival misunderstandings arose between the uncle and the nephew owing to the machinations of the courtiers. Some of them incited the Sulṭān to imprison the prince who would sooner or later try to usurp the throne. Others led by Udayaśrī organised a conspiracy to assassinate the Sulṭān and set up Ḥasan as ruler. But the plot was discovered. Ḥasan on the advice of Udayaśrī fled to Loharkōt, and strengthened the rebels. Udayaśrī was however imprisoned; but in consideration of his ability and past services he was released and forgiven on the mediation of Sura Rānī, Queen of Quṭbu'd-Dīn. In spite of this Udayaśrī tried to escape and join the prince. But he was caught and beheaded. Quṭbu'd-Dīn then secured the surrender of Prince Ḥasan by bribing the garrison, and had him thrown into prison.[56]

The most important event in the reign of Quṭbu'd-Dīn was the arrival of Sayyid 'Ali Hamadānī, commonly known as Amīr-i-Kabīr or 'Alī-i-Ṣ̤ānī, who was one of the most remarkable personalities of the fourteenth century Muslim world. Born in Hamadān on Monday the 22nd October, 1314, he descended from the famous family of the 'Alavī Sayyids of the town.[57] His father Sayyid Shihābu'd-Dīn was a governor of Hamadān. But Sayyid 'Ali did not show any interest in the affairs of his father; instead he came under the spell of his maternal uncle, Sayyid 'Alā'u'd-Dīn who was a learned Ṣūfī. Alā'u'd-Dīn was the first teacher of Sayyid 'Ali, and taught him Qur'ān at an early age.[58] Later, Sayyid 'Ali became the disciple of Shaikh Sharafu'd-Dīn Maḥmūd b. 'Abdu'llāh Mazdaqānī, the *Pīr* of his uncle.[59] He also read under Shaikh Ruknu'd-Dīn 'Alā'u'd-Daula and then under Quṭbu'd-Dīn Nīshāpūrī. After attending on Shaikh

Ruknu'd-Dīn for six years, he learnt at the feet of Taqīu'd-Dīn Dūstī for two years.[60] But after the latter's death he went back to his former teacher Sharafu'd-Dīn Maḥmūd who put the finishing touches to his education.[61]

After completing his education, Sayyid 'Ali set out on his travels on the advice of his teachers who regarded this as a valuable means of acquiring knowledge. Convinced of its usefulness, he later undertook many travels. According to some authorities he journeyed round the world three times.[62] He made several pilgrimages to Mecca, and visited various parts of the Muslim world.[63] But the most important of his travels was his visit to Kashmīr which had such far-reaching consequences for that country.

Sayyid 'Ali arrived for the first time in Kashmīr in September 1372. After a stay of four months, he proceeded to Mecca on a pilgrimage, and thence returned to Hamadān. The second time he came was in 1379 in the reign of Quṭbu'd-Dīn. He remained in the Valley this time for two and a half years, and returned to Turkistān *via* Ladākh. He came for the third and last time in 1383, and left after a stay of about a year for Turkistān.[64]

The third visit of Sayyid 'Alī was caused by the third invasion of Persia by Tīmūr in 1383 when he conquered 'Irāq, and decided to exterminate the 'Alavī Sayyids of Hamadān who, until his time, had played an important part in local affairs. Sayyid 'Alī, therefore, left Hamadān with 700 Sayyids, and set out towards Kashmīr where he expected to be safe from the wrath of Tīmūr.[65] On hearing the news that Sayyid 'Alī was approaching Srīnagar, Sulṭān Quṭbu'd-Dīn went out with his chief officials and received him with great warmth and respect, and brought him and his followers to the city. Sayyid 'Alī took up his residence in an inn in 'Ala'u'd-Dīnpūr. There he constructed a *ṣuffa* (raised floor) where he used to perform his prayers, which were also attended by Quṭbu'd-Dīn.[66]

At this time the number of Muslims in Kashmīr was very small; a majority of the population being still Hindu. Moreover, in dress, manners, and customs there was nothing to distinguish them from the Hindus.[67] In 'Ala'u'd-Dīnpūr, for example, there was a temple which was visited every morning both by the Sulṭān and his Muslim subjects.[68] To avert famine Quṭbu'd-Dīn once performed the *yagṅa*, and distributed large gifts to the Brahmans,[69] and in contravention of Islamic teachings he had two wives who were sisters.[70] Sayyid 'Alī denounced these practices and called upon Quṭbu'd-Dīn to divorce one wife and retain the other. The Sulṭān, in accordance with the saint's instructions, divorced the elder sister and re-married the younger named Sūra who became the mother of his two sons, Sikandar and Haibat. He also enjoined the Sulṭān to wear the dress common in Muslim countries. He held discussions with the Brahman priests and in this way secured many converts to his faith.[71]

Anxious not to antagonise his non-Muslim subjects, Quṭbu'd-Dīn did not follow every advice of the Sayyid, but he held him in great reverence, and visited him every day. Sayyid 'Alī gave him a cap which, out of respect, the Sulṭān always wore under his crown. The subsequent Sulṭāns followed the same practice until the cap was buried with the body of Fatḥ Shāh according to the latter's will.[72] After the Sayyid had been for about a year in the Valley, he decided to leave. The Sulṭān tried to persuade him to postpone his departure, but the Sayyid refused, and departed with some of his followers, leaving behind Maulānā Muḥammad Balkhī commonly called Mīr Ḥājī Muḥammad, at the request of the Sulṭān, to give him guidance in matters relating to the *Sharī'a*.[73] The Sayyid travelled to Pakhlī, and thence proceeded to Kunār near Kāfiristān. Here he fell seriously ill and died on January 19, 1385, and was buried in Khatlān.[74]

Sayyid 'Alī was a great scholar in Arabic and Persian. He is said to have been the author of more than one hundred works on logic, jurisprudence, philosophy, political science, ethics, Ṣūfism and commentaries.[75] He is said to have written a treatise on the science of physiognomy styled *Qiyāfat-nāma*.[76] Another work on the same subject called *Fī 'Ilmu'l-Qiyāfa* has been noticed in the Bodleian Catalogue.[77] *Ẓakhīratu'l-Mulūk* is his work on political science and ethics, and contains his ideas on government and the duties of subjects and rulers. Besides being a prolific prose writer, Sayyid, 'Alī also wrote Persian poetry.

According to a tradition among the Shī'ites of Kashmīr,

Sayyid 'Ali Hamadānī is said to have been a Shī'ite. Nūru'llāh Shūshtarī in his work *Majālisu'l-Mu'minīn* has included him in the list of Shī'ite saints. But Nūru'llāh Shūshtarī is not a sure guide on this question, for he regards all great Ṣūfīs, philosophers, and scholars of medieval Islam as Shiites. A modern scholar also thinks that Sayyid 'Alī was a Shī'ite on the ground that in some of his poetic compositions he has extolled the virtues of 'Alī and his successors.[78] But this is an insufficient proof, for many Sunnī saints have also written similar panegyrics, glorifying the family of the Prophet. Thus there is no sufficient evidence to support the view that Sayyid 'Alī was a Shī'ite; on the other hand, there is reason to believe that he was a Sunnī Muslim. In his work *Ẕakhīratu'l-Mulūk* he extensively quotes the traditions on the authority of 'Āisha, the wife of the Prophet, and the early Caliphs.[79] He has profound reverence for the first four Caliphs whom he regards, next to the Prophet, as the best of creation.[80] In one place he strongly says that it is the duty of every Muslim to spread the principles of *Sunnat va al-Jamā'at*.[81] Ja'far Badakhshī, a disciple of Sayyid, 'Alī, says that he was at first a Ḥanafite, but later he became a Shāfi'ite. However, he did not object if any of his followers wished to remain a Ḥanafite; nor did he oppose the practice of the Ḥanafite law in Kashmīr.[82]

As a Ṣūfī, Sayyid 'Ali belonged by two intermediaries to the Order of Shaikh Aḥmad 'Alā'u'd-Daula Samnānī (d. 1335-36), and attached himself to the Kubravīya Order.[83] But although the Sayyid did not himself found any order, his indirect disciple, Sayyid Muḥammad Nūrbakhsh, was the founder in the ninth century of the Nūrbakhshīya sect which played an important role in the religious and literary life of Persia for many centuries.[84] In reality, however, the real value of Sayyid 'Alī's work in Persia and Central Asia has yet to be properly assessed. But it appears that he achieved his greatest triumphs in the Valley of Kashmīr, where even today after the lapse of more than 450 years his influence continues to be felt.

Sulṭān Sikandar (1389-1413)

Quṭbu'd-Dīn was an old man when a son was born to him

and was named Sikandar. To celebrate the occasion festivities were held, gifts and Jāgīrs were conferred upon the courtiers, and prisoners were released.[85] Later his queen gave birth to another son who was named Haibat.[86]

On Quṭbu'd-Dīn's death in the year 1389, his eldest son Sikandar ascended the throne; but as he was a minor, his mother Queen Sūra acted as Regent.[87] The chronicles do not describe the events of her Regency clearly and fully. She, however, appears to have been a woman of ability and strong character. She ruled with a firm hand, and put to death her own daughter and son-in-law for conspiring against Sikandar.[88] Meanwhile Rāi Māgre, who was the prime minister, had grown powerful and ambitious. He had Prince Haibat, Sikandar's younger brother, whom he suspected of being his rival, poisoned.[89] Similarly he had a minister named Sāhaka treacherously killed.[90] The chronicles do not tell us if Sūra adopted any measures to check the growing power of Rāi Māgre. But when Sikandar took the reins of government in his hands, he decided to get rid of Rāi Māgre. He sent him with a force to invade Ladākh, hoping that he would be slain there. But instead Rāi Māgre succeeded in conquering Ladākh and returning victorious to Srīnagar. And as his relations with the Sulṭān worsened, he raised the banner of revolt. Sikindar first tried to persuade him to give up his refractory conduct, but having failed in the attempt, he sent Laddarāja to attack him from the front, while he himself advanced to attack him from the rear. On the approach of these forces, Rāi Māgre fled without offering any resistance. But he was seized by the chief of Bānihāl, and sent of Sikandar. The Sulṭān spared his life in consideration of his past services, but threw him into prison where, after sometime, he committed suicide.[91]

In 1398 the storm of Timūr's invasion burst on India.He had left Samarqand in April 1398, and encamped on the banks of the Indus on the 20th September, at the very spot where Jalālu'd-Dīn Khawārizm Shāh had fled before Chingīz Khān by crossing the river. Here ambassadors from various countries came to offer their allegiance. Sulṭān Sikandar too, in order to avert the invasion of his kingdom, sent an envoy to the conqueror, professing submission. Tīmūr was satisfied at this, and dismissed the envoy after issuing a *farman* that Sikandar should join him with his army at Dīpālpur.[92] Sikandar accordingly set out from Srīnagar, but on reaching the village of Jabhan he was informed that Tīmūr's ministers wanted from him a contribution of 30,000 horse and 100,000 *durusts* of gold, each weighing two and a half *misqāls*. He therefore returned to Kashmīr to collect the sum.[93]

When Tīmūr occupied Delhi after annihilating the army of Maḥmūd, the last Tughlaq ruler, he sent Uljāh Tīmūr Tufuqdār, Faulād Bahādur and Zainu'd-Dīn to Sikandar to demand explanation why he had not come to pay his homage.[94] The envoys proceeded to Srīnagar and, after meeting the Sulṭān, returned, accompanied by his representatives led by Maulānā Nūru'd-Dīn. Meanwhile Tīmūr had left Delhi, and they joined him in the neighbourhood of Jammu. On Ferbuary 24, 1399, Nūru'd-Dīn presented a letter from Sikandar, which was written in respectful terms and expressed his desire of waiting on him. On being asked why Sikandar had not proceeded to Dipālpūr as ordered, he explained that the Sulṭān had advanced as far as Jabhan, but returned to collect money and horses which he expected would be demanded from him. On hearing this Tīmūr rebuked his ministers, and told them that the tribute demanded from Sikandar was beyond his means, and that he should have been asked to pay according to his capacity. Tīmūr then sent the envoys accompanied by Mu'tamad Zainu'd-Dīn with the message that Sikandar should not consider himself bound to fulfil the demands made by his officers, but that he should proceed at once and meet him on the banks of the Indus after twenty-eight days.[95] On receiving these instructions, Sikandar again set out, but on reaching Bārāmula, he learnt that Tīmūr had crossed the Indus and proceeded towards Samarqand. He therefore returned to Srīnagar.[96]

Sikandar did not make any new conquests; he only tried to retain the kingdom left to him by his father. In the early part of his reign he led an expedition against the ruler of Ohind named Fīrūz, who had renounced his authority, and compelled him to recognize his suzerainty and give him his daughter Mīra in marriage.[97]

After reducing Fīrūz, Sikandar sent an army under Sūhabhaṭṭa and Laddarāja to subdue Pāla Deo, Rājā of Jammu, who had not paid him tribute. Realising the futility of resistance, the Rājā submitted, and sent his daughter as a present to Sikandar. But as soon after he again declared his independence, Sikandar sent Sūhabhaṭṭa and Jasrat Khokar,[98] with whom he had entered into an alliance, with a large force against the Rājā. They defeated him and sacked Jammu.

Of the Sulṭān's private life the chronicles tell us very little. They only mention that he abstained from wine and other intoxicants, and that on religious grounds he did not listen to music. He appears to have been a man of puritan temperament, and banned all the gay celebrations which were so common a feature of reigns of Zainu'l-'Ābidīn and other Sulṭāns.[99] He also never indulged in extra-marital relations, and kept within the legally prescribed limit. Sikandar first married Mīra, the daughter of the king of Ohind, who became the mother of his three sons, Mīr Khān, Shādī Khān and Mahmūd.[100] He then married Śobhā Devī[101] who gave birth to two sons named Muḥammad and Fīrūz,[102] and two daughters who were married to the rulers of Ohind and Sindh.[103] But Sikandar did not have the same affection for the sons of his second wife as for those by his first.[104] As a result when Fīrūz grew up, Sikandar exiled him from Kashmīr in order to prevent a war of succession with his step-brothers.[105] During his last illness he called his three sons in his presence, and advised them to avoid strife and remain united. He then appointed Mīr Khān, the eldest, as his successor and conferred upon him the title 'Alī Shāh. He breathed his last in 1413.[106]

Sikandar was an able generous and brave ruler, and looked after the welfare of his subjects. He put an end to many oppressive taxes like Bāj and Tamghā and others, which had hitherto been realised from the people.[107] He established schools for the education of boys, and founded hospitals where medicine and food were supplied free.[108] He endowed a number of villages for the benefit of travellers, scholars, Sayyids and other deserving persons. The Shaikhu'l-Islām was made responsible for the administration of these endowments.[109]

Sikandar was a great patron of learned men and Ṣūfīs; and during his reign many of them came to Kashmīr from Persia and Central Asia. The Sultan treated them with respect, and gave them Jāgīrs which could be inherited by their descendants. Some of the more prominent among those who entered the Valley during his period were Sayyid Ḥasan Shirāzī, formerly Qāẓī in Shiraz, whom Sikandar made Qāẓī of Kashmīr; Sayyid Aḥmad from Isfahān, who was the author of many books; Sayyid Muḥammad from Khwārizm who was a good poet; Sayyid Jalālu'd-Dīn, a saint from Bukhārā, who came with his followers; Bābā Ḥājī Adham, and his disciple Bābā Ḥasan, the logician, from Balkh.[110] Also at this time came Sayyid Muḥammad Hamadānī, the son of the great Sayyid 'Alī Hamadānī. He was born in Khatlān in the year 1572, and was twelve years of age when his father died. Sayyid 'Alī left a testament for his son with Maulānā Sarāi to be sent to Khwaja Isḥāq Khatlānī and Maulānā Nūru'd-Dīn Badakhshī, two of his most prominent disciples.In this will Sayyid 'Alī advised his son to travel extensively when he grew up, for this would help him to build up his character, broaden his mind and develop his personality.[111]

Muḥammad Hamadānī read under Khwāja Isḥāq and Maulānā Nūru'd-Dīn, and when he attained the age of sixteen the testament of his father was given to him. Muḥammad Hamadānī visited many places, and then in 1393, at the age of twenty-two, he arrived in Kashmīr with three hundred Sayyids and learned men. He wrote for Sulṭān Sikandar *Risāla-i-Sikandarī*, a work on Ṣūfism, in Persian.[112] He was also the author of a book on logic in Arabic.[113] He was greatly revered by the Sulṭān who regarded him as his teacher and guide. He converted a number of Hindus to Islām, but the most important man to embrace Islām under his influence was Sūhabhaṭṭa, Sikandar's chief minister and commander-in-chief, whom he named Ṣaifu'd-Dīn, and after the death of his first wife Bībī Tāj Khātūn, the daughter of Sayyid Ḥusain Baihaqī, married his daughter. Muḥammad Hamadānī stayed in Kashmīr for nearly twelve years.[114] He left Kashmīr owing to his differences with Sayyid Muḥammad Ḥiṣārī and proceeded on a pilgrimage to Mecca. From there he returned to Khatlān where he died on April 30, 1450, and was buried near his father.[115]

Sikandar was a great builder. He founded the town of Sikandarpūr,[116] and there built a magnificent palace and a grand Jāmi' Masjid. The latter's architect was Ṣadru'd-Dīn Khurāsānī. It had 372 wooden columns, each 40 yards in height and 6 yards in circumference. There were four archways, each of which contained 32 of these columns.[117] Sikandar also built a mosque in the town of Bījbehāra, and laid the foundation-stone of an 'Id-gāh in Srīnagar which was completed by his son. Sulṭān Alī Shāh.[118] Besides the mosques, he built *khānqāhs* (hospices) in the villages of Vachi and Trāl[119] and in the town of Sōpūr.[120] Sayyid 'Ali Hamadānī had built a raised floor in 'Alā'u'd-Dīnpūr for the congregational prayers. Sikandar constructed there in 799/1396-97 a hospice known as Khānqāh-Mu'allā. He endowed it with the three villages of Vachi, Shaura, and Nunahwānī, and appointed Maulānā Muḥammad Sa'īd as trustee.[121] Sikandar also constructed another mosque near the spring of Bavan. It was two-storeyed with a beautiful garden around it, having all kinds of flower plants and fruit trees. The place was so pleasant and picturesque that Sikandar used to spend his time there in spring. His example was followed by the subsequent rulers of Kashmīr until the time of Muḥammad Shāh.[122]

Sikandar was the first Sulṭān of Kashmīr to enforce the *Sharī'a* with great strictness in the country. He banned the use of wine and other intoxicants, and prohibited gambling, the dancing of women and the playing of musical instruments like the flute, lute, and guitar, allowing only the playing of drum and fife for military purposes.[123] And in order to see that the Islamic law was properly enforced, he established the office of the Shaikhu'l-Islām. These measures were adopted by Sikandar under the influence of Sayyid Muḥammad Hamadānī. It was also due to his advice that the Sulṭān imposed two *pals* of silver as *Jizya* upon the non-Muslims, and prohibited *Satī* and the application of *qashqa* (*tilak*—a religious mark made by the

Khanqah-i-Mu'alla, Srinagar

Jami' Masjid, Srinagar

Hindus of the forehead).[124] However, the chief person who prevailed upon Sikandar to adopt an intolerant attitude towards the non-Muslims was Ṣaifu'd-Dīn, who was in this respect his evil genius. The Sulṭān at first resisted him, but in the end gave in, and allowed himself to be used as an instrument of his minister's religious fanaticism. Ṣaifu'd-Dīn, with the zeal of a new convert, called upon the Brahmans to embrace Islām. As a result some became Muslim. Those who refused had to pay *Jizya*.[125] Others who would not or could not pay, decided to leave Kashmīr and take refuge in India. When Ṣaifu'd-Dīn heard of this, he ordered the guards on the frontiers not to allow any one to leave the Valley without a permit. But in spite of these restrictions many Brahmans succeeded in escaping from the country.[126]

In their misplaced zeal for their faith, Sikandar and Ṣaifu'd-Dīn were also responsible for the destruction of some images and temples. But the statement of Jonarāja that there was no village or town where temples were not razed to the ground, is fantastic.[127] It must be remembered that as Ṣaifu'd-Dīn had been a Brahman, Jonarāja resented his conversion to Islām and therefore magnified his iconoclastic activities. The Muslim chronicles also speak of the wholesale destruction of temples, but they distort facts owing to their anxiety to represent Sikandar and his minister as champions of Islām. The falseness of their view is evident from the fact that if we add up the list, given by them, of temples allegedly destroyed, then not a single one should have remained standing. In reality, however, even over a hundred years after Sikandar, a large number of temples were still in existence in the Valley. Mīrzā Ḥaidar Dughlat, who ruled Kashmīr for ten years, writing in about 1546 observed. "First and foremost among the wonders of Kashmīr stand her idol temples. In and around Kashmīr there are more than 150 temples.... In the rest of the world there is not to be seen, or heard of, one building like this. How wonderful that there should (here) be a hundred and fifty of them."[128] Abū'l-Faẓl also wrote that some of the temples were in a state of perfect preservation;[129] and similarly Jahāngīr remarked that "the lofty idol temples, which were built before the manifestation of Islām, are still in existence."[130]

Thus the iconoclastic activities of Sikandar have been greatly exaggerated. In many instances it was not Sikandar who pulled down the temples, but what really happened was that when the inhabitants of a certain locality embraced Islām, the temple was converted into a mosque, or it went into ruins due to sheer neglect. Many suffered because of earthquakes.[131] But these factors were ignored, and Sikandar was held responsible for any temple that was found in a crumbling state. Some writers have even gone to the extent of suggesting that he employed gunpowder to destroy temples. Stein, however, observes: "The early use of gunpowder in Kashmīr has been doubted by others, and I believe rightly. Earthquakes and the imperfect fitting of stone, observable in all Kashmīrian temples, are sufficient to explain the complete ruin, notwithstanding the massive character of the material."[132] Another writer similarly observes: "It is scarcely possible to imagine that the state of ruin to which they have been reduced (referring in particular to the temples of Avantipūr), has been the work of time or even of men, as their solidity is fully equal to that of the most massive monuments of Egypt. Earthquakes must have been the chief agents in their overthrow.[133]

Sulṭān 'Alī Shāh (1413-20)

Sikandar's eldest son, Mīr Khān, who ascended the throne under title of 'Ali Shāh, showed no ability as a ruler. He was weak and fickleminded, and allowed himself to be dominated by Ṣaifu'd-Dīn who continued as chief minister.[134] Other ministers who enjoyed 'Alī Shah's confidence, were Laddī Māgre and Śankar, the physician. But this roused the jealousy of Ṣaifu'd-Dīn who decided to destroy them. His plan was to strike at his rivals when all of them, including the sons of Laddī Māgre, particularly the eldest Muhammad Māgre, the governor of Bāngil,[135] would be present at the capital. To lull them into a false sense of security he began to bestow favours of Laddī Māgre's another son Tājī Māgre and to consult him on all important matters. He then invited Muḥammad Māgre to

Srīnagar under the pretext of seeking his advice. But the latter suspected treachery and fled. When Ṣaifu'd-Dīn heard of this, he had Laddī Māgre, who was ill, his remaining sons and Śankar, treacherously seized and thrown into prison. Meanwhile Muḥammad Māgre had taken refuge with Govind, chief of the Khaśas, who lived in the neighbourhood of Ohind, and whom he regarded as his friend. But Govind betrayed him to Ṣaifu'd-Dīn's men. Muḥammad Māgre was seized, shackled, and imprisoned in the fort of Bīru.[136] He, however, succeeded in making good his escape through the efforts of his foster-brothers. Ṣaifu'd-Dīn became alarmed at this news, and he had Laddī Māgre put to death. Laddī Māgre being a popular man, his execution caused considerable grief to the people.[137]

We have seen that Sikandar had exiled his son Fīrūz. But after the Sulṭan's death, the latter returned to Kashmīr to contest the throne with the support of the Turkish troops, supplied to him by the ruler of Hindustān.[138] Ṣaifu'd-Dīn at once despatched Laddarāja and Gaurabhaṭṭa who completely routed Fīrūz. In reward for their services, Ṣaifu'd-Dīn appointed Laddarāja as Mīr Bakhshī, and Gaurabhaṭṭa as governor of Kamrāj.[139]

Soon after, however, Laddarāja, having incurred the displeasure of Ṣaifu'd-Dīn, tried to flee the country. But he was seized by Hamsabhaṭṭa, Ṣaifu'd-Dīn's brother, and thrown into prison. Meanwhile, Ṣaifu'd-Dīn died of consumption, and his death was followed by a struggle for power between Hamsabhaṭṭa and Gaurabhaṭṭa whom he had entrusted with the government before his death. Hamsabhaṭṭa, in order to strengthen himself against his rivals, released Laddarāja, and with his help defeated and killed Gaurabhaṭṭa. At the same time realising that Laddarāja might prove a dangerous rival, he assassinated him. In this way he became the most powerful man in the kingdom.[140]

There was, however, one man whom he regarded as a thorn in his side. This was Shāhī Khān, 'Alī Shāh's younger brother, who was not prepared to submit to him. Hamsabhaṭṭa, therefore, made up his mind to destroy him too. But Shāhī Khān came to know of it, and with the consent of 'Alī Shāh and the support of the Thākurs,[141] he had assassinated him in the 'Īd-gāh on the day *'Īdu'z-Ẕuha*. 'Alī Shāh, who had been chafing under the yoke of Hamsabhaṭṭa, was glad at his fall, and in his place appointed Shāhī as prime minister. This appointment was hailed by the people, for the young Prince had endeared himself to them by his courage, intelligence, and tact.[142]

Not long after these events, 'Alī Shāh, who was of a religious bent of mind, decided to give up his throne and go on a pilgrimage to Mecca, and to spend the rest of his days there. Shāhī Khān, however, tried to dissuade him from this step by telling him that serving the people was the best form of devotion to God. But his advice had no effect, and 'Alī Shāh left Kashmīr after entrusting the kingdom to him, and giving him the title of Zainu'l-'Ābidīn.[143]

From Srīnagar 'Alī Shāh proceeded to Jammu to bid farewell to its rājā who was his father-in-law. On the way interested persons pointed out the difficulties and privations of the journey of Mecca; and, when he reached Jammu, his father-in-law disapproved of his decision.[144] 'Alī Shāh, who never possessed a strong will, yielded to these criticism. He gave up the idea of going on a pilgrimage, and returned to Kashmīr via Rajaurī, accompanied by the armies of the rulers of Jammu and Rajaurī to claim his throne.[145] Jonarāja states that Zainu'l-'Ābidīn was angry with 'Alī Shāh for having brought a foreign army, but that the affection for his brother got the better of him, and so he gave up the throne and left Kashmīr.[146] Another chronicler says that since Zainu'l-'Ābidīn had held the kingdom as a trust of 'Alī Shāh, he relinquished it in his favour and left the Valley.[147] But the truth appears to be that Zainu'l-'Ābidīn retired without offering any resistance because he did not find himself strong enough to fight 'Alī Shāh. He proceeded to Siālkōt and sought the help of Jasrat Khokar.[148] The latter promised to support him, but this angered 'Alī Shāh who set out to punish the Khokar chief. The ruler of Jammu, however, advised him not to descend from the mountains until he had arrived with his army, for the Khokars were clever fighters.[149] But 'Alī Shāh ignored him and continued his march. The result was that he was defeated by Jasrat at Thanna.[150] After this victory Zainu'l-'Ābidīn proceeded to Srīnagar, where he was welcomed by the people. This however did not end the civil war. Jonarāja does not record the subsequent events, but from a study of the Persian chronicles it appears that 'Alī Shāh reorganized his army, and, with the support of the Jammu forces, invaded the Valley to recover the throne. Zainu'l-'Ābidīn, hearing of this, advanced via Bārāmūla, and defeated his brother at Urī.[151] According to Ḥaidar Malik, 'Alī Shāh was captured and imprisoned in the fort of Pakhlī where he died after a few years.[152] But Srīvara, who is a contemporary authority, says that he was seized by Jasrat and put to death by him. He does not state if this was done by the orders of Zainu'l-'Ābidīn, but it is unlikely that Jasrat should have carried out the execution without the consent of the Sulṭān, his friend and patron.[153]

NOTES

1. Munich MS., 53b; T.A., iii, 426.
2. *Ibid.*
3. Jonar., 26-7.
4. Firishta, 649.
5. T.H., ii, 85b.
6. Jonar., 33. T.A., iii, 427; Munich MS., f. 54a.
7. Jonar., p. 33.
8. *Ibid.*, p. 26.
9. Jonar., pp. 24, 33; Munich MS., 50a.
10. N.A., 23a; G.A., f. 109a.
11. Jonar., p. 35.
12. *Ibid.*, Munich MS., f. 54a. The statement in T.A., iii, 427, that Jamshēd was suspicious of his brother from the beginning is not supported by Kashmīr chronicles.
13. It is a village situated in Lat. 33° 55′ Long. 75° 4′ on the right bank of the Jehlam about 17 miles south-east of Srīnagar. It lies on the site of the town of the same name founded by Rājā Avantivarman.
14. Munich MS., f. 54a.
15. *Ibid.*, ff. 54b-55b; Jonar., pp. 33-5.
16. Jonar., p. 35.
17. W.K., f. 16a.
18. Jonar., 37.

19. *Ibid.*, 37; B.S., f. 18b.
20. Jonar., 37; Munich MS. f. 55a.
21. Munich MS., ff. 55a-b.
22. Jonar., 37.
23. B.S., f. 18b.
24. Firishta, T.A., and the Munich MS., say that he was the son of Shāh Mīr and brother of 'Alā'u'd-Dīn. But this is wrong. Jonarāja calls him at one place the son of Shāh Mīr (p. 35) but at another place mentions him as the grandson of Shāh Mīr (p. 26). All other Persion chronicles state that Shihābu'd-Dīn was the son of 'Alā'u'd-Dīn.
25. Munich MS., ff. 55b-56a; B.S., ff. 20b-21b; H.M., f. 108b.
26. H.M., f. 108b. Later chronicles add Transoxiana to the list.
27. B.S., ff. 20a-21a; Ḥasan, ff. 105b-106b; H.M., ff. 108a-b.
28. Munich MS., ff. 56a-b; Jonar., p. 39; T.A., iii, 428.
29. B.S., f. 20b; Ḥasan, 106b; H.M., 108b-109b.
30. N.A., f. 28a; G.A., ff. 113a-b.
31. See Reinaud, *Memoire sur l'Inde*, pp. 190 sqq.
32. Munich MS., ff. 55b-56a; B.S., ff. 20b-21b; H.M., f. 108b. S.A., pp. 2-3, attributes these conquests to Sayyid Ḥasan, son of Tāju'd-Dīn, a cousin of Sayyid 'Ali Hamadānī.
33. J.R.A.S., xlvii, (1918), p. 453. There is some confusion regarding the date of Shihābu'd-Dīn's meeting with the Rājā of Nagarkōt and Fīrūz Shāh. From a study of Fīrūz Shāh's reign it appears that this meeting must have taken place either in 1360 or later for, before this period, Fīrūz was busy elsewhere. (M.T., i, 327-30). But the difficulty arises from the statement of Jonarāja that in 1360 a flood took place in Kashmīr, and that Shihābu'd-Dīn was present at the time in Srīnagar. Shihābu'd-Dīn might have left Kashmīr to meet Fīrūz after the flood, but according to the Kashmīr chronicles he proceeded directly from Ladākh to Nagarkōt, and the flood took place on his return from the campaign. This means that the meeting took place before 1360. But that was impossible as is clear from the movements of the Delhi Sulṭān. It may be that the flood occurred in about 1362 and not in 1360 as mentioned by Jonaraja. It is also possible the Shihabu'd-Dīn met Fīrūz early in 1360 and then returned to Srīnagar at the time of the flood.
34. Neither Jonar nor any history of Fīrūz Shāh's reign refers to this conflict or a marriage alliance. B.S. and Ḥaidar Malik's history too do not mention of the marriage alliance. It occurs only in the later chronicles of Kashmīr, which also describe Shihābu'd-Dīn's

marriage alliances with the rulers of Sindh and Kābul. But these are legendary accounts.

35. B.S., f. 19a; Ḥasan, f. 103a; H.M., f. 107a.
36. H.M., f. 107b.
37. N.A., ff. 29a-b; G.A., f. 110b.
38. B.S., f. 22a; Ḥasan, 107b; H.M., 109b.
39. Jonar., p. 44.
40. Jonar., p. 42; Munich MS., f. 56b; B.S., f. 21b. Shihābu'd-Dīnpūr is now called Shādīpūr (See p. 16 and n. 5, *supra*).
41. See p. 43n. 2 *supra* for a discussion of the date of the flood.
42. Jonar., p. 41; Munich MS. f. 56b.
43. Munich MS. f. 56; also T.H., cited in Ṣūfī, i, 139.
44. Jonar., p. 41; B.S., f. 231a, Udayaśri of Jonarāja is Udshahrawal of Persian chronicles.
45. Ḥasan, 105a.
46. Jonar., pp. 38, 41. Candra Ḍāmara of Jonarāja is Malik Chandra of Bahāristān and Chandra Dār of Ḥaidar Malik. Śura Lolaka of Jonarāja is Shahrāwal of the Persian chronicles.
47. B.S., f. 21b; Ḥasan, f. 107a; H.M., f. 109a. N.A. adds the name of Sayyid Ḥasan, the son of Sayyid Tāju'd-Dīn, a cousin of Sayyid 'Ali Hamadānī, as one of the Sulṭān's commanders.
48. Jonar., pp. 42 sqq; Munich MS., f. 57a.
49. Jonar., pp. 47-8; Munich MS., f. 59a.
50. W.K., f. 17b.
51. It is a part of Srīnagar consisting of the two Mohallas of Langarhatta and Pīr Ḥajī Muḥammad.
52. Jonar., p. 53; Munich MS., 59b.
53. *Ibid.*, f. 58-b; Jonar., pp. 47-8.
54. Munich M.S., f. 59a.
55. Jonar., 49.
56. *Ibid.*, pp. 59-2; Munich MS., ff. 58b-59a.
57. *Journal Asiatique*, ccxl, p. 54.
58. F.K., ff. 135a-b; also Ja'far, *Khulāṣatu'l-Manāqib*, f. 90a.
59. *Ibid.*, f. 136a; also *Nafaḥātu'l-Uns*, p. 515; *Riyāẓu'l-'Ārifin*, p. 169; *Ḥabību's-Siyar*, iii, p. 87.
60. F.K., ff. 136-b-37a.
61. *Nafaḥātu'l-Uns*, p. 515; *Ḥabību's-Siyar*, iii, p. 87.
62. *Ibid*.
63. F.K., ff. 135a-37a.
64. *Ta'rīkh-i-Kabīr*, pp. 12-4; also *Journal Asiatique*, ccxl, pp. 61-2.
65. *Ibid.*, p. 62.
66. B.S., f. 24a; Ḥasan, ff. 109-110a.

67. H.M., (B.N.) f. 36b.
68. F.K., f. 147a; also S.A., p. 8.
69. Jonar., 53.
70. F.K., f. 147b.
71. *Ibid.*, ff. 147b-48b; Ḥasan, f. 108b; H.M., 110b.
72. Ḥasan, 110a; H.M., 111a. It is a said that when a darwēsh heard that the cap had been buried with Fatḥ Shāh's body he prophesied that this would mean the end of the dynasty.
73. F.K., f. 151b; *Majmū'a dar Ansūb Mashā'ikh-i-Kashmīr*, f. 111b; Ḥasan, ff. 110b. One of the Kashmīrī nobles who accompanied the saint was Laddi Māgre. (S.A. pp. 13-4).
74. *Journal Asiatique*, ccxl, pp. 54-5.
75. See Ethe, i, p. 1021 and Rieu. ii. pp. 835b-36a for the list of his works. Also *Journal Asiatique*, ccxl, pp. 56 sqq and *Yaghmā*, iv, No. 8, pp. 337 sqq.
76. Ethe, ii, No. 3057.
77. Bodleian, i, No. 1241, 28.
78. *Journal Asiatique*, ccxl, pp. 54 sq.; and *Yaghmā*, iv, No. 8, pp. 337-38.
79. 'Alī Hamadānī, *Ẕakhīratu'l-Mulūk*, ff. 6a sqq.
80. *Ibid.*, f. 6b.
81. *Ibid.*, f. 52b.
82. Ja'far Badakhshī, *Manqabatu'l-Jawāhir*, ff. 30b-31a; also F.K., f. 147b.
83. *Journal Asiatique*, ccxl, pp. 55-6.
84. *Ibid.*, f. 56.
85. Jonar., p. 53; Munich MS., f. 59b. The author of this work calls him Sankar. Perhaps it was an abbreviation of Sikandar.
86. Jonar., p. 53.
87. Munich MS., ff. 59b-60a; Firishta, p. 562.
88. Jonar., (Bo. ed.), No. 668. Dutt's translation is here somewhat confused.
89. Jonar., p. 55, calls Rāi Māgre as Uddaka.
90. *Ibid.*
91. Jonar., pp. 55-6.
92. Sharafu'd-Dīn 'Alī Yazdī *Ẓafar-nāma*, pp. 46-7; *Malfūẓāt*, ff. 283a-b; See also Munich MS., ff. 60b-61b which gives a detailed account of Sikandar's relations with Tīmūr.
93. *Ẓafar-nāma*, p. 164; *Malfūẓāt*, f. 319a.
94. It was with these envoys that Tīmūr must have sent the two elephants as presents to Sikandar mentioned in B.S., Ḥaidar Malik's *Ta'rīkh* and other chronicles.

95. *Ẓafar-nāma*, pp. 164-5; *Malfūẓāt*, ff. 319a-b.
96. Munich MS., 61b; Firishta, p. 653. It is absurd to say that Tīmūr took with him Shāhī Khān, the future Zainu'l-Ābidīn. Shāhī Khān was not even born when Tīmūr invaded India.
97. Jonar., pp. 58-9; Munich MS., f. 62a.
98. He was the son of Shaikhā Khokar, the brother of Nuṣrat Khokar. He had been taken away into captivity by Tīmūr, and returned to the Punjāb on the conqueror's death. (See for more details about the Khokars, Rose's *Glossary of the Punjāb Tribes and Castes*, ii, pp. 546-7; and I.A., xxxvi, pp. 1-8.
99. See Chapters IV and V.
100. Jonar., pp. 58-9; Munich M.S., f. 62a.
101. We know from the chronicles that Sikandar married the daughter of the Rājā of Jammu (Jonar. Bo. ed. No. 729). Probably she was known of Śobhā Devī. But if she was a different person, then it means that Sikandar had three wives.
102. Fīrūz was Sikandar's son from Śobhā Rānī and was not an adopted son. (Jonar. Bo. ed. Nos. 737, 856; also Jonar., p. 64). Jonar., p. 59, wrongly says that the sons of Śobhā were adopted children.
103. Munich M.S., f. 63a.
104. Jonar. (Bo. ed.), No. 737.
105. *Ibid.*, No. 856; Munich M.S., f. 63a.
106. Jonar., p. 61; T.A., iii, 435; Firishta, p. 655.
107. T.A., iii, 433; T.H., ii, f. 89b. Bāj had been collected under Shihābu'd-Dīn (BS., f. 19a). Tamghā was a demand in excess of the land revenue but Bāj was simply a tax or toll. Tamghā seems to have been introduced into Kashmīr from Persia or Turkistān. Bāj and Tamghā were levied on horses, cows, goats, silken clothes etc., (Wilson's *Glossary* pp. 5 sq.).
108. B.S., f. 34b. These charitable institutions survived until the seventeenth century.
109. *Ibid.*
110. *Ibid.*
111. F.K., f. 155a.
112. *Ibid.* f. 156a; B.S., f. 25b; S.A., p. 18.
113. *Ibid.*; H.M., f. 112b.
114. S.A., p. 27; *Miskīn, Ta'rīkh-i-Kabīr*, p. 25, says Muḥammad Hamadānī stayed for 22 years.
115. *Ibid.*; B.S., f. 36b; Da'ūd Mishkāti, *Asraru'l-Abrār*, f. 45a. See also S.A., pp. 18 sqq. for Muḥammad Hamadānī's life in Kashmīr. The date of the Sayyid's death as 809/1377-8 given in W.K., f.

20b, is incorrect.

116. It was situated at the foot of the Kōh-i-Mārān. It is now called Nauhatta and is a part of Srīnagar.
117. B.S., f. 35a; H.M., 114a.
118. B.S., f. 35a; Ḥasan, f, 113b; H.M., f. 114a; see also T.H., i, 140b sq.
119. Vachi is a village situated at the eastern foot of Zainapūr Udar. Trāl is a small town situated in Lat. 33° 56′ Long. 75° 10′ on the sloping plateau at the foot of the mountains east of the Volur pargana of which it is a Tahsīl station.
120. T.H., i, ff. 140b sqq.
121. B.S., f. 35b; T.H., i, 113b-114a. According to a tradition Muḥammad Hamadānī gave a *Lāl-i-Badakhshān* to Sikandar in return for these villages. But this seems to be unreliable for the Sulṭān could not have accepted the *lāl* as payment for the endowment. *Futuḥāt-i-Kubravīya* says it was given as a present to Sikandar by the Sayyid.
122. B.S., 34b; Ḥasan, ff. 114a-b; H.M., f. 114b.
123. B.S., f. 26a; Jonar., pp. 67-7; H.M., f. 113b.
124. Jonar., p. 60; also Jonar., (Bo. ed.) No. 1077; Munich MS., f. 64b; B.S., f. 26a. For more details about *Jizya* see Chapter XI.
125. H.M., f. 113b; Jonar., p. 60, says the Hindus had to pay heavy fines for retaining their religion. This fine was nothing else but *Jizya*.
126. Jonar., pp. 65-7.
127. *Ibid.*, p. 60.
128. T.R., p. 426.
129. A.A., ii, 124.
130. *Tuzuk-i-Jahāngirī*, ii, 150.
131. Lawrence, *Valley*, pp. 162, 213.
132. Cited in Lawrence, *Valley*, p. 190 n. 1; see also J.A.S.B., xlv, p. 64, where Maclagen in his article "*On Early Asiatic Weapons*" says that gunpowder was not known in the time of Sikandar, and that the destruction was caused by earthquakes and Time. He illustrates his view by referring to the temples of Pāyech and Mārtand which, in about a quarter of a century since Cunningham expressed his view, have suffered owing to the fingers of Time and the moderate movements of the earth. The earthquakes of June and July 1828 caused considerable destruction of house property in Srīnagar, and large masses of rocks are said to have been detached from the hill sides and thrown down.
133. Mooreroft, ii, p. 150.

134. Jonar., p. 61; Munich MS. f. 66a.
135. It is a pargana in Kamrāj. Its old name was Bhangil. But by the time of Ḥaidar Malik its name had been changed to Bāngil.
136. Bīru is Bahurūpa of Jonarāja. It is a pargana on the south-west side of the Valley and is situated in Lat. 34° 1′ Long. 74° 38′.
137. Jonar., pp. 61 sqq; Munich MS., ff. 65a-b.
138. The name of this ruler is not mentioned in the chronicles. But perhaps he was Khiẓr Khān, the founder of the Sayyid dynasty, who was ruling Delhi at this time.
139. Jonar., p. 65; Munich MS., f. 66a.
140. *Ibid.*, 66b; Jonar., p. 69.
141. Thākkura was a title of the small nobility of Rājpūts from the hill territories to the south of Kashmīr. (Stein, BK. VII, No. 290n; Lawrence, *Valley*, p. 306).
142. Jonar., p. 69; Munich MS., f. 67a.
143. Jonar., pp. 70-1; Jonarāja does not say the Mecca was 'Alī Shāh's destination, but it is mentioned by the Persian chronicles.
144. Jonar., p. 71; Ḥasan, f. 115a; H.M., f. 115a-b.
145. Munich MS., f. 68a; T.A., iii, 434.
146. Jonar., p. 72.
147. Munich MS., f. 68a.
148. *Ibid.*, f. 68b; T.A., iii, 434.
149. Jonar., pp. 74-5; Munich MS., f. 69a.
150. Yaḥya as-Sirhindī, *Ta'rīkh-i-Mubārak Shāhī*, p. 194; T.A., i, 271.
151. H.M., f. 115b; Ḥasan, f. 115a; N.K., f. 28b.
152. H.M., f. 115b.
153. Śrīv, BK. I, Chapt. iii, No. 106 (Bo. ed.).

Chapter 5

Zainu'l-'Ābidīn the Great (1420-70)

Of all the Sulṭāns who sat on the throne of Kashmīr, Zainu'l-'Ābidīn was undoubtedly the greatest. He ushered in a period of nearly half a century of peace, prosperity and benevolent rule for his people. He introduced many arts and crafts for which Kashmīr has become famous ever since. He promoted learning, music, and painting, and made Kashmīr the centre of a great culture. He won the loyalty and affection of his subjects who called him Bud Shāh or the Great King, a name by which he is remembered even today by the people Kashmīr. He acquired a halo in popular imagination which still surrounds his name in spite of the lapse of nearly five hundred years.

Conquests

The reign of Zainu'l-'Ābidīn, unlike that of his grandfather Shihābu'd-Dīn, is not noted for any stirring military exploits, for he was not inclined to wage wars for self-aggrandisement; his main interest lay in developing the arts of peace. At the same time he was not prepared to give up his claims to the territories which had been reduced by his grandfather and were of strategic and commercial importance to Kashmīr. Ladākh and Baltistān had been conquered by Shihābu'd-Dīn, but they had become independent after his death. Although Sikandar had reconquered them, they had again asserted their independence during the weak rule of 'Alī Shāh. Zainu'l-'Ābidīn, therefore, collected a large army in the pargana of Lār, and set out accompanied by his commanders, Hilmet Raina, Aḥmad Raina and Muḥammad Māgre. Having crossed the Zōjī-

Lā Pass he compelled the Ladākhī chief 'aBumlde lV to acknowledge his sovereignty. He then secured the allegiance of the Baltī ruler.[1] The account in Persian chronicles that in this expedition Zainu'l-'Ābidīn met the ruler of Kāshghar in Ladākh, and that although his forces were numerically inferior, he defeated his rival who was in occupation of the province, appears to be spurious, for it is not supported by Jonarāja who is a contemporary authority for this period. This tradition is in reality nothing but a repetition of an earlier encounter between Sulṭān Shihābu'd-Dīn and the ruler of Kāshghar. However, it was probably in the course of this campaign that Zainu'l-'Ābidīn invaded Guge,[2] and in the village of Shel[3] saved a gold image of Buddha from the hands of some tribal people, whom Francke wrongly regards as Muslims.[4] He also captured the town of Kulū which was in the possession of the Ladākhīs (Bhauṭṭas). However, it appears that, shortly after, these territories renounced the authority of the Sulṭān, for we find that in 1451 he had to send his eldest son Adham Khān to conquer Ladākh;[5] and then again between 1460 and 1470, he himself led the expedition.[6] But the details of this last campaign have not been recorded in the chronicles.

Zainu'l-'Ābidīn next directed his attention towards Ohind whose chief had been subdued by Sikandar, but had declared his independence in the reign of 'Alī Shāh. Although he was supported by the ruler of Sindh, the Sulṭān defeated him and established his suzerainty over him.[7]

Relations with Foreign Countries

Zainu'l-'Ābidīn's reputation for justice and patronage of art and culture had spread far and wide. This led to the exchange of embassies and the establishment of friendly relation between him and the rulers of various countries. Thus Mīrzā Abū Sa'īd (1452-67), the Tīmūrid ruler of Khurāsān and Transoxiana, sent an envoy to the Sulṭān with Arab horses and Bactrian camels as presents. Zainu'l-Ābidīn in return sent him saffron, paper, musk, shawls, crystal cups and other articles.[8] According to the *Nawādiru'l-Akhbār*, Shāh Rukh (1407-47), son of Tīmūr, who was a great patron of literature and science, sent Zainu'l-'Ābidīn elephants and precious stones. The Sulṭān thanked him and sent presents in return, but wrote that he would have appreciated it better, if he had received learned men and books instead of precious stones. Shāh Rukh, thereupon, sent him six learned scholars, and a number of manuscripts.[9]

Zainu'l-'Ābidīn had friendly relations with the rulers of other countries, too. The Sharīf of Mecca, and the kings of Gilān and Egypt sent him presents.[10] Dongar Singh, Rājā of Gwalior, hearing that the Sulṭān was interested in music, sent him valuable works on the subject. After his death his son Kirat Singh maintained friendly relations with the Sulṭān.[11] There was also an exchange of embassies and gifts between Zainu'l-'Ābidīn and the rulers of Sindh, Bengal, and Tibet, Sulṭān Maḥmūd of Gujarāt, Maḥmūd I of Mālwa, and Buhlūl Lodī.[12]

Zainu'l-'Ābidīn's relations with Jasrat continued to be as friendly as before. Jasrat had carved out for himself an independent principality in the Punjāb on his return from Samarqand. But being very ambitious, he wanted to extend it.[13] As Zainu'l-'Ābidīn was indebted to him for his help in the fight against 'Alī Shāh, he gave him military assistance. Jasrat, taking advantage of the weakness of Mubārak Shāh, the Sayyid ruler of Delhi, conquered the whole of the Punjāb. But his attempt to conquer Delhi failed.[14] Alarmed at his activities, Mubārāk Shāh sent a force to crush him. Jasrat being defeated, fled to Kashmīr, and received the protection of Zainu'l-'Ābidīn.[15]

Rebellions

In the early part of the reign there was a rising led by Pāṇḍū Chak, the leader of the Chaks. He organised a strike as a protest against the corvée system, so that when Zainu'l-'Ābidīn visited Kamrāj, he found that no unskilled workers were available. The Sulṭān, however, forced them to work. But when he left, Pāndū and his followers set fire to the palace and other government buildings in Kamrāj. Fearing retaliation, Pāṇḍū sent away his family and the families of his followers of Drāva, while he himself fled to the hills of Trahgām.[16] When the Sulṭān heard that his palace had been burnt he sent a force which destroyed all the houses of the Chaks in Trahgām. Pāṇḍū escaped to

Drāva[17] and joined his family there. Meanwhile, the Sulṭān rebuilt the palace. But Pāṇḍū returned, and having again set fire to the palace, withdrew to Drāva. Zainu'l-'Ābidīn, thereupon, decided to attack Pāṇḍū in his retreat. He first won over the inhabitants of Drāva by giving them money and land, and then, with their help, succeeded in capturing Pāṇḍū. The latter along with the members of his family were brought before the Sulṭān, who ordered the execution of all men fit to bear arms. Only women and children were spared, and sent to live in the distant village of Trahgām. One of the sons of Pāṇḍū was Ḥusain Chak, a posthumous child, who became the father of ten sons.[18]

The last twenty years of Sulṭān's reign were disturbed by the rebellion of his sons, Adham, Ḥājī, and Bahrām. Zainu'l-'Ābidīn had designated, according to an earlier precedent in the family, his younger brother Maḥmūd as heir to the throne.[19] But as Maḥmūd died, he proclaimed Ḥājī heir-apparent. Since this aroused the jealousy of Adham, the eldest son, the Sulṭān, apprehending danger, thought it inexpedient to keep the brothers together at Srīnagar. He, therefore, in 1451, sent Adham to invade Ladākh which had become independent under its king bLo-gros-mchog-ldan (1440-70). The prince was victorious in the campaign, and having conquered the province, returned to the capital with the booty which he placed at the feet of the Sulṭān.[20] The latter then despatched Ḥājī to Lohara as its governor. There in 1452, at the instigation of some of his evil counsellors, Ḥājī decided to invade Kashmīr and usurp the throne. His wise and loyal officers, however, dissuaded him against such a course, pointing out that the advice to revolt was given by interested persons who were anxious to return home to their families, and that it would be a mistake to take up arms against the Sulṭān who was too powerful to be defeated. But Ḥājī ignored their suggestions, and, with the help of the Khaśas, entered Kashmīr *via* Hirapūr.[21] Hearing of this the Sulṭān set out with his army. He was however anxious to avoid the conflict, and so he sent a Brahman messenger to persuade his son to give up his refractory conduct. But Ḥājī's soldiers cut off the Brahman's ears. When Ḥājī came to know of it he felt ashamed at the behaviour of his men, and decided to make peace with his father. But his officers opposed him, reminding him that they had begged him not to rebel against the Sulṭān, but he had ignored their advice. If he were now to make peace, while he himself would be reconciled to the Sulṭān, they would be left in the lurch and suffer. Owing to this attitude of his followers, Ḥājī had no other alternative except to prepare for battle with his father.[22]

Meanwhile, the Brahman agent had returned to the Sulṭān. When the latter saw his condition, he was filled with great anger, and at once moved his army in order to punish Ḥajī and his followers. He encountered the rebels at Pallashilā.[23] The fight continued from morning till sunset, and led to a great loss of life. In the end Ḥājī's forces were defeated and fled, pursued by Adham, who killed many of them. He wanted to continue the pursuit and seize Ḥājī, but he was recalled by his father. Ḥajī, having collected the remnants of his army, escaped to Hirapūr and thence to Bhimbhar.[24] The Sulṭān returned to Srīnagar and there built a minaret of the heads of the enemy, and ordered the execution of the prisoners of war.[25] He then entrusted Adham to make inquiries about the conduct of those persons who had instigated Ḥājī to revolt. Adham confiscated their properties, and inflicted great sufferings on their families. In consequence many persons out of fear deserted Ḥājī and went over to Adham. The Sulṭān now proclaimed Adham his heir-apparent, and appointed him governor of Kamrāj.[26]

Soon after these events, in 1460, Kashmīr was subjected to a severe famine caused by a heavy fall of snow which destroyed the rice crop. This brought great misery to the people who were compelled to subsist on roots and leaves; and as a result large numbers died of starvation. The price of rice rose from 300 *dinārs* to 1,500 *dinārs* per *kharwār;* and even at that price it was not easily available. Taking advantage of the scarcity, grain merchants made huge profits. The Sulṭān was greatly distressed, and did his best to alleviate the sufferings of his subjects. He distributed rice from his own stores, and, after the famine was over, he cancelled the debts which the people had incurred in order to buy rice. Many persons had pawned their valuables in exchange for grain. The merchants were ordered to return the articles to their owners and receive money for the grain which they had supplied.[27]

Hardly had the inhabitants of the Valley recovered from the effects of the famine when, two years later, they fell victim to another calamity. This was the flood caused by a severe rainfall. Men and beasts alike perished, and thousands of houses were destroyed. Fortunately, however, the rice crop was not affected. The Sulṭān, apprehending the recurrence of a similar calamity, built on the high banks of the Jehlam the town of Zainatilak, near Andarkōt, which had been destroyed due to the flood. It was in this new city that Jai Singh of Rajaurī was received by the Sulṭān, and appointed Rājā of the kingdom of Rajaurī.[28]

Zainu'l-'Ābidīn had hoped that with the appointment of Adham as heir-apparent and governor of Kamrāj, all the internecine troubles would be over. But he was disillusioned. Adham spent his time in hunting or in the society of women. He was cruel, vain, and rapacious, and oppressed the inhabitants of Kamrāj. He resumed the lands which had been granted by the Sulṭān, and robbed the people of their wealth. Following his example, his officials also exploited the inhabitants, and indulged in rape and plunder.[29] When the Sulṭān learnt of this he felt grieved, and admonished Adham. But the latter instead of listening to him raised the banner of revolt. He arrived at Quṭbu'd-Dīnpūr, and then marched to attack his father in Zainagīr. Taken by surprise, the Sulṭān tried to persuade him to give up his refractory conduct. Wiser counsels prevailed, and Adham returned to Kamrāj.[30]

Zainu'l-'Ābidīn was not certain if Adham would long remain loyal and peaceful, and so he wrote to Ḥājī immediately come to his assistance. But before Ḥājī could arrive, Adham attacked Sōpūr in 1459. Its governor offered resistance, but Adham defeated and killed him and destroyed the town.[31] Hearing of this, the Sulṭān sent a large army of Sōpūr. After heavy fighting Adham was routed. And as his followers were fleeing across the Jehlam at Sōpūr, the bridge gave way, and three hundred of them were drowned in the river. After this the Sulṭān himself proceeded to Sōpūr and consoled the inhabitants of their sufferings.[32]

Meanwhile the Sulṭān, learning of the arrival of Ḥājī in the neighbourhood of Bārāmūla, at once despatched Bahrām to receive him. The two brothers greeted and embraced each other, and then proceeded to join their father.[33] When Adham came to know of this he became panic-stricken, and having crossed the Indus, sought refuge in the Sind Valley.[34] Zainu'l-'Ābidīn returned to Srīnagar with Ḥajī who was once again declared heir-apparent.[35] His followers were forgiven for their past conduct and were given *khil'ats* and jāgīrs by the Sulṭān.[36] Of fair complexion, polite, modest and energetic. Ḥajī was a favourite of Zainu'l-'Ābidīn.[37] The Sulṭān, however, did not like Ḥājī's excessive addiction to wine which was undermining his health. He tried to persuade him to give up the vice, but in vain.[38] In consequence he became disgusted with him. Some of the nobles, who favoured Adham, taking advantage of this state of affairs invited him to come to Srīnagar. Adham thereupon immediately set out towards Kashmīr.[39] But Ḥasan, Ḥājī's son, who was in Pūnch, marched to Rajaurī to intercept him. A severe engagement took place between the uncle and the nephew. Ḥasan was defeated and Adham reached Srīnagar safely. Here the brothers were reconciled to each other, and both Ḥājī and Bahrām welcomed Adham. But this did not improve matters, for their reconciliation was more apparent than real.[40] Moreover, Adham did not receive the welcome he and his supporters had expected from the Sulṭān. This was because the latter, having had bitter experience of both Adham and Ḥājī, had begun to bestow favours upon his youngest son, Bahrām, whom he wanted to declare as his successor. Zainu'l-'Ābidīn therefore called him to his presence, and told him that he should not trust Adham who would never forget the part he had played in the war against him. He also warned him against Ḥājī who, he pointed out, would be interested more in his own son Ḥasan than in him. But Bahrām paid no heed to his father's words, and replied that he was not prepared to give up the society of Ḥājī who would always help and protect him. This reply came as a great blow to the Sulṭān, for he had pinned his last hopes on Bahrām.[41] He became so disgusted with his sons that he refused to nominate any of them as his successor. Although his ministers advised him to declare one of them as heir-apparent, he remained adamant. Adham, the Sulṭān pointed out, was a miser and was surrounded by unscrupulous advisers; Ḥājī was a drunkard, while Bahrām was licentious. Under the circumstance, the Sulṭān thought, his sons should themselves decide the question of succession by force of arms after his death. The one who was the strongest would naturally secure the throne. It was the question of survival of the fittest.[42]

Meanwhile, as the Sulṭān had foreseen, the facade of friendship between the brothers began to crack. Bahrām in order to promote his own interest tried to foment dissension between Adham and Ḥājī. After succeeding in separating them, he made common cause with Ḥājī and plotted the destruction of Adham. The latter got alarmed and sought the protection of his father. But the Sulṭān called him a coward, and refused to help him. Adham therefore moved to Quṭbu'd-Dinpūr, and there kept himself on the alert.[43]

The closing phase of Zainu'l-'Ābidīn's life was clouded with private sorrows and public anxiety. He was grieved at the dissensions among his sons, and at their attitude of disloyalty towards him. His wife, Tāj Khātūn, to whom he had been very devoted, was dead. Many of his trusted friends and counsellors had also passed away,[44] and he had no able minister left who could give him useful advice.[45] His new courtiers were only opportunists and men with no principles, attending him during the day and intriguing with his sons in the night. Thus he saw that owing to the follies and selfishness of his sons and officers, the kingdom was heading towards a catastrophe, and the work of his lifetime was being destroyed.[46] All this saddened him and filled him with a sense of frustration. And as he was no longer strong enough either physically or mentally to fight against the dangerous tendencies around him, he took refuge in religion. He began to pray for his early death to be relieved of his sufferings, and to ask Śrīvara to recite the *Saṁhitā* which might give him some consolation.[47]

Meanwhile the mental powers of the Sulṭān were decaying. He began to suffer from loss of memory, and therefore gave up signing official papers, allowing his ministers to carry on the government. He became apathetic towards everything, so that when he was consulted by his officials about public affairs, he either did not reply, or uttered words without any meaning.[48] Moreover, he began to suffer from the persecution mania. He would not touch the food brought to him, suspecting that it was poisoned and imagining that his ministers were planning his overthrow.[49]

Bahrām, perceiving that the end of the Sulṭān was approaching, advised Ḥājī to proceed to the palace, imprison the ministers hostile to him, and seize the horses and the treasury. But Ḥājī rejected the advice, saying that he did not want to do anything to hurt his father; and although he went to the palace, he passed the night in attendance on the Sulṭān who lay dying.[50]

Adham, who was in Quṭbu'd-Dīnpūr, on hearing the reports of his father's approaching death, moved with his army to Naushahr to seize the throne. But instead of marching immediately on the capital, he procrastinated, and passed the night on the outskirts. Meanwhile the treasurer Ḥasan Kachhī took the oath of allegiance to Ḥajī and handed over the treasury to him. Moreover, Hajī on the advice of Ḥasan and Bahrām seized the horses. When Adham heard of this he became struck with panic, and realising that his cause was lost, he fled, pursued by Bahrām, who killed a number of his followers. Shortly after Ḥasan, who was the governor of Pūnch, hastened to the help of his father. This further strengthened Ḥājī's position.[51]

While the civil strife was going on, the Sulṭān lay unconscious, dying. In the end he expired at noon on Friday the 12th May, 1470, at the age of 69.[52] His body was carried to the *Mazār-i-Salāṭīn*, and was buried there amidst the loud lamentations of his subjects. On that day no one cooked food, and no smoke arose from the houses in the capital.[53] Ḥājī also displayed belated grief, and repented for the sufferings he had caused his father.[54]

Character

Of Zainu'l-'Ābidīn's physical appearance there is no description in the chronicles. Śrīvara says that he was handsome and had a black, flowing beard, but beyond this he does not mention anything.[55] However, it is evident from a close study of the accounts that the Sulṭān did not possess the physical strength, energy, and prowess of Shihābu'd-Dīn. Nor is there anything to show that he was a great soldier, for there are no military exploits to his credit. It is true that he defeated 'Alī Shāh, but this was due more to the help he received from Jasrat Khokar than to his own initiative and valour. And the armies which won victories in Ladākh, Baltistān, and Kulū, were led not by him but his commanders.

Zainu'l-'Ābidīn possessed a mild temper, and was very rarely provoked to anger.[56] He was affectionate by nature as is shown by his attitude towards his courtiers and members of his family. Thus when Śivabhaṭṭa, his minister, died, he was very grieved, and distributed a large sum of money in charity.[57] Similarly, as his other faithful counsellors passed away one by one, he felt lonely and sad. The Sulṭān was also very fond of his sons; and it was only when they repeatedly rebelled that he turned against them. However, he refrained from punishing them, although if he had adopted a harsher policy many of the troubles of his later reign might have been avoided.

The Sulṭān possessed a deeply religious nature. He was strict in the performance of his religious duties, praying five times a day and keeping the *Ramaẓān* fasts during which period he did not take meat.[58] He held the Ṣūfis, learned men, and Brahman pandits in great respect, and granted them lands.[59] He consulted the Shaikhu'l-Islām on affairs of state,[60] and his relations with the 'Ulamā' were in general cordial.

Our information regarding the private life of the Sulṭān is very scanty. From the Sanskrit chronicles it appears that he occasionally indulged in wine, but never in excess. He, however, abstained from other intoxicants.[61] There is also evidence to show that he led a moral life. He never kept any concubines; nor did he have more than three wives at a time. He first married Tāj Khātūn, the daughter of Sayyid Muḥammad Baihaqī.[62] She gave birth to two daughters, of whom one was married to her nephew Sayyid Ḥasan Baihaqī,[63] while the other to the ruler of Pakhlī. The Sulṭān was very devoted to Tāj Khātūn, and her death, which took place in his old age, greatly affected him. His two other wives were princesses from Jammu.[64] But it is not known if they were sisters; nor if they were in his harem together. By these Jammu princesses the Sulṭān had four sons, named Adham, Ḥājī, Bahrām and Jasrat.[65] But the last seems to have died young, because we do not find him mentioned either by Śrīvara or by the Muslim chroniclers.

According to a tradition of doubtful authenticity, Sunder Senā, Rājā of Rajaurī, sent his eldest daughter Rājya Devī to Zainu'l-'Ābidīn. The Sulṭān, who was engaged in sport on the Volur lake, seeing the lady's party coming, inquired "What mother's *doli* is that"? On being told that it was the Rajaurī princess sent to him, he said that, as he had called her mother, he could not receive her as a wife. She was, however, not sent back to Rajaurī, but was allowed to live in the palace. She became a Muslim, and built the Rajaurī Kadal, a bridge over the Mār canal in Srīnagar. Sunder Senā then sent his second daughter, who also embraced Islām. Her name was Sunder Devī, but was called by the people Sundermājī.[66]

No other Kashmīrī Sulṭān did so much to promote the welfare of his subjects as Zainu'l-'Ābidīn. He undertook tours to different parts of the country to find out the condition of the people, and how his officers were carrying on the administration. With the same object in view it was his practice, like that of the Caliph Hārūn ar-Rashīd, to disguise himself and roam about the streets of his capital.[67] His espionage system was very efficient, and kept him informed of the activities of his subjects and officers.[68] If he came to know that they were taking bribes or oppressing the people, he punished them.[69] He abolished the extra taxes and arbitrary fines which his officers realized from the peasants to fill their own pockets,[70] and ordered that land sold should be registered on the *bhūrja* (birch-bark) so that the sale might not be afterwards denied.[71] Like Aśoka, he had his code of laws inscribed on copper plates, which were placed in villages and towns for the enlightenment of the people.[72] The prices of different commodities too were inscribed on copper plates; and a decree was issued that the articles imported by merchants should not be kept hidden in their houses but should be sold to the public at a small profit. This was done to prevent cornering and black marketing.[73]

During the reign of Zainu'l-'Ābidīn copper mines were worked, and their income was set aside by him for his own expenses. Gold dust was also collected from the sandy banks of the rivers, and the government's share of this was one-sixth.[74] Since the melting of gold and silver idols in the reign of Sikandar had brought about a depreciation of these metals, the Sulṭān ordered coins to be minted from pure copper.[75]

Zainu'l-'Ābidīn had a high sense of justice, and no one who committed a crime was spared, however close he was to the throne. One Mīr Shāh, who was a favourite of the Sulṭān, killed his wife in a fit of rage. The Sulṭān refused to pardon him and ordered him to be put to death.[76] Similarly, when his two foster-brothers, Shēr and Mas'ūd, both of whom enjoyed his confidence, quarrelled, and the former killed the latter, the Sulṭān ordered the execution of Shēr.[77] In another instance Sa'du'llāh, a learned man, whom the Sulṭān respected, killed a Brahman yogī out of jealousy. Zainu'l-'Ābidīn consulted the Shaikhu'l-Islām about him and was told that he deserved the punishment of death. However, as Sa'du'llāh had committed the crime in a state of drunkenness, the Sulṭān commuted the death sentence, and instead ordered him to ride on an ass through the market, with his face towards the tail, his beard drenched in urine, his head shaved, his hands tied with the entrails of the deceased, and the spectators spitting on him."[78]

The Sulṭān did not, as a rule, favour the infliction of capital punishment, which he reserved for serious crimes. For ordinary offences he preferred to give milder punishments. Thus he decreed that thieves and robbers should not be executed, nor even be flogged, but were to be put in shackles, and then made to dig earth or work on public buildings.[79] Similarly, the caṇḍālas,[80] who earned their livelihood by thieving, were not to be sent to prison, but were to be compelled to carry on agriculture. To those who took to stealing for lack of employment, he gave food.[81] He built charity houses and hospitals for the poor and the sick.[82] If a robbery was committed in a village, the chief men of the place had to pay a fine. In this way robbery was stopped, and men slept in peace in their houses and travelled in safety even through forests and lonely places.[83]

Agriculture

Zainu'l-'Ābidīn took keen interest in agriculture. He built floating islands on which crops were sown. He drained the marshes and brought large areas which lay barren under cultivation.[84] He developed the irrigation system by making a number of tanks, canals, and dams.[85] The following is the list of important canals which were constructed by him:

The Lachhamkul carried the waters of the Sind river to the new town of Naushahr founded by the Sulṭān. The canal extended to the Jāmi' Masjid, and then emptied itself into the Mār canal.[86]

The Kākapūr canal irrigated the lands around the village of Kākapūr.[87]

The Chakdar canal originated from Nandmarg, and irrigated the plateau of Chakdar.[88]

The Karāla canal irrigated the Karāla country known by its present name of Adavin, lying between Shupiyan and Romuh.[89] It was on the banks of this canal that the Sultān built the town of Zainapūr[90]

The Avantipūr canal irrigated the lands around Avantipūr, and made possible the cultivation of rice crops.[91] A portion of this canal, running as far as the villages of Midpūr and Rājpūr, is still in existence.[92]

The Shāhkul or Safapūr canal carried the waters of the Sind river across the district of Lār to the lands around the Manasbal lake. Here on the banks of the lake the Sulṭān restored the ancient town of Andarkōt, and built at Safapūr a palace called Bagh-i-Safa, which later became the residence of Mīrzā Ḥaidar.[93]

The Lālkul or Pohur canal carried the waters from the Pohur river to the land around Zainagīr, a town which the Sulṭān founded. This was done by constructing a dam and diverting the waters of the river. As a result the cultivation of rice became possible in that area.[94]

The Shāhkul or Mārtand canal diverted the waters of the Lidar river to irrigate the arid plateau of Matan.[95] This enabled the Sulṭān to introduce the cultivation of sugar-cane on the plateau. The canal is still in existence.[96]

The Mār canal or Nalla Mār: Previously the surplus waters of the Dal lake flowed out into the Jehlam at Habbā Kadal.[97] But Zainu'l-'Ābidīn diverted the waters of the lake into the Mār canal which he extended up to Shādīpūr where it emptied itself at the confluence of the Jehlam and Sind.[98] In consequence a large tract of land was recovered for cultivation. The Sulṭān spanned the canal with seven bridges of masonry. Today it is an important highway of traffic between Srīnagar and the Dal.

Owing to these irrigation works, the draining of marshes, and the reclamation of large areas for cultivation, Kashmīr became self-sufficient in food, and rice was cheap.[99] According to Moorcroft, the annual produce of rice in Zainu'l-'Ābidīn's time was seventy-seven lakhs of *kharwārs*.[100] The revenue was realised in kind, and granaries were built to store the grain.[101] Whenever the price of rice went up or there was a famine, the government immediately brought out its stocks to bring down the prices and to feed the people. It is not known as to what was the normal rate of assessment. But from the fact that whenever there was a famine the rent was reduced to one-fourth and in some place even to one-seventh,[102] it can safely be concluded that the state's share must have been one-half or one-third of the produce. The state's share in the crops raised by the peasants on the land cleared and brought under cultivation at Zainapūr at the expense of the government was one-seventh of the gross produce. The Sulṭān had this inscribed on the copper plates so that in the future also rulers should realise the revenue at the same rate.[103]

Zainu'l-Ābidīn and his Non-Muslim Subjects.

One of the most outstanding features of Zainu'l-Ābidīn's reign was the just and liberal treatment that was meted out to the non-Muslims. The Sulṭān allowed the Hindus complete freedom of worship, and recalled those who had fled to Jammu and Kishtwār. He even permitted those Brahmans who had become Muslims under duress to return to their former religion.[104] He banned cow-slaughter, and gave Hindus the right to perform *Satī* and other customs which had been prohibited by his father.[105] He not only permitted the repair and rebuilding of the temples destroyed in the time of Sikandar, but in some cases he himself repaired and rebuilt them. He gave rent-free lands to Brahmans, endowed temples, and did not resume the grants made in the time of the Rājās.[106] In Rainwārī (Srīnagar), for example, there was a large building erected under the Hindu kings where food was supplied free to persons who came from outside on pilgrimage to various sacred places in the Valley. Zainu'l-'Ābidīn extended the endowment and constructed another building for the accommodation of pilgrims and travellers.[107]

We have seen that Sikandar had imposed two *pals* of silver as *Jizya* upon every non-Muslim. Realising that it was a heavy burden, Zainu'l-'Ābidīn, on the advice of Śiryabhaṭṭa, reduced it to the nominal amount of one *masha* of silver.[108] That he did not entirely abolish the *Jizya* was due to his respect for the opinion and sentiments of the 'Ulamā. In actual practice, however, it was as good as abolished, for it was never collected under him.[109] The Sulṭān also cancelled another exaction which fell only upon the Hindus. The Hindus of Srīnagar had to pay a tax to the owner of the land near the junction of the Mār canal and the Jehlam where they cremated their dead. When the Sulṭān was informed of this, he, at the request of Śrīvara, abolished it.[110]

The Sulṭān in order to win the goodwill of his Hindu subjects participated in their festivals. Thus when the monks of Śrī Jain monastery celebrated the worship of vessels, he took part in it, and fed the monks.[111] Similarly every year, on the day of *Nāgayātra* and during the festivity of *Gaṇacakra,* he fed the devotees for five days with rice, meat, vegetables and fruits. He dismissed them on the twelfth day of the moon after presenting them with quilt, money and other things. On the thirteenth he saw the display of lamps on both sides of the river on the occasion of the worship held to celebrate the birth of the

Jehlam. Seated in a boat on the river, the Sulṭān spent the whole night listening to songs and witnessing the worship performed by the citizens.[112] Another festival in which he participated was that of *Caitra,* celebrated in spring. He visited a number of towns on the occasion in order to witness the display of flowers and to enjoy music and dancing.[113]

During his reign non-Muslims held high positions and were trusted by him, for his criterion in making appointments was not the religion of the candidate but his ability.[114] Śivabhaṭṭa, a Brahman, was his physician and a confidant whom he always consulted on important matters.[115] Another person who was his counsellor and stood high in his favour was Tilakācārya, a Buddhist. Two other Brahmans, Siṁha and Rūpyabhaṭṭa, were the court astrologers. Karpūrabhaṭṭa was a Brahman physician, much respected by the Sulṭān.[116] Śiryabhaṭṭa was the superintendent of the king's court of justice. The Sulṭān was so much attached to him that on his death he distributed a large sum of money in charity.[117]

Patronage of Letters

Zainu'l-Ābidīn was a great patron of learning and surrounded himself with learned men with whom he was fond of holding discussions.[118] He conferred upon them grants of land and other privileges and, in order to be able to enjoy their constant company, he made arrangements for their residence at Naushahr.[119] That is why, attracted by his patronage, scholars like Sayyid Muḥammad Rūmī, Sayyid Aḥmad Rūmī, Qāẓī Sayyid 'Alī Shīrāzī, Sayyid Muḥammad Luristānī, Qāẓī Jāmāl, and Sayyid Muḥammad Sistānī left their countries and emigrated to Kashmīr during his reign.[120] Qāẓī Jāmāl, who had come from Sindh, was made Qāẓī by the Sulṭān.[121] Maulānā Kabīr had been Zainu'l-'Ābidīn's tutor, but had gone away to Herāt to seek knowledge. The Sulṭān recalled him, and made him Shaiku'l-Islām.[122] Mullā Aḥmad was a court poet, and was much respected by him. Other poets attached to the court were Mullā Nādirī and Mullā Fatḥī.[123] Mullā Aḥmad and Mullā Nādirī, besides being poets, were also historians, and each wrote a history of Kashmīr. Other persons whose society the Sulṭān enjoyed were Mullā Pārsā Bukhārī and Sayyid Muḥammad Madā'in.[124] Jonarāja and Śrīvara, authors of the Sanskrit chronicles, were also greatly trusted by the Sulṭān and were constantly in attendance. Yodhabhaṭṭa, another courtier of the Sulṭān, was not only a great Vedic scholar,[125] but was also conversant with Persian, and had learned Firdausī's *Shāh-nāma* by heart.[126] He wrote a book on music and a play in Kashmīrī verse named *Jainaprakāśa* giving an account of his master's reign.[127] Notthosoma Pandit was another Kashmirī poet who composed a book in Kashmīrī verse called *Jainacarita* in which he described the life and achievements of Zainu'l-'Ābidīn.[128] Bhaṭṭāvatāra, influenced by the *Shāh-nāma* and other Persian works which he has studied, composed the *Jainavilāsa* which contained the sayings of the Sulṭān.[129] Manṣūr b. Muḥammad was a great scholar and wrote the *Kifāya-i-Mujāhidiyyah*, a work on medicine, which he dedicated to Zainu'l-'Ābidīn to whose court he had been attracted by the widespread fame of his justice and liberality. He was also the author of the *Tashrīḥ bi'ṭ-taṣwīr*, a treatise on the anatomy of the human body with illustrations, which was dedicated to Mīrzā Pīr Muḥammad, grandson of Tīmūr.[130]

Zainu'l-'Ābidīn established a translation bureau in which Persian works were translated into Sanskrit and Sanskrit works into Persian. In this way knowledge was made accessible to those who knew either of these languages.[131] Śrīvara began the translation of Jāmī's *Yūsuf u Zulaikhā* into Sanskrit in the Sulṭan's reign, and completed it in 1505, and named it *Kathā-Kautuka.*[132] Mullā Aḥmad, who was a scholar in both Persian and Sanskrit, translated by the Sulṭān's order the *Mahābhārata*[133] and Kalhaṇa's *Rājataraṅgiṇī*[134] into Persian. The latter work was also translated for Akbar by Shāh Muḥammad Shāhābādī. Later, the Persian translation was rewritten by 'Abdu'l-Qādir Badā'ūnī by order of the Emperor.[135]

Education

Zainu'l-'Ābidīn took great interest in the spread of education in Kashmīr. He opened a school near his palace in Naushahr, and placed it in charge of Mullā Kabīr. Sometimes he himself used to go there to attend the lectures of the Mullā. For its maintenance, and for granting scholarships to deserving students, he created an endowment with the Mullā as its trustee. The institution survived until the seventeenth century.[136] Another place where education was imparted was the hospice of Shaikh Ismā-'īl Kubravī, who later in the reign of Ḥasan Shāh became Shaikhu'l-Islām. Students came from Herāt and Transoxiana to learn at his feet.[137] A large *madrasa* was founded at Sir near Islāmābād, and Mullā Ghāzī Khān was made its principal.[138] At Siālkōt there was a Madrasatu'l-'Ulūm to which the Sulṭān contributed six lakhs of rupees, while his queen gave away her valuable necklace.[139] Zainu'l-'Ābidīn also built a number of hostels where board and lodging were free for poor students.

The Sulṭān was very fond of books, and spent large sums of money in collecting them. Before his time the number of Persian and Arabic manuscripts in Kaṣhmīr was very small. He, therefore, sent his agents to India, Persia, 'Irāq, and Turkistān to purchase them.[140] In case their owners refused to sell them, his instructions were to secure their transcribed copies and pay the copyists generously.[141] Sanskrit manuscripts were also purchased in large numbers, and those works which during the reign of Sikandar had been removed to India, were by Zainu'l-'Ābidīn's efforts brought back.[142] In this way the Sulṭān built up a big library which existed until the time of Fatḥ Shāh. It perished in the civil wars and foreign invasions of the later Shāh Mīr period.[143]

Zainu'l-'Ābidīn was not only a patron of learned men, he was himself a scholar and a poet. He knew Sanskrit, Persian, and Tibetan besides Kashmīrī which was his mother tongue.[144] Pandits read out to him from various *Śāstras*,[145] while Śrīvara recited to him the *Vaśiṣtha Brahmadarśana* of Vālmīki and the *Saṁhitā* along with their explanations and annotations.[146]

The Sulṭān is said to have been the author of two works in Persian. One of them was on the manufacture of fireworks in the form of a dialogue—a method which became a model for the Kashmīrī writers.[147] Towards the end of his life, disillusioned on account of the revolt of his sons and the disloyalty of his ministers, he wrote another book named *Shikāyat* in which he discussed the vanity and transitoriness of this world.[148]

Ths Sultan also composed poetry in Persian under the *nom de plume* of *Quṭb*, and was in the habit of exchanging repartees in improvised verse with his poet-laureate, Mullā Aḥmad. Once due to the intrigues of some of the courtiers, who were jealous of the poet, the Sulṭān turned against him and exiled him. On reaching Pakhlī, Mullā Aḥmad composed four couplets and sent them to the Sulṭān, who was so delighted with them that he immediately ordered his recall.[149]

Arts and Crafts

No Kashmīrī ruler ever did so much for the promotion of arts and crafts as Zainu'l-'Ābidīn. In fact it will not be too much to say that whatever arts we see in Kashmīr today owe their existence to him. No doubt the Valley had been famous in Hindu times for its arts and crafts, but they had greatly suffered in the chaos which lasted for over two hundred years preceding the establishment of the Sultanate. Besides, a large number of artists and craftsmen had perished in the course of Zuljū's invasion.[150] Zainu'l-'Ābidīn, however, revived the old industries which had either disappeared or declined, and at the same time introduced new ones.

The Kashmīrīs were hitherto ignorant of the art of paper-making and book-binding. The Sulṭān, therefore, sent two persons to Samarqand at government expense to receive training in these arts; and in their absence he supported their families. During their stay in Samarqand one of them learnt the art of manufacturing paper, while the other learnt the art of book-binding. On their return to Srīnagar they taught these arts to others.[151] In the Phāg pargana the Sulṭān made arrangements for one of them to make paper, and he was given a village as jāgīr. The book-binder was also assigned a village. The villages remained in the possession of the descendants of these craftsmen until the time of Ḥaidar Malik, the historian, in the first half of the seventeenth century.[152]

The great interest which Zainu'l-'Ābidīn took in the development of arts and crafts is further evident from the fact that if he came to know that an artist or a craftsman from 'Irāq,

Khurāsān or Turkistān was on a visit to the Valley, he would induce him to teach his people whatever he knew. In fact, sometimes, the Sulṭān would not permit him to leave Kashmīr until he had done so.[153] It was perhaps in this way that the Sulṭān introduced for the first time in Kashmīr the use of the weaver's brush and loom, and the weaving of silk cloth. The patterns on the silk cloth were so exquisitely made that the Valley became famous for it. Kashmīr also became well-known for its shawls in the Sulṭān's time.[154] From the account of Śrīvara it appears that Zainu'l-'Ābidin was endowed wth a spirit of inquiry and inventiveness. Thus he knew how to make fireworks, and he trained one Ḥabīb in the art. Before his time the powder used for fireworks was imported from outside, and was not easily obtainable. But the Sulṭān taught the people how to manufacture it, and, as a result, it became a common thing.[155] It was under his influence that his mechanics invented new weapons of war.[156] However, there is no evidence to suggest that these weapons were guns or cannons using gunpowder.[157]

Music

Unlike his father Sikandar, who had banned music, Zainu'l-'Ābidīn was a great patron of it, and, as we have seen, he used to spend some of his evenings in the company of singers and dancers. He liberally rewarded them, and in his reign Kashmīr became famous for its musicians.[158] Yodhabhaṭṭa was a well-known musician, and wrote a book on music which he dedicated to the Sulṭān.[159] Mullā 'Ūdī, who had come from Khurāsān, was another great musician.[160] Mullā Zāda too had came from Khurāsān, and was an expert in playing the lute made of tortoise shell. Śrīvara also played on the lute. He possessed a melodious voice and sang Persian songs in chorus. Jamīl was not only a poet and a painter, but also a musician and sang beautifully in Persian.[161]

Buildings

Zainu'l-'Ābidīn was a great builder, but unfortunately, with the exception of the tomb of his mother and the tomb and mosque of Madanī, which are in a dilapidated condition, not a single building of his time has survived. He founded the new town of Naushahr, now a part of Srīnagar, and made it his capital. He adorned it with splendid houses for his officers, courtiers, and learned men.[162] But the most magnificent edifice which he constructed there was a palace of wood which, as described by Mīrzā Ḥaidar Dughlat, had twelve storeys, each containing fifty rooms, halls, and corridors. It was surmounted by a golden dome, and its spacious halls were lined with glass.[163]

Besides Naushahr, Zainu'l-Ābidīn founded the towns of Zainapūr, Zainakōt and Zainagīr,[164] and in all these places he constructed magnificent buildings. In Zainagīr a spacious palace was built and was surrounded by a picturesque garden.[165] The construction of the Jāmi' Masjid in Srīnagar, started by Sikandar, was completed by Zainu'l-'Ābidīn.[166] The latter also, like his brother 'Alī Shāh, constructed a bridge, and named it after himself as Zaina Kadal.[167] A great achievement of the Sulṭān was the construction of a causeway along the Dal lake to the Phāg pargana.[168] Another causeway was built from Andarkōt to Sōpūr, and the income of a village was set aside for its maintenance.[169]

In ancient times there existed an island in the north-east corner of the Volur lake, but it had become submerged in water. Zainu'l-'Ābidīn decided to reclaim the island in order to make it a storm-refuge for boats. He had stones poured into the lake, and in this way, after great efforts, land was raised above the water level. He named the island Zainalānk, and on it, in 847/1443-4, he built a palace, a mosque, and a garden.[170] The palace had four storeys. The first was constructed of stones; the second of bricks and the third and fourth of timber. The mosque was built of stones.[171] The *hānjīs,* carpenters, masons and others who had been employed in the construction of the buildings, were awarded the income of the parganas of Khuyahōm in perpetuity.[172]

During the later part of his reign the town of Sōpūr was destroyed by fire. The Sulṭān built there a palace with the materials of the one at Bārāmūla, which was pulled down. He also constructed in the town a swinging bridge.[173] As already mentioned, he built for himself in important villages and towns

Inscription on a stone slab to commemorate the founding of Zainalank. Dated 847/1443-4. Directorate of Records, Srinagar

rest houses where he stayed during his tours to the different parts of the kingdom.[174] Besides, inns were constructed for travellers on the main roads. Villages were endowed for their maintenance, and food was supplied free.[175].

NOTES

1. B.S., ff. 50a-51a; Ḥasan, f. 121b; H.M., f. 121a. See for more details about 'aBumlde, Francke, *History of Western Tibet*, pp. 75sqq. But the name of the Baltī chief who was Zainu'l-'Ābidīn's contemporary is not known.
2. Guge lies north of Garhwāl and Kumaun and is now part of Tibet.
3. Shel is 8 miles south-east of Leh on the Indus. It is Shaya of Jonarāja.
4. Jonar., (Bo. ed.), Nos. 1106-7. Francke in I.A., xxxvii, p. 188, identifies the *mlecchas* with the Muslims. But this is incorrect, for it is unlikely if there were any Muslims in Shel at that time, or at any rate, even if there were any, they could not have been strong enough to seize the gold image of Buddha. Jonarāja does not give the date of the event, but probably it took place between 1430 and 1440. (See I.A. xxxvii, p. 188).
5. See *infra*, p. 74.
6. Jonar., p. 103; I.A., xxxvii, p. 188.
7. Jonar., (Bo. ed.), No. 1105.
8. Munich MS., f. 73a; T.A., iii, 440.
9. N.A., ff. 46-47a; also G.A., f. 126b.
10. Srīv., p. 151; Munich MS., f. 73a; T.A., iii, 440.
11. Munich MS., f. 73a; T.A., iii, 440.
12. Śrīv., p. 151; T.A., iii, 440.
13. *Cam. Hist. Ind.*, iii, 209.
14. Munich MS., ff. 69a-b; T.A., iii, 435.
15. Jonar., p. 79. See *Cam. Hist. Ind.*, iii, 209-12, for Jasrat's activities.
16. Trahgām or Trigamma is a big village in the Lōlāb Valley. It is about 25 miles north-west of Bārāmūla. It should not be confused with Trigām which is in Paraspūr pargana opposite the junction of the Jehlam and the Sind.
17. This was the name for the Kishangangā Valley from below Shardi as far as Karnāv.
18. B.S., ff. 52a-53a.
19. Munich MS., f. 74a; T.H., ii, f. 103b.
20. Śrīv, pp. 105-6; Munich MS., f. 74b; I.A., xxxvii, p. 189.

21. Śrīv., pp. 106–8.
22. *Ibid.*, 109-10; Munich MS., f. 74b.
23. It is a *karēwa* near Shupiyan at a distance of about 33 miles south of Srīnagar on the route to Rajaurī. In the time of the Mughals there was an inn where travellers changed horses and halted.
24. Munich MS., ff. 75a-b; T.A., iii, 442-3; also Jonar., 112 sqq.
25. Munich MS., f. 75a; T.A., iii, 443.
26. *Ibid.*
27. Jonar., pp. 117-19; Munich MS., 75b.
28. Jonar., pp. 120-3.
29. *Ibid.*, 125-6; Munich MS., f. 75b.
30. Śrīv., 126-8; Munich MS., f. 75b.
31. *Ibid.*, Śrīv., pp. 128-9.
32. Munich MS., f. 75b; T.A., iii, 444.
33. Munich MS., f. 76a; T.A., iii, 444.
34. It is a narrow valley opening into the north side of Kashmīr, a few miles north-west of Srīnagar. It lies between Lat. 75° 30′ Long. 74° 50′.
35. Śrīv., p. 131; Munich MS., f. 76a.
36. *Ibid.*, Śrīv., p. 137.
37. *Ibid.*, p. 132.
38. *Ibid.*, pp. 158-60; Munich MS., ff. 76a-b.
39. Adham had gone to the Sind Valley and from there had moved on to outer Hills.
40. Śrīv., pp. 160-1; Munich MS., f. 76b.
41. Śrīv., pp. 161-2.
42. *Ibid.*, 162-3.
43. *Ibid.*, 168-9; Munich MS., f. 76b.
44. Śrīv., p. 158.
45. *Ibid.*, p. 163.
46. *Ibid.*
47. *Ibid.*, pp. 165-7.
48. *Ibid.*, 169-70.
49. *Ibid.*, 170-71.
50. *Ibid.*, 172.
51. *Ibid.*, 172-4; Munich MS., f. 77a.
52. *Ibid.*, Śrīv., p. 175.
53. *Ibid.*, p. 178.
54. *Ibid.*, pp. 177-8.
55. *Ibid.*, pp. 174-5.
56. *Ibid.*, p. 167.
57. Munich MS., f. 74a.

58. Śrīv., p. 170. According to Śrīv., p. 175, the Sulṭān's lips quivered at the time of his death, and it appeared that he was praying. Probably he was reciting the *kalima*.
59. Jonar., p. 90; Munich MS., f. 71a.
60. Jonar., p. 80.
61. For the Sulṭān's view on the bad effects of alcohol see Śrīv., p. 159.
62. Śrīv., p. 157. Śrīvara calls her Vodhā Khātonā. Perhaps Vodhā is a corruption of Makhdūm, which was also her name, or of Bōd which means big.
63. B.S., ff. 29b-30b.
64. Jonar., p. 86. Śrīv., p. 194, mentions of only one princess who was the sister of Mānik Dev, the Rājā of Jammu, and the mother of Adham Khān.
65. Jonar., p. 86.
66. J.P.H.S., ix, part ii, p. 145. This account is based on Cunningham who does not give any authority. *Tazkira Rājgān-i-Rajaur* does not mention of any such marriage.
67. Ḥasan, f. 122a; H.M., f. 121b.
68. Śrīv., p. 101.
69. Jonar., p. 96.
70. Munich MS., f. 70a; T.A., iii, 436.
71. Jonar., p. 88.
72. Munich MS., f. 69b.
73. *Ibid*., ff. 69b-70a; T.A., iii, 436.
74. Jonar., pp. 88-9; Munich MS., f. 72b. It is not recorded as to where these mines were situated. But copper may have been extracted from the mountain on which 'Aishmakān in the Lidar Valley stands. (Lawrence, *Valley*, p. 62).
75. Munich MS., f. 70b; T.A., iii, 437.
76. Jonar., p. 80.
77. Munich MS., f. 74a; T.A., iii, 441.
78. Jonar., pp. 85-6.
79. *Ibid*., p. 95; Munich MS., f. 72a.
80. See chapter XII for the Caṇḍālas.
81. Śrīv., p. 101.
82. Jonar., pp. 82, 88.
83. Munich MS., f. 69b; T.A., iii, 436; also Śrīv., p. 102.
84. *Ibid*., p. 142; B.S., f. 51b.
85. Śrīv., p. 141; N.A., f. 46a.
86. *Ibid*., f. 45b.
87. Jonar. p. 86. See also Munich MS., f. 71a and T.A., iii, 437. Kākapūr

is the ancient Utpalapura. (Stein, ii, p. 474).

88. Jonar., p. 87. Nandmarg is a pass in the Pīr Panjāl Range situated south-east extremity of the Shāhābād Valley. It is Nandashaila of Jonarāja. Chakdar is Chakradhara of Jonarāja.
89. It is a village about 10 miles north of Shupiyan, on the west side of the road to Srīnagar, in Lat. 33°52' Long. 74°53'.
90. Jonar., p. 87. Zainapūr was a pargana in the Shupiyan dist. of Marāj division. Now it is in Anantnāg dist.
91. Jonar., p. 87.
92. Kāk, *Ancient Monuments of Kashmīr* p. 37. I have not been able to trace Midpūr either in the settlement records or on the maps. The inhabitants of Avantīpūr are also ignorant of the existence of such a village.
Rājpūr is a village about 12 miles south-east of Srīnagar. It is well-known for its apple orchards and is a packing centre for apples.
93. Jonar., p. 87. Safapūr is a small village situated on the bank of the Mansabal where Akbar had constructed a garden.
94. B.S., ff. 51a-b., S.A., p. 38; T.H., 1, f. 99b. Zainagīr is a pargana in Kamrāj division.
95. Jonar., (Bo. ed.), Nos. 1232 sqq; also N.A., ff. 45a-46a, and G.A., f. 127a.
96. Jonar., p. 87.
97. Lawrence, *Valley*, p. 191; T.H., i. 99b
98. Śrīv., p. 143; S.A., p. 37.
99. H.M., ff. 120b-21a.
100. Moorcroft, *Travels*, ii, p. 135. When Moorcroft visited Kashmīr the annual produce was only twenty lakhs of *kharwārs.*
101. Śrīv., p. 140.
102. Munich MS., f. 75b; T.A., iii, 443.
103. Śrīv., p. 156.
104. *Ibid.*, p. 437.
105. Śrīv., p. 143; Munich MS., f. 70a; B.S., ff. 48b-49a.
106. Śrīv., p. 142; Jonar., p. 87; Munich MS., f. 70a; B.S., f. 48b.
107. *Tuḥfatu'l-Aḥbāb*, pp. 226-27; F.K., f. 200b.
108. Jonar., (Bo. ed.), Nos. 1077-78. The Calcutta text and its English trans. by Dutt is vague and confused on this point. S.A., p. 30, says a very small sum was imposed as *jizya* on the non-Muslims.
109. Munich MS., f. 70a; Firishta, p. 657, and other Persian chronicles say that *Jizya* was abolished probably on the ground that it was not realised.
110. Śrīv., p. 143.

111. *Ibid.*, p. 142.
112. *Ibid.*, pp. 123-5.
113. *Ibid.*, pp. 132-4.
114. Jonar., p. 77.
115. *Ibid.*, p. 82; Munich MS., f. 69b.
116. Jonar., p. 83.
117. *Ibid.*, p. 97; Munich MS., f. 74a.
118. Srīv., pp. 146, 181.
119. B.S., ff. 46b-47a.
120. *Ibid.*, 48b-56a.
121. Ḥasan, ff. 119a-b; H.M. ff. 118-19b.
122. Ḥasan, f. 120a.
123. B.S., f. 56a.
124. *Ibid.*, f. 46b.
125. R.S. Pundit, Trans, of *Kalhaṇa's Rājat.*, pp. 25n., 176.
126. Munich MS., ff. 72b-73a.
127. Śrīv., p. 136.
128. *Ibid.*, (Bo. ed.), BK. 1, chap. iv, No. 37; Munich MS., f. 72b.
129. Śrīv., (Bo. ed.), BK. 1, chap. iv, No. 39. In the Cal. ed. of the text as translated by Dutt, it is stated that he had "perused the *Shāh-nāma*". But the Bo. ed. says: "He had mastered the ocean-like texts that existed in the country of *Shāh-nāma.*"
130. Rieu, ii, pp. 467b-68a, 470b; also Ethe, i, Nos. 2296-7.
131. Śrīv., p. 146; Munich MS., f. 73a.
132. Published in Bombay in 1901. See Ṣūfī, *Kashīr*, i, 167.
133. Munich MS., f. 73a.
134. *Ibid.*
135. M.T., ii, 380; see for more details, Ṣūfī, *Kashīr,* i, pp. 163-64. But Ṣūfī confuses Kalhaṇa's *Rājataraṅgiṇī* with *Baḥru'l-Asmār* which is a quite different work. (See Storey, *Persian Literature,* Section ii, p. 438).
136. Ḥasan, f. 119b; H.M., f. 119b.
137. W.K., f. 41a.
138. *Ṣūfī, Kashir,* ii, 348. Sir is a large village about 7 miles north-east Anantnāg in Lat. 33° 47' Long. 75° 17'.
139. *Ibid.*
140. B.S., f. 47b; Ḥasan, f. 120b; H.M., f. 120a.
141. B.S., f. 48a.
142. Śrīv., p. 145.
143. Ḥasan, f. 120b., H.M., f. 120a.
144. Munich MS., f. 73a; T.A., iii, p. 439.
145. Śrīv., pp. 145, 166.

146. Jonar., p. 91.
147. Śrīv., p. 135.
148. *Ibid.*, p. 167.
149. H.M., ff. 117b-118a.
150. Ḥasan., ff. 121a-b; H.M., f. 120b.
151. B.S., ff. 47a-b; Ḥasan, f. 120b; H.M., f. 120a.
152. *Ibid.;* Ḥasan, ff. 120b-121a. Lawrence, *Valley*, p. 380, says the paperworkers were settled by the Sulṭān in Naushahr (Srīnagar) and in his time there were 30 such families.
153. B.S., f. 47a; Ḥasan, f. 120a; H.M., f. 120b.
154. Śrīv., p. 151.
155. *Ibid.*, p. 135.
156. *Ibid.*, p. 105.
157. See for more details Chapter XI under section of Weapons.
158. B.S., ff. 49a-b; H.M., f. 113a.
159. Śrīv., p. 135; Munich MS., f. 72a. Śrīvara calls him Sujjya. It may be a corruption of Shujā. But Persian chronicles call him Mullā 'Ūdī, perhaps because he could play well on the 'Ūd.
160. Munich MS., f. 73a.
161. *Ibid.*, f. 72a; Śrīv., pp. 135-6; T.A., iii, 439.
162. B.S., f. 46b.
163. T.R., p. 429; Śrīv., pp. 137-8.
164. For Zainapūr and Zainagīr see p. 85 *supra*. Zainakōt is a village 4 miles west of Srīnagar. Ḥasan Shāh in T.H., ii, f. 98a, gives the names of other villages like Zainadab in Naushahr (Srīnagar), Zaina Danaib on the Volur lake and Zaina Kadal in Srīnagar.
165. B.S., ff. 51b-52a. The statement in S.A., p. 38, that the royal buildings in Zainagīr were destroyed by the Chaks is not corroborated by other chronicles. They were probably destroyed in the course of civil wars and foreign invasions of the later Shāh Mīr period. Mīrzā Ḥaider does not mention the existence of any buildng in Zainagīr during his time.
166. N.A., f. 45a.
167. *Ibid.*
168. *Ibid.*, f. 46a.
169. Lawrence, *Valley*, p. 191.
170. Jonar., p. 94; T.R., p. 429. See J.A.S.B. (1880), pp. 16 sq, for the inscription upon a stone near a mosque on the island.
171. S.A., p. 30.
172. Ḥasan, f. 117b.
173. Śrīv., pp. 155-6.
174. Ḥasan, ff. 117b-118a; H.M., f. 117a.
175. Munich MS., f. 71a.

Chapter 6

Dynastic Troubles and Rebellions

Ḥaidar Shāh (1470-72)

Under Zainu'l-'Ābidīn the Shāh Mīr dynasty reached the meridian of its power and glory. But after his death, under his weak successors, it started on its downward course until it met its final overthrow at the hands of the Chaks. Ḥājī Khān ascended the throne under the title of Sulṭān Ḥaidar Shāh. To celebrate the occasion festivities were held in Sikandarpūr, and gifts were bestowed on nobles and tributary chiefs.[1] Bahrām, his younger brother, was conferred upon the jāgīr of Nāgam, while his son Ḥasan Khān was given the jāgīr of Kamrāj and declared heir-apparent.[2]

Meanwhile, Adham Khān, who was in Jammu, proceeded to Pūnch and decided to invade Kashmīr. The Sulṭān was advised by Pūrṇa, the barber,[3] who was his favourite, and by other counsellors, that it was at the invitation of Ḥasan Kachhī, the treasurer, that Adham was planning the invasion of the Valley. Ḥaidar Shāh, thereupon, sent for Ḥasan and his seven accomplices and had them put to death. The ministers of Sulṭān Zainu'l-'Ābidīn, who had opposed Ḥaidar Shāh's claim to the throne, were also executed.[4]

When Adham heard the news of Ḥasan's execution, he was struck with fright, and returned to Jammu. Bahrām too became alarmed and decided to flee, but gave up the idea on being assured of safety by the Sulṭān who wanted to keep him near himself as he was useful in checkmating the designs of Adham.[5] Soon after, news reached Ḥaidar Shāh that Adham Khān had lost his life while fighting along with his maternal uncle Mānik Dēv, the ruler of Jammu, against the Turks.[6] The Sulṭān was grieved to hear this, and he caused his body to be brought from Jammu and had it buried near the grave of Sulṭān Zainu'l-'Ābidīn.[7]

Ḥaidar Shāh, like his father, pursued a liberal policy towards the Hindus. But some of the Brahmans, provoked by the barber, caused damage to the Khānqāh-i-Mu'allā[8] and began to harass the Muslims of Srīnagar.[9] When the Sulṭān heard of this he inflicted severe punishments on the persons guilty of the outrage. Their arms and legs were cut off, and their properties were confiscated, including the lands which had been given to them by Zainu'l-'Ābidīn.[10]

Owing to the Sulṭān's neglect of the administration, the states of the Outer Hills, which had been tributary to Kashmīr since the time of Shihābu'd-Dīn, now declared their independence. Prince Ḥasan was therefore despatched with an army to reduce them to obedience. Jai Singh, the ruler of Rajaurī, submitted without offering any resistance, and gave Ḥasan handsome presents and his daughter in marriage. The ruler of Jammu and the chief of the Gakkhars also submitted, and they were spared. But those chiefs who refused to recognise the sovereignty of ths Sulṭān, were attacked, and after being defeated, were executed and their capitals were destroyed. After campaigning in this way for six months, Prince Ḥasan decided to return to Kashmīr, as alarming news had reached him from Srīnagar.[11]

During the absence of Ḥasan, Bahrām Khān had succeeded in strengthening his position by winning the confidence of the Sulṭān, and bringing him under his influence. Taking advantage of Ḥaidar Shāh's deteriorating physical and mental powers caused by excessive drinking, he even began to plot with the nobles to usurp the throne. It was on hearing this news that Ḥasan had returned by forced marches to Srīnagar. But as he had come without the Sulṭān's permission, Bahrām and other interested persons succeeded in alienating the Sulṭān from him by insinuating that he had arrived in order to seize power.[12] The result was that he was at first refused audience by the

Sulṭān, and it was only at the request of the army chiefs that he was finally received. But his services in suppressing the refractory chiefs were ignored, and he was given only an ordinary *khil'at*.[13] Soon after, Ḥaidar Shāh, while carousing on the top floor of the palace in a glass room, fell down and bled through his nose. As he had already been for some time past spitting blood and suffering from gout, he fainted and had to be carried to his bed. When his condition grew worse, and it became certain that he would not recover, his ministers headed by Aḥmad Aitū, the Wazīr, proceeded to Bahrām Khān and requested him to proclaim himself as Sulṭān and appoint Ḥasan as his heir-apparent.[14] But he refused to accept the second condition. Thereupon Aḥmad, with the consent of the nobles, declared Ḥasan as ruler, and made preparations to attack Bahrām. The latter alarmed at this fled the city. Bahrām had in reality behaved in a cowardly manner and shown a great lack of energy and enterprise, for, if he had taken prompt action by seizing the treasury, the horses, and the palace, he would have secured the throne.[15]

Ḥaidar Shāh died on April 13, 1472, after a reign of one year and ten months, and was buried near his father's grave.[16] He was generous and cultured, and a patron of art and learning. He was himself a poet and wrote a book of songs in Persian.[17] He was fond of the society of Mullā Dā'ūd, a great musician, whose pupil Khwāja 'Abdul'l-Qādir taught the Sulṭān to play on the lute. He acquired such proficiency in it that, according to Śrīvara, "he gave lessons even to the professors". He also learned to play well on other instruments from persons who were attached to his court.[18]

Like his father and uncle, Ḥaidar Shāh also built a bridge across the Jehlam in Srīnagar and named it Nau Kadal.[19] He was a man of tolerant disposition, and enjoyed the society of learned Brahmans who read out to him passages from the Purāṇas, the Dharmaśāstras and the Saṁhitās. Although very generous to the poor and liberal in bestowing gifts and jāgīrs on the courtiers, he was not of a forgiving nature and punished severely anyone guilty of even the most trifling offence.[20] At the same time he possessed a weak nature, and allowed himself to be dominated by persons of a stronger will. In particular he was under the influence of the barber Pūrṇa who was rapacious, unscrupulous, and a great intriguer. He spent most of his time in his wine cups and in the society of women and musicians, and as a result left the management of the state to corrupt and worthless favourites who misgoverned the country.

Sulṭān Ḥasan Shāh (1472-84)

Ḥasan Shāh signalised his accession to the throne by leaving Sikandarpūr, the capital of his father, and proceeding to live at Naushahr.[21] Since he had become ruler through the efforts of Aḥmad Aitū, he conferred upon him the title of Malik, gave him the jāgīr of Nāgām, and made him his Wazīr.[22] His son Naurūz was appointed Amīri-iDar or Lord Chamberlain, given the title of Bahādur Mulk,[23] and granted the jāgīr of Ikshikā.[24] Jahāngīr Māgre was entrusted with the chief command of the army and given the title of Shaukat Jung, while Khwāja Nūru'd-Din was given the post of Shaikhu'l-Islām, and Khwāja Muḥammad 'Ālam that of Ṣadr.[25]

Soon after Ḥasan Shāh became Sulṭān, Bahrām, who had fled to India, invaded Kashmīr at the invitation of some of the nobles and arrived in the province of Kamrāj. Learning of the invasion, Ḥasan Shāh, who was at this time at Avantipūr, at once proceeded to Sōpūr.[26] He, however, did not know what course to follow, as treachery was rife in his camp, and conflicting advices were being offered to him by his ministers. Some were even suggesting that resistance was futile, and that the Sulṭān should retire to the Punjāb. But Malik Aḥmad, the Wazīr, opposed all defeatist tactics and advised resistance to the enemy. The Sulṭān finally agreed with him and sent Tāzī Baṭ against the pretender.[27] Thereupon Bahrām hastened to Dūlipūr[28] to attack Tāzī Baṭ, expecting to be joined by the nobles who had invited him and promised him support. But on reaching Dūlipūr, he was disappointed to find that none came over to his side. He therefore had to fight without any allies. As a result, his forces were defeated and scattered and he himself escaped to Zainagīr. From there again he fled, but was pursued and, having been struck by an arrow, was captured along with his son.[29] They were both brought before the Sulṭān who ordered them to be confined in Bahrām's own palace. But soon after, apprehending that Bahrām might form a rallying point for the discontented nobles, Ḥasan Shāh had him shackled and blinded.[30] Three years after this Bahrām died.[31] He was mean, ungrateful, an opportunist, and an intriguer. Zainu'l-'Ābidīn had bestowed favours on him, yet he had opposed him and neglected him during his last illness; and to achieve his own ends he had tried to play his two brothers against each other. He had then conspired the overthrow of Sulṭān Ḥaidar Shāh, and finally attempted to seize the throne from his nephew, Ḥasan Shāh.

Meanwhile two-persons, named Abhimanyu and Malik Zāda, had risen high in the Sulṭān's favour. Abhimanyu had belonged to Ḥājī's party, and had helped him in his rebellion against Zainu'l-'Ābidīn.[32] Later he had served Ḥaidar Shāh, and now Ḥasan Shāh reposed great confidence in him and placed him in charge of Divasar pargana.[33] But Abhimanyu being ambitious, became jealous of Malik Aḥmad, and began to plot his overthrow. But the minister succeeded in counteracting his machinations, and by the Sulṭān's order had him blinded and thrown into prison, where he died in great misery after two years.[34]

The Malik Zāda, too, like Abhimanyu, had an unhappy end. He was dishonest and enriched himself by robbing the people. He was very friendly with Pūrṇa, the barber, and with his help organised a plot to overthrow the Sulṭān. But the conspiracy was discovered, and both he and the barber were thrown into prison where they died. Their ill-gotten wealth was confiscated by the Sulṭān.[35]

Having removed his rivals, Malik Aḥmad turned his attention to making his position stronger by entering into marriage alliances with the important families in the kingdom. He adopted Tāzī Baṭ,[36] a man of humble origin, as his son and married him to the eldest sister of Jahāngīr Māgre, the commander-in-chief, and then had him appointed minister and guardian of Prince Muḥammad.[37] But the result of this was that Malik Aḥmad's sons, particularly Naurūz, became jealous of

Tāzī Baṭ. They accused him of arrogance, favouritism, and rapacity, and pointed out to their father that the advancement of Tāzī would lead to the ruin of their family.[38] Their instigations had the desired effect, and Malik Aḥmad became hostile to Tāzī. He sent him to the Outer Hills against some of the tributary chiefs who had declared their independence and had not paid any tribute to the Sulṭān. He hoped thereby to keep him away from Srīnagar, and in his absence to secure his overthrow.[39]

Tāzī Baṭ, unaware of the designs of Malik Aḥmad, marched with an army. He succeeded in reducing Jammu, Rajaurī, and other neighbouring states; and then, supported by the Jammu army, he marched on Saīlkōt, which belonged to Sulṭān Buhlūl Lodī. The town being practically defenceless, Tāzī plundered it.[40] When Tātār Khān, Buhlūl Lodī's governor of the Punjāb, heard of this he set out with an army to invade Kashmīr. He occupied some of the villages at the foot of the mountains, but owing to the high barriers which barred his passage, he did not advance any further. Moreover, as the prestige of the rulers of Kashmīr was still great, he thought that serious resistance would be offered to him, and his invasion would end in failure. In reality however the country was no longer as strong as it had been in former days, and could have been easily overrun by an enterprising general.[41]

Meanwhile, Malik Aḥmad had succeeded in poisoning Ḥasan Shāh's mind against Tāzī Baṭ. He had the guardianship of Prince Muḥammad transferred from him to his own son, Naurūz;[42] and although Tāzī Baṭ returned from the campaign successful with the spoils of war, he persuaded the Sulṭān not to confer any honours on him. Not satisfied with this, and still fearing Tāzī Baṭ as a rival, he decided to destroy him. For this purpose he recalled the Baihaqī Sayyids from India in spite of the opposition of some of the nobles who looked upon all foreigners with suspicion, and entered in league with them. Finally he secured the Sulṭān's order by which Tāzī Baṭ's property was confiscated, and he was interned in his own house and given a small allowance.[43]

After bringing about the fall of Tāzī Baṭ, Malik Aḥmad directed his attention to other ministers whom he suspected of being his possible rivals. He had them dismissed, and in their place appointed his own favourites. As a result Aḥmad's power enormously increased, and every one began to fear him. Even Jahāngīr Māgre, the commander-in-chief, was filled with apprehension.[44]

Ḥasan Shāh, who was watching these developments closely, did not approve of Aḥmad's conduct and turned against him. Observing the change in the attitude of the Sulṭān, the minister's ememies felt encouraged, and suggested to him to take away the guardianship of Prince Yūsuf from Aḥmad.[45] The Sulṭān, acted on their advice; but fearing rebellion, he won over the Sayyids and sought the support of Jahāngīr Māgre to crush Aḥmad. The latter, hearing of these developments, marched with his followers to the palace and entered it. Meanwhile, Jahāngīr, having arrived from his estate, released Tāzī Baṭ, and set out with him and the Sayyids to attack Aḥmad. Tāzī Baṭ's supporters set fire to the western gate of the palace, causing the destruction of a large number of houses in the neighbourhood. Aḥmad, finding himself surrounded on all sides, and realising that he was not strong enough to resist Jahāngīr for his troops began to desert him, threw himself at the mercy of Ḥasan Shāh. The latter, remembering his past services, gave him protection against his enemies who would otherwise have put him to death. However, urged by Jahāngīr and other courtiers, Malik Aḥmad and his sons and prominent followers were thrown into prison, and their properties were confiscated.[46] In his place Sayyid Ḥasan Baihaqī, Ḥasan Shāh's father-in-law, was appointed Wazīr, and the jāgīr of Nāgām was transferred to him. Malik Aḥmad had been Wazīr for ten years. He had been loyal to Ḥasan Shāh, who in turn had placed great confidence in him and acted on his advice. He was generous and tolerant, and granted villages to the Brahmans, while for the Muslims he built and endowed hospices.[47] In the beginning he ruled the country well, but later on, filled with the lust for power, he became tyrannical, neglecting the administration and pursuing a policy of intrigue and nepotism.

Baltistān and Ladākh had again become independent, and so, in 1483, Ḥasan Shāh despatched Jahāngīr Māgre and Sayyid

Ḥasan to reconquer them. Jahāngīr suggested to Sayyid Ḥasan to march together and act jointly. But the latter did not agree to this, and undertook the campaign separately. He invaded Baltistān, and having reduced its chief to obedience, returned to Srīnagar in triumph. But Jahāngīr, who had proceeded to Ladākh, was defeated by its ruler Lhachen Bhagan (1470-1500). The Ladākhīs (Bhauṭṭas) fell upon his rear and destroyed his army. Jahāngīr himself, however, succeeded in making good his escape and returning to Srīnagar. The reverse was due to the disunity of the Kashmīrī commanders, for if they had carried on the campaign jointly, Jahāngīr's army would not have met with such a disaster.[48] This defeat was taken advantage of by the Sayyids to incite the Sulṭān against Jahāngīr whom they regarded as a serious rival. Jahāngīr, disgusted with the court intrigues and alarmed for his life, went away to Loharkōt.[49]

Like his father, Ḥasan Shāh also indulged in excessive drinking. This in the end undermined his health, and he had a serious attack of diarrhoea.[50] Realising that he would not recover, he sent for Sayyid Ḥasan, his Wazīr and father-in-law, and asked him to recall Adham's son Fatḥ Khān, who was living in exile in the Punjāb, and appoint him his successor, as his own sons, Muḥammad, Ḥasan, and Yūsuf, were only minors. But in case the Queen did not approve of this, she was free to make any other arrangement. The Queen was at first agreeable to the Sulṭān's suggestion, but, under the influence of her father, she changed her mind, and, when the Sulṭān died on April 19, 1484, she at once declared her son Muḥammad, who was seven years of age, as Sulṭān.[51]

As a prince Ḥasan Shāh had shown some energy and enterprise but ever since he became ruler, he took little interest in public affairs, and not even once led an army. Instead, he applied himself more or less exclusively to pleasure. Malik Aḥmad, the Wazīr, at first governed the country well, but later, he too neglected his duties, and appointed to responsible positions in the government his own men who were corrupt and inefficient. Aḥmad's conduct aroused the anger and jealousy of the nobles, and led to an armed conflict. This weakened the administration, and adversely affected law and order. Taking advantage of this the outlying provinces of the kingdom became independent, and only the Valley was left in the possession of Ḥasan Shāh. An attempt to reduce Ladākh ended in disaster; and although Baltistān, Jammu, and Rajaurī were reduced, they soon relapsed into independence owing to the weakness of the central government.

Although politically Ḥasan Shāh's reign was a failure, culturally it was of great significance. Ḥasan Shāh was, next to Zainu'l-'Ābidīn, the most cultured ruler of the Shāh Mīr dynasty. He patronised men of learning, and under him some Persian works were translated into Sanskrit. He was interested in the spread of education, and founded schools which were liberally endowed. He was not only a great patron of music, but was himself well versed in it. He possessed a sweet voice, and sang Persian, Kashmīrī, and Sanskrit songs. His court was adorned with skilful musicians of whom some had come from distant places, attracted by the Sulṭān's love of music. In all, there were 1,200 musicians in his court.[52]

Ḥasan Shāh's reign was characterised by great building activity. He built palaces at Didamar[53] and Sōpūr, and repaired those which had been erected by his predecessors at various places. In Srīnagar he built a *khānqāh* and dedicated it to his father'[54] and when his mother Gul Khātūn died, he constructed a new bridge of boats in her memory at the end of Shihābu'd-Dīnpūr. But the most important edifices which he rebuilt were the Khānqāh-i-Mu'allā and Jāmi'Masjid, which had been erected by Sikandar, but a great fire had destroyed them in 1479.[55]

The example of the Sulṭān was followed by his nobles. The Wazīr, Malik Aḥmad, constructed a number of buildings at Didamar, including a *khānqāh* which was endowed with the village of Satipusha,[56] and where foreigners were given free accommodation and food. His wife Shāh Bēgum also built a *khānqāh* on the road leading to Kherī.[57] His sons, the nobles, and princes vied with each other in the erection of *khānqāhs.* Hindus and Buddhists too constructed many religious buildings. Sayyabhāṇḍapati built a *vihāra* at Bījbehara,[58] while his brothers erected a beautiful stone temple of Gaṇeśa. Many other similar edifices were erected by the Hindus.[59]

Sulṭān Muḥammad Shāh (i) 1484-6

Muḥammad Khān ascended the throne under the title of Muḥammad Shāh. But as he was too young to exercise any authority, the affairs of the government were conducted by his maternal grandfather, Sayyid Ḥasan.[60] Within a short period, however, Sayyid Ḥasan and other members of his family, owing to their foreign origin and the superior and arrogant attitude which they adopted towards the Kashmīrī nobles,[61] combined with their opposition to the caste system[62] and their discouragement of the use of Sanskrit and Kashmīrī,[63] became very unpopular in the country.[64] The Kashmīrī nobles, therefore, organised a plot against them with the help of Paraśurām, the ruler of Jammu, who, apprehending an attack from Tātār Khān, had fled to Srīnagar. One night about three hundred men, including some Jammu soldiers, secretly entered the fort of Naushahr by bribing the guards.[65] Early next morning, while Sayyid Ḥasan was holding court in the fort, they came out of their hiding places and attacked him and his followers, killing him and thirteen others. A servant, though seriously wounded, escaped through a drain in the fort, and informed Sayyid Ḥasan's son, Sayyid Muḥammad, of the tragedy.[66] Hearing of this Sayyid Muḥammad with his brother Sayyid Hāshim at once attacked the fort and occupied it. He also seized all the treasure which was there, and distributed it among his troops.[67]

Meanwhile, 'Idī Raina tried to secure the release of Yūsuf Khān, the son of Bahrām Khān, and to set him up on the throne. But Sayyid 'Alī Baihaqī, one of the Sayyid nobles, came to know of the plot, and he immediately put Yūsuf Khān to death.[68] Sītan Devī, Yūsuf's mother, kept the body of her son with her for three days, and then had it buried. Near his grave she built a cell where she passed the rest of her days.[69]

Hearing of these events, Jahāngīr Māgre returned to Srīnagar from Loharkōt at the request of the Kashmīrī nobles. The Sayyids offered to come to terms with him. But he refused, and sent his son Dā'ūd, accompanied by Ṣaifdār, across the bridge to attack the Sayyids in Naushahr. But Dā'ūd was defeated and killed. To celebrate their victory, the Sayyids erected a minaret of the heads of the slain.[70] Encouraged by this success, the Sayyids themselves decided to take the offensive. Informed of this the Kashmīrīs also advanced and encountered the enemy on the bridge. But suddenly it gave way, and as a result many soldiers from both the armies were drowned in the river.[71]

Realising that the Kashmīrī nobles were getting bolder and stronger every day, the Sayyids sought the help of Tātār Khān, the Lodī governor of the Punjāb. The latter sent to their aid some troops. But when these reached Bhimbar, its Rājā checked their advance, and compelled them to retreat.[72] This news raised the spirits of the Kashmīrīs whose attacks on the Sayyids became more frequent. But they were indecisive, being only in the nature of skirmishes. The victory sometimes lay with the Kashmīrīs and sometimes with Sayyids. After two months, however, the Kashmīrī nobles with a large army crossed the Jehlam and attacked the Sayyids. The latter, being outnumbered, were defeated. They fled, but were pursued, and many of them were killed and the city of Naushahr was set fire to.[73] The Kashmīrī nobles entered the fort of Naushahr, and saluted Muḥammad Shāh as Sulṭān. The Sayyids were once again banished from the country. Their Jāgīrs were confiscated and distributed among the nobles who had brought about their overthrow.[74] Paraśurām, who had played an important part in the conflict against the Sayyids, was given presents and allowed to depart.[75] Jahāngīr Māgre was appointed prime minisiter.

The facade of unity in the country lasted as long as the Sayyids were in power. But as soon as the latter were overthrown, the nobles restarted quarelling. Some of them invited Fatḥ Khān, the son of Adham Khān, who was living in Jalandhar, and promised him support.[76] On receiving the invitation, Fatḥ Khān proceeded to Rajaurī, and although he was dissuaded from the step by Jahāngīr Māgre, he, in the middle of 1485, having won over Mas'ūd Nāyak, the Guardian of the passes, entered Kashmīr *via* Hirapūr, where he was joined by his supporters.[77] Jahāngīr at once set out with Muḥammad Shāh and encamped at Gūs Udar.[78] But on hearing that Fatḥ Khān had reached Kalampūr, he marched to attack him, leaving behind Muḥammad Shāh at Gūs Udar. Heavy fighting took place at Kalampūr.[79] The royal forces were on the point of being defeated, when Jahāngīr rallied them by spreading a false rumour that Fatḥ Khān had been captured. This demoralised the latter's followers and they fled. Fatḥ Khān, despairing of success, also left the battle-field and finally managed to escape to the Punjāb.[80] Some of his leading supporters were, however, seized and thrown into prison and their houses were plundered.[81]

Although defeated and driven out of Kashmīr, Fatḥ Khān organised his forces at Bahrāmgala,[82] and again invaded Kashmīr the following year. Jahāngīr Māgre encountered him on the *karēwa* in the Nāgām pargana. Meanwhile Zīrak Baṭ, a follower of Fatḥ Khān, entered Srīnagar with a small following and secured the release of Malik Ṣaifdār and others who had been imprisoned because they had supported Fatḥ Khān.[83.] Jahāngīr became alarmed at these developments and made peace with Fatḥ Khān through the mediation of the Rājā of Rajaurī[84] Meanwhile he began his intrigues, and having succeeded in alienating the Rājā from Fatḥ Khān and in separating the latter from his other supporters, he attacked him. Fatḥ Khān, finding himself completely isolated, fled, pursued by Jahāngīr as far as Hirapūr.[85]

From Hirapūr, Fatḥ Khān proceeded to Jammu which he occupied, and then again made an attempt to seize the throne of Kashmīr. Jahāngīr Māgre advanced to offer him battle with the support of Sayyid Muḥammad and other Sayyid chiefs whom he had recalled from their exile in India.[86] Fatḥ Khān being defeated at Gūs Udar, retired to Rajaurī along with his adviser and commander Ṣaifdār. However, he did not lose heart. A few months after he again organised an army and entered the Valley. He met the royal forces at Dāmadar Udar,[87] and this time he was victorious. Jahāngīr escaped with a wound, Sayyid Muḥammad deserted and joined Fatḥ Khān. Muḥammad Shāh tried to escape but was seize by Fatḥ Khān's supporters (October 14, 1486).[88] He was confined in his own palace, but was provided with all comforts. Fatḥ Khān was proclaimed ruler, and ascended the throne under the title of Sulṭān Fatḥ Shāh. The Khaśas who had come with him sacked the city; and although order was restored after three days, yet, for about six months, the kingdom was at their mercy.[89]

Sulṭān Fatḥ Shāh (i) (1486-93)

Fatḥ Shāh was religious and possessed simple habits. He abstained from wine, did not play dice, and led a strictly moral life.[90] He was intelligent, brave, and enterprising, and tried his best to curb the power of the nobles, but he was not successful. The result was that while he reigned the nobles ruled in his name, and the decline of the dynasty continued.

Since Fatḥ Shāh had secured the throne through the efforts of Ṣaifdār, he made him his prime minister. Soon however he became dissatisfied with him for keeping all power in his own hands and treating him only as a figure-head. He therefore secured the support of Nuṣrat Raina, Sarhang Raina, Mūsā Raina, and Shams Chak and decided to overthrow Ṣaifdār. In order to carry on his preparations undisturbed he destroyed all the bridges of the town, and then, after a few days, attacked Ṣaifdār at the village of Ramlana.[91] A fierce hand to hand fight ensued. Ṣaifdār was killed by Sarhang Raina, but the latter himself was mortally wounded by him. However, Ṣaifdār's death completely demoralised his troops, and they fled. Fatḥ Shāh was glad at this victory and rewarded Mūsā Raina and Nuṣrat Raina with gifts, while Shams Chak was appointed prime minister.[92]

Shams Chak was the son of Hilmat Chak who with his tribe had come from the direction of Gilgit and had settled in Kopwārā. Kopwārā is situated 55 miles north-west of Srīnagar. He had served in turn Sayyid Muḥammad, Malik Naurūz, and Ṣaifdār. He was brave and had earned fame in the civil wars. He married the daughter of Pāṇḍū Chak's son Ḥusain Chak who was living in Gawāril.[93] This united the two families which had hitherto been hostile to each other, and greatly strengthened the position of Shams Chak, for all the followers of Ḥusain Chak joined him.[94]

After two and a half years of peace, dissensions among the nobles revived. The relations between Sayyid Muḥammad and Shams Chak became estranged. Ibrāhīm Māgre, the son of

Jahāngīr Māgre, and 'Īdī Raina also turned against Shams Chak, and, with the help of Sayyid Muḥammad, made preparations to overthrow him.[95] They then attacked him in the vicinity of Bulbul Shāh's tomb and defeated him. Shams Chak, however, succeeded in crossing the bridge of 'Alī Kadal over to Ziāldakar where he was joined by Kājī Chak who had also fought his way through the ranks of the enemy. Shams Cak, at first, thought of again making a stand, but as his forces were smaller and many of his supporters had deserted him, he retired to Kamrāj. Since Fatḥ Shāh had allied himself with Shams Chak he had to give up his throne and retire to Naushahrā.[96] Muḥammad Shāh, who had been confined in his own palace, was released and declared Sulṭān for the second time.[97]

Sulṭān Muḥammad Shāh (ii) 1493-1505

Immediately on ascending the throne, Muḥammad Shāh, accompanied by his prime minister, Sayyid Muḥammad, Ibrāhīm Māgre, and Mūsā Raina, set out against Shams Chak. When he reached the village of Trahgām, Shams Chak moved to Drāva.[98] Muḥammad Shāh, having destroyed the houses of Shams Chak's partisans in and around Trahgām, proceeded to Sōpūr. When Shams Chak heard of this he returned to Trahgām; and since he had a smaller army than that of his opponents, he decided to make a night attack and marched to Sōpūr, reaching there early in the morning.[99] Muḥammad Shāh was taken by surprise and fled across the bridge, leaving behind some of his baggage which fell into the hands of the enemy. He then destroyed the bridge, and encamped on the other side of the river. But Mūsā Raina, being stationed at some distance from the main army, learnt of the night attack after the bridge had been destroyed, and so he could not cross the river. However, though he had a small force he refused to surrender, and when he was attacked by Shams Chak, he made a brave stand and, with the help of Kājī Chak, 'Īdī Raina, and Sayyid Muḥammad, defeated him. Shams Chak fled to Trahgām, and thence to Naushahrā, where he joined Fatḥ Shāh.[100] Muḥammad Shāh returned to his capital in triumph, and conferred upon Mūsā Raina a jāgīr in reward for his services.[101] But this did not please Mūsā, as he felt he had been assigned a smaller jāgīr than what he deserved.[102] Moreover at this time arrived Shamsu'd-Dīn[103] for the second time in Kashmīr and Mūsā became his devoted follower. But Sayyid Muḥammad did not approve of Shamsu'd-Dīn's ideas, and compelled him to retire to Skārdu. Mūsā was therefore very angry with Sayyid Muḥammad, and having won over Ibrāhīm Māgre and Ḥājī Padar, invited Fatḥ Shāh, who was in Naushahrā, to Kashmīr. Fatḥ Shāh, accordingly, entered the Valley, and on reaching Hirapūr was joined by Mūsā, Ibrāhīm, and Hājī.[104] Hearing of this Muḥammad Shāh accompanied by Sayyid Muḥammad marched against them, and defeated them at Zainakōt. The next day, however, Fatḥ Shāh after reorganising his army again offered battle. He was on the point of losing when suddenly Sayyid Muḥammad was killed. This demoralised the royal forces, and they fled. Muḥammad Shāh nearly escaped capture, and succeeded in making his way to Naushahrā. Fatḥ Shāh was thereupon proclaimed Sulṭān.[105]

Sulṭān Fatḥ Shāh (ii) 1505-14

On ascending the throne Fatḥ Shāh raised Shams Chak, who had been with him in exile, to the office of prime minister. But partly out of jealousy and partly because of the arrogant attitude of Shams Chak, Ibrāhīm Māgre and Mūsā Raina resented his appointment. And shortly afterwards, they joined hands with Fatḥ Shāh who also had begun to chafe under the yoke of his minister. A plot was therefore organised against Shams Chak and he was seized and thrown into prison. Since Shams Chak had been responsible for the assassination of Ṣaifdār and the overthrow of the Dangres, Mūsā Raina employed Bahrām Dār and Dati Malik for putting him to death.[106] Although Shams Chak was in chains, and had no weapons to defend himself with, except a small knife, yet he fought with his assassins like a tiger, killing three of them and wounding others. In the end, however, he was overpowered by a shower of arrows and killed along with his son. He had remained Wazīr only for four months.[107]

The first act of Mūsā Raina, who now replaced Shams Chak, was to exile the Dangre tribe which had turned against him.[108] He then recalled Shamsu'd-Dīn from Skārdu, and helped him in his missionary activities. Mūsā Raina was able and efficient and ruled Kashmīr with a strong hand.[109] But Ibrāhīm Māgre, who had so far been friendly with him, now became hostile. He won over Fatḥ Shah as well as some of the nobles who did not approve of Mūsā's religious policy.[110] He then with his supporters proceeded to the palace at Sikandarpūr (Srīnagar), and having destroyed the bridge of the city, prepared to attack Mūsā. The latter, on the other hand, encamped in the field of Ziāldakar; but finding that his forces were smaller than those of his rivals, he decided to retire to India.[111] Meanwhile, Malik 'Uṣmān and Dati Malik, chiefs of the Dangre tribe, who had been exiled by Mūsā Raina, set out towards Srīnagar *via* Hirapūr at the invitation of Ibrāhīm Māgre. Mūsā, in order to avoid encountering them, took the route of Chīra Hār, but on the way he was killed by a soldier.[112]

Fatḥ Shāh now appointed Ibrāhīm Māgre his prime minister. But Ibrāhīm remained in power only for forty days, because the Dangre chiefs, whom he had recalled from India to his aid, became alienated, and, with the help of some nobles, succeeded in overthrowing him. Ibrāhīm fled to India. He was a past master in the art of intrigue, but was incompetent as an administrator; and during his short tenure of office there was utter lawlessness in the country.[113]

After the flight Ibrāhīm, Malik 'Uṣmān became Wazīr. But two months after, Kājī Chak, Jahāngīr Padar, and Gadā'ī Malik formed a plot against him with the support of Fatḥ Shāh. They surprised Dati Malik, who was in the palace administering justice, and killed him. They seized Malik 'Uṣmān, who was in another room with Fatḥ Shāh, and threw him into prison. Thereupon, Jahāngīr Padar was set up as Wazīr. But only a month had elapsed when Ibrāhīm Māgre returned from the Punjāb with an army, and defeated Jahāngir Padar and Kājī Chak. The latter, accompanied by Fatḥ Shāh who had supported him, left for the Punjāb. But Ibrāhīm recalled Fatḥ Shāh, who had reached as far as Hirapūr, and acknowledged him as Sulṭān.

Coins were struck and the *khuṭba* was recited in the name of Faṭh Shāh.[114]

Ibrāhīm Māgre had enjoyed office only for a year, when Malik 'Uṣmān, who had been released by him from prison, Shankar Raina, and Nuṣrat Raina formed a league in concert with Fatḥ Shāh and seized Abdāl and Fīrūz, the two sons of Ibrāhīm. This made the latter so demoralised that he fled to Pūnch. Thereupon Malik 'Uṣmān became Wazīr, and the kingdom was divided into three parts among 'Uṣmān, Shankar, and Nuṣrat.[115]

Peace, however, lasted only for five months, after which Ibrāhīm Māgre and the Chaks, who were in the Punjāb, patched up their differences and decided to enthrone Muḥammad Shāh. They advanced from Pūnch to Bārāmūla, and established themselves at Sōpūr. Thereupon Malik 'Uṣmān with Fatḥ Shāh set out towards Sōpūr, and encamped opposite the enemy forces with only the Jehlam between them. But as 'Uṣmān could not cross the river and attack the enemy, he left behind Fatḥ Shāh and Shankar Raina to keep watch over their movements, while he himself marched by way of Khuyahōm[116] to attack them from the rear. But Lohar Māgre and Rēgī Chak came to know of his plan, and they tried to intercept him.[117] They were however defeated at the village of Pushkaranāga,[118] and retreated to join Muḥammad Shāh's forces. When Malik 'Alī Sarkhail heard of this defeat, he decided to play a ruse. He spread the news through some of the trusted men of Fatḥ Shāh that Malik 'Uṣmān had been defeated and killed, and that Muḥammad Shāh's forces would cross the river next day to seize Fatḥ Shāh. The latter should, therefore, escape to Pūnch while there was still time. On being informed of this Fatḥ Shāh was seized with panic and, leaving behind part of his baggage, made good his escape in the night by the Tōshamaidān route. Thus the victory, which Malik 'Uṣmān had gained over Lohar Māgre, was thrown away and turned into defeat by the pusillanimity of Fatḥ Shāh.[119] This disheartened him, and he too fled. But he was pursued by Ibrāhīm Māgre and captured. He was then thrown into prison and there put to death.[120] Shankar and Nuṣrat, however, having submitted, were pardoned.[121]

Muḥammad Shāh (iii) 1514-15

After the flight of Fatḥ Shāh, Muḥammad Shāh became Sulṭān for the third time. He appointed Ibrāhīm Māgre his chief minister, because it was due to his efforts that he had secured the throne. Meanwhile Fatḥ Shāh, having again decided to invade Kashmīr, sent his son Ḥabīb Khān to find out the chances of his success. Ḥabīb Khān was joined by Jahāngīr Padar, and was promised support by the Chak nobles who were related to his mother.[122] With these assurances Fatḥ Shāh entered the Valley, and many nobles, including the Chak chiefs led by Kājī Chak, rallied to him. Owing to these defections Muḥammad Shāh and Ibrāhīm Māgre did not offer any resistance, and left Kashmīr for the Punjāb.[123] Fatḥ Shāh thus recovered the throne after nine months of exile.[124]

Fatḥ Shāh (iii) 1515-17

Although Fatḥ Shāh was the Sulṭān, he was only a figure-head, for the real power was in the hands of the nobles. Moreover, his prime minister, Jahāngīr Padar, and the two chiefs Shankar Raina and Kājī Chak had assigned him only the revenues of the crown lands, while they had divided the rest of the Valley among themselves.[125]

In the autumn of 1515 Muḥammad Shāh with Ibrāhīm Māgre entered Kashmīr to claim the throne. They were met by the royal forces at Bāngil. Ibrāhīm Māgre was killed with his two sons, but Muḥammad Shāh managed to escape to Pūnch. After wandering for nearly two years he proceeded to the court of Sulṭān Sikandar Lodī (1489-1517) to seek his help. He was received with respect and supplied with a force of 3,000 men. With these Muḥammad Shāh set out towards Kashmīr.[126] When he reached Danaor,[127] he received messages of loyalty and promises of support from Kājī Chak, Shankar Ṛaina, and Nuṣrat Raina.[128] And shortly after, these nobles raised the banner of revolt against Fatḥ Shāh and occupied the fort of Harshīn.[129] Fatḥ Shāh and Jahāngīr Padar besieged them, but were repulsed. Fatḥ Shāh thereupon fled to the Punjāb.[130] There he died in August 1517. His body was brought to the Valley, and Muḥammad Shāh had it buried with all due ceremonies near the grave of Sulṭān Zainu'l-'Ābidīn.[131]

Muḥammad Shāh (iv) 1517-28

Meanwhile, hearing the news of Fatḥ Shāh's overthrow and convinced of the loyalty of his own supporters, Muḥammad Shāh decided to dispense with the aid of the foreign troops whose presence in the Valley would not only make him unpopular but would also be unnecessary burden upon the country. He therefore left behind the Indian troops at Danaor, and with 2,000 of his followers proceeded towards Srīnagar. On arriving there he appointed Kājī Chak his Wazīr, but suspecting Shankar Raina of treachery, he threw him into prison.[132] He then returned to Danaor to dismiss the Indian troops. He accompanied them as far as Naushahrā, and there he bid them farewell. But as winter had set in, and the routes to Kashmīr were blocked by snow, he himself decided to remain in Naushahrā.[133]

During Muḥammad Shāh's absence the Valley was plunged into civil war. Nuṣrat Raina was angry at the imprisonment of Shankar and the appointment of Kājī Chak as chief minister, and so he revolted with the help of Lohar Māgre. Kājī, on the other hand, was joined by Jahāngīr Padar who had hitherto been his rival. Each faction thus prepared for a conflict. Nuṣrat Raina finding himself not strong enough to fight a pitched battle with Kājī Chak, decided upon a night attack. But his plan miscarried, for Kājī came to know of it and was ready to oppose him. The engagement took place at Ziāldakar. Kājī was wounded, but Nuṣrat's fall demoralised his supporters and they fled. The Chaks were thus victorious. Early in spring Muḥammad Shāh entered Kashmīr accompanied by Sayyid Ibrāhīm, the son of Sayyid Muḥammad Baihaqī.[134]

Kājī Chak's friendship with Jahāngīr Padar was only short-lived. Early in 1520 he despatched his son Mas'ūd with a large force to seize Jahāngīr Padar who was in the village of Pāmpūr.[135] Jahāngīr warned of this fled to Dārdu, where he joined Gadā'ī Malik. Mas'ūd having plundered his house returned to Srīnagar.[136]

Next year in May 1521 there was another rising led by Malik Abdāl, the son of Ibrāhīm Māgre, Lohar Māgre, and 'Īdī Raina. They joined Fatḥ Shāh's son Sikandar, and, having proclaimed him ruler, seized the fort of Nāgām. Jahāngīr Padar and Gadā'ī Malik, who were in Dārdu, also set out towards Nāgām in order to support Sikandar. Kājī Chak sent Daulat and Mas'ūd, to intercept them, while he himself marched to attack Sikandar. He defeated him at Lulpūr,[137] and when Sikandar after this reverse retreated to the fort of Nāgām, he besieged him there. Meanwhile Daulat Chak attacked Gadā'ī Malik near Shādīpūr and killed him.[138] But Mas'ūd Chak did not fare well against Jahāngīr Padar. Being struck by an arrow in the eye, he fell from his horse and died.[139] But in spite of this temporary setback the victory lay in the end with the Chaks. Daulat after defeating Gadā'ī Malik, crossed the river at Shādīpūr, and joined Sayyid Ibrāhīm and Tāzī Chak who had been sent by Kājī Chak to the help of Mas'ūd. Together they prevented Jahāngīr Padar from crossing the river and joining Sikandar in the fort of Nāgām.[140] Meanwhile Sikandar, finding his position untenable, since no help could reach him, made overtures of peace to Kājī and then fled to the Punjāb. Soon after Jahāngīr Padar too made good his escape.[141] Lohar Māgre and 'Īdī Raina however submitted and were pardoned by Muḥammad Shāh. Daulat Chak, Kājī's nephew, received the jāgīr of Mas'ūd for his success against Jahāngīr and Gadā'ī Malik.[142]

In 1522 the Māgres again invaded and brought with them this time Fatḥ Shāh's second son, Ḥabīb Khān, as pretender. But as their forces were small they failed to achieve anything. Moreover, 'Īdī Raina went over to the enemy. This disheartened them, and they retired from the Valley. On the way Ḥabīb died. His body was brought to Srīnagar and buried near the grave of his father. Soon after Kājī recalled the Māgre chiefs and entered into marriage alliances with them.[143]

Kājī Chak having pacified his enemies became very powerful. But this aroused the resentment of Muḥammad Shāh who found himself to be a ruler only in name. He therefore won over some of the important nobles like Malik Abdāl, Lohar Māgre, Malik 'Alī Chādura, and Rēgī Chak, and plotted Kājī's overthrow. He left the city and proceeded to Lār with Naurūz Chak, a cousin of Kājī, to organise resistance. There was however no conflict, for when Kājī saw that the nobles on whom he depended had deserted him, he got disgusted and went away to Naushahrā in 1527.[144]

Soon after these events, Kashmir was threatened by an invasion of the Mughals under Kūchak Bēg and Shaikh 'Alī Bēg who were despatched by Bābur to help Sikandar in securing the throne.[145] When Kājī Chak heard of this his patriotism was strirred, and although he had received no orders from Muḥammad Shāh, he prepared to repel the invasion. He collected a force from the surrounding area and sent Tāzī Chak, Ḥusain Chak, and his son Ghāzī, who was at this time only about eighteen years of age, against them. Both Ghāzī and Tāzī fought bravely and defeated the Turks in the neighbourhood of Naushahrā. Kājī then seized Sikandar who had invited the Mughals.[146]

When Muḥammad Shāh heard of this, he expressed his gratitude to Kājī, and requested him to forget the past and return to Srīnagar. Kājī accordingly returned in 1527, and brought with him Sikandar whom he handed over to Muḥammad Shāh. Sikandar was blinded by the Sulṭān's orders, although Kājī Chak opposed the infliction of such a cruel punishment. Sikandar died in prison after a few days.[147]

Muḥammad Shāh again appointed Kājī his Wazīr. But this led to the revival of old feudal rivalries. The Māgres and Malik 'Alī Chādura revolted against Muḥammad Shāh for having shown favour to Kājī. They entrenched themselves in the village of Kichhāmā,[148] and prepared for resistance. Muḥammad Shāh despatched Kājī and Sayyid Ibrāhīm against the rebels. The Māgre forces were completely routed, and Malik 'Alī was captured. He was made over to Tāzī Chak who confined him in his house. But shortly after he managed to escape to the Punjāb with the connivance of Tāzī. Meanwhile differences had arisen between Kājī and Muḥammad Shāh. As a result Kājī deposed him in favour of his son Ibrāhīm. Muḥammad Shāh with some of the nobles was imprisoned in the village of Lad.[149]

Sulṭān Ibrāhīm Shāh 1 (1528-29) and Nāzuk Shāh (1529-30)

Ibrāhīm Shāh[150] was a ruler only in name, for it was Kājī who exercised real power. Soon after Malik 'Alī Chādura, Rēgī Chak, and the Māgre chiefs, who were in exile, conferred at Naushahrā and decided to send Abdāl Māgre to the court of the Emperor Bābur to seek his help against Kājī Chak. Abdāl proceeded to Delhi and was received with honour by the Emperor who gave him an army under his two commanders, Shaikh 'Alī Bēg and Muḥammad Khān.[151] With this Mughal force the Kashmīrī chiefs set out to invade Kashmīr. But realising that the people of the Valley would look upon the coming of the Mughals with distrust, Abdāl Māgre declared Nāzuk Shāh also called Nādir Shāh, the son of Fatḥ Shāh, as Sulṭān.[152]

Early in the spring of 1528 the rebel chiefs with Nāzuk Shāh and the Mughal army entered Kashmīr. Kājī Chak, hearing of this, at once marched against them, and met them at Tāpar.[153] Although he and his followers fought with great courage, they were defeated. Many of the Chak nobles, including Tāzī Chak, lost their lives. Kājī however succeeded in escaping to the Salt Range, while Sayyid Ibrāhīm, Ghāzī Chak, and Daulat Chak were made prisoners and sent under a guard to the city. But on the way, at nightfall, Daulat Chak escaped in a boat, and remained in the neighbourhood, immersed in water up to his chin with his head covered with water-lilies. His guards searched for him until midnight with the help of a large number of boats but without success. After the guards left, Daulat made good his escape. Ghāzī and Sayyid Ibrāhīm, however, remained in custody, and with them the Māgres and the Mughals entered the capital in triumph.[154]

Owing to the victory of the Māgres, Ibrāhīm Shāh, who had been set up by Kājī and was the son of his sister Ṣāleḥ Mājī,[155] was deposed and Nāzuk Shāh was enthroned. Nāzuk transferred his capital to Naushahr, and gave assurance of safety to the Kashmīrīs who were apprehensive of the Mughals. Abdāl Māgre assumed the office of Wazīr.[156] But Nāzuk Shāh remained in power only for a year,[157] for Muḥammad Shāh, who was in prison at Lad, was brought from there and enthroned in the summer of 1530. But he was a ruler in name, for the real power was wielded by the nobles who had been responsible for his recall. He was given the crown lands for his expenses, while the rest of the kingdom was divided equally among Abdāl Māgre, Lohar Māgre, Rēgī Chak, and Malik 'Alī Chādura.[158]

Muḥammad Shāh (v) 1530-37

After these changes the Mughal troops were given presents and requested to leave, for it was felt that their permanent stay in the country would not be good for it. Malik 'Alī was deputed to escort them as far as Naushahrā.[159] Meanwhile, Bābur died and was succeeded by Humāyūn. When the Mughal commanders returned to Lahore they informed Kāmrān, Humāyūn's governor of the Punjāb, that owing to the disunity in Kashmīr it was not difficult to conquer it.[160] Kāmrān, therefore, in 1531, set out towards the Valley accompanied by Mahṛam Bēg and Shaikh 'Alī Bēg. On reaching Naushahrā, Kāmrān sent his two commanders with 3,000 horse to undertake the invasion, while he himself stayed behind.[161] Owing to the absence of any strong government in the Valley the passes were left undefended, and so the Mughals easily entered the country. However, the Kashmīrīs tried to check their advance on the capital, but were defeated, and had to retreat to the fort of Chīraodar.[162] The Mughals thereupon marched on Srīnagar and occupied it. They sacked the city, set fire to it, and slew the Kashmīrīs who had come down from the hills to fight them.[163] After this they marched on the fort of Chīraodar, which was also occupied, the Kashmīrī forces having withdrawn to Athwājan[164] without putting up a fight. When Kāmrān, who was still in Naushahrā, heard the news of these victories he returned to Lahore, convinced that Kashmīr had finally been reduced, and that there would be no further resistance.[165]

At first the Kashmīrī nobles thought that Kājī Chak was supporting the Mughals, but learning that he was neutral, they appealed to him to return from the Salt Range, where he was at the moment living, in the hour of his country's need, and save it from falling under foreign domination. Kājī, in response to this request, at once set out towards the Valley and joined the

Kashmīrī forces at Athwājan.[166] His arrival raised their morale and spirit so that, when they were attacked by the Mughals at Athwājan, they put up a fierce fight and defeated them. Encouraged by this success, the Kashmīrīs established themselves on the Takht-i-Sulaimān, and from there began to lead attacks on the enemy in the city. The Mughals resisted for some time, but as they could not hold out much longer, they made overtures of peace.[167] After an hour's negotiations carried out between Kājī Chak and Maḥram Bēg in a boat on the Jehlam, the Mughals agreed to quit Kashmīr. They received presents, and after a few days left for Lahore *via* Bārāmūla, escorted by Daulat Chak and Jahāngīr Māgre up to Pakhlī.[168]

After the withdrawal of the Mughals, the Valley was divided by the nobles into five parts, excluding the crown lands belonging to Muḥammad Shāh and the jāgīr of Sayyid Ibrāhīm. Abdāl Māgre, who continued as Wazīr, Lohar Māgre, Kājī Chak, Rēgi Chak and Malik 'Alī Chādura each received one part.[169] But hardly had Kashmīr recovered from the effects of the Mughal invasion when, after a year, it was subjected to another attack. This time from the north-east, from Kāshghar, by Mīrzā Ḥaidar Dughlat.

NOTES

1. *Ibid.*, f. 77b; Śrīv., pp. 183-4.
2. Śrīv. (Bo. ed.), BK. II, No 15; Munich MS., f. 77b.
3. Śrīv., p. 186, calls him Riktetara, but subsequently he is mentioned as Pūrṇa. See also Śrīv. (Bp. ed.), Nos. 30, 52, where he is called Rikitara and Pūrṇapatī respectively. Munich MS. calls him Pūnī, while Niẓāmu'd-Din and Firishta refer to him as Lūlī. In Arabic characters Pūnī can be easily read as Lūlī.
4. Śrīv., pp. 190-3; Munich MS., f. 78a.
5. Śrīv., p. 189.
6. *Ibid.*, p. 194; Munich MS., f. 78a. It seems Adham Khān had married a Jammu princess. After his death his son Fatḥ Khān was brought up by the Jammu Rājā. (Śrīv., p. 309).
7. Munich MS., f. 78a; T.A., iii, p. 447.
8. Śrīv., (Bo. ed.), BK. ii, No. 127, refers to Saida Khānqāh which must be the Khānqāh-i-Mu'allā.

9. *Ibid.*, No. 122 sq.
10. Śrīv., pp. 195-6.
11. *Ibid.*, pp. 198-9.
12. *Ibid.*, p. 199; Munich MS., f. 78b.
13. Śrīv., p. 200.
14. The story that Bahrām had the Sulṭān poisoned and prevented him from receiving proper medical treatment is unreliable. (See Śrīv., p. 203).
15. *Ibid.*, pp. 200-3.
16. N.A., f. 49b.
17. Śrīv., p. 204.
18. *Ibid.*, p. 188.
19. N.A., f. 49b.
20. Munich MS., f. 77b.
21. Śrīv., p. 206, calls it Zain-nagar.
22. B.S., f. 58b calls him Malik Aḥmad Aitū, but T.H., ii, f. 107a, calls him Malik Aḥmad Yatu. Niẓāmu'd-Din and Firishta refer to him as Malik Aḥmad Aswad. Aswad in Persian means black or powerful. G.A., f. 135b, says he was given the title of Quṭbu'd-Daula.
23. Śrīv., p. 208, uses the term *Dvārapāla* instead of *Amīr-i-Dar* or *Ḥājib-i-Dar* of Persian chronicles.
24. Ikshikā is the Sanskrit name for Yech pargana north of Nāgām pargana. (Stein, ii, 475).
25. G.A., f. 135b.
26. Śrīv., p. 210.
27. *Ibiḍ*, p. 211; Ṭ.A., iii, 448.
28. Śrīv., p. 211. Dūlipūr is a village lying on the edge of the forest about 2 miles south-east of Shalūra, on the road to Sōpūr.
29. Śrīv., pp. 212-3; T.A., iii, 449.
30. Śrīv., pp. 217-8.
31. *Ibid.*, p. 219; T.H., ii, f. 107b; T.A., iii, 449. Firishta is wrong in saying that Bahrām died three days after. *Cam. His. Ind.*, iii, p. 285, follows Firishta.
32. Śrīv., p. 110.
33. *Ibid.*, pp. 203, 217.
34. *Ibid.*, p. 200; T.H., ii, f. 107b, calls him Zain Padar, and says that he had been a Wazīr of Zainu'l-'Ābidīn. See also T.A., iii, 449 and n. 4.
35. Śrīv., p. 221. Śrīvara thinks the charge of treachery was false.
36. *Ibid.*, pp. 223, 240. Tāzī Baṭ had served Ḥasan Shāh in his wars outside Kashmīr in the time of his father and so was favoured

by him (*Ibid.*, p. 208). He also enjoyed the confidence of the queen. (*Ibid.*, p. 238).

37. Śrīv., BK. iii, Nos. 226–7; T.A., iii, 450. At another place Śrīv. wrongly says that Prince Ḥusain was under the guardianship of Tāzī Baṭ (No. 328). Actually it was Naurūz who was the guardian of Prince Ḥusain (See T.A., iii, 450). The youngest son Prince Yūsuf was under Malik Aḥmad (Śrīv., (Bo. ed.) BK. iii, No. 373).
38. Śrīv., p. 238.
39. *Ibid.*, p. 239.
40. B.S., f. 59a; H.M., ff. 123b–24a. The statement in T.A., iii, 449 that there was an engagement between Tāzī and Tātār is not corroborated by Kashmīr chronicles.
41. B.S.,ff. 59a-b; Ḥasan, f. 123a; H.M., ff. 123b–24a.
42. Śrīvara is very confusing on this point. At one place he says that Tāzī was in charge of Prince Muḥammad, while at another place he says that he was in charge of Prince Ḥusain. Actually Tāzī was the guardian of Prince Muḥammad and Nauruz of Prince Ḥusain (See above, note 2). When Malik Aḥmad became angry with Tāzī, he had the guardianship of Prince Ḥusain as well transferred to his son. He himself of course remained in charge of the education of Yūsuf till his fall.
43. Śrīv., pp. 241-44.
44. *Ibid.*, p. 245.
45. *Ibid.*, (Bo. ed.), BK. iii, No. 373.
46. *Ibid.*, pp. 246-8.
47. *Ibid.*, p. 209.
48. I.A., ii (1908), p. 191. Also Śrīv., p. 253, but Śrīvara wrongly calls Sayyid Ḥasan as Sayyid Naṣīr who had by this time died.
49. Śrīv., p. 253.
50. *Ibid.*, p. 262; T.A., iii, 450.
51. *Ibid.*, pp. 450-1; Śrīv., pp. 263 sqq.
52. *Ibid.*, pp. 130-2; B.S., f. 58b; H.M., f. 123b.
53. The palaces at Didamar were built in 1474 (Śrīv., p. 224). Didamar is Diddāmatha of Śrīvara. It is now a quarter of Srīnagar and is situated below the seventh bridge on the right bank of the river. Stein, Bk. VI, No. 300n. wrongly says that it is between the sixth and seventh bridges.
54. Śrīv., pp. 224-5.
55. S.A., pp. 39-40; W.K., f. 36b; T.H., i, ff. 139a-b; Śrīv., p. 235.
56. The locality cannot be traced. Either its name has changed or it has disappeared.
57. The name Kherī is the older form of Khur used by both Kalhaṇa

and Śrīvara. Khur is a large village situated about 2 miles from the Vishokā, in Lat. 33° 37' Long. 74° 56' 45' (Stein, ii. p. 470).

58. This town was founded by Rājā Vijay, and its ancient name was Vijayeshvara. It is 25 miles south-east of Srīnagar in Laṭ. 33° 48' Long. 75° 9'.
59. Śrīv., p. 227.
60. B.S., f. 61a.
61. *Ibid.*, f. 61b; Śrīv., p. 252.
62. *Ibid.*, p. 302.
63. *Ibid.*, p. 268.
64. *Ibid.*, pp. 268-70; B.S., f. 61b.
65. Śrīv., pp. 270-1; Firishta, 668; B.S., ff. 62a-63a. But B.S., does not refer to the part played by the ruler of Jammu.
66. B.S., ff. 62a-63a. The number 30 given by Śrīv., p. 272, is exaggerated.
67. B.S., ff. 63b sqq.
68. Munich MS., f. 79a; T.A., iii, 452. See also Śrīv., pp. 274-5. Edarājānaka of Śrīvara is 'Īdī Raina of Persian chronicles.
69. Munich MS., f. 79a; T.A., iii, 452; Śrīv., p. 276, calls her Sobāna.
70. Munich MS., f. 79a; T.A., iii, 452.
71. *Ibid.*, 453; Munich MS., f. 80a.
72. *Ibid.*, f. 80a; T.A., iii, 453.
73. *Ibid.*, Munich MS., ff. 80a-b.
74. *Ibid.*, Śrīv., pp. 302-3. The account in B.S., ff. 65b-66b is partial to the Sayyids. It is wrong to say that peace was brought about by the mediation of the 'Ulamā and that the Kashmīrī nobles repented for their part in the assassination of Sayyid Muḥammad's father.
75. Śrīv., p. 302.
76. T.A., iii, 454, says that Fatḥ Khān after Tātār Khān's death became governor of the Punjab. But this is not supported by any other authority. Śrīv., p. 309 only says that after Tātār Khān's death his son gave protection to Fatḥ Khān, who after some time went to live in Jalandhar.
    Munich MS., f. 80b says that after Tātār's death Fatḥ Khān proceeded to Rajaurī. Probably this was done at the invitation of the Kashmīrī chiefs.
77. Śrīv., pp. 311 sqq.
78. It is a plateau south of Srīnagar, crossed by the road from Shupiyan. Śrīvara calls it Gusikoddāra. (See Stein, ii, 474).
79. Śrīvara calls it Kalyānapura. It is situated in Lat. 33° 48' Long. 74° 54'. Being on the high road from the Pir Panjāl Pass to Srīnagar

it has been the scene of many battles.

80. Śrīv., pp. 315-8.
81. Munich MS., f. 81a.
82. It is a small village in Lat. 33° 36' Long. 74° 27' on the road between Bhimbhar and Kashmīr. It is situated in a deep gorge at the foot of the Ratan Pīr Pass. Its old name was Bhairavagala.
83. Śrīv., pp. 322-3; Munich MS., f. 81a; T.A., iii, 455.
84. Śrīv., p. 325.
85. *Ibid.*, Munich MS., f. 81b. Zirak Bat had also deserted to Muḥammad Shāh. But later he was put to death by Jahāngīr Māgre. (Śrīv. p. 327).
86. *Ibid.*, pp. 328 sqq.; Munich MS., f. 81b.
87. It is a plateau south of Srīnagar and is called Damodaroddara by Śrīvara and Dāmodarasūda by Kalhaṇa (Stein, Bk. 1, No. 156n; vol. ii, 475).
88. Śrīv., pp. 328-32; also Munich MS., ff. 81b-82a.
89. Śrīv., pp. 334-5.
90. Prāj., pp. 338-9.
91. It was a village near Srīnagar, but now it has disappeared and is not found on the maps.
92. B.S., f. 68a; H.M., ff. 124b-25b.
93. It is not traceable on any map. There is, however, a village of the name of Garūra on the Volur lake.
94. B.S., ff. 67a-b.
95. B.S., f. 68a; H.M., f. 125b. N.A., f. 53b says that Fatḥ Shāh was also a party to the coalition against Shams Chak. But this is not corroborated by earlier accounts.
96. It lies on the Pīr Panjāl route to Kashmīr, and is distant about 122 miles south-west of Srīnagar. It is situated in Lat. 33° 10′ Long. 74° 18'.
97. H.M., ff. 125b-27a; B.S., ff. 68a-70a.
98. It is the modern name of the Kishangaṅgā Valley from below Shardi as far as Karnāv. Its ancient name was Durānda, but the Persian chronicles call it Dārdu. (Stein, BK. viii No. 2709n).
99. B.S., ff. 70a-b; H.M., ff. 127a-b.
100. B.S., ff. 71a-b; H.M., ff. 127b sqq; N.K., ff. 30a-b.
101. H.M., f. 129a.
102. *Ibid.*
103. See Appendix A for more details of his life.
104. B.S., ff. 71b-72a; *Tuḥjatu'l-Aḥbāb*, pp. 68-9; *Majmū'a dar Ansab Mashā'ikh-i-Kashmīr*, f. 11b.
105. B.S., ff. 72a sqq; H.M., f. 129b.

106. B.S., f. 77a.
107. B.S., ff. 77a-b. H.M., f. 130a, says Shams Chak remained in office for two months.
108. B.S., f. 78a.
109. *Ibid.,* H.M., ff. 131a-b. These chronicles state that Mūsā Raina remained in power for nine years, but this seems incorrect, for Fatḥ Shāh himself reigned for nine years, and during this period ministerial changes occurred seven times.
110. T.H., ii, f. 115a.
111. B.S., ff. 80b-81a; H.M., f. 131a.
112. H.M., f. 131b. B.S., ff. 81a-b says his death was caused by a fall from his horse. According to T.H., ii, f. 115b, his neck got entangled in a vine creeper and he fell from the horse and died on the spot. But this manner of death is also attributed to 'Īdī Raina by Ḥaidar Malik and Nārāyan Kaul.
113. B.S., f. 81b; H.M., f. 131b; I.A., xxxvii, p. 192.
114. B.S., ff. 81b-82a; H.M., ff. 131b-32a.
115. B.S., ff. 83a-b; H.M., f. 132a; Prāj. pp. 343-4.
116. It is a pargana on the northern shore of the Volur lake. Śrīvara calls it Khūyāshrama.
117. B.S., ff. 83b-84a.
118. *Ibid.,* f. 84a; H.M., f. 132b. Pushkaranāga is a village situated in Lat. 34° 2' Long. 74° 33' at the foot of the hill of the same on its east side.
119. B.S., ff. 84b-5a; The route followed by Fatḥ Shāh is mentioned in B.S. as being *via* Jawail. I cannot find this place on maps. In T.H., ii, f. 117a it is the Tōshamaidān route. In Śuka, p. 346, it is the Hirapūr route.
120. B.S., f. 85a; H.M., f. 132b. Śuka, p. 347, calls Malik 'Uṣmān as Utsa Malik.
121. N.A., f. 58b.
122. H.M., f. 132b.
123. *Ibid.,* 85b.
124. B.S., f. 85b.
125. *Ibid.;* H.M., f. 132b.
126. B.S., ff. 86a-b; H.M., f. 133a; Śuka, pp. 384-9. Munich MS., f. 83a and T.A., iii, p. 458, wrongly state that Muḥammad Shāh proceeded to the court of Sikandar Khokar. T.A., borrowed it from Munich MS.
127. It is marked on Stein's map as lying north-east of Rajaurī (J.A.S.B., lxviii, 1889).
128. B.S., f. 86a.

129. Harshīn is a village about 10 miles south-west of Shupiyan.
130. H.M., f. 133a. According to B.S., f. 85a, Fatḥ Shāh's overthrow was brought about by Mīr Shamsu'd-Dīn.
131. B.S., f. 88a; H.M., f. 135a; Munich MS., f. 84a.
132. Shankar was later killed in prison (N.A., f. 60a). But Śuka, p. 355, says that he died a natural death. Rājāna Śriṅgāri of the Sanskrit chronicles is no other than Shankar Raina.
133. B.S., ff. 86b-7a; H.M., ff. 133a-b; also Śuka, pp. 351-3.
134. B.S., ff. 87a-b; H.M., ff. 134a-5a; Śuka, pp. 351-2.
135. H.M., f. 135a; T.H., ii, 119a. Pāmpūr is situated on the right bank of Jehlam about 8 miles south-east of Srīnagar. Its ancient name was Padmapura.
136. H.M., f. 135b; N.A., f. 60b; B.S., f. 89b, says that Jahāngīr fled to Kamrāj.
137. It is an important place near Chrār Sharīf in Badgām Taḥsīl, about 9 miles south of Śrīnagar. It is famous for its springs.
138. B.S., f. 89b; Munich MS., ff. 84a-b; Śuka, pp. 355-7.
139. *Ibid.;* H.M., f. 135b.
140. B.S., f. 90b.
141. H.M., f. 136a.
142. *Ibid.;* Śuka, p. 358.
143. *Ibid.,* pp. 358-9.
144. B.S., 91a; H.M., f. 136a.
145. Bābur does not refer to this event in his *Memoirs* But T.A., iii, 460, says that Sikandar returned with a party of the Mughals; and Firishta, 673, says that the Mughals belonged to Bābur. See also B.S., f. 91a.
146. B.S., ff. 91a-b; H.M., f. 136a. See also N.A., ff. 61b-2a. N.K., ff. 32a-b.
147. B.S., f. 91a; Munich MS., f. 85a; Śuka, pp. 361-2.
148. It is about 5 miles south-west of Bārāmūla. It is the point where the Jehlam is said to leave the Valley.
149. B.S., f. 92a; H.M., (B.N.), f. 137a. Also Śuka, p. 364, who calls Lad as Gaggada. But Munich MS., f. 86a, says Muḥammad Shāh was imprisoned in Loharkōt. T.A., iii, 462, follows Munich MS.
Lad cannot be traced. Probably it is a *nūr* (narrow value) with Lad as its local name.
150. Ibrāhīm Shāh had accompanied his father to Ibrāhīm Lodi. Muḥammad Shāh after receiving the aid had left, but Ibrāhīm had remained behind with the Lodī Sulṭān. After the battle of Pānipat in which Ibrāhīm seems to have fought on the side of the Lodīs against Bābur, he returned to Kashmīr. (Munich MS.,

f. 85a; Firishta p. 674; Śuka, p. 363).

151. B.S., f. 92a; H.M., f. 137a; Munich MS., ff. 85a-b. T.H., ii, f, 120b, says that Bābur gave Abdāl 20,000 troops. But this is absurd. Śuka, p. 364, gives the figure as 1,000. T.A., and Firishta do not give any figures.
152. Munich MS., f. 85a; Śuka, p. 365. H.M. and B.S. do not mention Nāzuk Shāh at all. Firishta wrongly says that Nāzuk Shāh was the son of Ibrāhīm Shāh.
153. Briggs, iv. p. 491. Tāpar is a considerable village situated on the high road from Bārāmūla to Srīnagar in Lat. 34° 12' Long. 74° 34'. Its ancient name was Pratāpapura. (Stein, ii, 482). Śuka, p. 365, mentions Nīlāshva as the place of the battle. This place cannot be identified. But according to Stein, BK. vii, No. 163n, it was probably a territorial division in Kashmīr. Firishta and T.A. have Sīlāh, but it is really Nīlā. B.S., and H.M. merely say that the battle took place in Bāngil pargana. Nīlā must have been situated near Tāpar.
154. B.S., ff. 92a sqq; H.M., ff. 137b-8a; Munich MS., ff. 85a-6a.
155. W.K., f. 42b.
156. Munich MS., ff. 86a-b; T.A., iii, 462.
157. Munich MS., f. 86b.
158. H.M., f. 138b.
159. Munich MS., f. 86b; B.S., f. 95b; H.M., f, 138b.
160. B.S., f. 96a; T.A., iii, 363. N.A., f. 64b, is wrong in saying that Bābur sent Kāmrān, because Bābur had died in December 1530.
161. B.S., f. 96a; H.M., f. 138b.
 The date 937/1530 as given by B.S. and H.M. is incorrect, because when the expedition took place Bābur was no longer alive. (See T.A., iii, 363). The expedition therefore must have taken place in 1531.
162. B.S., f. 96a. Chīraodar is *karēwa* situated to the south-west of Srīnagar on the road to Shupiyan. It is a local name not commonly known.
163. Śuka, p. 370; T.A., iii, 463.
164. It is a hamlet situated on the right bank of the Jehlam at the southern base of Takht-i-Sulaimān.
165. B.S., ff. 96a-b; H.M., f. 139a.
166. Munich MS., f. 87a; T.A., iii. 463-4; N.A., ff. 65a-b.
167. B.S., f. 96b; H.M., f. 139a.
168. B.S., ff. 97a-b. Śuka's account of the invasion is very brief.
169. B.S., f. 97b.

Chapter 7

Mīrzā Ḥaidar Dughlat and his Conquest of Kashmīr

Mirza Muḥammad Ḥaidar Dughlat was born in 1499-500 at Tāshqand, the capital of the province of Shāsh, where his father was governor. He descended from the Dughlat tribe, a subdivision of the Chaghatāy branch of the Mongols. On his mother's side he was related to Bābur, their mothers being sisters.

Mīrzā Ḥaidar's father possessed a treacherous and intriguing nature; and it was owing to his constant intrigues that Shaibānī Khān, the Uzbeg chief, had him assassinated at Herāt. Mīrzā Ḥaidar, who had been with his father, was carried away to Bukhārā by some of the relatives who felt that his life was in danger. From Bukhārā he was taken to Badakhshān and thence, after a year, was brought to Kābul where he remained with Bābur for two years and accompanied him in his campaigns. Then, in the beginning of 1514, he was summoned by his uncle Sulṭān Aḥmad, the Khān of Mughalistān. Shortly afterwards Sulṭān Aḥmad died, and Mīrzā Ḥaidar entered the service of the Khān's son, Sulṭān Sa'īd Khān, and remained with him for nineteen years.[1]

Mīrzā Ḥaidar participated in Sulṭān Sa'īd's wars against the Kirghiz, the Uzbegs and oher tribes, and was sent to distant expeditions. But among these campaigns the most important was the one in which he was despatched along with Prince Sikandar Mīrzā, Sulṭān Sa'īd's second son, to conquer Ladākh which had already been many times raided by parties sent by

Sulṭān Sa'īd.[2]

Mīrzā Ḥaidar set out in July 1532.[3] He occupied Nubra, a province of Ladākh, and then proceeded to Māryul, near Leh. Meanwhile, severe winter had set in; and as there was no place in Ladākh which could be regarded as suitable for winter quarters, Kashmīr was selected for the purpose. At this time Mīrzā Ḥaidar was informed that the Khān was proceeding towards Māryul, and that he was afflicted with *dam-gīr*. Mīrzā Ḥaidar, therefore, leaving his troops behind advanced to meet him, and then together they entered Nubra. Mīrzā Ḥaidar pointed out that in Ladākh there was no district which could provide winter quarters for more than 1,000 men. Kashmīr, on the other hand, could support a larger army; but, as the Khān was not strong enough to cross the high passes leading into the Valley, he should with 1,000 men proceed to Baltistān which could be easily reached without causing *dam-gīr*. The rest of the troops, Mīrzā Ḥaidar suggested, should spend their winter in Kashmīr under his command.[4]

The total number of men which the Mongols had at this time was 5,000. Of these 3,000 belonged to the Khān, and 2,000 to Mīrzā Ḥaidar. The Khān, according to Mīrzā 'Ḥaidar's advice, retained 1,000 and advanced towards Baltistān, while Mīrzā Ḥaidar with 2,000 men proceeded to join his own army of 2,000 and, having effected the junction, set out towards Kashmīr.[5] On the road the Ladākhī chiefs submitted and joined him with their forces, while the Baltī Tibetans living in the villages of Kashmīr acted as his guides. Mīrzā Ḥaidar crossed the Zōjī-Lā and entered Kashmīr early in January, 1533.[6] He then sent 400 experienced men under Tumān Bahādur Qābuchī against the Kashmīrī forces which had advanced to offer resistance in the defile of Lār.[7] At dawn they attacked the Kashmīrīs, stationed as outpost at the upper end of the defile. Taken by surprise the Kashmīrīs fled, and were pursued by the Mongols. When the main body saw this, they too fled. Meanwhile, Ḥaidar's remaining force arrived and joined in the pursuit.[8] The Kashmīrīs took refuge in the fort of Hānjik.[9]

The Mughals, having crossed the defile of Lār, marched on Naushahr, which they occupied without any difficulty. Mīrzā

Ḥaidar took up quarters in Zainu'l-'Ābidīn's palace of Rājdān and fortified it.[10] After staying there for twenty-four days he proceeded towards Marāj. His followers set fire to the villages and towns and destroyed the grand edifices built by the former rulers of the country.[11] They massacred the men, and made the women and children their slaves. They made no distinction between Muslims and non-Muslims, for all alike suffered at their hands. As a result of these atrocities many of the inhabitants fled from the Valley to the safety of the mountains.[12]

From the month of January to March 1533, Mīrzā Ḥaidar's forces carried on their ravages. Meanwhile, the Kashmīrīs had recovered from the first shock of invasion and defeat. Their spirits were aroused by the 'Ulamā who, from their refuge in the island on the Volur, issued a decree that the killing of the invaders was not only permissible but obligatory, and that any one who died fighting against them would be a martyr.[13] This pronouncement provoked the Kashmīrīs to effective action, and they began to organise resistance. They hung on to the Mughal forces, and harassed them by cutting down stragglers and striking at their baggage and thus hindering their movements. Mīrzā Ḥaidar tried to avoid the enemy, but early in spring his troops were forced into an engagement at Bāgh-i-Bavan.[14] Bābā Sharq Mirzā, his commander, with 500 horse encountered Malik 'Alī Chādura. But he was wounded and fled. Seeing this, Dā'im 'Alī from the right and Mīrzā Ḥaidar from the left, each with 1,000 horse, advanced to attack. The Kashmīrīs fought with great courage but, after Malik 'Alī Chādura and some other chiefs were killed, they became demoralised and fled.[15]

This defeat did not dishearten the Kashmīrīs, who, under the leadership of Kājī Chak and Abdāl Māgre, again prepared for resistance. They however avoided pitched battles and, instead, began to harass the Mughals by descending from the hills and making surprise attacks. These tactics proved successful, for they began to wear down Mīrzā Ḥaidar and his followers.[16]

Alarmed at these developments, Mīrzā Ḥaidar took counsel from his officers. Mīr Dā'im 'Alī, a distinguished noble, advised him to attack the Kashmīrī chiefs who had established themselves on the mountains and from where they swooped down to harass the Mughals. But Mīrzā 'Alī Taghā'i, another noble, was opposed to this plan on the ground that as the Kashmīrīs were occupying strong positions, it would be disastrous for the Mughals to advance against them. He therefore suggested that the best course would be to attack their families in the Valley. The result of this would be that those whose families were in the Valley would come down to defend them, while those whose families were on the hill-tops would remain behind. Thus the enemy forces would be divided, and they could then be easily overpowered. Mīrzā Ḥaidar followed 'Alī Taghā'i's advice and rejected that of Dā'im 'Alī. But the consequence was that he had to move from place to place chased by the Kashmīrīs. In the end, however, he halted at Chādura.[17]

Meanwhile 'Alī Taghā'i began suggesting that it would be difficult to conquer Kashmīr, and the Mughals should therefore withdraw from the country. The soldiers, tired of continuous warfare and longing for their homes, were won over to this point of view. Mīrzā Ḥaidar could have put 'Alī Taghā'i to death, as suggested by Dā'im 'Alī, for carrying on these intrigues, and then completed the conquest of Kashmīr. But he decided to quit the country and accordingly made overtures of peace to the Kashmīrī nobles.[18] As a result of the negotiations it was agreed that the *khuṭba* was to be read in the name of Sa'īd Khān;[19] that Muḥammad Shāh's brother's daughter was to be given in marriage to Prince Sikandar Sulṭān;[20] that presents were to be given for Sa'īd Khān; that Kashmīrīs who were prisoners in the hands of the Mughals, were to be released;[21] and that, in return, the Mughals were to give woollen cloth and other articles as presents to Muḥammad Shāh.[22] After concluding the treaty Mīrzā Ḥaidar left Kashmīr at the end of May 1533 by the same route by which he had come.[23]

After the withdrawal of the Mughals Kashmīr was visited by a severe famine, because owing to continuous fighting and the ravages of the Mughals not much cultivation had been possible.[24] Fortunately, the famine lasted only for a year, and as during this period the nobles remained united, the sufferings of the people caused by starvation were not aggravated by civil war. Perfect peace reigned in the country for three years.[25]

Sulṭān Shamsu'd-Dīn (1537-40).

In about the middle of 1537 Muḥammad Shāh died, and was succeeded by his second son, Shamsu'd-Dīn.[26] Shortly afterwards the civil war flared up. Kājī Chak, who was living at his jāgīr of Zainapūr, proceeded to the city with his followers to attack the Māgres and Rēgī Chak. But the latter, learning of his approach, withdrew to Bārāmūla. Kājī Chak followed him, but as Daulat Chak and other chiefs, who were his supporters, went over to his enemies, he left for the Punjāb.[27]

Early in the spring of 1538 Rēgī Chak went to Jammu to marry the daughter of its ruler. Kājī Chak took advantage of his absence and returned to the Valley, assisted by the Gakkhars,[28] in order to overthrow he Māgre faction. He encamped at the village of Gaisū,[29] and then proceeded to besiege the fort of Sōpūr, where Abdāl Māgre, Lohar Māgre, and the chiefs of Chādura had shut themselves in, as they did not think they were strong enough to fight Kājī a pitched battle without the help of Rēgī. While the siege was in progress, Rēgī returned from Jammu, Kājī therefore left Daulat Chak, Ghāzī Khān, and Sayyid Ibrāhīm to blockade the fort, while he himself with a strong force marched against Rēgī who had arrived in Srīnagar. Rēgī prepared himself for resistance in 'Alā'u'd-Dīnpūr, but after a severe engagement he was defeated. Meanwhile the Māgres, hearing that Kājī had proceeded to the city, left Sōpūr. But they were attacked by the troops left behind by Kājī and routed. The Māgre chiefs tried to reorganise their forces, but failed and so fled to Rajaurī[30]

After the fall of Abdāl Māgre, Kājī Chak became prime minister; and when, shortly after, Shamsu'd-Dīn II died he set up Muḥammad Shāh's another son, Ismā'īl, who was his son-in-law, on the throne. Kājī was able and efficient, and ruled the country with justice. He promoted the welfare of the peasants and treated the nobles generously. In spite of this the latter conspired to assassinate him. But they were discovered and imprisoned. After some time, however, Kājī released them and restored to them their jāgīrs which he had confiscated.[31] He then divided the kingdom into three equal parts between himself, Sayyid Ibrāhīm, and Sulṭān Ismā'īl Shāh. But Kājī could not remain long in power, for Kashmīr was threatened by a fresh Mughal invasion.

Mīrzā Ḥaidar's Conquest of Kashmīr

After his withdrawal from Kashmīr Mīrzā Ḥaidar carried on war in Tibet and Ladākh. Meanwhile, news reached him that Sulṭān Sa'īd had died and had been succeeded by his son Rashīd Sulṭān, who had begun his reign by putting to death all those whom he suspected of plotting in favour of his brother Sikandar. Mīrzā Ḥaidar feared that, since he was also known to be on friendly terms with the prince, he would incur the displeasure of Rashīd Sulṭān. He therefore gave up the idea of returning to Kāshghar or continuing the campaign. Instead he left Ladākh, and, after a hazardous journey, went to Badakhshān.[32] From there he proceeded to Lahore and served Kāmrān for some time. He then entered the service of Humāyūn, who treated him with honour and called him 'brother' after the Mughal fashion.[33]

While he was in Lahore, Mīrzā Ḥaidar had received an appeal for help from Abdāl Māgre and Rēgī Chak against Kājī Chak through Khwāja Ḥājī who was acting as their agent with the Mughals.[34] Mīrzā Ḥaidar wanted to help them, and pleaded on their behalf with Kāmrān, but without any success. When, however, Kāmrān marched to deal with the rebellion of his brother Hindāl, Mīrzā Ḥaidar accompanied him to Agra, and there managed to raise an army.[35] This was placed under Bābā Jujak, one of Kāmrān's superior officers,[36] who was instructed to proceed with Khwāja Ḥājī. But as Bābā Jujak possessed neither courage nor initiative, he did not move beyond Lahore, and under one pretext or another postponed his march. And when he heard of Humāyūn's defeat at the Ganges, near Qanauj, by Shēr Shāh (May 17, 1540), he finally gave up the expedition, keeping the Kashmīrī chiefs waiting for him in vain in the hills of Rajaurī[37]

After the retreat of the Mughals from Qanauj to Lahore as a result of Humāyūn's defeat, Abdāl Māgre and Rēgī Chak again appealed for assistance through Khwāja Ḥājī, assuring Mīrzā Ḥaidar that Kashmīr could easily be conquered and pointing out the advantages of such a conquest.[38] At this time the Mughal nobles were discussing the general policy the Emperor should adopt. Mīrzā Ḥaidar proposed that he should be allowed to proceed to Kashmīr which he knew from personal experience and from the assurances of Abdāl and Rēgī could be occupied in two months. After the conquest of the Valley the Mughals should send their familes and baggage there for safety, while they themselves should take up strong positions on the Outer Hills of Kashmīr, extending from Sirhind to the Salt Range. This would be a safe position because Shēr Shāh would not be able to bring his infantry owing to the difficult nature of the terrain.[39] Mīrzā Ḥaidar and the Mughal nobles in general agreed to the proposal, but Kāmrān rejected it and suggested that the women and baggage should be sent to Kābul, while the men should remain in the hills or go to Kashmīr. Meanwhile news came that Shēr Shāh had reached the banks of the Beas, and as a result the Mughals were struck with panic. Mīrzā Ḥaidar, on being consulted by Humāyūn, again suggested the Kashmīr plan. Humāyūn agreed and gave him 400 men and permitted him to proceed to Naushahrā. Mīrzā Ḥaidar was assured that as soon as the Kashmīrī chiefs would join him, Sikandar Tūpchī, a fief-holder in the neighbourhood, would come to his assistance. When Mīrzā Ḥaidar would reach the pass, Khwāja Kalān, a high officer of Humāyūn, would enter Naushahrā. When Mīrzā Ḥaidar would enter Kashmīr, the Khwāja would advance to the foot of the pass. Humāyūn would then himself proceed towards the Valley.[40]

In accordance with this plan Mīrzā Ḥaidar marched to Naushahrā and was joined by Abdāl and Rēgī. But neither Sikandar Tūpchī nor Khwāja Kalān moved to his help.[41] In fact they did not render any aid even to Humāyūn when he, at the end of October 1540, proceeded from Lahore to Siālkōt with the object of going to Kashmīr. Khwāja Kalān went away from Siālkōt and joined Kāmrān at Behra,[42] while Sikandar Tūpchī, frightened at the news of Shēr Shāh's approach near Lahore, took refuge in the Sārang hills.[43] The cowardly and treacherous conduct of his officers greatly disgusted Humāyūn who, therefore, gave up the idea of going to Kashmīr, and turned to the west.[44] Mīrzā Ḥaidar was thus left with a handful of retainers in his own pay and about 400 men given to him by Humāyūn at Lahore.[45] He was, however, not disheartened, knowing that owing to the disunity in Kashmīr he would be able to conquer it even with the small force at his disposal.

Kājī Chak, hearing that Mīrzā Ḥaidar had arrived in Rajaurī and that he had been joined by Abdāl and Rēgī, at once proceeded to the Kapartal Pass[46] to prevent his entry. But Mīrzā Ḥaidar abandoned that route, and on the 22nd of November, 1540, entered Kashmīr by the Pūnch Pass.[47] Kājī was baffled at the turn of events, and so, instead of organising resistance to the invaders, he along with Ismā'īl Shāh left the country *via* Hirapūr, and proceeded to Shēr Shāh to seek his help.[48] As there was no one to offer him any opposition, Mīrzā Ḥaidar occupied the Valley without even striking a blow.

Mīrzā Ḥaidar set up Nāzuk Shāh on the throne and made Abdāl Māgre Wazīr. He then divided the kingdom into three equal parts between himself, Abdāl Māgre and Rēgī Chak. But early in spring, on the first day of *Naurūz,* Abdāl Māgre died of paralysis.[49] Thereupon his son Ḥusain Māgre was given his jāgīr and the Wizārat.[50]

Meanwhile Kājī Chak had reached the court of Shēr Shāh.[51] The Afghān ruler, impressed by the scars of numerous wounds which Kājī had received in various battles, welcomed him graciously and conferred upon him the title of Khān-i-Khānān and gave him 5,000 horse and two elephants under the command of 'Ādil Khān and Ḥusain Khān Shērwānī.[52] With these forces, early in the spring of 1541, Kājī entered Kashmīr *via* Hirapūr.[53] Hearing of this, Mīrzā Ḥaidar left his family in the fort of Andarkōt, and with Ḥusain Māgre, Rēgī Chak and 'Īdī Raina marched against Kājī.[54] He encountered him at Watanār,[55] but the battle was indecisive. For a month after this the parties engaged with each other in skirmishes and then, owing to the floods and rains, they withdrew. While Kājī established himself at Girdār,[56] Mīrzā Ḥaidar encamped at Kōthēr.[57] But after the floods had subsided, the combatants took their stand at Vahatōr,[58] and on August 13, 1541, fought a severe battle. Although the Chaks had 5,000 cavalry and several thousand foot-soldiers while Mīrzā Ḥaidar had only 3,000, they were defeated and Kājī with Daulat Chak, Sayyid Ibrāhīm, and the Afghāns fled to India. But Malik Nājī, who had been wounded, submitted and was received with honour by Mīrzā Ḥaidar.[59]

In the beginning, Mīrzā Ḥaidar's relations with the Kashmīrī nobles had been cordial. He had treated them with respect, and sought their advice on all matters of the state. But after some time he became arrogant and began to look down upon them and to ignore them. Rēgī Chak was the first to resent his attitude. Mīrzā Ḥaider, apprehending mischief, won over Ḥusain Māgre and 'Īdī Raina and set out to seige Rēgī Chak who was at the moment in his jāgīr of Kamrāj. But Rēgī, warned in time of his intentions, fled to the hills of Rajaurī and joined Kājī Chak (1543).[60] Mīrzā Ḥaidar, not finding Rēgī at Kamrāj, razed to the ground his house, and then returned to Andarkōt. Next year, early in spring, Rēgī and Kājī again entered Kashmīr to drive out the Mughals, and encamped at Gulmarg. Mīrzā Ḥaidar with the Mughal and Kashmīrī forces advanced against them, and having made a surprise night attack, defeated Kājī and Rēgī, who again fled to the Punjāb hills.[61] On Friday, September 12, 1544, Kājī Chak died of fever at Thanna.[62] Although left alone Rēgī again invaded Kashmīr in 1546. But he was defeated and killed by a force sent by Mīrzā Ḥaidar. His head was cut off and brought before the Mīrzā.[63]

These victories made Mīrzā Ḥaidar the *de facto* ruler of Kashmīr. He, however, retained Nāzuk Shāh as Sulṭān in whose name the *khuṭba* was recited and coins were struck. Mīrzā Ḥaidar's relations with Ḥusain Māgre and 'Īdī Raina also remained cordial.[64]

After overpowering his enemies Mīrzā Ḥaidar decided to recover the territories which had been a part of the kingdom of Kashmīr until the time of Ḥasan Shāh. He first attempted the conquest of Kishtwār and advanced from Lār in 1548. He himself remained in the village of Jhālū,[65] and sent Bandagān Kōkā and 'Īdī Raina with an army to reduce Kishtwār. On arriving at the village of Dahut, situated on the river Mārma,[66] they found the Kishtwār army entrenched on the other side, ready to prevent their passage. There was an exchange of arrows and musket shots, but the Mughals could not cross the river. The next day, however, they tried to enter Kishtwār by a detour from the main road. When they arrived at the village of Dār it became dark and they were attacked by the enemy. Bandagān Kōkā, the commander of the Mughal force, Muḥammad Māgre and many others lost their lives. In fact the casualties on the Mughal side were so heavy that ever since the place has been called Mughal Maidān or Mughal Mazār. Only a few persons managed to escape and join the Mīrzā after suffering great privations.[67]

Although Mīrzā Ḥaidar failed against Kishtwār, he was more fortunate in other directions. In 1548 he occupied Baltistān and Ladākh and placed them in charge of Mullā Qāsim and Mullā Bāqī respectively. He then conquered Rajaurī from the Kashmīrī chiefs and entrusted it to Muḥammad Naẓar and Ṣabr 'Alī. Finally, he reduced Pakhlī and appointed Mullā 'Abdu'llāh as its governor.[68]

In 1549 Haibat Khān Niyāzī, the governor of Lahore, revolted against his overlord, Islām Shāh Sūr. Being defeated at Dungot,[69] near Sambhal, he took refuge in the Sārang hills with the Gakkhars. Islām Shāh, thereupon, made war upon the latter and crushed them.[70] Haibat Khān then fled to the outer mountains of Kashmīr, pursued by Islām Shāh as far as Bhimbhar. Mīrzā Ḥaidar was alarmed at the move of the Afghān chiefs, and so advanced to prevent them from entering the Valley. When Haibat Khān found that his way was blocked in the front by the Mughals and in the rear by Islām Shāh, he moved towards the hills of Rajaurī.[71] There he met Daulat Chak and Ghāzī Chak,[72] who proposed that he should accompany them to Kashmīr in order to overthrow Mīrzā Ḥaidar.[73] His followers were agreeable to the proposal, but Haibat Khān rejected it and sent a Brahman agent to Mīrzā Ḥaidar to come to terms with him. Having received a large sum of money from the Mīrzā, Haibat Khān gave up the idea of invading Kashmīr and went away to Birna near Jammu. The Kashmīrī chiefs, getting disgusted at his attitude, separated from him and went over to Islām Shāh.[74] But Mīrzā Ḥaidar, in order to win over the latter to his side, sent to him, in 1550, Khwāja Shams Mughal with a large quantity of saffron. After a year the Khwāja returned to Kashmīr, accompanied by Yāsīn Afghān, with rich presents from the Afghān ruler. Mīrzā Ḥaidar presented Islām Shāh's *wakīl* with shawls and saffron, and then gave him leave to depart.[75]

Although a strong champion of orthodoxy, Mīrzā Ḥaidar had been, at first, owing to reasons of political expediency, very liberal towards the followers of the Nūrbakhshīya sect. In fact, to please Rēgī Chak and other chiefs, who were Nūrbakhshiyās, he had even visited the tomb of Mīr Shamsu'd-Dīn and paid homage like a devotee. But after the revolt of Rēgī Chak his attitude changed, for he became convinced that in order to maintain peace in the Valley, uniformity of religion was essential.[76] He therefore, on the advice of Maulānā Jamāl and Shaikh 'Umar, banned the Nūrbakhshīya sect.[77] He then destroyed the tomb of Shamsu'd-Dīn, and in 1545 put to death Ḥaẓrat Rishī.[78] He also executed Ṣūfī Dā'ūd, Mullā Ḥājib Khaṭīb and many other Nūrbakhshīyas; while some like Qāẓī Mīr 'Alī were exiled and their houses destroyed.[79] Shaikh Dāniyāl, the son of Shamsu'd-Dīn, who had gone away to Skārdu owing to Mīrzā Ḥaidar's intolerance, was brought back in 1549 and thrown into prison. After this false witnesses were obtained to testify that he had reviled the first three Caliphs, and on that charge, on March 14, 1550, he was executed by the decree of Qāẓī Ḥabīb, Qāẓī Ibrāhīm, and Qāẓī 'Abdu'l-Ghafūr.[80] His trunk and head were taken away by his followers and secretly deposited and, after Mīrzā Ḥaidar's death, they were collected and buried in the tomb of his father Shamsu'd-Dīn.[81]

The execution of Dāniyāl was a great mistake committed by Mīrzā Ḥaidar because he was a pious man and much respected in the country. The Mīrzā had been warned by Mullā 'Abdu'llāh, one of his confidants, against this step, but he had ignored him replying that Dāniyāl's execution was necessary for the stability and welfare of the kingdom.[82] In reality, however, the effect of his policy was contrary to his expectations.

Malik 'Īdī Raina and Malik Muḥammad Nājī, who had embraced Shī'ism, became inimical towards the Mīrzā for his persecution of their co-religionists and they decided to overthrow him.[83] They won over Nāzuk Shāh, Ḥusain Māgre and Khwāja Ḥājī who not only disapproved of Ḥaidar's intolerance but also his arrogance and nepotism. In the beginning he had treated the Kashmīrī nobles with respect and associated them in the government of the country, but later on he began to look down upon them, ignoring their claims, concentrating all power into his own hands, and appointing his own followers as governors of different provinces.[84] The result of this policy was that even those Kashmīrī nobles who had hitherto remained loyal to him were now alienated and began to conspire his overthrow.

Meanwhile trouble had broken out in the Outer Hills, and therefore, in 1551, Mīrzā Ḥaidar sent an army of Mughals and Kashmīrīs *via* Bārāmūla under his cousin Qarā Bahādur accompanied by Ḥusain Māgre, 'Īdī Raina, and Khwāja Ḥājī.[85] When it reached Mānkōt[86] the Kashmīrī chiefs decided to attack the Mughals,[87] and having separated from Qarā Bahādur, they proceeded to the top of the hill and sent a small force supported by the hill people to cut off his communications with Kashmīr. Early next morning the Kashmīrīs descended from the hill and attacked the Mughals. The latter resisted till mid-day, but in the end fled, pursued by the Kashmīrīs who killed many of them and seized their baggage. Those who escaped took refuge in the fort of Barbal.[88] Thereupon, 'Īdī Raina despatched about 500 horse under Ḥusain Māgre, Nājī Malik, and Khwāja Ḥājī to besiege the fort, while he himself proceeded to Pūnch. As the Kashmīrīs, who were being helped by the hill people, outnumbered the Mughals, Qarā Bahādur got disheartened and decided to make peace with them, but some of the chiefs like Sayyid Mīrzā and Mīrzā 'Alī Kōka were against it and wanted to fight their way to the Gakkhar country. Qarā Bahādur ignored their advice, and left the fort with some of his followers in order to negotiate with the Kashmīrīs. But as he advanced he was attacked by the enemy. Seeing this the rest of the garrison also came out of the fort and made for the Gakkhar country.

Although they were pursued by the Kashmirīs, they succeeded in making good their escape. But those belonging to Qarā Bahādur's party were either killed or taken captives. The latter were taken to 'Īdī Raina who was in Pūnch. Qarā Bahādur, Quṭb 'Alī Kōkā, and Muḥammad Naẓar were imprisoned while others had their hands cut off. After this victory 'Īdī Raina sent a message to Daulat Chak, who was in Naushahrā, to join him. Daulat at once set out and met 'Īdī Raina who had entered the Valley *via* Hirapūr. A large number of people flocked under their banner, and together they marched towards Srīnagar.[89]

These happenings caused great anxiety to Mīrzā Ḥaidar. After consulting his followers, he left his family in the fort of Andarkōt with a Mughal garrison and some Kashmīrīs, and then marched against 'Īdī Raina. But just at this time serious revolts broke out in Baltistān and Ladākh against Mullā Qāsim and Mullā Bāqī respectively. Mullā Qāsim with his followers was killed, but Mullā Bāqī succeeded in escaping and joining Mīrzā Ḥaidar near Andarkōt. Risings also took place in Pakhlī, and its governor, 'Abdu'llāh Samarquandī was defeated by the rebels. Meanwhile, learning of the disaster that had befallen Qāra Bahādur, he became so demoralised that he decided to withdraw to the Valley. But when he reached Bārāmūla, he was killed by the Kashmīrīs.[90] Similarly, Kōkā Mīr, who had been sent to establish order in Kishtwār, was defeated and killed with 1,500 of his troops in the pargana of Adavin.[91] On receiving these distressing news from all sides, Mīrzā Ḥaidar proceeded to Srīnagar and thence moved to Vahatōr,[92] to engage with the Kashmīrī chiefs who, led by 'Īdī Raina, had fortified themselves in the fort of Manār, near Khāmpūr.[93] But as Mīrzā Ḥaidar had a small force, he decided upon a night attack. Although some of his officers dissuaded him from such an hazardous undertaking,[94] Mīrzā Ḥaidar ignored them, and after designating his brother 'Abdu'r-Raḥmān to succeed him, he marched against the enemy with about 700 or 800 horse. When he reached the base of the fort he left his troops behind, and with only thirty men proceeded to the top of the buttress. But on the way most of his followers fell out, and he was left with only seven men. While he was trying to enter the fort, he was killed by an arrow (October 1551).[95]

This is the only contemporary account of Mīrzā Ḥaidar's death known to exist, and there is no reason to doubt its authenticity, for Sayyid 'Alī, its author, was in the Mīrzā's service, and participated in this campaign. It is true that he was not present on the spot when Mīrzā Ḥaidar was killed, but he must have written on the basis of information gathered from reliable witnesses.

Besides the account of Sayyid'Alī, there are other versions also about the manner of Mīrzā Ḥaidar's death. According to one version, he was slain by Kamāl Dūbī with a sword;[96] according to another, a butcher is said to have shot an arrow which hit him in the thigh and killed him.[97] Ḥaidar Malik, however, relates that Mīrzā Ḥaidar was killed with an axe by a butcher who suspected him to be a Mughal spy.[98] All these versions, it must be remembered, are based on hearsay, and may therefore be discounted as spurious. However, there may be some ruth in the tradition contained in the *Ṭabaqāt-i-Akbarī* that, while he was leading the attack, Mīrzā Ḥaidar was accidentally struck by an arrow discharged by Shāh Naẓar, a cuirassier, belonging to his own army.[99] This statement does not in any way conflict with that of Sayyid 'Alī, who is silent over the question whether Mīrzā Ḥaidar lost his life at the hands of the enemy or one of his own men.

When in the morning Mīrzā Ḥaidar's body was discovered, the Chaks wanted to insult it, but Ḥusain Māgre and Sayyid Muḥammad Baihaqī had it buried near the grave of Sulṭān Zainu'l-'Ābidīn, and protected it for a month.[100] The Mughals, on Mīrzā Ḥaidar's death, had fled to Andarkōt. There they were besieged by the Kashmīrīs. But after three days of fighting Mīrzā Ḥaidar's widow decided to make peace with the enemy saying that, as the Mīrzā was dead, it was useless to continue the conflict. She accordingly sent Amīr Khān, the architect, to negotiate the terms of surrender. Ḥusain Māgre exercised a moderating influence on those Kashmīrī nobles who were in favour of continuing hostilities, and finally secured a settlement. Qarā Bahādur and others who were in prison were released. The Kashmīrīs gave an undertaking that they would not molest the family and followers of Mīrzā Ḥaidar. After this his family was brought from Andarkōt to Srīnagar and treated with respect. They were then sent *via* Pakhlī and Kābul to Kāshghar. But some of the Mughals, like Ṣabr 'Alī and others, who took the route *via* Ladākh, were killed by the Ladākīs.[101]

The exploits and career of Mīrzā Ḥaidar is reminiscent of his cousin Bābur. Like him he possessed great adventurous spirit, and was always active both in body and mind. Like him also he was generous and affectionate, a fearless fighter and a great general.[102] But he did not have the same insight into human nature, and he lacked the tact and prudence and the broad humanity of his great cousin. He was, however, not petty-minded and could rise to great heights of magnanimity. Thus he could have easily declared himself as Sulṭān of Kashmīr, but did not do so as an act of self-denial. Instead, he raised Nāzuk Shāh to the throne as a stop-gap until Humāyūn's return from exile. And as soon as, in 1545, he heard that Humāyūn had occupied Kābul and Qandahār, he transferred to him the sovereignty with which he had invested Nāzuk Shāh. He read the *khuṭba* and struck coins in the name of Humāyūn, and even invited him to Kashmīr, suggesting that it would serve as a useful base for the invasion and reconquest of Hindustān.[103]

In the beginning Mīrzā Ḥaidar ruled Kashmīr with justice and ability. He recovered some of the territories which had been subject to Kashmīr in the time of Zainu'l-'Ābidīn. He established good government, and tried to promote trade, agriculture and industry. But later on, with the worsening of his relations with the Kashmīrī nobles, the administration gradually deteriorated, and he failed to protect the peasants from the high-handedness of the Mughals.[104]

Few medieval rulers of Kashmīr did so much for the promotion of art and culture of Kashmīr as Mīrzā Ḥaidar. He was, in this respect, a great admirer of Zainu'l-'Ābidīn, and tried to follow in his footsteps. He sent for artists and craftsmen from different countries, and revived arts which had been languishing due to continuous civil wars.[105] He patronized men of learning, and appointed teachers in every village for the education of children.[106] He built a number of mosques in Srīnagar with baths, which kept the prayer-rooms warm in winter so that even in extreme cold weather people could pray there and take rest. He also constructed magnificent edifices, and laid out beautiful gradens in Andarkōt. He introduced new types of windows and doors, and made innovations in dress and food.[107]

Mīrzā Ḥaidar was very versatile and a man of many accomplishments. He excelled in penmanship, painting, and various kinds of handiwork.[108] He was a great lover of music, and introduced into Kashmīr various types of musical instruments.[109] According to Jaḥāngīr, Mīrzā Ḥaidar's court was celebrated for skilled musicians.[110] Mīrzā Ḥaidar was also an excellent poet in Turkī and a good poet and prose writer in Persian.[111] Besides the *Ta'rīkh-i-Rashīdi* which he composed in Persian while he was in Kashmīr, he is also regarded as the author of the anonymous *Jahān-nāma*, a metrical treatise on Geography in Turkī, which he is said to have written during his stay in Badakhshān in 1508-9.[112]

But these qualities of Mīrzā Ḥaidar were offset by his excessive religious fanaticism. In his zeal to preserve the Islamic orthodoxy he banned Shī'ism and the Shāfi'ite school.[113] Moreover, he secured a decree from the 'Ulamā of Hindustān that the Nūrbakhshīyas were heretics, and that it was perfectly lawful to destroy them if they persisted in their beliefs and refused to accept the teachings of Abū Ḥanīfa. Accordingly he began to persecute them, and put to death many of their leaders. He also placed a ban on other Ṣūfī orders on the ground that Ṣūfīs led immoral lives, ate and drank forbidden things, and spent their time interpreting dreams, displaying miracles, and prostrating themselves before one another. In this way Mīrzā Ḥaidar compelled every Muslim to conform to the Sunnī faith.[114] But his success was only short-lived, for the Kashmīrī nobles resented his religious bigotry and joined hands to bring about his overthrow.

During his stay in Kashmīr Mīrzā Ḥaidar felt as if he was in exile, and the thought of his own country never left his mind.[115] In 1547, when an ambassador arrived from Kāshghar, he proceeded to Lār to welcome him.[116] In fact all through the period he kept himself in touch with his relations and friends in Kāshghar. This failure to regard Kashmīr as his home and to identify himself with its people proved disastrous for him. For it made him arrogant, and prevented him from making serious efforts to win the affection and good-will of the Kashmīrīs. He began to lean more and more upon the support of his own followers, thereby alienating the Kashmīrī chiefs. This eventually led to his downfall.

NOTES

1. For more details of Mīrzā Ḥaidar's life, see T.R., Intro., pp. 1-27.
2. *Ibid.*, pp. 403, 417.
3. T.R. (MS.), iii, f. 12a has the end of Z̲ū'l-Ḥijja, 938/end of July, 1532. But T.R. (trans.), p. 417, just gives Z̲ū'l-Ḥijja, 938.
4. T.R., pp. 417-21.
5. *Ibid.*, p. 421. According to H.M., f. 139a, Mīrzā Ḥaidar had 14,000 horse and 20,000 foot. According to T.A., iii, 464, Śuka, p. 370, and Munich MS., f. 87b, he had 12,000.
6. T.R., p. 423. According to the *S.O.S. Bulletin*, viii, p. 988, Mīrzā Ḥaidar arrived in Kashmīr on Jumāda ii, 28, 939/Dec. 26, 1532. But as the 1st of Jumāda ii, 939, corresponds to the 29th Dec., 1532, the Mīrzā must have invaded Kashmīr early in January 1533. The date of Sha'bān 4, 932/March 1, 1533, given in A.N., i, 404, is incorrect.
7. T.R. (MS.), iii, f. 14b, but T.R., p. 423, has Kaluchī. The defile is about 3 miles above the village of Gagangīr. (See Stein, ii, 490).
8. T.R., pp. 423-4.
9. It is a village about 4 miles west of Srīnagar in Lat. 34° 5' Long. 74° 47'.
10. T.R., p. 437.
11. B.S., f. 98a; Munich MS., f. 87b; T.A., iii, 464.
12. B.S., f. 98a; also Śuka, p. 371.
13. B.S., ff. 98b-9a.
14. T.R. (MS.), iii, f. 21b. Bāgh-i-Bavan was situated on the plateau of Mārtand. The village of Bavan, containing a magnificent spring, is situated on the left bank of the Lidar. It is in Lat. 33° 46' Long. 15°. The plateau is the Sahrā-i-Bābel of the Persian chronicles. Ross in his trans. of T.R., p. 438, wrongly calls it Bāgh-i-Navīn.
15. B.S., ff. 99b-100b; H.M., ff. 140a-41b; Munich MS., f. 88a.
16. B.S., ff. 101a-b.

17. T.R. (MS.), ii, f. 22a. The trans. has Jarura which is wrong.
18. T.R., pp. 439-41.
19. *Ibid.*
20. *Ibid.*, B.S., f. 101b.
21. Munich MS., f. 89a; T.A., iii, 465.
22. *Ibid.;* Also Suka, p. 373 for the terms of the treaty.
23. T.R., p. 373; *S.O.S., Bulletin,* viii, p. 938; Śuka, p. 373.
24. B.S., ff. 102a-b; Śuka, pp. 373-74.
25. B.S., ff. 102a-b.
26. *Ibid.;* Śuka, p. 375.
27. B.S., f. 102b.
28. B.S. (B.M.), f. 77a.
29. It is a village south-east of Nāgām.
30. B.S., ff. 103a sqq.; H.M., ff. 142a sqq.
31. B.S., ff. 106a-b; H.M., f. 144b.
32. T.R., pp. 450 sqq.
33. *Ibid.*, pp. 473.
34. *Ibid.*, p. 481. A.N., i, 359, is wrong in saying that the Kashmīrī chiefs came down from Rajaurī to Lahore.
35. T.R., p. 482; A.N., i, 359.
36. A.N., i, 359.
37. T.R., p. 482; A.N., i, 359.
38. T.R., p. 482; A.N., i, 360; B.S., f. 107a. Ross in his trans. wrongly calls Rēgī Chak as Zangī Chak, although in T.R. (MS.), iii, f. 50a, it is Rēgī Chak.
39. T.R., pp. 479-80.
40. T.R., p. 483; A.N., i. p. 360.
41. T.R., p. 483.
42. A.N., i, 402; Banerjee, *Humāyūn*, ii, 16.
43. This is in the Gakkar country, south-west of Kashmīr. It lay on the Indus and extended from the Siwālik hills to the borders of Kashmīr. (I.A., xxxvi, p. 8).
44. A.B., i, 360; Banerjee, *Humāyūn*, ii, 13.
45. A.N., i, 402.
46. Kapartal Pass or Kandal is 9 miles east of Rajaurī. It is on the Hirapūr route. Another variant of Kapartal is Karanbal. (See A.N., iii, 746n. 3).
47. T.R., p. 485; A.N., i, 402. B.S., f. 107a gives 21 Rajab 947/21 Nov., 1540. The year 948 A.H. given in T.A., iii, 467 is incorrect. The Pūnch Pass of Abū'l-Fazl is the Chīra Hār route of the Kashmīr chronicles. (See H.M., f. 145a; S.A., p. 50).
48. B.S., ff. 107a-b; H.M., f. 145a; also T.R., p. 485.

49. B.S., ff. 107a-b; also T.R., p. 485.
50. B.S., f. 107b.
51. A.N., i, 403, says that Kājī presented his niece, who was Muḥammad Shāh's grand-daughter, to Shēr Shāh. But Kashmīrī chroniclers do not mention it. T.H., ii, f. 125b, follows A.N.
52. A.N., i, p. 403; S.A., p. 50. B.S., f. 108a says Kājī was given a small force. According to T.A., iii, 468, it numbered 5,000. The number given by A.N. appears to be correct.
53. B.S., f. 108a; also S.A., p. 80.
54. T.R., p. 484; H.M., f. 145a.
55. It is a village in a grassy valley in the range of hills between Shāhābād and Bring parganas.
56. It is a village situated in the Anantnāg Tahṣīl, about 5 miles south-east of Islāmābād.
57. B.S., f. 108a; N.K., f. 34b. Kōthēr (ancient Kapateshvara) is a village situated in Lat. 33° 40' Long. 75° 18'. It is in Kutahār pargana.
58. B.S., f. 108a; H.M., f. 145b. Vahatōr is 7 miles south of Srīnagar on the high road towards Shupiyan in Lat. 33° 58' Long. 74° 51'.
59. B.S., ff. 108a-b; H.M. ff. 145a-b; A.N., i, 403. Ross in his trans. gives the date of battle as 8 Rabī' ii, 948/Aug. 1, 1541.
60. B.S., f. 110a; H.M., ff. 146a-b. T.A., iii, 468, assigns the year 950/1543 for Rēgī's flight.
61. B.S., f. 110a.
62. *Ibid.*, ff. 110a-111a. B.S. is wrong in saying that Kājī died at Dānagalla. (See H.M. (B.N.), f 47b and N.A., f. 69b).
63. T.A., iii, 469.
64. B.S., f. 111a; N.K., f. 34b.
65. It is situated near the boundary of Kishtwār and is locally known, but cannot be traced on the maps.
66. Mārma is a rivulet in Kishtwār which swells during the rainy season. As regards the localities of Dār, Dahut, and Jhālū, they are locally known, but they cannot be traced on the maps.
67. J.P.H.S., iv, p. 37.
68. T.A., ii, p. 470. T.A. says Ladākh was placed under Muḥsin, while according to Firishta it was placed under Mullā Ḥasan.
69. It is a village on the Indus in Lat. 71° 40' Long. 32° 58'.
70. *Ta'rīkh-i-Dā'ūdi*, ff. 191b-92a; T.A., ii, p. 113. See I.A., 1907, pp. 8 sq. for the Gakkhar tribe.
71. *Ta'rīkh-i-Dā'ūdi*, f. 195a.
72. T.A., iii, 471. *Ta'rīkh-i-Dā'ūdī*, f. 195b incorrectly mentions Muḥammad Naẓar and Ṣabr 'Alī also, although they were loyal to Mīrzā Ḥaidar.

73. T.A., iii, 713 (trans), and Firishta, p. 680, are wrong in saying that the Kashmīrī chiefs took Haibat Khān to Bārāmūla. There is no mention of this in either the Afghān or Kashmīrī accounts. The Persian text of T.A., iii, 471 has, instead of Bārāmūla, Damlah which cannot be identified.
74. *Ta'rīkh-i-Dā'ūdi* f. 196a; T.A., iii, 471. But both these chronicles are incorrect in stating that Ghāzī Chak went to Mīrzā Ḥaidar. Ghāzī was against Mīrzā Ḥaidar and so he could not have gone to him.
75. T.A., iii, 472.
76. B.S., f. 111b.
77. See *infra* p. 144.
78. B.S., f. 111b. S.A., p. 51; T.H., ii, f. 193b and W.K., f. 45a, say that Shamsu'd-Dīn's bones were taken out and burnt and his tomb was turned into a public latrine. But B.S. and H.M. do not mention this.
79. N.A., f. 71a; N.K., f. 34b; T.H., ii, f. 127b.
80. B.S., ff. 111b-12a; S.A., p. 51; T.H., ii, f. 127b.
81. B.S., ff. 112a-b.
82. *Ibid.*, f. 112b.
83. N.A., ff. 71a-b.
84. H.M., f. 146b.
85. H.M., f. 147, and T.A., iii, 472 assign the year 958/1551 for these happenings. But B.S., f. 112b gives Sept.-Oct., 1550.
86. A village and fort in the province of Pūnch and situated on the right bank of the Mandel stream in Lat. 33° 38' Long. 74° 6'.
87. T.A., iii, 472, wrongly states that Ḥusain Māgre sent his brother to inform Mīrzā Ḥaidar of the treachery of the Kashmīrīs, for the Māgres themselves were a party to the conspiracy against the Mīrzā.
88. B.S., f. 113a; also H.M., ff. 147a-b where the account is given somewhat differently. Barbal was a fort near the Tōshamaidān Pass on the route to Pūnch (See for more details, Stein, ii, 399 and n. 59).
89. B.S., ff. 114a-15a; H.M., ff. 147a-48a.
90. S.A., p. 52; B.S., ff. 115b-16a; H.M., f. 147b.
91. H.M., f. 147b.
92. S.A., p. 52; B.S., f. 116a. H.M. has Aunpūr.
93. Khāmpūr is situated 10 miles south of Srīnagar on the high road leading to the Pīr Panjāl Pass. T.A. and S.A. wrongly call it Khānpūr. B.S. and T.H. have Khāmpūr Cunningham, according to Stein, is wrong in identifying it with the ancient Kanishkapura. (Stein, ii, 482n.).

94. S.A., pp. 52-3. Sayyid 'Alī says that he and his father advised the Mīrzā not to make a night attack.
95. S.A., pp. 52-3. B.S., ff. 116a-b, agrees with this account. S.A. and B.S. give the date of Mīrzā Ḥaidar's death as 6 Z̲ū'l-Qa'da 957/ Nov. 18, 1550. But A.A. (Blochmann), p. 313, and T.R., p. 22, say that the Mīrzā was killed in Oct. 1551. See also T.A. and H.M. which give the year 1551. I have followed these authorities, for the chronology of S.A. and B.S. is not always reliable.
96. A.N., i, 406; see also T.A. (trans.), iii, 718n. 1.
97. T.A., iii, 475.
98. According to H.M., f. 148a, Mīrzā Ḥaidar set out alone to find out the condition of the enemy force. A butcher, who was skinning a cow, saw him and questioned who he was. The Mīrzā replied that he was neither a Persian nor a Kashmīrī. The butcher, suspecting him to be a Mughal spy, delivered such a severe blow upon his head with his axe that he fell down from his horse and died. But this story appears to be apocryphal. In the first place it is incredible that a butcher should have been engaged in his work in the night near the scene of conflict. Secondly, Mīrzā Ḥaidar who was a brave soldier and was well armed, could not have been killed by a butcher with an axe.
99. T.A., iii, 475.
100. S.A., p. 53; W.K., f. 46a; T.H., ii, f. 130a.
101. T.A., iii, 478; see also H.M., ff. 148b-49a.
102. Rāzī, *Haft Iqlīm,*, f. 365a. Author of *Ta'rīkh-i-Dā'ūdi*, f. 196a says Mīrzā Ḥaidar was "a courageous youth".
103. T.R., Intro., pp. 24-5.
104. H.M., f. 146b.
105. A.N., i, 404; H.M., f. 146a.
106. *Risālah dar Manāqib-i-Khulafa*, f. 513b.
107. N.A., f. 70b.
108. *Bābur-nāma*, i, 22.
109. A.A., i, 404.
110. *Tuzuk-ī-Jahāngīrī*, ii, 148.
111. *S.O.S. Bulletin*, viii, pp. 987-8; *Bābur-nāma*, ii, 22; also Rāzī, *Haft Iqlīm*, f. 365a for an appreciation of Mīrzā Ḥaidar's character.
112. *S.O.S. Bulletin*, viii, 987-8; Storey, *Persian Literature*, Sec, ii, Fasc. 2, p. 274.
113. B.S., f. 120a.
114. T.R., pp. 435-6; Firishta, 646-7; also B.S., f. 120b.
115. T.R., Intro., p. 19.
116. *Ibid.*, p. 469.

Chapter 8

End of the Shāh Mīr Dynasty and the Chak Ascendancy

Nāzuk Shāh, who had been raised to the throne by Mīrzā Ḥaidar, was allowed to continue as Sulṭān by the nobles. But it was in reality 'Īdī Raina, his prime minister, who was the virtual ruler. The latter treated the nobles with respect, and did his best to win their favour. Since the Chaks had suffered considerably under Mīrzā Ḥaidar and were in economic difficulties, he rewarded them generously.[1] The pargana of Divasar was allotted to Daulat Chak, the pargana of Vihī was given to Ghāzī Chak and Kamrāj to Yūsuf Chak and Bahrām Chak, while Khwāja Ḥājī received one lakh *kharwārs* of paddy.[2]

In about the middle of 1552 news came that Haibat Khān Niyāzī, whom the Gakkhars could no longer give protection, was advancing to invade Kashmīr. Thereupon 'Īdī Raina, Daulat Chak, and Ḥusain Māgre marched against him, and met him in the Bānihāl pargana. Severe fighting continued from morning till sunset. The Afghāns fought valiantly. Bībī Rābi'a, the wife of Haibat Khān, in particular displayed great courage. But in the end, owing to their inferiority in numbers, the Afghāns were routed. Haibat Khan, Bībī Rābi'a, Shahbāz Khān and many other chiefs were slain. Their heads were sent by the Kashmīrī nobles to Islām Shāh.[3]

Soon after this, civil war flared up in Kashmīr. Already before the invasion of the Niyāzīs, the nobles under the leadership of Daulat Chak and 'Īdī Raina had fought one another in Srīnagar. 'Īdī Raina had even employed the help of Qarā

Bahādur and other Mughals who had not yet left the country. Bābā Khalīl, the Shī'ite divine, however, by explaining to 'Īdī Raina the disastrous consequences of placing trust in foreigners, had brought about peace between him and Daulat Chak.[4] But in reality it was nothing more than a truce, for, after the destruction of the Niyāzīs, dissensions in the Valley were revived. On the one side were the Māgres, the Kopwārā Chaks and the Baihaqī Sayyids headed by 'Īdī Raina, and on the other were the Chaks led by Daulat Chak.[5]

Towards the end of 1552, 'Īdī Raina decided to overthrow Daulat Chak.[6] But the latter anticipated his move by taking Ḥusain Māgre and Sayyid Ibrāhīm prisoner. The rest of 'Īdī Raina's followers, however, managed to escape and join their chief. After a few days 'Īdī with the Māgres and Yūsuf Chak set out to attack Daulat. But before they could do so, Daulat forestalled their move by himself crossing the Jehlam in Srīnagar and attacking them. 'Īdī Raina was defeated and put to flight.[7] But at Rāwalpūr,[8] while in a hurried flight on horseback, his neck got entangled in a vine creeper and he was killed on the spot.[9] Thereupon, Daulat Chak assumed the duties of prime minister. He deposed Nāzuk Shāh and set up in his place Ibrāhīm Shāh, the son of Muḥammad Shāh, who, before Mīrzā Ḥaidar's invasion, had already once reigned for a short time.[10] Nāzuk Shāh, finding no hope of recovering the throne, left for the Punjāb.[11]

Daulat Chak's rise to power marks the beginning of the Chak ascendancy in the Valley which lasted for over thirty years. The Chaks, as we have seen, had entered Kashmīr in the time of Sūhadeva and were raised to prominence by Sulṭān Shamsu'd-Dīn I. But it was not until the time of Muḥammad Shāh that they began to play an active part in the affairs of the kingdom. They increased their prestige and power by entering into marriage alliances with the principal landowning families of the Valley and the ruling dynasty; and by their tact, energy, perseverance, and valour they eventually succeeded in defeating all their rivals and making themselves supreme in the country.

Mīrzā Ḥaidar had banned Shī'ism, the Nūrbakhshīya sect,

the Shāfi'ite school and the various Ṣūfī orders, having declared that no religion except the Ḥanafite was to be practised. But Daulat Chak lifted the ban, and issued a proclamation that people were free to profess any religion they liked, and that no one was allowed to impose his own beliefs upon others.[12]

Daulat Chak then built three mausoleums. One for Shaikh Dāniyāl, whose body was brought there and buried. Another he constructed over the grave of Mīr Shamsu'd-Dīn, which had been destroyed by Mīrzā Ḥaidar, and endowed it for the maintenance of Shamsu'd-Dīn's descendants and the servants of the hospice. In the third mausoleum the body of Bābā 'Alī Najjār was brought and buried. An endowment was created, and his son Bābā Ḥasan was made its trustee.[13]

The ruler of Ladākh had not paid his tribute for many years. Moreover, his subjects had entered the Valley and driven away the flocks of sheep from the pargana of Khawārpara, which was included in the jāgīr of Ḥabīb Chak, brother of Nuṣrat Chak. Daulat Chak therefore sent Ibrāhīm Chak and Ghāzī Chak's son Ḥaidar Chak to invade Ladākh. Meanwhile Ḥabib Chak had himself invaded Ladākh. He defeated the Ladākhīs and, after occupying a number of their forts, compelled them to pay a tribute of 3,000 horses, 500 pieces of leather, 100 sheep, and 30 yaks.[14]

Daulat Chak treated the nobles kindly; and to win over the rival faction he released Ḥusain Māgre and Sayyid Ibrāhīm whom he had imprisoned for joining 'Īdī Raina against him. However, some members of his own family, incited by interested persons, became jealous of him. Matters came to a head when he married Ghāzī Chak's mother, the widow of his uncle, Kājī Chak. Ghāzī Chak, Ḥusain Chak and other of his relations greatly resented this marriage and made up their minds to overthrow him.[15] Towards the end of 1555, when Daulat Chak had gone in a boat for shooting on the Dal lake, Ghāzī made a sudden attack on his troops who were in Ḥusainābād. Taken by surprise, they fled. Thereupon, Ghāzī seized all the Horse and set out in pursuit of Daulat Chak.[16] But the latter escaped to the hilly parts of the Phāg pargana. He was, however, seized by a shepherd and brought before Ghāzī, who had him blinded.[17] Ghāzī now replaced Daulat Chak as prime minister.

In the spring of 1556, some chiefs, headed by Nuṣrat Chak and Yūsuf Chak, conspired to put Ghāzī and his brother Ḥusain Chak to death. But Ghāzī discovered the plot and sent for the leaders. Not suspecting any danger they obeyed the summons. He remonstrated with them for their treacherous conduct and then detained them for the night.[18] Hearing of this Ḥabīb Chak, Shams Raina, and Muḥammad Māgre took up arms against Ghāzī. They destroyed the bridge of the town and assembled in the field of Ziāldakar. Ghāzī proceeded to the river on the opposite side; and for a few days there was exchange of arrows and musketry between his forces and those of the enemy. But finding that the rebels were daily gaining in strength by fresh reinforcements, Ghāzī crossed the river and attacked them in Ziāldakar. After heavy fighting he defeated them. Ḥabīb Chak was killed, Yūsuf Chak, the son of Rēgī Chak, was seized and thrown into prison, while Shams Raina and others escaped to India.[19]

Not long after these events, other Chak nobles like Ghāzī's own brother Shankar Chak, Bahrām Chak and Fatḥ Chak organised a rising in Sōpūr. But Ghāzī marched against them and defeated them. Bahrām escaped to Khuyahōm, but was captured there. He was brought to Srīnagar and put to death. Ibrāhīm Chak, another son of Rēgī Chak, was also seized and executed. But Fatḥ Chak and Shankar Chak escaped.[20] Orders were given to blind Yūsuf Chak, who was in prison, but he managed to escape.[21]

The Kashmīrī chiefs, who had fled to India, sought the help of Humāyūn. The Emperor was willing to give them assistance, but soon after he died on January 24, 1556. Thereupon, they made advances to Abū'l-Ma'ālī. He had been a great favourite of Humāyūn, who had called him his son. But Akbar after his accession ordered Abū'l-Ma'ālī's imprisonment owing to his arrogance, and sent him to Lahore.[22] From there, however, Abū'l-Ma'ālī escaped to the territory of the Gakkhars. Although he was seized by Kamāl Khān Gakkhar and thrown into prison, he managed to escape with the help of Yūsuf Chak to

Naushahrā. There he entered into an alliance with Shams Raina, Fatḥ Chak, Khwāja Ḥājī, and the blind Daulat Chak;[23] and, having collected a force of 300 Mughals and 800 Kashmīrīs, he entered Kashmīr *via* Pūnch and Bārāmūla and encamped at Patan (1558).[24] When Ghāzī heard of this he released Nuṣrat Chak and Sayyid Ibrāhīm, and with them set out against the enemy. He encountered Abū'l-Ma'ālī at Hānjīvera.[25] After heavy fighting, which lasted from morning till sunset, the invaders gave way. Shams Raina, realising that Abū'l-Ma'ālī would fall into the hands of the enemy, sent him away with an escort of twelve men, and himself continued to resist, in spite of the severe wounds he had received. He then tried to commit suicide, but did not succeed. He was captured alive; and although his daughter was married to Ghāzī's son, he was not spared but was executed.[26] A number of Mughals were also taken prisoners. They were beheaded, and their heads built up into minarets.[27]

After this victory Ghāzī sent Nuṣrat Chak on a goodwill mission to Akbar. Nuṣrat was received with honour by Bairam Khān.[28] Meanwhile, the Emperor had received a request for help through Qarā Bahādur from the Kashmīrī nobles who were opposed to Ghāzī.[29] He welcomed this opportunity, and gave a large force to Qarā Bahādur, who had previous experience of Kashmīr, to lead the invasion. Qarā Bahādur marched *via* Naushahrā in the summer of 1560.[30] But he did not get any response from the nobles. On the contrary, Fatḥ Chak and Lohar Chak, who were in Pūnch, deserted and went over to Ghāzī. Similarly Nuṣrat sent a message to Ghāzī that he was not on the side of the Mughals. The nobles who had promised to help Qarā Bahādur, now backed out because they found that his army was not strong and he would be defeated. But the result of their attitude was that Qarā Bahādur got disheartened, and did not move from Rajaurī. Ghāzī Chak, however, marched to Hirapūr, and thence proceeded *via* Thanna to Loharkōt. He sent a force of infantry which defeated the Mughals near Rajaurī.[31] He then himself attacked Qarā Bahādur who had marched to Danaor. Here, after a severe engagement lasting from morning till sunset, he routed the Mughals. Qarā Bahādur escaped and joined Akbar at Agra. The Kashmīrī chronicles say that Ghāzī

Chak had announced before the battle that anyone who brought the head of a Mughal would get an *ashrafī*, and so over 700 heads were brought. Ghāzī Chak gave them the promised reward, and in some cases even five times as much. He then returned to Srīnagar, and constructed a bigger minaret of the skulls of his enemies.[32]

Ghāzī Chak, on seizing power from Daulat Chak, deposed Ibrāhīm Shāh and enthroned his brother Ismā'il, another son of Muḥammad Shāh.[33] But when Ismā'īl Shāh died in 1557, he proclaimed his son Ḥabīb Shāh, who was his own nephew, as king.[34] In the year 1561, however, under the pretext that Ḥabīb Shāh was incompetent, Ghāzī Chak set him aside, and with the consent of the nobles himself ascended the throne, assuming the title of Sulṭān and laying the foundation of the Chak dynasty.[35]

In 1560-61, again, the nobles revolted under the leadership of Fatḥ Chak and Lohar Chak. Ghāzī despatched his brother, Ḥusain Chak, against them. Meanwhile, winter had set in, and as a result many of the rebels perished in snow. The rest proceeded to Kishtwār, but as they were in great distress they surrendered to Ḥusain Chak. He mediated on their behalf with Ghāzī Shāh who pardoned them and granted them jāgīrs.[36]

In 1562-63 Ghāzī proceeded to Lār, and from their sent his son Aḥmad with Fatḥ Chak to the conquest of Ladākh. Fatḥ Chak leaving Aḥmad behind on the frontier, raided the country and returned safely. As the Ladākhīs did not want to fight they sent tribute. But Aḥmad became jealous of Fatḥ Chak's exploit and decided to emulate him. And although he was dissuaded by him, he invaded Ladākh with only 500 men. But he was defeated by the Ladākhī troops and pursued. This made him so panic-stricken that he did not even stop at the camp of Fatḥ Chak to unite with him in order to resist the enemy. His example demoralised the followers of Fatḥ Chak and they also fled. Fatḥ Chak tried to rally them against the enemy, but was slain. When Ghāzī Shāh heard of the disaster, he remonstrated with his son.[37]

In his old age Ghāzī Shāh was afflicted with leprosy which affected not only his general health but also his eyesight. He, therefore, entrusted the work of government to his brother

Ḥusain Khān, who had been his constant adviser during his rule, and designated him to be his successor.[38] He then divided equally all his personal belongings into two portions. One half he gave to his son while the other half he sent to the merchants for sale. But as the merchants regarded the price demanded by him as too high, they appealed to Ḥusain Khān. The latter prohibited them from paying the price asked for. This angered Ghāzī Shāh so much that he decided to regain his powers and to nominate his son Aḥmad as heir-apparent. But his plan miscarried for Ḥusain Khān deposed him and himself ascended the throne at the end of 1563.[39] Ḥusain Shāh then issued orders for putting out the eyes of Aḥmad. Ghāzī Shāh interceded on his behalf, but without success. He lingered henceforth a futile wreck for four years until he died in 1566-67[40] at the age of fifty-eight.[41]

Ghāzī Shāh possessed all those qualities necessary to found a dynasty—vigilance, courage, energy, tenacity of purpose, and ability to take advantage of opportunities. He began his career as a soldier under his father, Kājī Chak, at the age of eighteen. He fought in all his wars, and shared with him exile and all kinds of privations. After Kājī's death he served under other senior members of his family, and impressed the Chaks so much with his abilities that when they became dissatisfied with Daulat Chak they chose him as their leader. On assuming power Ghāzī Chak suppressed the refractory chiefs and established law and order. But his most notable service to his country was that he successfully protected it from the Mughal invasions, which, twenty years later, overwhelmed his successors. Ghāzī Shāh had a rough exterior, but he was a cultured man and composed verses in Persian.[42] He was generous to those who were loyal to him, but he showed no mercy to traitors, and inflicted cruel punishments on them. He was the first Sulṭān of Kashmīr to have introduced the practice of blinding the political opponents and cutting off their limbs.[43] At the same time he was brave and admired brave men, and forgave them even if they were his enemies. Thus when Kūchak Bahādur, belonging to Qarā Bahādur's army, was taken prisoner, having been seriously wounded by an arrow, Ghāzī Shāh spared his life, treated him with kindness, and made him over to the physicians.[44]

Ghāzī Shāh had a high sense of justice. Once a servant of his favourite son, Ḥaidar Khān, while accompanying him, picked up a jujube from the ground. He observed this and had the hands of the servant cut off. When Ḥaidar Khān heard of this, he was so angry that he refused to visit his father. Ghāzī Shāh felt hurt, and sent Ḥaidar's uncle, Muḥammad Malik, to remonstrate with him. Ḥaidar got enraged and stabbed his uncle to death. Ghāzī Shāh, thereupon, caused Ḥaidar to be hanged. His body was exhibited on the gibbet for eight days, and then thrown into the river.[45]

Ghāzī Shāh was a Shī'ite, but he allowed freedom of belief to persons of all religions. The author of the *Nawādiru'l-Akhbār* says that Ghāzī was intolerant, and because of this many Sunnī chiefs like Nuṣrat Chak, Yūsuf Chak, and Nājī Malik proceeded to Kāshghar and brought Qarā Bahādur in order to overthrow him.[46] But there is no reliable evidence to support the view that the Kashmīr nobles ever went to Kāshghar. Moreover, when Qarā was sent by Akbar to invade Kashmīr, many of the Sunnī nobles refused to help him and professed their loyalty to Ghāzī Shāh. Similarly it is wrong to say that rebellions in the latter's reign were due to religious differences. Their main cause was the scramble for power among the nobles. Neither from Ḥaidar Malik's account nor from the *Bahāristān-i-Shāhi* does it appear that Ghāzī Shāh was a fanatical Shī'ite.

Sulṭān Ḥusain Shāh (1563-70)

On ascending the throne Ḥusain Shāh was called upon to deal with a number of conspiracies and risings one after another. The first conspiracy against him was organised by Ghāzī's son, Aḥmad Khān, Muḥammad Māgre, and Nuṣrat Chak. But Ḥusain Shāh discovered it, and sent for the malcontents under the pretext of obtaining pledges of loyalty from them. When they came he had them seized and thrown into prison.[47]

In 1565, Ḥusain Shāh was faced with the revolt of his younger brother, Shankar Chak, who fled from Kashmīr and began to create trouble in the Naushahrā area by occupying villages and oppressing the peasants. Ḥusain Shāh thereupon sent Muḥammad Nājī and his younger brother 'Alī Khān Chak to Pūnch. They attacked Shankar and defeated him.[48] But soon after he again raised the banner of revolt. He was once more defeated by 'Alī Chak near Rajaurī.[49]

In 1565-66 while Ḥusain Shāh had gone away shooting on the Vethnār lake,[50] Fatḥ Khwāja Baqqāl and his son, on whom the Sulṭān had conferred the titles of Khān-i-Zamān[51] and Bahādur Khān respectively, decided to seize power with the help of Fatḥ Chak, Shams Dūnī, and other nobles. Their plan was to enter the palace, put to death their rivals, and secure the release of Aḥmad Khān, Muḥammad Māgre, and Nuṣrat Chak. But Nājī, who was in charge of the capital, came to know of the plot, and so, when the rebels entered the palace, they met with stiff resistance, and were finally repulsed. Fatḥ Chak and Bahādur Khān were killed, while Khān-i-Zamān was taken prisoner. Meanwhile, Ḥusain Shāh saw from a distance the fire in the palace caused by the rebels. He immediately returned and ordered the limbs of Khān-i-Zamān and his accomplices to be cut off.[52]

Soon after, the Wazīr Mubāriz Khān hatched a plot against Ḥusain Shāh in collaboration with Lohar Chak. But the conspirators were seized and their hands and feet were cut off. Nuṣrat Chak, who was in prison, was blinded.[53]

After the fall of Mubāriz Khān in 1567-68, Malik Lūlī succeeded him, but on the charge of embezzling 40,000 *kharwārs* of paddy belonging to the government he was dismissed and in his place 'Alī Kōkā was appointed.[54] It was during 'Alī Kōkā's term of office that an incident took place which had far-reaching effects on the subsequent history of Kashmīr.

One day, in 1568-69, Qāẓī Ḥabīb, a fanatical Sunnī, while riding along in Srīnagar, came across one Yūsuf Aindar, an equally fanatical Shī'ite. The Qāẓī vilified the Shī'ites; Yūsuf retorted by abusing the Qāẓī. Thereupon, Qāẓī Ḥabīb struck him with a whip. Yūsuf retaliated by drawing his sword and wounding the Qāzī, who fell from his horse. When 'Alī Kōkā, who was a staunch Sunnī, heard of this he at once brought the matter to the notice of Ḥusain Shāh, and with his permission called a council of important 'Ulamā like Qāzī Mūsa, Mullā

Yūsuf Almās, and Mulla Fīrūz Ganā'ī. This body passed a decree condemning Yūsuf to death.[55] The execution of Yūsuf created great resentment among the Shī'ite divines. Some of the Sunnī 'Ulamā also did not approve of the decision, contending that none of the Four Schools sanctioned death penalty for the offence committed by Yūsuf.[56] Even Qāẓī Ḥabīb was opposed to the infliction of such a punishment on the ground that he had not died of the wound.[57]

It was at this time that Akbar sent Mīrzā Muqīm as his ambassador to Kashmīr. Ḥusain Shāh sent his high officials to meet him at Hirapūr, and then he himself came out of Srīnagar to receive him.[58] As he was at the moment very perturbed by the controversy over the execution of Yūsuf, he referred the matter to Mīrzā Muqīm. The Mīrzā sent for all the prominent 'Ulamā, including those who had condemned Yūsuf to death. Everyone came except Qāẓī Mūsā, who fled from the city and hid himself. Qāẓī Zainu'd-Dīn and Mullā Rāzī questioned Mullā Yūsuf Almās and Mullā Fīrūz as to the justice of the penalty of death inflicted on Yūsuf, when Qāẓī Ḥabīb had not been killed. They replied that they had given their verdict at the suggestion of Ḥusain Shāh, who wanted Yūsuf's execution on account of political reasons and had sent them word through 'Alī Kōkā. But the Sulṭān denied having had anything to do with the affair, except that, instead of deciding the case himself, he had entrusted it to the Qāẓīs. In the end, the Sunnī and Shī'ite 'Ulamā decreed the execution of Mullā Fīrūz and Mullā Yūsuf Almās according to the Shāfi'ī law. Qāẓī 'Abdu'l-Ghafūr, a Ḥanafite, and Qāẓī Zainu'd-Dīn, a Shāfi'ite, agreed with this judgement.[59]

Soon after Mīrzā Muqīm left Kashmīr. Ḥusain Shāh sent with him Ya'qūb Mīrzā,[60] the son of Bābā 'Alī, as his *wakīl* with valuable presents for the Emperor and his daughter to be married to Prince Salīm. Meanwhile, 'Alī Kōkā had despatched some nobles and Ulamā headed by Mullā 'Abdu'llāh to the Imperial Court to complain to Akbar against Mīrzā Muqīm. By misrepresenting the whole affair of Qāẓī Ḥabīb and Yūsuf, they succeeded in stirring Akbar's anger to such a pitch that as soon as Mīrzā Muqīm returned to Agra, he was at once put to death on the advice of Shaikh 'Abdu'n-Nabī and other 'Ulamā. The

Emperor also ordered the execution of Ya'qūb, though he was an envoy, and sent back the presents and Ḥusain Shāh's daughter to Srīnagar.[61]

Towards the end of his reign, while Ḥusain Shāh was seriously suffering from the cancer of the mouth, 'Alī Kōkā and Nājī Malik advised him to set up one of his sons on the throne and imprison his brother 'Alī Khān along with Sayyid Mubārak. But before Ḥusain Shāh could act, 'Alī Khān, warned of the plan, fled to Sōpūr where he was joined by Sayyid Mubārak and other disaffected chiefs. Then, having gathered a sufficient force, he marched on Srīnagar and encamped at Fathyārī. He repelled a night attack of the royalists, and the following morning entered the capital. As Ḥusain Shāh was not strong enough to offer resistance, he decided, on the advice of Nājī Malik and 'Alī Kōkā, to abdicate, and sent the crown to 'Alī Khān through Bābā Khalīl.[62]

Ḥusain Shāh was by far the best ruler of the Chak dynasty. His rule, though efficient and strong, was tempered with mildness and justice, so that his subjects called him *Nūshīravān-i'Ādil* after the great Sāsānid Emperor of Persia. He attended to their complaints, protected them from robbers and rapacious officials, and endeavoured to promote their prosperity.[63] He was of a generous disposition, and every day, after morning prayers, he distributed money to the poor and needy.[64] Though a Shī'ite, he allowed the practice of the Ḥanafite law, and appointed Sayyid Ḥabīb, a Sunnī jurist from Khwārizm, as Qāẓi of Srīnagar and Preacher of the Jāmi Masjid.[65] His attitude towards his non-Muslim subjects was also very liberal. He granted them complete freedom to practice their religion and customs and to celebrate their festivals. In fact, in some of the festivals, like the Spring and Śrīpancamī, he himself participated.[66] He was a man of cultured tastes. He was fond of music, wrote verses in Persian,[67] and enjoyed the society of artists and scholars. He divided the day in the following manner: On Monday he attended court with the Qāẓīs and Mīr 'Adls. On Tuesday he went out hunting. Wednesday he spent with his army. Thursday he passed in the company of musicians and friends. On Friday he held discussions with the 'Ulamā. Saturday was passed in the society of Hindu and Buddhist priests, and Sunday he spent with the Ṣūfīs.[68]

The last days of Ḥusain Shāh's reign were clouded with personal grief and public anxiety. First there was the affair of Yūsuf Aindar and Qāẓī Ḥabīb which caused him endless worries. Then his brave and able son Ibrāhīm, whom he was very fond of, died of small-pox.[69] This affected him so much that he became consumptive.[70] After his abdication some of the courtiers advised 'Alī Shāh to imprison and blind him. But 'Alī Shāh refused to listen to them and gave Ḥusain Shāh complete freedom of movement and the use of his treasure.[71] Ḥusain Shāh went to live in Zainapūr, and there he died of fever after a year.[72]

Sulṭān 'Alī Shāh (1570-78)

On his accession 'Alī Shāh made Sayyid Mubārak Baihaqī, who had been for a long time his faithful friend, his Wazīr. To strengthen further the bonds of friendship with him he gave his daughter in marriage to Mubārak's son, Sayyid Abū'l-Ma'ālī.[73]

For about two years peace reigned in the kingdom. But at the end of 1571, 'Alī Khān Chak, son of Naurūz Chak, entered into league with some nobles in order to seize the throne. Warned of the plot, 'Alī Shāh decided to execute him. But Sayyid Mubārak interceded on his behalf and sent him away to his home in Kamrāj. 'Alī Khān, however, did not stay there long. He fled to Lahore and sought the help of Ḥusain Qulī Khān, Akbar's governor of the Punjāb.[74] When this news reached Srīnagar, some of the courtiers who were jealous of Mubārak, made him responsible for 'Alī Chak's escape, and accused him of treason. Meanwhile 'Alī Chak, having failed to get on well with Ḥusain Qulī Khān, had fled to Mānkōt. A force was, thereupon, at once despatched against him by 'Alī Shāh. He was seized, brought to Srīnagar, and thrown into prison. But after a year and a half he was released on presenting the Sulṭān one hundred gold *dīnārs*.[75]

In 1572-73 took place the revolt of Prince Yūsuf Khān, 'Alī Shāh's son and successor. As Aiba Khān, Ghāzī Shāh's son, was also a claimant to the throne, Yūsuf's relations with him became inimical. Incited by Muḥammad Baṭ he proceeded to Aiba Khān's house with his followers and assassinated him, and then out of fear of the Sulṭān he went away to Sōpūr, where he raised the banner of revolt. 'Alī Shāh was very angry with Yūsuf for causing Aiba Khān's death and organising a rising. He, therefore, sent a force unde his brother Abdāl Khān against him. Abdāl was anxious to attack Yūsuf and destroy him in order to clear the way for his own succession. But Sayyid Mubārak opposed this fratricidal war and brought about reconciliation between father and son. Muḥammad Baṭ, however, was not forgiven, but was thrown into prison.[76]

Soon after this event Shams Dūnī and Muḥammad Marāj, two nobles of Kashmīr, began to create trouble in the country. But when 'Alī Shāh sent an army against them, they got frightened and took refuge with Sayyid Mubārak. The latter interceded on their behalf with the Sulṭān who forgave them.[77]

In 983/1575-76 'Alī Shāh was faced with a serious danger on account of the invasion of Kashmīr by Nāzūk Shāh's sons, Ḥājī Ḥaidar Khān and Salīm Khān.[78] They were living in exile in the Punjāb, but having entered into correspondence with some Kashmīrī chiefs who promised to help them, they set out towards the Valley in order to contest the throne. 'Alī Shāh, learning that the pretenders had reached Naushahrā and had been joined by their supporters, at once sent a force under his brother Lohar Chak and Muḥammad Chak against them. When the army reached Thanna, Muḥammad Chak took Lohar prisoner, and surrendered him to the enemy. On hearing this 'Alī Shāh became greatly alarmed, and despite the fact that Nājī Malik assured him that Muḥammad was not a traitor, but a loyal servant, his fears were not dispelled. But events turned out as Nājī had foreseen. Muḥammad Khān, having lulled Ḥājī Ḥaidar and Salīm into a false sense of security by surrendering Lohar, made a surprise attack on them at Singpūr while they were proceeding to Rajaurī from Naushahr. Salīm Khān was killed, but Ḥājī Ḥaidar succeeded in making good his escape to India. Muḥammad Khān then secured Lohar Chak's release and with him returned to Srīnagar.[79]

In 1572 'Alī Shāh decided to reduce Kishtwār whose ruler

Bahādur Singh had renounced his authority. Accordingly, he sent three armies, each under the command of Abdāl Khān, 'Alī Khān, and Naurūz Chak, to invade Kishtwār from three sides, while he himself encamped at Singpūr.[80] Bahādur Singh, realizing that he would not be able to resist the Kashmīrī forces, decided to come to terms. He acknowledged 'Alī Shāh as his suzerain, agreed to pay tribute, and presented the wife of one of his relations with whom the Sulṭān was in love. 'Alī Shāh married her and named her Fatḥ Khātūn.[81] But as Bahādur Singh did not pay his tribute, 'Alī Shāh, in 1574, again sent a force under Ismā'īl Ganā'ī against him. But as before Bahādur Singh agreed to come to terms. He promised to pay his tribute regularly in future, and sent his sister Śankar Devī to be married to 'Alī Shāh's grandson, Ya'qūb.[82]

On about July 3, 1578,[83] Akbar, from the neighbourhood of Kalānaur, sent Mullā 'Ishqī and Qāẓī Ṣadru'd-Dīn as ambassadors to Kashmīr ostensibly with the object of proposing a marriage between Prince Salīm and Ḥusain Shāh's daughter, but in reality to find out if the conditions were favourable for a Mughal invasion of the country. 'Alī Shāh accepted the proposal and sent his *wakīl* Muḥammad Qāsim with his niece and presents of shawls, musk, and saffron to the imperial court. He also had the *khuṭba* recited and the coins struck in the name of Akbar.[84]

'Alī Shāh was an able and just ruler, and looked after the welfare of the peasants. When the *rabī'* crops failed in 1578 owing to the heavy fall of snow and caused famine in the country, he brought out his treasure, and distributed it freely among the poor and needy.[85] He was kind and of a humane disposition, and forgave even those who took up arms against him. He discontinued the practice of the blinding and cutting of limbs of political opponents prevalent since the time of Ghāzī Shāh.[86] He was a liberal ruler and did not discriminate between Shī'ites and Sunnīs . He appointed Sayyid Mubārak, a Sunnī, as his Wazīr and held the Ṣūfīs like Ḥamza Makhdūm and his two disciples, Bābā Dā'ūd Ganā'ī and Bābā Rishī Harvī in great respect. Shaikh Ya'qūb Ṣarfī and Khwāja Muḥammad Rafīq were also respected by him.[87] He was fond of playing polo every morning and afternoon. But one day, early in 1579, during a game, he was mortally injured. He returned to the palace and, realizing that his end was near, he crowned his eldest son, Yūsuf Khān, as Sulṭān.[88]

NOTES

1. H.M., f. 150a.
2. T.A., iii, p. 476.
3. *Ta'rīkh-i-Dā'ūdi*, ff. 196a-b; T.A., iii, 478-9; also *Ta'rīkh-i-Khān-i-Jahāni*, f. 109b and B.S., f. 117b. *Ta'rīkh-i-Dā'ūdī* wrongly states that it was Mīrzā Ḥaidar who sent the Kashmīrī chiefs against the Niyazīs. M.T., i, 500, however, does not refer to Mīrzā Ḥaidar in this connection.
4. T.A., iii, 478.
5. B.S., f. 117b.
6. B.S., f. 118b gives the year 958 but it should be 959/1552. (See J.R.A.S., 1918, p. 462).
7. B.S., f. 118a.
8. It is a village about a mile south-west of Srīnagar, on the road leading to the areodrome.
9. H.M., f. 151b; N.K., f. 35b. The statement in B.S., f. 118a, that 'Īdī Raina, having fallen ill on the way, returned to Srīnagar where he died, appears to be apocryphal.
10. Firishta, p. 685 says that Ibrāhīm was the son of Nāzuk Shāh. But this is incorrect. Daulat Chak would not have raised to the throne a person belonging to the collateral branch which was hostile to the Chaks. Ibrāhīm Shāh was in fact the son of Muḥammad Shāh. (T.A., iii, 480). He was the same person who had reigned before from 1528-29. (See p. 121, *supra*). B.S. and H.M. skip over the reign of Ibrāhīm Shāh, and state that Nāzuk Shāh was succeeded by Ismā'īl Shāh.
11. B.S., f. 121b.
12. *Ibid.*, ff. 120a-21b.
13. *Ibid.*, ff. 120b-21a.
14. T.A., iii, 481, and trans. p. 727n. 1.
15. H.M., ff. 151a-b.
16. *Ibid.*, f. 152b; B.S., f. 122a. The date assigned to this event in H.M. (I.O) as 961 A.H. is wrong. H.M.(B.N.), f. 51a, and B.S. give the year 962/1555. T.A. agrees with them.
17. H.M., f. 153b.

18. B.S., f. 122b.
19. *Ibid.*, f. 123a; H.M., ff. 155a-56b.
20. B.S., f. 123a. See also T.A., iii, 485, where the account is given with slight variation.
21. B.S., f. 123a.
22. For Abū'l-Ma'ālī's career see A.N., ii, 154-56; M.T., ii, 2-6; and T.A., ii. 127 sqq.
23. T.A., iii, 486; A.N., ii, 153-4; M.T., ii, p. 10, is wrong in saying that Abū'l-Ma'ālī was treated with honour by Kamāl Khān, and the two set out to conquer Kashmīr. Kamāl Khān was loyal to Akbar and so could not have welcomed Abū'l-Ma'ālī. See A. A. (Blochmann), pp. 507-8; T.A., ii, 161; and *Ma'āṣiru'l-Umarā'*, ii, 144 sq. for Kamāl Khān's relations with Akbar.
24. A.N., ii, pp. 154-5. H.M. wrongly places the invasion of Abū'l-Ma'ālī before the rebellion of the nobles. The date of the invasion assigned by B.S., T.A., and M.T., is 965/1558.
    Patan is a large village in Lat. 34° 10' Long. 74° 36', distant 17 miles north-west of Srīnagar on the high road between Srīnagar and Bārāmūla.
25. Hānjīvera is a large village in Lat. 34° 8' Long. 74° 38', 2 miles east of Patan on the road towards Srīnagar.
26. H.M., ff. 154a-55a. A.N. and T.A. say that Abū'l-Ma'ālī's life was saved by a Mughal.
27. Kashmīrī accounts say that 4,000 were killed on both sides, and 1,700 Mughals were taken prisoners. But these are exaggerated estimates. According to A.N. Abū'l-Ma'ālī had only 300 Mughals with him.
28. H.M., f. 154a.
29. Suka, p. 384 says that Nāzuk Shāh also joined Qarā Bahādur. But he wrongly calls the latter as the son of Humāyūn.
30. T.A., ii, 488; A.., ii, 197. Śuka wrongly places the invasion of Qarā Bahādur before that of Abū'l-Ma'ālī and in the summer of 1561. He also wrongly says that Qarā twice invaded Kashmīr.
31. B.S., ff. 124a-b; A.N., ii, 197-8; T.A., iii, 488.
32. H.M., f. 157a; also Suka, pp. 384–6.
33. T.A., iii, 482–83.
34. B.S., f. 125a; T.A., iii, 483. According to H.M., f. 151b, it was Daulat Chak who had enthroned Ḥabīb Chak. Śuka's account is confused and unreliable.
35. B.S., f. 125a; H.M., f. 153b. See T.A. for dates which, I think, are reliable. According to N.A, f. 76b, one day in the court, 'Alī Khān, Ghāzī's younger brother, removed the crown from Ḥabīb's head

and placed it on Ghāzī's. Ḥabīb Shāh ws imprisoned. From an inscription outside the walls of the Mazār-i-Salāṭīn it appears that he died in 1573.

36. T.A., iii, 488-89.
37. *Ibid.*, 489-90.
38. B.S., ff. 125a-b; H.M., ff. 158a-b.
39. T.A., iii, 490-1.
40. *Ibid.*, iii, 493.
41. Ghāzī Chak was 18 years of age in 1527 when Bābur's troops invaded Kashmīr in 1527. (see p. 120, *supra*). He was thus 58 years of age at the time of his death in 1567.
42. Suka, p. 383; T.H., ii, f. 136b.
43. B.S., f. 124b.
44. A.N., ii, 199.
45. H.M., ff. 157b-58a.
46. N.A., f. 78b.
47. B.S., ff. 125a-26b; T.A. iii, 491-2.
48. H.M., ff. 160b-62a; T.A., iii, 491.
49. *Ibid.*, iii, 492. In the trans. of T.A., iii, p. 742, 'Alī Khān is wrongly referred to as 'Ālam Khān.
50. A lake lying on the left bank of the Jehlam, about 5 miles south-east of Srīnagar.
51. From B.S., f. 126b it appears that Khān-i-Zamān was the Wazīr.
52. *Ibid.*, ff. 126a-b; T.A., iii, 492. H.M. says Khān-i-Zamān was only reprimanded.
53. B.S., f. 126b.
54. T.A., iii, 493-4.
55. B.S., ff. 127a-b; T.A., iii, 494.
56. B.S., f. 127b.
57. T.A., iii, 494.
58. *Ibid.*; B.S., f. 128a.
59. B.S., ff. 128a-29b. T.A. says Zainu'd-Dīn was a Shī'ite.
60. B.S, f. 130a; M.T., ii, 128. T.A., iii, 494 is wrong in stating that Ya'qūb had been sent by Akbar. Ya'qūb was the son of Bābā 'Alī, a Shī'ite divine of Kashmīr.
61. B.S., f. 130; M.T., ii, 128, see also Briggs, *Rise of Muhammadan Power in India*, iv, 519. T.A. and Firishta mention only of Mīrzā Muqīm's execution, but it is not improbable that Akbar in a fit of anger may have also put to death the envoy of Ḥusain Shāh.
62. B.S., ff. 131a-32b.
63. *Ibid.*, f. 125b; H.M., f. 158b; Śuka, pp. 391-2.
64. H.M., f. 159b.

65. W.K., ff. 52a, 60a. N.A., ff. 81a sq. unjustly accuses him of intolerance towards the Hindus.
66. Śuka, p. 393.
67. W.K., f. 52b.
68. H.M., f. 159b.
69. B.S., f. 128a; H.M., f. 165a.
70. H.M., f. 165a.
71. B.S., ff. 133b-34a; Śuka, p. 393. According to B.S. it was Sayyid Mubārak who advised Ḥusain Shāh not to blind his brother.
72. Śuka, p. 393, says Husain Shāh died of epilepsy, but this is not supported by other authorities. The Sulṭān was consumptive, and probably died of fever.
73. B.S., f. 133a.
74. Ḥusain Qulī Khān was Bairam Khān's sister's son. He was treated with great favour by and held high offices under Akbar. He was governor of the Punjāb from 1569 to 1576. See for more details of his life, Ma'āṣiru'l-Umarā', i, pp. 645 sqq.
75. *Ibid.*, f. 134a; also T.A., iii, 498.
76. B.S., f. 135a; T.A., iii, 499, wrongly calls Aiba Khān as Ibrāhīm Khān.
77. B.S., ff. 136a-b.
78. H.M., f. 165b. According to T.A., iii, 499, Ḥaidar Khān was the son of Muḥammad Shāh while Salīm Khān was his cousin.
79. H.M., ff. 165b-66b; also T.A., iii, 499-500.
80. It is a small village in Lat. 33° 28' Long. 75° 37', situated above the left bank of the Kasher Khol stream on the Kishtwār side of the Marbal Pass.
81. H.M., f. 167a. According to T.A., iii, 498, she was Bahādur Singh's daughter.
82. H.M., ff. 167a-b; J.P.H.S., iv, 37.
83. A.N., iii, 356; Elliot, v, 411; Badā'ūnī, ii, 276. The date 980/1572-3 as given by Firishta and T.A. is incorrect.
84. W.K., f. 53a; T.A., iii, 498-99. T.A. is wrong in stating that the lady sent was 'Alī Shāh's nephew's daughter.
85. H.M., ff. 167b-68a.
86. B.S., f. 137a.
87. N.A., ff. 87a-88a; A.A. (Blochmann), p. 651 and n.2.
88. H.M., ff. 168b-69a; B.S., ff. 137b-38a.

Chapter 9

Yūsuf Shāh and Akbar

On 'Alī Shāh's death his brother Abdāl Chak decided to contest the throne. Sayyid Mubārak, however, tried to avert hostilities, and, with the consent of Yūsuf Shāh, sent Bābā Khalīl, a Shī'ite divine, to Abdāl, requesting him to give up all thoughts of war and to come and participate in the burial ceremonies of 'Alī Shāh. But as Abdāl did not trust Yūsuf on account of his part in the assassination of Aiba Khān, he refused to go. Thereupon, Sayyid Mubārak himself went to Abdāl accompanied by Muḥammad Baṭ and Bābā Khalīl. On behalf of Yūsuf and on their own behalf they gave a pledge to Abdāl guaranteeing his personal safety if he attended the funeral ceremonies. They also pleaded with him to give up the idea of contesting the throne, for Yūsuf had a better claim to it than anyone else.[1] But their requests fell on deaf ears. Having thus failed in their mission, they returned and advised Yūsuf to immediately attack Abdāl. Yūsuf, accordingly, organised an army with the advance-guard under Muḥammad Khān, the centre under Sayyid Mubārak, and the rear under himself. Hearing of this Abdāl moved out to Nauhattā, and there encountered Muḥammad Khān. Although he was wounded by a bullet he kept on fighting. Meanwhile, Mubārak came up to the help of Muḥammad Khān with over 2,000 horse. After a heavy engagement Abdāl was killed by Sayyid Mubārak.[2] This demoralised his followers. Shams Chak and Ḥabīb Chak escaped.[3] Sayyid Jalāl, son of Sayyid Mubārak, lost his life while pursuing them. Yūsuf Shāh, who was in the rear with a small force, came up to the battle-field after the fighting was over and forbade the burial of Abdāl's body. But Qāẓī Mūsā, the Qāẓī of Sōpūr, defied the order, and buried it in the ancestral graveyard the same day. The next day Yūsuf Shāh, after performing the last rites in connection with his father's death, proclaimed himself Sulṭān.[4]

Yūsuf Shāh had been in power only for two months[5] when he was faced with a serious revolt which brought about his abdication. The leader of the uprising was Abdāl Baṭ who had become alienated because instead of him Muḥammad Baṭ had been made Wazīr.[6] He won over the nobles who were dissatisfied with Yūsuf Shāh for spending his time in the society of women and singers and neglecting the administration of the country.[7] He then decided to depose Yūsuf and enthrone Mubārak in his place. The latter at first refused to take up arms against Yūsuf, and tried to reconcile the two groups through the good offices of Bābā Khalīl. But having failed in the attempt, owing to the intransigence of Yūsuf, who refused to forgive his opponents, Mubārak agreed to join the rebels.[8] At this time Nājī Malik advised Yūsuf to open his treasury, and distribute it among the people who would rally to is support. But Yūsuf did not follow the advice.[9] Nāji also suggested to Yūsuf that he should himself march against the rebels instead of entrusting the command to Muḥammad Khān who was young and inexperienced. Despite this Yūsuf sent a force under Muḥammad Khān to the 'Īd-gāh where the rebels had assembled, while he himself proceeded to the field of Ziāldakar.[10] Muḥammad Khān crossed the bridge of Naukadal and attacked the enemy. But after hard fighting in which both sides lost 300 men, he was killed. This spread panic among his followers who fled. Some escaped and joined Yūsuf in the field of Ziāldakar, while others went over to the enemy.[11] According to the *Bahāristān-i-Shāhī* Yūsuf Shāh's position was so precarious at this time that, if Mubārak had attacked him as advised by some of his supporters, he would have easily seized him. But Mubārak refrained from this step. In fact, when Yūsuf sent him Mullā Ḥasan Aswad, 'Alī Shāh's tutor, to ask forgiveness for his previous mistakes, he forgave him and advised him to leave Kashmīr, assuring him that he would be recalled after a few months.[12] Yūsuf Shāh, therefore, went away to Thanna.[13] But this account is very partial to Mubārak, for, as his subsequent attitude towards Yūsuf Shāh shows, he could not have played the magnanimous role assigned to him by the author of the *Bahāristān-i-Shāhī*. In reality Yūsuf left for Thanna because his forces had been defeated and he found further resistance to be useless.

Mubārak, who now replaced Yūsuf Shāh as Sulṭān, led a very simple life, being averse to all pomp an show. He sold off the crown and the royal parasol (*chatr*), which were studded with precious stones, and distributed the money among the poor and the soldiers.[14] He was just and generous, and though a good soldier, he was a man of peace, and only in the last resort unsheathed his sword. He detested the shedding of blood, and, as we have seen, always advised 'Alī Shāh and Yūsuf Shāh to forgive the malcontents.

The nobles had set up Mubārak in order to rule in his name. But when they found that he would not allow himself to be dominated by others, they turned against him and invited Yūsuf Shāh to return to Kashmīr.[15] Assured of their support, Yūsuf left Thanna, but when he reached the village of Barbal, he received proposals of peace from Mubārak through Dā'ūd Mīr. He, therefore, sent his sons, Ya'qūb and Ibrāhīm, to Mubārak, accompanied by Dā'ūd Mīr and Mullā Ḥasan Aswad, and then he himself got ready to meet him. Meanwhile, Abdāl Baṭ, the leader of the faction against Mubārak, became alarmed at these developments and sent Yūsuf a message, warning him against trusting Mubārak's words or meeting him. Yūsuf believed Abdāl and broke off the talks.[16] However, when he was attacked by Mubārak, the Chak nobles, despīte their promises, did not come forward to help him. The result was that he was defeated, and had to return to Thanna *via* Barbal.[17]

Abdāl had foiled the peace negotiations between Yūsuf and Mubārak, but as the latter was still in power, he made another plan to bring about his overthrow. On the one hand he had 'Alī Khān, son of Naurūz Chak, treacherously seized and imprisoned by telling Mubārak that it was he who had invited Yūsuf Shāh to invade the Valley and had thus been responsible for causing so much chaos. On the other hand he told the Chak nobles that it was by Mubārak's order that 'Alī Chak had been imprisoned, and warned them that their lives too were in danger. In this way Abdāl Baṭ tried to incite the rival parties against each other.[18] Deceived by his machinations, the Chak nobles again invited Yūsuf to return, and meanwhile they prepared for a revolt. Hearing of this Mubārak, although ill, marched to the 'Īd-gāh and sent a challenge to Abdāl for a personal combat. Abdāl knew that he was no match for Mubārak in personal valour and so he decided upon a ruse. He sent Bābā Khalīl to him with a message that the Chak nobles were anxious for peace, but were driven into hostility because of 'Alī Chak's imprisonment, and suggested negotiations in the hospice of Bābā Khalīl. Mubārak was beguiled by these words, and, having released 'Alī Chak, proceeded to the hospice.[19] There the Chak nobles, who had gathered in large numbers on the occasion,[20] compelled him to abdicate, and in his place set up Lohar Chak, son of Shankar Chak, on the throne, with Abdāl Baṭ as Wazīr. The latter in order to consolidate his position at once threw 'Alī Chak and his son Yūsuf into prison, and sent word to Yūsuf Shāh not to come to Srīnagar.[21] Yūsuf Shāh was disgusted with the insincerity of the Kashmīrī nobles, and so decided to invoke the aid of the Emperor Akbar. He proceeded to Lahore to Rājā Mān Singh and Mīrzā Yūsuf Khān, who took him to Agra, and there in January 1580 he was presented to the Emperor.[22]

Akbar received Yūsuf Shāh cordially, and deputed Rājā Mān Singh and Mīrzā Yūsuf Khān Shāh to help him in the recovery of his throne.[23] Accordingly, in the month of August, 1580, Yūsuf Shāh proceeded to Lahore with them. When Muḥammad Baṭ, his former Wazīr, got this news he left his force of one thousand men at Buhlūlpūr and joined him at Lahore. There it was decided not to employ the Mughal troops who would be unpopular in the country, and who, after its conquest, would take over the administration and enforce their own laws.[24] Yūsuf Shāh, therefore, borrowed some money from the merchants of Lahore and with about 800 men, whom he enlisted there, he marched towards Buhlūlpūr under the pretext that he was going to find out the conditions existing in Kashmīr.[25] At Buhlūlpūr he managed to raise another body of 3,000 men with the help of some Kashmīrī nobles, and then set out to Bhimbhar. After defeating Yūsuf Dār,[26] who was posted at Naushahrā by Lohar Chak, Yūsuf Shāh advanced on Rajaurī. Its ruler, Rāi Bahādur, seeing how Yūsuf Shāh Dār had fled, submitted to him. He was received with honour and made commander of the vanguard of the army.[27] Yūsuf Shāh then moved to Thanna. Lohar Chak now sent Yūsuf Khān, the son of Ḥusain Shāh Chak, and Nāzuk Baṭ, the son of Abdāl Baṭ, against Yūsuf Shāh. On reaching the village of Sidau,[28] Yūsuf Khān, having seized Nāzuk Baṭ, handed him over to Yūsuf Shāh, and himself entered his service.[29] Owing to the defection of Yūsuf Khān, Lohar Chak's army became demoralized and began to disintegrate. Shams Dūnī, Malik Ḥasan and many other chiefs fled and joined Yūsuf Shāh at Thanna.[30]

Lohar had stationed Ḥaidar Chak at Hirapūr with a large force, thinking that Yūsuf Shāh would follow the Pīr Panjāl route. But Yūsuf Shāh left behind a small force to conceal his movement, and with the rest of his army moved towards Pūnch and entered Kashmīr through the Tōshamaidān Pass.[31] He defeated Lohar's forces at Chīra Hār and again at Sōpūr. He then crossed the Jehlam, and after destroying the Sōpūr bridge, occupied the surrounding country.[32] When Lohar heard the news of the defeats of his armies and the desertion of his officers, he became extremely anxious. He, therefore, on Abdāl's advice, released 'Alī Chak from prison in order to secure his help in the war against Yūsuf Shāh.[33] He then recalled Ḥaidar Chak from Hirapūr to Srīnagar, and having collected his forces from all sides, set out with a large army towards Sōpūr.[34] But finding that the Sōpūr Bridge had been destroyed, he tried to cross the river by means of boats. However, owing to the resistance of the enemy from the other bank he was not successful. He therefore, detached a force of 2,000 men under Ḥaidar Chak by the route of Khuyahōm to attack Yūsuf Shāh from the rear, while he himself stayed behind to watch the movements of the enemy.[35] Meanwhile, he sent a message to Yūsuf Shāh through Bābā Khalīl that, since he would soon be attacked both from the front and from the rear and defeated, he should leave

Kashmīr in return for which he would be given the jāgīr of Dachün-Khovūr.[36] Yūsuf Shāh for a moment became nervous because of the numerical inferiority of his forces, but encouraged by Ḥasan Malik, who assured him of victory, he rejected Lohar's overtures.[37] And in the early morning of November 8, 1580,[38] he crossed the Jehlam in order to make a surprise attack on the enemy. A force of over 2,000 men under 'Alī Baṭ tried to prevent the crossing, but was beaten back.[39] Yūsuf Shāh's army then proceeded to attack Abdāl Baṭ. As the flower of Lohar Chak's force had been sent away under Ḥaidar Chak, Abdāl was at a disadvantage.[40] After a severe fight he was defeated and killed. Lohar retreated and made a final stand at the village of Brathana.[41] But having again suffered a reverse, he fled to Srīnagar. Yūsuf Shāh at once marched on the capital, which he entered without any opposition.[42] Hearing of Lohar's defeat, the forces under Ḥaidar Chak became demoralized, and dispersed. Ḥaider Chak himself escaped by way of Chīra Hār.[43]

On occupying Srīnagar Yūsuf Shāh entrusted Muḥammad Baṭ with the duties of prime minister, and ordered a search to be made for Lohar Chak and his followers. Lohar was discovered concealed in the house of Qāẓī Mūsā, Qāẓī of Sōpūr; Lohar's brother, Muḥammad, was seized in Bārāmūla, and Ḥasan Chak was captured in Mamosa[44] in the pargana of Bāngil. Besides these many other chiefs were also seized, and they were brought before Yūsuf Shāh.[45] He accused them of having joined Lohar Chak in spite of the fact that both he and his father had treated them kindly and bestowed favours on them. He pointed out that several times they had called him to Kashmīr, yet on each occasion they had betrayed him. Under the circumstance pardon was out of the question. Lohar Shāh, his brother, Muḥammad Khān, and Ḥasan Chak were blinded.[46] Some had their limbs amputated, while others were executed. 'Alī Khān Chak and his son Yūsuf Khān were, however, imprisoned. But a general amnesty was given to the common soldiers and villagers who had joined Lohar Chak.[47]

Ḥaidar Chak and Shams Chak Kopwārā[48] had fled to Karnāv after Lohar Chak's defeat. Ḥaidar Chak had pointed out to Shams Chak that it would be dangerous for them to stay there long, as Yūsuf Shāh would soon send a strong army which they would not be able to resist. But Shams Chak did not accept this advice and stayed on. Ḥaidar, however, separated from him and proceeded to Ladākh.[49]

As Ḥaidar had foreseen, Yūsuf Shāh ordered Lohar Malik Qorchī to march against Shams Chak. Learning of this, Shams left Karnāv[50] and occupied the fort of Fīrūz near Pakhlī.[51] But as he had antagonised the garrison by his cruelties, the commandant sent a message to Lohar to come immediately and seize Shams. Lohar made a rapid march, and arrived before the fort. Shams Chak was surrendered and taken to Yūsuf Shāh, who had him blinded.[52]

Early in 1581, Shams Chak, son of Daulat Chak, 'Ālam Shēr Māgre, and other nobles began to make plans for the overthrow of Yūsuf Shāh. Informed of this, the latter threw the conspirators in prison. Alarmed at these developments, Ḥabīb Khān fled to the hills and was joined by Ḥaidar Chak. Yūsuf Khān, who was in prison, succeeded in escaping and joining the rebels.[53] They then approached the ruler of Ladākh named Jamyang Namgyal (1560-90),[54] and secured from him the aid of about 4,000 horse. When Yūsuf Shāh heard of this he sent an army against them. As there was no unity among the rebel chiefs, they failed to put up any resistance. They were seized with panic and dispersed. The Ladākhī forces also withdrew. Ḥaidar Chak went away to Kishtwār, while Ḥabīb Chak, finding his way blocked on all sides by the royal forces, secretly returned to Srīnagar, and began to foment trouble there.[55] But he was seized in the village of Sonawar.[56] Yūsuf Khān was captured with his brothers in the Bring pargana. Yūsuf Shāh ordered Ḥabīb Chak to be blinded, while Yūsuf Khān and his brothers had their limbs cut off.[57]

Soon after these events, Yūsuf Shāh had to deal with the revolt led by his chief minister, Muḥammad Baṭ. The latter wanted to punish Shams Dūnī because of some personal grudge; but since Yūsuf Shāh opposed him, he decided to assassinate him with the help of Yūsuf Khān. But as the plot was discovered, Muḥammad Baṭ fled. He was pursued by Yūsuf Shāh who seized him and some of his followers. But the rest escaped to swell the forces of Ḥaidar Chak in Kishtwār.[58]

Meanwhile Prince Ya'qūb, who was only a youth, came under the influence of the malcontents and escaped with Aiba Khān, son of Abdāl Baṭ, to Kishtwār. He was, however, brought back by Mullā Ḥasan Aswad deputed for the purpose by Yūsuf Shāh. But Aiba Khān remained with Ḥaidar Chak.[59] Another important person to join Ḥaidar Chak at this time was Shams Chak who had escaped from prison while Yūsuf Shāh was away in Lār.[60]

These defections greatly alarmed Yūsuf Shāh, and so in 1582 he despatched Shēr 'Alī Baṭ and Nājī Malik with a large force against Ḥaidar Chak in Kishtwār. But Shēr 'Alī was killed and Nājī Malik captured in a night attack by Ḥaidar Chak.[61] Thereupon, Yūsuf Shāh himself advanced with his son Ya'qūb, who was entrusted with the command of the advanceguard, to crush the rebels. As the latter were in a defile occupying a strategic position, Ya'qūb's forces, which encountered them, suffered reverse and fled to join the main army. However Ya'qūb rallied them and, after a severe engagement, defeated Ḥaidar Chak who fled together with Shams Chak and Aiba Khān. Yūsuf came up to the battle-field after the victory had been won. He rewarded Ibrāhīm and Abū'l-Ma'ālī, the sons of Sayyid Mubārak, with *khil'ats* and jāgīrs for the courage they had displayed in the battle.[62]

This defeat convinced Shams Chak and Aiba Khān of the futility of resistance, and so they opened negotiations with Yūsuf Shāh who, on the mediation of the Rājā of Kishtwār, pardoned them and gave them jāgīrs.[63] Ḥaidar Chak, however, refused to surrender, and leaving Kishtwār, proceeded to Lahore, where he received the protection of Rājā Man Singh, and was assigned the jāgīrs of Bhimbhar and Naushahrā.[64] When Yūsuf Shāh learnt of this he sent Khwāja Qāsim, the grandson of Khwāja Ḥājī, to counteract the intrigues of Ḥaidar Chak. But Khwāja Qāsim returned unsuccessful to Srīnagar. Rājā Mān Singh, being angry with Yūsuf Shāh for not having employed the Mughal troops in the recovery of his throne, wanted to use Ḥaidar Chak as a pawn to promote the imperial interests in Kashmīr.[65]

Towards the end of 1581, Akbar, on his return from Kābul,

sent from Jalālābād Mīrzā Ṭāhir and Ṣāliḥ 'Āqil as ambassadors to Kashmīr. They were received by Yūsuf Shāh at Bārāmūla with every mark of respect, and then brought to Srīnagar.[66] They delivered to him an imperial command that he had not kept the Mughal court informed of the conditions in Kashmīr, and that if there was no internal trouble he should immediately proceed to do personal homage to the Emperor.[67] When Yūsuf Shāh discussed this order with his ministers, they advised him that, since Akbar appeared to be anxious to annex Kashmīr, he should prepare for resistance, give up the life of ease and luxury which he was leading, and strengthen the frontier forts.[68] But Yūsuf Shāh paid no heed to these words, and instead tried to placate the Emperor by sending him costly presents and his third son Ḥaidar Khān with Mīrzā Ṭāhir and Ṣāliḥ 'Āqil, who shortly after left Srīnagar.[69] But these professions of loyalty failed to satisfy Akbar, who insisted that Yūsuf Shāh should himself come to court. After a year, therefore, he sent back Prince Ḥaidar with Shaikh Ya'qūb Ṣarfī with a *farmān* that Yūsuf Shāh should at once proceed to Fatḥpūr Sīkrī, otherwise an army would be sent against him.[70] Shortly after Tīmūr Bēg was despatched by Rājā Mān Singh as Mughal ambassador to Kashmīr, carrying the same order. Yūsuf Shāh got frightened by these repeated summons, and so, when Tīmūr Bēg took leave of departure from Srīnagar, he sent with him his eldest son Prince Ya'qūb and the choicest articles of Kashmīr to Akbar.[71] Ya'qūb arrived in Fatḥpūr Sīkrī and was presented to the Emperor on February 9, 1585.[72] But instead of expressing his approval, Akbar was displeased and complained that, although he had twice ordered Yūsuf Shāh to appear at court, he had not come. Yūsuf Shāh had at first sent his third son Ḥaidar, a mere boy, who was unfit for military service, and had then deputed Ya'qūb, who was both mad and wicked. He had been spending his time in ease and luxury ever since he had recovered his throne, and had not given any proofs of his loyalty to the Emperor.[73]

Akbar had always regarded Kashmīr as part of the Mughal Empire. This was probably because it had been conquered by Mīrzā Ḥaidar Dughlat on behalf of Humāyūn. Although Mīrzā Ḥaidar had been overthrown, the Mughal title to the Valley had not been allowed to lapse. In 1560, as we have seen, Akbar sent Qarā Bahādur against Ghāzī Chak in order to "uproot that tyrant" whose injustices had been brought to the notice of the Emperor.[74] But Qarā Bahādur's invasion of the Valley ended in a fiasco. Despite this, the Chak Sulṭāns continued to send occasionally to the Emperor rich gifts, which were looked upon by him as tribute and recognition of his suzerainty.[75] Moreover, in 1580, Yūsuf Shāh, who had been driven out of his kingdom, was given assistane by Akbar to recover his throne; and although the help was not employed, and Yūsuf Shāh regained his kingdom by his own efforts, yet the very fact that a Mughal force had been placed at his disposal was a sufficient justification for the Emperor to regard him as his vassal. But such a view was not held by Yūsuf Shāh, and that is why he had repeatedly evaded Akbar's summons to court. However, in order not to antagonise the Emperor, he had sent him valuable presents and his sons to represent him at the imperial court. Akbar resented his attitude, and would have liked to send an army for the conquest of the Valley, but his hands were too full with the affairs of Hindustān. It was not until about 1585 that he found himself sufficiently free to adopt a more active policy towards Kashmīr. He knew that there was disunity in the country which he could exploit to his own advantage. Moreover, Mīrzā Ḥaidar had shown that, although the Valley was surrounded by huge mountain barriers, its conquest was not difficult.

On August 22, 1585, Akbar left Fatḥpūr Sīkrī in order to effect the settlement of the province of Kabul, as his half-brother Mīrzā Muḥammad Ḥakīm had died and there was a danger of an Uzbeg invasion.[76] When he reached Kalānaur on the 1st October, he deputed Ḥakīm 'Alī Gīlānī and Baha'u'd-Dīn Kambū to proceed to Srīnagar and bring Yūsuf Shāh with them. They were to tell the Kashmīr Sulṭān that he had until now made distance a pretext for not coming to court; but now that the Emperor was in the Punjāb, he should at once come to pay his homage.[77]

Yūsuf Shāh had been receiving reports from his son Ya'qūb, who was at the Mughal court,[78] about the Emperor's plans with regard to Kashmīr. They had caused him considerable anxiety.

But when he came to know that Akbar had despatched two envoys, he completely lost his nerves and consulted his counsellors. They begged him, as before, to pay more attention to public affairs, to organise his army, and be ready to defend his country against a Mughal invasion.[79] But Yūsuf Shāh was opposed to resisting the Mughals. He argued that Akbar's army was too numerous and strong to be fought successfully, and that it could overrun the whole of the Valley in a few days' time. Moreover, Prince Ya'qūb was with Akbar who, if displeased, might order his execution. Under these circumstances it would be beter if he should himself proceed to Lahore, and by submitting to the Emperor save his country from an invasion.[80] But the nobles and high officials warned him against following such a course, pointing out that, if he left Kashmīr, he would never again get back his throne. At this time there was a general upsurge in the country, and everyone, rich and poor, old and young, was ready to fight against the invaders to the last man, and they appealed to Yūsuf Shāh to remain in Kashmīr.[81]But their appeals fell on deaf ears, for Yūsuf Shāh had lost the will to resist and had made up his mind to wait on Akbar.

While these discussions were in progress, Ya'qūb suddenly appeared in Srīnagar. On account of the disrespect shown to him by Akbar,[82] and the petty allowance of thirty or forty rupees which he had received for his expenses,[83] he had been very unhappy at the Mughal court. Moreover, having despaired of Yūsuf Shāh's appearance at court, he had become alarmed for his own safety. He had, therefore, when the imperial camp had reached Khawāṣpūr, secretly escaped from the custody of his guards.[84] He had proceeded towards Naushahrā, but finding that it was in the hands of Ḥaidar Chak, he had skirted the town on his right, and taken another route to Rajaurī. He had then entered Kashmīr and had reached Srīnagar before Ḥakīm 'Alī, Yūsuf Shāh was very angry with Ya'qūb for having come away without the Emperor's permission and wanted to imprison him, but was dissuaded by his ministers.[85]

Shortly after Yūsuf Shāh heard of the arrival of the Mughal envoys in Kashmīr. He went to receive them at Khāmpūr, and gave them a warm welcome.[86] He promised to accompany them, and send back Ya'qūb to the imperial court with his hands and feet bound.[87] However, owing to the opposition from the public, the nobles, and the army his plans were checkmated.[88] In fact, he was even threatened that if he attempted to leave Kashmīr, they would kill him and set up Ya'qūb in his place.[89]

Ḥakīm 'Alī and Baha'u'd-Dīn remained for two months in Srīnagar, but did not succeed in their mission owing to the hostile attitude of the Kashmīrī people who would not let Yūsuf Shāh go with them. They, therefore, took their leave, and joined the imperial camp at Ḥasan Abdāl on December 13, 1585.[90]

When Akbar heard of their report his anger was aroused, and on December 20, 1585, from the neighbourhood of Attock, he despatched an army of about 5,000 horse under Mīrzā Shāh Rukh, Rājā Bhagwān Dās, and Shāh Qulī Maḥram to invade Kashmīr, and deputed Ḥaidar Chak and Shaikh Ya'qūb Ṣarfi to act as guides.[91] The Mughal commanders wanted to undertake the invasion early in spring when the passes would be clear of snow. Moreover, they preferred the Bhimbhar route partly because it was easier, and partly because the chiefs along that route were favourably disposed towards the Mughals. Akbar was, however, opposed to any delay and ordered them to immediately march *via* Pakhlī, pointing out that since the Kashmīrīs did not expect any invasion from that direction at that time of the year, the passes would not be well-guarded. The Emperor's forecast proved to be correct, for, when the Mughal force advanced, it practically met with no resistance and easily entered Kashmīr.[92]

When this news reached Srīnagar, the people came to Yūsuf Shāh and reminded him of the sufferings which the Kashmīrīs and endured at the hands of the Kāshgharians, and how his ancestors had delivered the country from their oppression. He should also, they urged, prepare to resist the enemy in the narrow defiles and passes. Yūsuf Shāh ostensibly agreed with them, but in reality he had become convinced of the futility of resistance, and had resolved to surrender himself to the Mughals.[93]

However, in order to conceal his plan, he made

arrangements for the defence of the kingdom. He released Muḥammad Baṭ and 'Ālam Shēr Māgre from prison and proceeded with the latter to Bārāmūla, leaving the former in charge of the capital.[94] At Bārāmūla he organised three armies. The advance-guard was placed under Ḥasan Malik and 'Ālam Shēr Khān; the right was commanded by Ya'qūb and Abūl-Ma'ālī; and the left was under Bābā Ṭālib Isfahānī[95] and Ḥasan Baṭ, the brother of Muḥammad Baṭ. After making these appointments Yūsuf Shāh proceeded to Kōh Kuārmast.[96]

When the Mughals arrived at the pass of Būliāsa,[97] the Kashmīrīs moved forward to check their advance. The Mughal forces, partly owing to the stiff resistance which was offered to them, and partly because of snow, rain, and scarcity of supplies, failed to make any progress.[98] Rājā Bhagwān Dās therefore sent two of his agents with a letter to Yūsuf Shāh.[99] But they were seized by the Kashmīrī soldiers who wanted to kill them, but they were rescued by the army chiefs, who pointed out that according to the common usage the life of an envoy was sacred. The letter stated that although the Mughals had been defeated at present owing to snow and rain, yet another army would soon arrive, and then it would be impossible for the Kashmīrī forces to continue resistance. Yūsuf Shāh should, therefore, proceed with the Rājā to the Emperor's presence.[100] Yūsuf Shāh held talks with the envoys the whole night, and finally entered into an understanding with them.[101] Early next morning, under the pretext that he was going to inspect the troops, he left the Kuārmast Pass, and went to the village of Barzala.[102] After cheering up the inhabitans and the soldiers there, he proceeded to Būliāsa where he inspected the army, and was told by the Mīr Bakhshī that it consisted of 15,000 horse, 25,000 foot and 7,000 musketeers. He then with a few horsemen escaped to the Mughal camp, which he joined on February 14, 1586.[103]

Although the Kashmīrīs had been betrayed by their ruler, their spirit was not broken. In place of Yūsuf Shāh they set up Ya'qūb as their Sulṭān and resumed the struggle against the invaders.[104] The Mughals suffered great hardships on account of snow, cold, rain, and scarcity of food. Taking advantage of this Bābā Ṭālib Isfahānī, Muḥammad Salim Kāshgharī, and other Kashmīrī commanders inflicted great loss upon them. Realising the terrible state of his army and also affected by the news of Zain Khān's defeat in the North-Western Frontier, Rājā Bhagwān Dās made peace overtures to Ya'qūb by sending Mīrzā Akbar Shāhī to him.[105] Ya'qūb agreed to cease hostilities, but the final treaty was concluded by the Rājā with Yūsuf Shāh.[106] It was agreed that Yūsuf Shāh would retain his throne,[107] but that the coins would be struck and the *khuṭba* recited in the name of the Emperor;[108] that the mint, saffron cultivation, shawl manufacture, and game laws would be placed under the control of three imperial officers, Khwāja Mīrakī, Qalandar Bēg, and Mullā Maẕharī;[109] that the daughter of Mubārak Khān Gakkhar would be given in marriage to Prince Ya'qūb;[110] and lastly, that Yūsuf Shāh would be responsible for bringing Prince Ya'qūb to the presence of the Emperor.[111] Akbar did not approve of the treaty, but realising the conditions under which it had been concluded, he accepted it.[112]

After the conclusion of peace the Mughal army withdrew from Kashmīr, and on March 28, 1586, at Attock, Yūsuf Shāh was presented to Akbar by Rājā Bhagwān Dās.[113] He was received with respect, but was imprisoned, and given in charge of Rām Dās Kachwāhā.[114] This was a clear violation of the treaty according to which Yūsuf Shāh, after paying homage to the Emperor, was entitled to return to his country. Bhagwān Dās was so much affected by this breach that he attempted suicide to vindicate his honour as a Rājpūt.[115] When Akbar reached Lahore, Yūsuf Shāh was placed in charge of Rājā Todar Mal, and for two and a half years he remained in his custody. But when Rājā Mān Singh returned from Kābul, the Emperor at his request released Yūsuf Shāh.[116] He conferred on him a *manṣab* of 500 horse, a rank carrying a salary ranging from 2,100 to 2,500 rupees a month, and sent him with Rājā Mān Singh to Bīhār.[117]

Of handsome appearance, an expert in the science of music, fond of Persian and Kashmīrī poetry, patron of poets, scholars and musicians, and himself a poet, Yūsuf Shāh was one of the most cultured rulers of the Sultanate period. Though not possessed of any personal valour, he displayed, when he first ascended the throne, promptness and energy in suppressing the revolt of his uncle Abdāl Chak. On being driven out of Kashmīr, he again displayed enterprise, initiative, and resource in his attempts to recover the throne. After regaining the kingdom he tried to promote the welfare of his people. He prohibited the soldiers from taking corvée from the peasants, and, unlike his predecessors, he gave up the practice of exacting corvée and *Ẕakāt* from the *hānjīs*. He also abolished *Jizya* and taxes of an oppressive nature imposed on gardens, cattle, and artisans.[118] But despite all this he brought about his downfall through his own follies. Finding himself secure on the throne, he began to neglect the administration, spending more and more of his time over the wine cups and in the company of women and musicians. Moreover, he became so obsessed with the threat of a Mughal invasion that no amount of assurances of loyalty from his people could dispel the fear from his mind. But instead of adopting measures for the defence of the country, he was convinced that resistance was futile, and that only by a policy of submission could he save his kingdom. This was, however, a mistake, for he should have realised that Akbar was longing to annex Kashmīr, and that once he was in his power he would lose both his freedom and his throne.

In exile, the lot of Yūsuf Shāh was very tragic. The allowance which he received from the Emperor, though enough to support a life of comfort, was not sufficient to maintain his dignity; and, being of a generous nature and accustomed to luxury, he found himself always short of money. Moreover, in the scorching heat of the plains of Bihār, he longed for the cool and bracing climate and the picturesque sceneries of the Valley. In exile he missed the society of poets, scholars and musicians, but, above all, he pined for his beloved queen, Habba Khātūn. She was the daughter of a peasant of the village of Chandahār in the Vihī pargana. She had been unhappy with her first husband who was a drunkard and a debauchee and who ill-treated her. A poetess and a musician, possessed of a sweet voice, she captivated the heart of Yūsuf Shāh who fell in love with her and married her.[119] He built for her mountain resorts in Gulmarg, Sonamarg and other beautiful spots, which he was wont to visit with her.[120] But now as a royal prisoner he knew he would never see her again. All this so much affected him that his mind gave way and he died on Wednesday, the 14th Ẕū'l-Ḥijja, 1000/22nd September, 1592, after an illness of six days, and was buried in the pargana of Biswak.[121]

NOTE

1. B.S., ff. 138a-b; also H.M., ff. 169b-70b.
2. H.M., f. 171a; A.A. (Blochmann), p. 535. A.N., iii, 408, says that he was killed by a bullet. But according to B.S., ff. 140b-41a Abdāl was hit by an arrow from Sayyid Abū'l-Ma'ālī, and was finally killed by Sayyid Ḥusain Khān. But B.S. is inclined to exaggerate the exploits of the Baihaqī Sayyids.
3. Shams Chak was the son of Daulat Chak and Ḥabīb Chak was the son of Abdāl Chak.
4. B.S., ff. 139a-42b; H.M., ff. 170a-71b.
5. B.S., f. 142b. Firishta and T.A. also say that Yūsuf remained in power for two months. But H.M., f. 171b gives the period of one month and two days.
6. B.S., f. 142b.
7. H.M., f. 172a.
8. *Ibid.*, B.S., ff. 143b-44a.
9. H.M. says that Yūsuf Shāh ignored the advice because he was a miser. But no other authority holds the view that Yūsuf possessed a miserly disposition. Ḥaidar Malik is inclined to run down Yūsuf in order to exalt his grandfather, Nājī Malik.
10. HM., ff. 172b-73a; see also B.S., f. 144a. But B.S., unlike H.M., completely ignores the part played by Nāji Malik in these events.
11. H.M., ff. 173a-74a; B.Ṣ, ff. 145a-b.
12. B.S., ff. 146a-47a.
13. H.M., f. 174a; A.N., iii, 409.
14. B.S., f. 148b.
15. Ḥ.M., f. 174b.
16. B.S., ff. 149-50a.
17. *Ibid.*, f. 150b. According to H.M., f. 174b, Yūsuf Chak retired without giving a fight.
18. B.S., ff. 151a-b.
19. *Ibid.*, ff. 152a sqq.
20. H.M., f. 175a.
21. B.S., ff. 155b-56a.

22. H.M., f. 175b; A.N., iii, 409. According to B.S., f. 157a, Akbar presented Yūsuf Shāh two ladies.
23. B.S., f. 157a; T.A., iii, 503. According to H.M. (B.N.), f. 57b and N.A., f. 92b Yūsuf was refused help. But this is wrong.
24. B.S., f. 157b. According to A.A. (Blochmann), p. 535, the Mughal army accompanied Yūsuf as far as Pinjar; according to T.A., iii, 503 it went up to Siālkōt.
25. H.M., f. 176a.
26. H.M. (L.O.), N.A., and N.K. call him Yūsuf Dār, but H.M., (B.N.) calls him Muḥammad Yūsuf, while B.S. calls him Yūsuf Khān. His father was 'Alī Khān, who was the son of Naurūz Chak.
27. H.M., f. 176a; See also H.M. (B.N.), f. 58a, where additional information is given.
28. It is a village in Lat. 33° 40' Long. 74° 50', situated at the foot of the ascent to the Būdil or Sidau Pass.
29. H.M., f. 176b. These defections were due to Abdāl's despotic rule. (B.S., f. 157a).
30. H.M., ff. 176b-77a; B.S., f. 158a.
31. H.M. (B.N.), f. 58a.
32. B.S., f. 158b; H.M., f. 177a.
33. B.S., f. 159b.
34. H.M., ff. 177a-b.
35. *Ibid.*, f. 177b; B.S. 160b.
36. H.M., f. 178b; B.S., ff. 160b-61a. Dachün-Khōvur is Dachhin Khāwarah of A.A. and of the Persian chronicles of Kashmīr. It is the valley lying on both the banks of the Jehlam below Bārāmūla. (See Stein, ii, 493).
37. H.M. (B.N.), f. 58a.
38. A.N., iii, 465.
39. H.M., f. 179a.
40. A.N., iii, 465.
41. It is in Badgām Taḥṣīl, about 3½ miles north-west of Srīnagar.
42. H.M., ff. 178a-80a.
43. B.S., ff. 162b-63a.
44. It is a village about 11 miles north-west of Srīnagar, on the road connecting Srīnagar with Gulmarg.
45. *Ibid.*, f. 164a; H.M., ff. 180a-81b.
46. B.S., ff. 164b-65b.
47. *Ibid.*, f. 166a.
48. Shams Chak belonged to the Chaks of Kopwārā and should not be confused with Shams Chak, son of Daulat Chak, who was related to the ruling dynasty.

49. H.M., ff. 181a-b.
50. Ancient Karnaha. This territory lies between the Kishangangā and the Kājnāg Range.
51. H.M., f. 181b. N.A., f. 95b.
52. H.M., ff. 181b-82a.
53. B.S., ff. 166b-67b; T.A., iii 504.
54. He was the ruler of Ladākh at this time. (See Francke, *History of Western Tibet,* p. 90). But the Ladākhī chronicles do not refer to his relations with Ḥaidar Chak.
55. B.S., ff. 167b-68a.
56. It is now a part of Srīnagar, and is situated to the south-east, near Takht-i-Sulaimān.
57. B.S., f. 168b; T.A., iii, 504.
58. B.S., ff. 169a-b.
59. *Ibid.,* ff. 169b-70a.
60. *Ibid.,* f. 170a; T.A., iii, 505.
61. B.S., f. 170b. T.A., iii, 505 wrongly says that the royalists were victorious.
62. B.S., ff. 170b-71a.
63. T.A., iii, 505; also B.S., f. 172a.
64. B.S., f. 172a; H.M., f. 182a.
65. B.S., ff. 172a-b.
66. T.A., iii, 504.
67. H.M., f. 183a.
68. *Ibid.,* 183a-b.
69. *Ibid.,* f. 183b; A.N., iii, 550; T.A., iii, 504.
70. A.N., iii, 576; T.A., iii, 504; see also H.M., ff. 184b-85a.
71. B.S., ff. 173a-b; also H.M., f. 185a.
72. A.N., iii, 676.
73. H.M., f. 185a.
74. A.N., ii, 197.
75. T.A., ii, 342.
76. A.N., iii, 705; T.A., ii, 396.
77. A.N., iii, 707. B.S., f. 174a, mentions Ṣāliḥ 'Aqil also as one of the envoys.
78. According to Persian chronicles of Kashmīr, Ya'qūb remained at the imperial court for 2 years. But A.N. and T.A. give the period of his stay as one year.
79. H.M., f. 185b.
80. *Ibid.,* f. 186a.
81. *Ibid.,* f. 186b.
82. Akbar was angry with Yūsuf Shāh for not coming to court and

so wrecked his anger on Ya'qūb by calling him wicked and mad. (See H.M., f. 185a).

83. M.T., ii, 365.
84. H.M., ff. 186b-87a; also B.S., f. 173b. But B.S. says Ya'qūb escaped from Buhlūlpūr. The statement in A.N., iii, 707, that Ya'qūb escaped first and the envoys were sent afterwards, is not corroborated by other authorities.
85. H.M., f. 187a.
86. *Ibid.*, f. 187b; Firishta, ii, 699 says that Yūsuf came as far as Thanna. But this seems wrong, for the nobles would not have allowed him to proceed so far.
87. H.M., f. 187b.
88. *Ibid.*, f. 188a.
89. T.A., iii, 505-6.
90. A.N., iii, 714; also T.A., iii, 504. H.M., f. 187b is wrong in stating that Yūsuf dismissed Ḥakīm 'Alī when he heard that Bhagwān Dās had been appointed to invade Kashmīr. Actually the appointment was made on Ḥakīm 'Alī's return.
91. A.N., iii, 715; T.A., ii, 398; M.T., ii, 360. H.M., f. 187b says that the Mughal troops numbered 50,000. But this is an exaggeration.
92. A.N., iii, 722-3.
93. H.M., f. 188a; Śuka, pp. 400-1.
94. B.S., f. 174b.
95. See A.A. (Blochmann), p. 676 and n. 3.
96. H.M., ff. 188a-b. Kuārmast is the last pass on the road to Srīnagar, and is described by Murray as the Bārāmūla Pass (A.A. iii, 724n. 1).
97. Būliāsa or Peliāsa, formerly Bolyasaka, lies on the right bank of the Jehlam, about 50 miles away from Bārāmūla. Jahāngīr called it Bhūlbās (*Tuzuk*, ii, 131) and A.N., iii, 723, calls it Būlyās. See Stein, ii, 403, for the strategic importance of this pass.
98. H.M., f. 189a.
99. *Ibid.*, (B.N.), f. 62a.
100. *Ibid.*, f. 189a.
101. *Ibid.*, f. 189b. H.M. and A.N. do not give the names of the envoys. But B.S. refers to one envoy as Mīrzā Qāsim, the grandson of Khwāja Ḥājī.
102. It is in the Badgām Taḥṣīl, Bārāmūla dist.
103. H.M., f. 189b; A.N., iii, 724. But A.N. wrongly says that it was Yūsuf who sent an envoy to the Mughal camp expressing his desire to submit.
104. B.S., f. 176a. Fighting mostly took place in the pass of Būliāsa.

Jahāngīr in his *Tuzuk*, ii, 132, says that it was in this pass that Ya'qūb fought against Bhagwān Dās. According to B.S., f. 177b, the Mughal camp was established in the village of Būliāsa.

105. B.S., f. 177a; H.M., ff. 199a-b; T.A., ii, 401. A.N., iii, 725, is incorrect in stating that "Kashmīrīs came forward with entreaties and proposed peace." See also M.T., ii, 363.
106. T.A., ii, 401; M.T., ii, 363.
107. M.T., ii, 363.
108. B.S., f. 177a; A.N., iii, 725.
109. A.N., iii, 725 and n.2.
110. H.M., f. 191a.
111. B.S., f. 177b.
112. According to M.T. ii, 363, Akbar did not accept the treaty. T.A., ii, 401 even says that the Emperor so much disapproved of the treaty that he did not allow the officers to appear before him. However, it seems that afterwards Akbar accepted the treaty. (A.N., iii, 725).
113. A.N., iii, 738; see also T.A., iii, 506. Smith, *Akbar*, p. 239, is incorrect in saying that Ya'qūb also surrendered along with his father. Smith is sometimes wrong in his sequence of events.
114. H.M., f. 191a.
115. B.S., f. 177b; M.T., ii, 364. But A.N., iii, 745, says he committed this in a fit of insanity. Smith, *Akbar*, p. 240 regards it as a correct explanation.
116. Mān Singh was replaced as governor of Kābul by Zain Khān and was appointed to the government of Bihār.
117. Smith, *Akbar*, pp. 240-1; H.M., f. 191a. According to H.M. (B.N.), f. 62b Yūsuf received Rs. 100/- a day for his expenses.
118. H.M., f. 182b. Zakāt was not realised from the *hānjīs* probably because of their poverty.
119. T.H., ii, f. 142b. It is strange that contemporary authorities like B.S. and H.M. do not mention Habba Khātūn at all. Our information about her is based on local tradition. But unfortunately all kinds of romantic tales are current about her in the Valley, so that it is difficult to separate fact from fiction.
120. T.H., ii, f. 143a.
121. A.A., ii, 121 (Niwal Kishore) has Biṣwak. A.S.B., 1885, p. 166, has also Biswak, and the place is still called by this name. But A.A., ii, 166 (English trans.) has Basok, while B.S. has Basang or Basank. I am extremely grateful to Professor Ḥasan 'Askarī of Patna University for taking the trouble of visiting Biswak and obtaining information for me from the local people about the graves of

Yusuf Shāh and Ya'qūb Shāh. Here is what he says:

"Biswak is situated some 3 miles north-east of Islāmpūr (Patna dist.). Adjacent to the village there is a mound which is said to have been a *garh,* although no historical information is available about it. The site has often yielded copper and gold coins in the course of minor diggings for domestic purposes. In one instance clay *chukkas* containing gold mohurs of Shāhjahān's reign are reported to have been found. There are two tombs of "Pīr-Shāh Ya'qūb" and "Yūsuf Shāh respectively near this *garh.* The villagers know nothing about the antecedents of these two personages. At a short distance from Biswak there is a village called Kashmīrīchak, which is now completely deserted and in ruins. According to local tradition, however, the Muslims belonging to this village came from Kashmīr, as is indicated by the name which the place bears. There is a mosque in this village near which the tomb of Yūsuf Shāh is situated. Only a mound now remains which, some time ago, the peasants tried to level with the ground in order to bring the land under cultivation. On finding, however, that it was a tomb, they, out of superstition, left it half demolished. If local tradition is passed together with the relevant historical information, it can definitely be established that these tombs are those of Yūsuf Shāh, the ruler of Kashmīr, and his son and successor, Ya'qūb Shāh. According to the *Akbar-nāma* and other chronicles Akbar defeated Yūsuf Shāh and imprisoned him. He was released later and granted a jāgīr in the pargana of Biswak, where both he and his son Ya'qūb settled and died. The existence of a village named Kashmīrīchak with a Kashmīrī Muslim population is also suggestive and significant. Authentic history and tradition thus corroborate each other, and there is no doubt that these tombs are those of Yūsuf Shāh and Ya'qūb Shāh."

Chapter 10

Fall of the Sultanate

Since the treaty had been concluded with the Mughals by Yūsuf Shāh, who had fled the country and ceased to be the Sulṭān, Ya'qūb Shāh and the Kashmīrī nobles did not regard it as binding on them. And so when, after the Mughal withdrawal, Ya'qūb Shāh returned to Srīnagar, he had the coins struck and the *khuṭba* recited in his own name. He however did not rule with tact, ability, and justice. He made the mistake of appointing 'Alī Dar, who was incompetent and addicted to intoxicants, his prime minister.[1] Ya'qūb Shāh also became arrogant,[2] treating the nobles with disrespect, and ignoring their advice. Moreover, having defeated the Mughals he was lulled into a false sense of security, and neglected the defence of the passes leading into Kashmīr.[3] But the greatest mistake which he made was that he adopted a hostile attitude towards the Sunnīs. He sent Mullā 'Ainī, whom he had given the title of Khān,[4] to Qāẓī Mūsā with the message to mention henceforth the name of 'Alī in all public prayers. As the Qāẓī refused to comply with it, Ya'qūb Shāh sent for him and tried to argue with him. Qāẓī Mūsā pointed out that rulers should not concern themselves with religious matters, but should devote their time and attention to the affairs of state. Furthermore, they should be tolerant, for intolerance leads to chaos and confusion in the kingdom. Ya'qūb Shāh was greatly displeased by these insolent replies, but for the time being he spared Mūsā, contenting himself only with showering abuses on him.[5]

Owing to Ya'qūb's arrogance and religious fanaticism, some of the nobles like Shams Chak, Malik Ḥasan Chadura, 'Ālam

Shēr Māgre, and the Wazīr, 'Alī Dar, were driven into hostility against him, and they decided to proceed to Lahore to seek the help of Akbar.[6] But when they reached Hirapūr, Ḥasan Malik suggested that, since the rainy season was about to commence, they should give up the idea of going to India, and, instead, march on Srīnagar and occupy it as Ya'qūb was absent in the village of Phāg.[7] Ya'qūb, hearing of the plan, released Muḥammad Baṭ, and appointed him Wazīr in place of 'Alī Dar, and on his advice immediately set out to the capital, which he reached before the rebels. The later encamped at Ziāldakar, while Ya'qūb established himself in the field of 'Īd-gāh.[8] But after a week of desultory fighting Shaikh Ḥasan, son of Mīr Shamsu'd-Dīn, and Bābā Khalīl, who were the *pīrs* of Ya'qūb Shāh, brought about a settlement. The rebels were given the province of Kamrāj and they left for Sōpūr which was to be their seat.[9] But on the way Shams Chak and 'Ālam Shēr Māgre decided to put Bābā Khalīl and Shaikh Ḥasan, who were accompanying them, to death in revenge for Ya'qūb's policy of intolerance towards the Sunnīs. But Ḥasan Malik intervened, and sent them back safely to Srīnagar. When Ya'qūb heard that Shams Chak and 'Ālam Shēr Māgre had made an attempt on the lives of the Shī'ite divines, he was furious. Moreover, he came to know that Shams Chak had destroyed the Sōpūr Bridge and was preparing for hostilities.[10] He, therefore, set out from Srīnagar with a large force, and having crossed the Jehlam near Sōpūr, he attacked the rebels and routed them. Shēr Māgre escaped to the hill of Kichhāmā, while 'Alī Dar fled to Barbal. Shams Chak took refuge in Srīnagar, but was captured and imprisoned.[11]

After suppressing the rebellion, Ya'qūb once more began to press Qāẓī Mūsā to include the name of 'Alī in the prayers. But Mūsā was adamant, and refused to comply. Partly due to this refusal, and partly because Ya'qūb regarded Mūsā as being solely responsible for the recent rising, he, contrary to the advice of his counsellors, ordered Mūsā's execution.[12] This was an extremely unwise act on his part, for it antagonised the Sunnīs and paved the way for the Mughal annexation of Kashmīr.[13] Another mistake which he committed was that, on the advice of Mullā Ḥasan Aswad, he dismissed Muḥammad Baṭ, his prime minister, who was a capable man, and threw him into prison. Nāzuk Baṭ, who was appointed in his place, was not competent enough to solve the problems, both internal and external, which faced the country.[14]

Owing to Ya'qūb Shāh's intolerance and harshness, Bābā Dā'ūd Khākī with his followers went away to Multān, while a number of chiefs headed by Shaikh Ya'qūb Ṣarfī proceeded to the court of Akbar and requested him to invade Kashmīr and annex it. They entered into the following agreement with the Emperor:[15]

1. There shall be complete freedom of worship and no interference in religious affairs.
2. There shall be no interference with the purchase and sale of commodities, and the rates of cereals.
3. Kashmīrīs shall not be made slaves.
4. Kashmīrīs shall not be molested or oppressed; nor will they be required to do *begār* (corvée).
5. Those Kashmīrī nobles who are a source of mischief shall not be associated with the administration of the country.

We have seen that Akbar did not approve of the treaty concluded by Rājā Bhagwān Dās with Yūsuf Shāh, but that he had accepted it as a matter of expediency. When, therefore, he learnt of the dissensions in Kashmīr and was assured by Shaikh Ya'qūb Ṣarfī of the support of Kashmīrī chiefs, he resolved upon its conquest. He first sent an army under Mīrzā Shāh Rukh, but as the latter did not prosecute the campaign effectively owing to his anxiety to return to India, he was relieved of the command,[16] and in his place Mīr Qāsim Khān Mīr Baḥr[17] was appointed along with Fatḥ Khān and Mīrzā 'Alī Akbar Shāhi,[18] while Ya'qūb Ṣarfī and Ḥaidar Chak were deputed to act as their guides and to win over the Kashmīrīs to the side of the Mughals.[19] Qāsim Khān set out from Lahore on June 28, 1586,[20] and passed through the defile of Bhimbhar on the 1st of September, 1586.[21] When he reached Rajaurī, Bahrām Nāyak, Ismā'īl Nāyak, and Shanki Chādura,[22] who were entrusted with the defence of the passes leading into Kashmīr, came and submitted, and assured him of the support of the Kashmīrī nobles.[23]

Learning of the Mughal invasion, Ya'qūb Shāh marched towards Hirapūr to repel it. But on all sides he saw nothing else but defection. He had sent a force under Bahādur Khān Chak and Naurang Khān Chak, but Bahādur Chak imprisoned Naurang Chak and proceeded to join the Mughals.[24] He was, however, met by Ẓafar Khān Nāyak who rescued Naurang Chak; but Bahādur Chak succeeded in going over to the Mughals at Karanbal.[25] Since there were other defections besides, Yūsuf Khān, Aiba Khān, and Sayyid Mubārak found it impossible to check the Mughal advance, and returned to join Ya'qūb Shāh at Hirapūr.[26] Ya'qūb was so disheartened by these developments that he decided to retire to Kishtwār. By the time he reached the pargana of Bring only a few of his followers had remained with him.[27]

Qāsim Khān felt encouraged by these desertions. Moreover he was assured by Ya'qūb Ṣarfī that many other chiefs too were waiting to join him at Hastivanj.[28] He therefore sent a force under Ya'qūb Ṣarfī and Jai Tawāchībāshī, with instructions to effect a junction with them. During their march the Mughals suffered great privations on account of snow and cold, and then when they reached Hastivanj, they discovered to their surprise, instead of friendly Kashmīrī nobles, a hostile force determined to check their advance.[29] What had happened is that the Kashmīrī chiefs like Ḥusain Khān, Shams Ganā'ī and others, having felt ashamed for causing the defeat and flight of Ya'qūb, had changed their minds and decided not to submit to the Mughals. Accordingly they had marched to Hastivanj to check their advance. They defeated the Mughals and took Ya'qūb Ṣarfī and Jai Tawāchībāshī prisoners.[30] But thinking that their victory had been decisive, they did not follow it up and, instead of making arrangements for the defence of the passes, they returned to Hirapūr. Here they enthroned Ḥusain Khān Chak, the son of Aiba Khān, in place of Ya'qūb Shāh.[31]

Meanwhile Shams Chak, who had been imprisond by Ya'qūb, taking advantage of the chaos escaped from prison, and set out towards Kamrāj.[32] But when he reached Chādura he was met by Malik Ḥasan who advised him to proceed towards Hirapūr, and fight the Mughals. He accepted the advice, and with Malik Ḥasan marched to Hirapūr. On arriving there, he, with the consent of the nobles, declared himself Sulṭān, and deposed Ḥusain Khān, who had been raised to the throne only four days before.[33]

Owing to their internal dissensions the Kashmīrīs had not been able to direct their attention to the enemy. It was only when the latter, having crossed the Karanbal hill, had arrived at the pass of Hastivanj that Shams Chak advanced to offer them battle.[34] On October 10, 1586, he had an engagement with their advance-guard. As the Kashmīrīs were on a height occupying an advantageous position, they repulsed the Mughals by discharging muskets and rolling down heavy stones, Qāsim Khān, thereupon, himself went forward to meet the Kashmīrīs. The latter put up a stiff resistance, but after their commanders, Moḥammad Qāsim Khān Nāyak, his son Ẓafar Khān Nāyak, and Muḥammad Chak, the son of Shams Chak, were killed they became demoralised and fled, pursued by the Mughals. Yādgār Ḥusain, on instructions from Qāsim Khān, at once advanced to occupy Srīnagar. He entered it on October 14, without meeting any resistance, and had the *khuṭba* read in the name of Emperoṛ. The next day Qāsim Khān himself arrived at the capital.[35]

We have seen that Ya'qūb Shāh, betrayed by his supporters, had fled to Kishtwār. But as Rājā Bahādur Singh of Kishtwār, who was his father-in-law, criticised him for his cowardice in having run away without fighting the Mughals, Ya'qūb Shāh returned to the Valley with a small following. He was joined by Yūsuf Khān, Ibrāhīm Khān, and Malik Ḥasan.[36] Many other persons also, owing to the oppressive rule of Qāsim Khān, rallied to Ya'qūb.[37] His force swelled to 8,000 horse, and he made Chandrakōt[38] his headquarters. Shams Chak, on the other hand, established himself at Sōpūr. He had an army of 3,000 horse and 7,000 foot, and was supported by Ḥusain Khān and Abū'l-Ma'ālī. From Chandrakōt and Sōpūr the Kashmīrīs set out in parties to attack the Mughals. They avoided pitched battles and instead harassed them by making surprise attacks, cutting down stragglers, and intercepting their supplies. These tactics were so successful that it became impossible for the Mughals to leave the city.[39]

After a month and a half, during which period the Mughals had been subjected to continuous harassment, Qāsim Khān decided to attack Ya'qūb. But on approaching his camp he was informed that Ya'qūb had proceeded to make an attack on the city. Qāsim Khān, therefore turned back and sent a force in advance under Muḥammad 'Alī. Ya'qūb Shāh, who lay in wait for him near a hill in Vular, south-east of Srīnagar, attacked him and gained a victory.[40] Encouraged by this success, he made a night attack on the western side of the town. Many houses were set on fire, including the palace of Yūsuf Shāh in which Qāsim Khān was residing. As a result he had to take refuge in the garden of Malik Muḥammad Nājī. From there he issued instructions to organise resistance, and ordered the execution of Ḥaidar Chak lest he should escape and join Ya'qūb.[41] When the Kashmīrīs heard the news of Ḥaidar Chak's death they were roused to fury, and determined themselves to take their revenge.[42] They attacked the Mughals in every nook and corner of the city and killed many of them. And they would have gained the day had it not been for an act of indiscretion committed by Ya'qūb. Elated with initial success he ordered the execution of Ḥusain Khān, who had been set up as ruler at Hirapūr, and of his supporters. This news filled the troops of Ya'qūb Shāh with consternation, and many of them retired from the battle-field, thus weakening his position.[43] Meanwhile the Mughals, having received reinforcements under Muḥammad Khān, the son of Fatḥ Khān Faujdār, from across the Jehlam, took the offensive. Ya'qūb's followers were unable to withstand the attack, and they fled, pursued by 'Alī Akbar Shāhī.[44]

This victory strengthened the morale of the Mughals, and Qāsim Khān began to send scouring parties to reduce the various parts of Kashmīr. At the same time he sent a force under Shaikh Daulat Bakhtiyār against Shams Chak who was at Sōpūr. When the Mughals reached Dānāwarī, Shams Chak with Sayyid Ḥusain Baihaqī and Shams Dūnī made a night attack on them, but were defeated and withdrew to Sōpūr. From there, on account of winter, they left for the hills of Karnāv.[45] Other Kashmīrī chiefs also dispersed to the hills, while Ya'qūb Shāh retired to Kishtwār.[46] But Yūsuf Khān Khān-i-Khānān, Ḥusain Khān, and Muḥammad Baṭ, perceiving the futility of resistance, made overtures to Qāsim Khān; and, on being assured of personal safety, they submitted on December 9, 1586. They were sent to Lahore with Bābā Khalīl, Bābā Mehdī, and Sayyid Mubārak, who were suspected of inciting the Kashmīrīs against the Mughals, and presented to the Emperor on March 2, 1587.[47]

For two months during the winter fighting ceased. But at the approach of spring Ya'qūb Shāh returned from Kishtwār, and established himself at the foot of a hill in the Vular pargana,[48] while Shams Chak returned from Karnāv to Sōpūr.[49] For some time there were daily skirmishes between the Mughals and the Kashmīrīs, but they did not lead to any decisive result. Eventually, early in 1588, Qāsim Khān despatched a force under Mīrzādā 'Alī Khān and Sayyid 'Abdu'llāh Khān,[50] with Shēr Khān Māgre to act as a guide. They met Ya'qūb at Gusu.[51] The Mughals, being handicapped by a heavy fall of snow, the narrowness of the defile, and the slipperiness of the road, were defeated. Mīrzāda 'Alī Khān was killed with 300 of his men, while the rest were either taken prisoners or escaped to Qāsim Khān.[52] Encouraged by this victory, Ya'qūb moved to the Takht-i-Sulaimān and encamped there. Shams Chak was also roused to action, and occupied the fort of Hānjik, four miles west of Srīnagar.[53]

The next day Qāsim Khān himself advanced to attack Ya'qūb, and encountered him at the foot of the Takht-i-Sulaimān. The Mughals would have again suffered defeat, but fortunately for them, Naurang Chak, Ya'qūb Shāh's commander-in-chief, was killed by an arrow which pierced his eye. This demoralised the Kashmīrīs and led to their rout.[54]

In spite of this defeat Ya'qūb was not disheartened. He made overtures to Shams Chak to forget the past and unite against the common enemy. Since Shams Chak responded favourably, Ya'qūb, accompanied by Ḥasan Malik, joined him in the fort of Hānjik. The two chiefs then set out to attack the Mughals whom they encountered near Hānjik.[55] The Mughals were completely routed and lost 1,500 men. They were pursued by Ḥasan Malik up to the field of Ziāldakar in Srīnagar.[56]

The victory achieved by the Kashmīrīs enabled Ya'qūb and Shams to establish themselves on the Kōh-i-Mārān. The Mughals, on the other hand, were reduced to a sad plight. For two months they dared not come out of the city, being subjected to continuous harassment. The Kashmīrīs grew even so bold as to attack the enemy in the town, and to carry away their horses and supplies.[57] This state of affairs made Qāsim Khān very despondent, and so he requested the Emperor for his recall. Akbar, accordingly, ordered Yūsuf Khān Riẓvī[58] to proceed to Kashmīr with Mullā Ṭālib Isfahānī, Bābā Khalīl and Muḥammad Baṭ, who were to act as guides and to win over the guardians of the passes. Yūsuf Riẓvī set out from Lahore in about the middle of 1588.[59]

When Ya'qūb Shāh heard that a strong army was coming to reinforce Qāsim Khān, he deputed Shams Chak's brother Lohar Chak to prevent them from entering Kashmīr.[60] Ḥasan Malik, however, opposed the appointment on the ground that Lohar Chak, being a friend of Bābā Khalīl, would go over to the Mughals, and suggested that Shams Chak be sent against Yūsuf Riẓvī, while Ya'qūb himself should stay behind to blockade Qāsim Khān, who was sure to perish owing to the want of supplies. But his advice was not followed; and, as Ḥasan Malik had predicted, Lohar Chak, instead of intercepting the Mughal force, joined it along with Bahrām Nāyak. This news spread consternation among the Kashmīrī troops in Hānjik, and when they heard of the arrival of Yūsuf Riẓvī at Hirapūr, many of their chiefs deserted and submitted to him.[61] The Kashmīrī forces thus completely disintegrated. Ya'qūb Shāh in disgust went away to Kishtwār, while Shams Chak retired to the Bring pargana.[62]

Yūsuf Riẓvī adopted a policy of conciliation and won over many chiefs. He then sent a force under Sayyid Bahā'u'd-Dīn and Muḥammad Baṭ against Shams Chak. But the latter made a night attack on them from the village of Trigām and obtained much plunder. At dawn, however, he suffered a crushing defeat at the hands of the Mughals and had to retire to the hills of

Kamrāj.[63] Meanwhile, Ya'qūb Shāh had returned from Kishtwār and encamped at Panjyārī in Dachün Khōvur. Yūsuf Riẓvī, thereupon, sent a force under Muḥammad Baṭ and Ḥājī Mīrakī against him. The Mughal commanders sent a messenger to persuade Ya'qūb to submit. But Ya'qūb, on the advice of Abū'l-Ma'alī, rejected these overtures, and determined to fight the enemy and die a hero's death. He accordingly attacked the Mughals, but although he obtained a victory over the advance-guard led by Muḥammad Mīr, the battle was indecisive, as hostilities had to be suspended on account of heavy rains. After this Ya'qūb Shāh withdrew to the pargana of Vular to reorganise his army. But he found that treachery was rife in his camp, for his troops were going over to the Mughals. That is why when Muḥammad Baṭ and Muḥammad Mīr advanced to attack him, he escaped to Kishtwār without offering any resistance.[64] But Abū'l-Ma'alī, who tried to put up a fight, was taken prisoner in the village of Chrār.[65] These unexpected developments convinced Shams Chak that any further resistance to the Mughals was futile, and so through the mediation of Sayyid Bahā'u'-Dīn he surrendered. Shortly after he was sent to the Emperor.[66] The submission of Shams Chak greatly disheartened Ya'qūb Shāh. And so when Akbar arrived in Kashmīr early in June, 1588, he too decided to give up the struggle and submit. Accordingly, he returned from Kishtwār, and, towards the end of July, did personal homage to the Emperor,[67] who sent him with Ḥasan Bēg Turkmān to Rājā Mān Singh at Rohtās. On the way Ya'qūb and his followers planned that his brother Ibrāhīm should assassinate Ḥasan Bēg and then all should escape. But the plan miscarried, for when Ḥasan Bēg, was attacked by Ibrāhīm, the Mughal guard came to his rescue and killed Ibrāhīm. Ya'qūb Shāh, having repented for his part in the affair, was forgiven by Ḥasan Bēg and was conducted safely to his father at Jaunpūr. From there, after taking a letter of guarantee from Yūsuf Shāh, Ḥasan Bēg sent Ya'qūb Shāh to Rājā Mān Singh at Rohtās.[68] Here he was kept virtually a prisoner, for it was thought that he might again make an attempt to escape. But when Yūsuf Shāh died, Mān Singh transferred his rank to Ya'qūb, and allowed him to proceed to his jāgīr. Before leaving

Rohtās, Ya'qūb Shāh went to bid farewell to Qāsim Khān, who claimed to be the son of Yūsuf Shāh. He ate the poisoned betel leaves that were offered to him by Qāsim Khān. By the time he reached Behīra[69] his condition grew worse and he died in the month of Muḥarram 1001/October 1593. His body was carried by Abū'l-Ma'ālī to Biswak, and buried there near the grave of his father Yūsuf Shāh.[70]

NOTE

1. B.S., f. 178a.
2. A.N., iii, 762, says that Ya'qūb became so arrogant as to adopt the title or Shāh Ismā'īl. This he probably did in imitation of the founder of the Ṣafavid dynasty.
3. H.M., f. 192a.
4. H.M. (B.N.), f. 63a.
5. H.M., ff. 192a-b; N.A., ff. 106b-107a. Śuka. p. 403 also refers to these religious discords.
6. H.M., f. 192a.
7. *Ibid.,* f. 193a.
8. *Ibid.,* B.S., f. 179a.
9. H.M., f. 193b.
10. *Ibid.,* f. 194a. But B.S., f. 178a sq. gives a slightly different version of the conflict.
11. H.M., ff. 194a-b; B.S., f. 180a.
12. *Ibid.,* f. 195a.
13. *Ibid.*
14. B.S., f. 181b.
15. W.K., f. 58a.
16. A.N., iii, 747.
17. For his career, see A.A. (Blochmann), pp. 412-3.
18. A.N., iii, 747; also B.S., f. 182a.
19. B.S., f. 182a.
20. A.N., iii, 752; also B.S., f. 184b; and M.T., ii, 364-65. The difference between the dates of A.N. and M.T. is only of a few days. B.S. also says that Qāsim occupied Srīnagar in 994/1586. But according to A.N. (Blochmann) p. 412, and T.A., ii, 403, Qāsim Khān left Lahore in early Sha'bān 994/1st half of July 1587.
21. A.N., iii, 764.
22. Abū'l-Fazl's Cārwarah is the village of Chādura, the home of Ḥaidar Malik.
23. A.N., iii, 764; B.S., f. 182b; see also Śuka, pp. 405-6.
24. H.M., f. 195b. According to H.M. (B.N.), f. 64a, only 30 or 40 horsemen remained with Ya'qūb by the time he reached Hirapūr.
25. H.M., f. 196a, Karanbal is the same as Kapartal Pass. See p. 133n. 1, *supra.*
26. B.S., f. 182b. Aiba Khān, son of Abdāl Khān, is the same person as Abiya Khān of A.N., iii, 768.
27. H.M., f. 183. Bring is in the Anantnāg dist.
28. See p. 24, *supra,* for Hastivanj.
29. A.N., iii, 766–7; H.M., 196a.
30. B.S., f. 183b; H.M., f. 196b. According to A.N., iii, 767 Ya'qūb

was wounded but was saved by his friends. Jai was, however, taken prisoner. This battle took place after Ya'qūb's departure for Kishtwār, and not before as A.N. says. A.N. is not always correct in its sequence of events.

31. H.M., f. 196b. Ḥusain Shāh was a cousin of Ya'qūb Shāh. (H.M. (B.N.) f. 64a).
32. Ya'qūb Shāh finding his affairs in chaos had released Shams Chak and Muḥammad Baṭ, his former Wazīr, so that they might help him. But pressed by his counsellors, Ya'qūb had again imprisoned them. However, taking advantage of the chaos, they now managed to escape. (A.N., iii, 768).
33. H.M., ff. 196b-97b.
34. B.S., f. 184a wrongly states that Shams Chak proceeded to the top of the Kanarbal hill to fight the Mughals, and that when he was defeated the Mughals encamped at Hastivanj.
35. A.N., iii, 769-70; H.M., f. 198a; also H.M. (B.N.), f. 64a.
36. H.M., f. 198b.
37. A.N., iii, 796.
38. It is an important village in the Bārāmūla Taḥṣīl, about 29 miles north-west of Srīnagar.
39. H.M., ff. 198b-99a.
40. A.N., iii, 786-7.
41. B.S., f. 186a; Śuka, p. 409, H.M., f. 199b says that Ḥaidar Chak was put to death by his guards. But it seems unlikely that the execution should have taken place without Qāsim's orders.
42. B.S., 186a; A.N., iii, 776.
43. H.M., f. 199b.
44. A.N., iii, 776.
45. H.M., f. 200a; also B.S., ff. 187a sqq.
46. B.S., f. 188a.
47. B.S., ff. 188a-b; A.N., iii, 787; Śuka, p. 411. B.S. says that Sayyid Mubārak was leading a retired life at this time.
48. It was a pargana comprising a long narrow valley which stretches from the north side of the Jehlam, between Avantīpūr and Bījbehāra. Its ancient name was Holada. (Stein, ii, 460; Bates, *Kashmīr Gazetteer*, p. 405).
49. B.S., f. 189a; H.M., f. 200b.
50. These two commanders had been sent by Akbar to the aid of Qāsim Khān. (A.N., iii, 788).
51. It is a village in the Pulwāna Taḥṣīl (Avantīpūr).
52. H.M., ff. 200b-1a; A.A. (Blochmann), pp. 491, 518. *Ma'āṣiru'l-Umarā'*, ii 258, agree with A.A. and A.N. in assigning the date of Mīrzā 'Alī Khān's death as 995/1587. But Badā'ūnī, who was a friend of Mīrzā, 'Alī Khān, gives 996/1588 as the year of his death.

53. H.M., f. 201a.
54. *Ibid.*, f. 201a.
55. *Ibid.*, ff. 201b-202a.
56. *Ibid.*, ff. 202b-3a.
57. *Ibid.*, f. 203b.
58. He was a Sayyid of Mashhad. For details of his life, see A.A. (Blochmann), pp. 369 sqq.
59. A.N., iii, 798; H.M., f. 203b. Sayyid Mubārak was also asked to accompany them in order to help in the general pacification of the country. But as he refused to go, Akbar became angry and sent him as a prisoner to Shahbāz Khān Kambū in Bengal. After a year when Shahbāz Khān was proceeding to Lahore to pay his respects to the Emperor and had reached Fīrūzābād, Sayyid Mubārak, who was with him, was taken ill and died. (See B.S., f. 190a).
60. H.M., f. 203b.
61. *Ibid.*, ff. 203b-4a.
62. A.N., iii, 798; B.S., f. 191a.
63. A.N., iii, 798-99; also B.S., ff. 191a-b. But B.S. says Shams Chak retired to the Bring pargana.
64. B.S., ff. 192a-93b.
65. *Ibid.*, f. 194a.
66. B.S., ff. 194b-95a; A.N., iii, 799. Shams Chak subsequently died at Burhānpūr in the Deccan. (B.S., f. 205b).
67. A.N., iii, 846; B.S., f. 196a; H.M., f. 204b; also Śuka, p. 418. But M.T., ii, 365, and T.A., ii, 404, say that Ya'qūb submitted to Qāsim Khān. This is incorrect, for it was not the latter but Yūsuf Riẓvī who was in command in Kashmīr at this time.
68. B.S., ff. 199b-200a.
69. A.A., ii, 120 (Niwal Kishore ed.) has Behīra. But A.A., ii, 166 (Eng. trans.) and J.A.S.B., 1885, p. 166, has Pahrā. It was in the Bihār Sarkār under Akbar.
70. B.S., ff. 201a-202b; see also p. 180 f.n. 3 *supra*. Ṣūfī, i, 236-7, is wrong in saying that Ya'qūb was buried in Kishtwār.

Chapter 11

The Administrative System

THE CENTRAL GOVERNMENT

In the absence of any treatise on administration, and with only a few stray references in the chronicles, it is difficult to present a comprehensive picture of how the Valley was governed during the Sultanate period. We can, at best, make out only a general outline, without any details.

From the little evidence that is at our disposal, it appears that Shāh Mīr and his immediate successors did not replace the governmental organisation of the Hindu kings. What they did was to infuse vigour and efficiency into the administration, and in this way tried to protect the peasants from rapacious officials, promote agriculture, suppress refractory chiefs, and establish law and order. From the time of Sulṭān Sikandar, however, under the influence of Persians and Turks, the tendency was to model the administration on the system prevalent in other countries under Muslim rule. The result was that new institutions began to be imported and designations of the old ones to be changed. However, although minor innovations continued to be introduced till the end of the Sultanate, the main lines of administrative development seem to have been completed during the reign of Sulṭān Zainu'l-'Ābidīn.

The Sulṭān

The Sulṭān of Kashmīr, like his predecessors, was an autocrat. He was the supreme executive, legislative and judicial authority in his kingdom. He could make laws and interpret the *Sharī'a.* He was his own commander-in-chief, and led the campaigns either personally or appointed other commanders in his place. He was the highest court of appeal, and had the power of life and death over his subjects.

The Sulṭān had a council consisting of his ministers and high officials whom he consulted on all matters relating to administration, foreign policy, and war and peace. Although the ultimate decision rested with him, yet, since the council was composed of members drawn from the leading landowning families, who were very powerful, it prevented his rule from turning into despotism. But otherwise the rule of the council was not directed towards the promotion of the good of the country. When the Sulṭān was weak, the real power was in the hands of the nobles who were members of this council and who set up or pulled down rulers, declared war or made peace, and even parcelled out the kingdom among themselves. The great authority which they wielded, proved disastrous to the country, for it not only prevented the establishment of a strong, centralised government, but it also led to the formation of cliques, to constant scramble for power, and to civil wars and rebellions. It was a repetition of the conditions which had existed under the Lohara dynasty.

In ordinary matters involving the *Sharī'a* the Sulṭān consulted the *Shaikhu'l-Islām.*[1] But when some serious question of conscience was involved, he convened a council of all the leading jurists of the kingdom and sought their advice. This was done by Mīrzā Ḥaidar when he banned the Nūrbakhshīya Order and put to death many of its leaders.[2] Similarly, it was after consulting the *'Ulamā* that Ḥusain Shāh Chak ordered the execution of Yūsuf and, later, of Qāẓī Ganā'ī and Qāẓī Almās.[3]

Symbols of Sovereignty

Apart from these powers, the Sulṭān also enjoyed certain special prerogatives to distinguish him from the nobles and his other subjects. These prerogatives or symbols were necessary to maintain his dignity and inspire awe and fear in the hearts of his people.

(a) *Titles* : All the rulers of the Sḥāh Mīr and Chak dynasties adopted the title of Sulṭān. Other common titles were Shāh, Pādshāh, and Sulṭānu'l-A'ẕam. But in addition, each ruler also assumed special titles. Thus Zainu'l-Ābidīn called himself Nā'ib-i-Amīru'l-Mū'minīn, and Ghāzī Chak as Muḥammad Humāyūṇ. Sulṭān Ḥusain Shāh Chak took the title of Naṣīru'd-Dīn Pādshāh Ghāzī, and the same title was assumed by Yūsuf Shāh. But 'Alī Shāh called himself Ẕahīru'd-Dīn Muḥammad 'Alī Pādshāh. But Ya'qūb Shāh assumed the title of Ismā'īl Shāh.[4] Evidently the Chak rulers had adopted these titles in imitation of the Mughal Emperors of India and the Ṣafavī Shāhs of Persia.

(b) *Khuṭba and Sikka* : At first it was only the prerogative of the Caliph to have his name recited in the *khuṭba* or sermon before the Friday prayers, and any attempt to introduce other names was regarded by the jurists as *bid'a* (innovation). But from the end of the third century *Hijra,* it became a common practice of the local rulers to have their names also inserted side by side with the name of the Caliph.[5] After the collapse of the Caliphate at Baghdād, however, although the Muslim rulers in general strictly enforced the insertion of their own names in the *khuṭba,* they gave up the custom of putting in the names of the puppet Abbasid Caliphs of Cairo.[6] We do not know in what relation the Sulṭān of Kashmīr stood with the Egyptian Caliphs, for beyond a reference to an exchange of embassies between Zainu'l-'Ābidīn and the ruler of Egypt the chronicles do not throw any light on this matter. But there is sufficient evidence to show that in Kashmīr, as in other countries under Muslim rule, the name of the reigning monarch was recited in the *khuṭba,* for the Kashmīr Sulṭāns regarded it as an important symbol of authority;[7] and it was only three times during the Sultanate period, that they had to surrender it.[8] Another exclusive privilege of the Sulṭān was the right to issue money bearing his name and titles.[9] Although the Sulṭāns allowed the names of their predecessors or of the great saints to be inscribed on the coins, they never gave up the right to strike coins except when they had to surrender their sovereign powers. None of the coins of this period bear the name of a Caliph.

(c) *Crown and Throne :* To sit on the throne[10] and wear the *Tāj* (crown) was the exclusive privilege of the Sulṭān; and whenever he abdicated, he handed over the crown to his successor.[11] Thus when Yūsuf Shāh was compelled to give up his throne, he sent the *Tāj* to Sayyid Mubārak who was declared by the nobles as Sulṭān.[12] Similarly, when Ghāzī Chak wanted to assume royal powers, the *Tāj* was removed from the head of Ḥabīb Shāh and placed on that of Ghāzī who took his seat on the throne.[13]

(d) *Chatr and Chaurī* : The *Chatr* (umbrella) and the *Chaurī* (flywhiskers) could not be used by any one except the Sulṭān. These had been the insignia of sovereignty under the Hindu kings and were adopted by the Sulṭāns.[14]

(e) *Khil'at* : The right of bestowing robes of honour on nobles, officials and tributaries was reserved for the Sulṭān. It was an old Persian custom which had been borrowed by the Abbasid Caliphs.[15] Later it had spread to other countries. Other insignia of royalty in Kashmīr were the Treasury,[16] the Royal Stable[17] and the Standard.[18] The Chariot had been an emblem of royalty under the Hindu rulers,[19] but it does not seem to have had any significance during the Sultanate period.

The Wazīr

Under the early Shāh Mīr rulers the chief minister was called by the old name of *Sarvādhikāra.*[20] It was probably in the reign of Zainu'l-'Ābidīn that he began to be designated as *Wazīr,* and by the time of Ḥasan; Shāh and Muḥammad Shāh the new title was in full vogue.[21] The *Wazīr* was the head of the civil administration and the highest official in the state. He was the constant adviser of the ruler, and enjoyed his utmost confidence. His powers were great, and therefore upon his ability and wisdom depended the welfare of the people and the stability of the kingdom. Owing to the great importance and prestige of the office, there was a keen competition for it among the nobles. But this aroused jealousies and rivalries which often led to armed conflicts. Since there was no separation of powers, the *Wazīrs* were often called upon to lead the campaigns. In the reign of Sulṭān Sikandar, for example, Sūhabhaṭṭa was not only the head of the civil administration, but also of the army. This was, however, not always the case. Thus under Shihābu'd-Dīn while the *Wizārat* and Finance were placed in charge of Udayaśrī, the command of the army was entrusted to Candra Ḍāmara and Laula.[22] During the period of decline of the Shāh Mīrs the *Wazīrs* were invariably military leaders. In fact their ascendancy in the state was due to their military prowess. They were so powerful that they reduced the Sulṭāns to the status of puppets and themselves became *de facto* rulers, presiding over the highest courts of appeal in company with the *Sharī'a* magistrates,[23] conferring jāgīrs upon the nobles, appointing or dismissing officers, and declaring war or concluding peace. In the end the Chaks, who acted as *Wazīrs* of the Shāh Mīrs, found themselves sufficiently strong to depose the Shāh Mīr Sulṭān and assume sovereign powers. In lieu of their services the *Wazīrs* were assigned big jāgīrs. But it is not known if in addition to this they also recceived any salary.

Dīwān-i-Kul

Next to the *Wazīr*, the *Dīwān-i-Kul* was the most important officer in the kingdom. But this office does not seem to have existed under the early Shāh Mīrs; it was introduced by Fatḥ Shāh who was anxious to reduce the power of the *Wazīr*. The latter retained the military, executive and judical functions, but the power to control the finances was taken away from him and placed in the hands of the *Dīwān-i-Kul*.[24] This separation of powers, however, did no serve any purpose for the *Wazīrs* remained as powerful as before. Nothing is known of the history of the *Dīwān-i-Kul* under the Chaks.

Ministry of Religious Affairs

The *Shaikhu'l-Islām* was the head of the eccelesiastical department of the state. It was during the reign of Sulṭān Sikandar that this office was for the first time established in Kashmīr.[25] The *Shaikhu'l-Islām* was the representative of the *'Ulamā*, and his duty was to see that the *Sharī'a* law was enforced. Under the circumstance only a person distinguished for his learning and piety was appointed to this office. The *Shaiku'l-Islām* performed the coronation ceremony, and was the constant adviser of the Sulṭān on legal and religious matters. Sometimes he also issued decrees on political questions, and these had great weight. Thus when, in 1532, Mīrzā Ḥaidar invaded Kashmīr and his soldiers began to devastate the Valley, the *Shaiku'l-Islām* issued a decree that to fight the invaders and to kill them was a righteous act, and that if any Kashmīrī lost his life while resisting the enemy, he would be a martyr. The effect of this pronouncement was that the Kashmīrī nobles were roused from their lethargy and began to organise strong resistance to the Mughals.[26]

Besides being an adviser to the Sulṭān, the *Shaikhu'l-Islām* was also in charge of the *waqfs* for charitable and educational purposes. From the income of these endowments schools were run, and stipends were given to deserving students, while strangers in the country were provided with food and accommodation until they were able to find some employment.[27] Under the Chaks the duties of the *Shaikhu'l-Islām* were taken over by the *Qāẓī* of Srīnagar, also known as *Qāẓī'l-Quẓāt*.[28]

Administration of Justice

The *Qāẓī* was the highest judicial authority in the state. His office was introduced into Kashmīr by Sulṭān Sikandar, probably at the same time as that of the *Shaikhu'l-Islām*. And the first *Qāẓī* whose name is mentioned in the chronicles was Sayyid Ḥasan Shīrāzī, who was appointed as *Qāẓī* of Srīnagar by Sikandar.[29] During the Chak period the prestige and powers of the *Qāẓī* greatly increased, for he was not only the head of the judicial department but also of the ecclesiatical department. He led the prayers, acted as the chief judge, looked after the charitable and educational endowments, and gave advice to the Sulṭān on religious matters. He was assisted by a *Muftī*, whose duty was to give rulings according to the Ḥanafite law.[30] Another officer under the *Qāẓī* was known as *Mīr 'Adl* who performed semi-magisterial functions. The parties, before going to the *Qāẓī*, approached the *Mīr 'Adl*, who drew up the case, and if it was not a complicated one and the parties agreed, he himself settled the dispute.[31]

Justice was also administered by the Sulṭān as well as by the *Wazīr*. The former acted both as a court of first instance and a court of appeal, trying civil as well as criminal cases. But there were no fixed regulations for appeal. Justice was dispensed with by the Sulṭān sitting in the *Dīwān-Khāna* in the open durbar every day. Ḥasan Shāh Chak, however, had fixed Monday as the day of the week when he attended court with the *Qāẓī* and *Mīr 'Adl.*[32] But the other Sulṭāns had no fixed days for holding court; they were accessible to the people on every day of the week. They dealt out justice impartially, but the punishments which they inflicted upon the criminals were not always according to the *Sharī'a*. Zainu'l-'Ābidīn, for example, did not favour either the execution of thieves and robbers or the mutilation of their limbs. Instead he made them work on public buildings.[33] Later under his successors capital punishment was re-introduced. For those who were guilty of treason the penalty was prison, death, or mutilation. The last form of punishment was introduced by Ghāzī Shāh Chak, but later 'Alī Shāh abolished it.[34]

The Royal Stable

This was an important department. Rival claimants to the throne always tried to seize the horses first. This was because, the cavalry being the most important arm of the army, it was felt that once the royal horses were taken possession of, victory would be easy. Thus we find that Ḥājī Khān, in making his bid for the throne on the eve of his father's death, first seized the Royal Stable.[35] As a result, Adham Khān despaired of success and fled to India. Similarly, to overthrow Daulat Chak, Ghāzī Chak had to seize the royal horses.[36] During the Hindu times the office was called *Mahāśvaśālā* (office of the Chief Master of Horse),[37] but it is not known as to what his designation was under the Sulṭāns. Whether he was called *Akhūrbek,*[38] as under the Delhi Sulṭāns, the chronicles give us no indication.

Mīr Bakhshī

The *Mīr Bakhshī* was the head of the military department, and was therefore an important officer. He kept the register of the soldiers, distributed their pay, and was responsible for their recruitment.[39] Under the Mughals he possessed considerable powers and influence,[40] but he does not seem to have enjoyed the same position and prestige under the Sulṭāns of Kashmīr. The first mention of a *Mīr Bakhshī* in the chronicles in the reign of 'Alī Shāh.[41]

Amīr-i-Dar

Amīr-i-Dar[42] or Lord Chamberlain, whom Jonarāja calls *Dvārapāla*,[43] was an important officer. His post commanded great prestige and was reserved for the Sulṭān's most trusted nobles. His importance arose from the fact that he was constantly in the company of the Sulṭān. All petitions to the latter were presented through him, and no one was allowed to enter the royal presence without being introduced by him. He also made arrangements for important celebrations at the court, and was thus the Master of Ceremonies.[44]

Nāyaks

The *Nāyaks*[45] were the guardians of the passes leading into Kashmīr. During the rule of Hindu kings the control of the passes was vested in a single officer who was known as *Dvārapati* or Lord of the Gate.[46] Under the Sulṭāns they were placed under a number of officers called *Nāyaks*, who were appointed by the Sulṭān, and were directly under the central government Their appointments were sometimes hereditary and, in return for their services, they were given jāgīrs. They had at their disposal a force which was stationed at fortified outposts, and their duty was to see that no one entered the Valley or left it without a *Khaṭṭ-i-Rāh* (permit).[47] They were also required to defend the Valley from foreign invasions and from the inroads of turbulent hill tribes, the Dards in the north and the Khaśas in the south-west.[48] Furthermore, they were to prevent smuggling and collect customs duties on goods exported and imported.[49] Whenever the passes were well defended and in the hands of trustworthy commanders, Kashmīr enjoyed immunity from foreign invasions. But whenever their defence was neglected or the *Nāyaks* turned traitors, the Valley was easily invaded.

Espionage System

The Sulṭāns kept themselves informed of the activities of their subjects and officials by means of spies. Thus it was through his spies that Ḥaidar Shāh came to know of the treacherous designs of his Treasurer, Ḥasan, and was able to nip the conspiracy in the bud.[50] Under Zainu'l-'Ābidīn the espionage system was very efficient, and it kept him in touch with the happenings in the remotest parts of the kingdom.[51] Sometimes he himself, like Hārūn ar-Rashīd, changed his dress and roamed in the streets of the capital to find out the condition of his subjects.[52] It was usual to employ prostitutes for spying and securing information.[53] Queens and princes had their own agents.[54] Spies were also kept by the Sulṭāns on the frontiers of the Valley to keep an eye on the activities of the *Nāyaks* and to report on the enemy movements beyond.[55]

Khazānchī[56] or Khazāna-dār

As the name implies, the *Khazānchī* was in charge of the treasury. In Hindu times he was called *Gañjavara*[57] after the Persian *Ganjwar,* and he continued to be called by the same title under the early Shāh Mīrs, but later on he was named *Khazānchī.* The importance of the office depended upon the personality of the man at the head. Thus Ḥasan, who was the Treasurer of Sulṭān Zainu'l-'Ābidīn, played a decisive part in securing the succession for Ḥājī Khān,[58] and, when the latter ascended the throne, he put the mark of royalty on his forehead.[59] There is no evidence of any other Treasurer having played an equally significant role in the affairs of state.

Police : Kotwāl and Muḥtasib

In the time of the Rājās, Srīnagar had a Prefect who was called *Nagarādhipa* or *Nagarādhikṛta.*[60] His duty was to collect fines levied on the people by the government, and to look after their morals. He also supervised weights and measures, the trades, and other matters relating to the town. Under the Sulṭāns these duties were performed by the *Kotwāl* and the *Muḥtasib.* The *Kotwāl* was responsible for maintaining law and order in the city, and for protecting the citizens from thieves and robbers.

His powers were great, and he could put the thieves to death.[61] In order to discharge his duties efficiently he had a police force at his disposal. The *Muḥtasib* supervised the markets, inspected weights and measures, and looked after the morals of the people. In addition, it was his duty to see that the public prayers were conducted properly; that intoxicating liquors and drugs were not manufactured or sold publicly; that no one was found drunk in public places; and that gambling and immoral living were not carried on. His powers were great in the time of Sikandar and those rulers who were anxious that the practices of the people should conform to Islamic teachings Under Mīrzā Ḥaidar Dughlat every part of Srīnagar, and every village and pargana in the kingdom had a *Muḥtasib* who was required to see that the people prayed five times a day and did not deviate from the precepts of Islām.[62] The *Muḥtasib* had no right to hold a formal trial, which could only be done by a *Qāẓī*. But he could initiate cases, and could also give light punishments for ordinary misdemeanours after a summary trial. Serious cases, however, which required proper investigation and legal exposition, were referred to the *Qāẓī* and *Muftī*. The *Muḥtasib* was really an executive officer.[63]

Central Record Department

All the official documents were kept in a separate record office at Srīnagar. Until the reign of Sulṭān Zainu'l-'Ābidīn, owing to the scarcity of paper, they were written on *bhūrja* (the inner bark of the Himālayan birch) with the ink made of powdered charcoal of almonds boiled in *gomutra (Urina Bovis).* The ink thus obtained is not spoilt by damp or water.[64] From the time of Zainu'l-'Ābidīn paper began to be manufactured in Kashmīr, and so, henceforth, the documents were written both on the birch-bark and on paper.[65] Besides Srīnagar there was also a record office at Sōpūr, the capital of Kamrāj. But during the reign of Zainu'l-'Ābidīn all the previous records were destroyed.[66]

In addition to the above, there were also many other officials and minor departments of the central government. Every department had a secretary called *Dabīr*.[67] The king's court of justice, which Jonarāja calls *Dharmādhikara*, had a superintendent who appears to have been a responsible officer.[68] He was a confidant of the Sulṭān, but his duties are not known. The guardianship of the royal princes was a coveted post for which there was a keen competition. The holder of the office had the status of a minister, and was a member of the Sulṭān's council. Then there was the Court Astrologer and the Court Physician both of whom enjoyed the Sulṭān's utmost confidence.[69] There was a separate department of music with an officer at its head.[70] The *Purohita* or the Brahman priest was an important person under the early Shāh Mīrs, but later his importance declined as his functions were taken over by the *Shaikhu'l-Islām*.[71]

Provincial and Local Government

The only part of the kingdom of Kashmīr that was directly governed by the Sulṭān or his agents consisted of the Kashmīr Valley and Lohara. The rest was ruled by its own chiefs who were independent in their internal affairs. The Valley of Kashmīr was divided into two provinces, Marāj on the east and Kamrāj on the west.[72] Marāj comprised the districts on both sides of the Jehlam, and Kamrāj those below.[73] Sōpūr was the headquarters of Kamrāj, while Srīnagar was the chief city of Marāj.[74]

The government of Srīnagar was directly under the Sulṭān, while the two provinces were administered by governors called *Ḥākims*, who generally belonged to the royal family.[75] Thus Zainu'l-'Ābidīn appointed his son Adham as governor of Kamrāj, and later Ḥaidar Shāh conferred upon his son Ḥasan the same province as jāgīr.[76] Under the later Shāh Mīrs, the Valley was divided among three or four feudal chiefs who were responsible for the administration of their respective areas. But the general supervision of the kingdom continued to be vested in the *Wazīr* who ruled in the name of the puppet Sulṭān.

The provincial government was a replica of the central government. The *Ḥākim* was required to maintain law and order, collect revenue and dispense justice. Being the head of the civil and military administration of the province, his powers were great; and as there were no constitutional checks on him, it was not unusual for him to defy the authority of the centre. To prevent this the Sulṭāns appointed such persons as governors whom they could trust. But they were not always successful in their choice, and consequently rebellions were a matter of common occurrence.

The *Qāẓī* was the head of the judiciary of the province, and was appointed by the centre. Under him there were *Qāẓīs* and *Muftīs* in every town and pargana. But there was no *Mīr 'Adl* who was only appointed in Srīnagar. The *Kotwāl* and *Muḥtasib* were in charge of the safety and morals of the inhabitants of the town. The espionage department kept the Sulṭān informed of the affairs of the provinces and of the activities of the provincial and local officials. The records of the government were kept in a record office under the care of a special officer.

The provinces were divided for administrative purpose into small districts called parganas,[77] each under a *Shiqdār*.[78] The number of these parganas was not constant but was changed from time to time by splitting them up or amalgamating them owing to reasons of administration. It is not known what was the number of parganas under Zainu'l-'Ābidīn or before him. According to *Lokaprakāśa* the Valley was divided into twenty-seven *Viṣayas,* but it is difficult to say to which period this list refers. Moreover, it gives only nineteen names of which only a few can be identified.[79] Under Muḥammad Shāh, however, the number of parganas was twenty-seven, but their names have not been mentioned.[80] Under Mīrzā Ḥaidar Dughlat, the number was increased to thirty.[81] According to Abū'l-Faẓl, under Akbar, the return of Āṣaf Khān showed thirty-eight parganas, whilst the earlier one of Qāẓī 'Alī contained forty-one.[82] Probably the last seems to be the number which existed during the Chak period.

Each pargana comprised a number of villages, whose total in the Valley amounted to 60,000.[83] Each village had an accountant or *paṭwārī* who was called in the Hindu times *Grāmakāyastha.*[84] What he was designated under the Sulṭāns is not known. For the maintenance of law and order there was a police officer called *Sarhang Zāda* who had under him a group of villages.[85] Under him were the Caṇḍalas who swept the houses in the day and acted as village watchmen in the night, and for this service they were given food by the villagers.[86] In the time of Mīrzā Ḥaidar every village had also a *Muḥtasib* whose duty was to see that the inhabitants lived a life in conformity with Islamic teachings. The chronicles do not tell us if the institution of *panchāyat* existed, nor do they mention the existence of the village headman.

Vassal Chiefs

The vassal chiefs belonged to the landowning families like the Māgres, Rainas, Chaks, Baṭs, and Dārs. They were assigned big jāgīrs, which could be passed on from father to son. In return they were required to pay revenue to the Sulṭān, to serve in the government, and to render him military aid in time of war. But since the chiefs were very powerful, possessing a large body of retainers, they were a great source of danger to the state. They constantly rose in rebellion and prevented the growth of a strong, centralised government. Under weak Sulṭāns they even appropriated large areas of the country to themselves.[87] And since they were exempted from paying land revenue and other taxes,[88] the income derived from the rest of the kingdom could not have been enough to run an efficient administration.

Khāliṣa Lands

These were the crown lands which were directly administered by Sulṭan. Even when the latter was deprived of all his powers, and the Valley was divided by the nobles among themselves as their private estate, he was still left in possession of the crown lands.

Lohara

The territory of Lohara had been subject to the Hindu kings of Kashmīr since ancient times, but during the period of their decline it had become independent. It was reconquered by Sulṭān Shihābu'd-Dīn only to reassert its independence during the last years of his reign. Quṭbu'd-Dīn tried to bring it under his rule, but without success; and it was not until the time of Zainu'l-'Ābidīn that it was once again reduced. It was he who abolished the reigning dynasty, and henceforth, till the end of the Sultanate, Lohara was directly governed from Srīnagar through a governor. Ḥājī Khān, the Sulṭān's second son, was appointed its first governor in 1452.[89]

Tributary States

The tributary states comprised Pakhlī, the Kishangangā Valley, Ladākh, Baltistān, Kishtwār and all the territory of the outer hills from the Rāvi on the east to the Jehlam on the west. The rulers of these states looked upon the Kashmīr Sulṭān as their suzerain, paid him tribute, gave their daughters in marriage to him or to the heir-apparent, and secured from him sanction for the succession to the throne.[90] They also supplied him with troops in case of war, presented themselves at the court on the occasion of the accession of a new Sulṭān, and participated in the coronation ceremonies at the conclusion of which they received gifts and *khil'ats*.[91] In the internal administration of their states, however, they were entirely free. Interference was only deemed necessary in case of a rebellion when an army was sent to reduce them to obedience. During the reigns of weak Sulṭāns, the chiefs invariably asserted their independence and withheld payment of tribute.

The Army

The army under the Sulṭāns consisted of (1) The Standing Army (2) Provincial Troops (3) Feudal Levies (4) Volunteers.

The first category of troops was under the Sulṭān's direct control and employment, and was recruited from amongst the Khaśas, Rājpūts, Sayyids, Māgres, Chaks, Rainas and others, who had the reputation of being good soldiers. The Ḍombas, too, were enlisted and were known to be stubborn fighters, but they had one great defect. They were unreliable, and at the least opportunity they turned aside from the battle and started plundering. The standing army was stationed at the capital, and in the time of war the Sulṭān marched at its head to repel the enemy, and detached a part of it under a separate commander. The army comprised foot and cavalry. The horsemen rode on ponies, but the officers rode on horses imported from Turkistān and 'Irāq, for Kashmīr itself did not breed horses of good quality.[92] Owing to the mountainous nature of the country, the cavalry was the most important arm of the fighting forces, and that is why an attempt to seize the throne was usually preceded by the capture of the royal stable. Elephants were also employed,[93] but as they had to be imported from India through difficult passes, their number was necessarily small, and their role in the army was therefore not important.

The provincial troops were stationed in the various provincial towns. Their number varied according to the strategic importance of the place. Then there were the garrisons in the frontier forts or watch-stations *(drangas)* at the head of the passes,[94] which were under their respective commanders called *Nāyaks*. There were also garrisons in the forts built inside the Valley at strategic places like Nāgām, Lār, Andarkōṭ, Chiraodar, Manār and Birū.

The feudal levies were the forces which the nobles supplied the Sulṭān in the time of war. Each contingent was under the command of its own chief. The rulers of Rajaurī, Jammu, Kishtwār and other tributary states also furnished troops. Volunteers were called out in times of emergency when the Valley was threatened by a foreign invasion. Usually the response to the Sulṭān's appeal was favourable, and the people rallied to the defence of their country.

Weapons

The weapons commonly employed were sword, bow and arrow, spear, battle-axe and mace. The soldiers wore coats of mail, while the horses were caparisoned with steel. Śrīvara refers to a weapon, made for the first time in Kashmīr in the time of Zainu'l-'Ābidīn, which "destroys forts, pierces the hearts of men, strikes horses with terror, throws balls of stone from a distance, and remains unseen by the soldiers from encampments".[95] At another place he says that the Sulṭān's army was "furnished with weapons like lightning, showering forth arrows with deep and prolonged roar".[96] This account gave occasion to the surmise in later times that these weapons were cannons using gunpowder.[97] But it must be remembered that Śrīvara, being a poet, was very often carried away by his imagination, and so his description must not be taken too literally. Moreover, he nowhere mentions *ayoguda* (gunpowder); he only refers to the use of *kṣara.*[98] Thus there is no reliable evidence to show that gunpowder was known in the time of Zainu'l-'Ābidīn. What really must have been employed is the Greek Fire of naphtha which also produced, like the gunpowder, considerable sound;[99] and the weapon invented was not a cannon but some kind of a mechanical device by which fire-missiles or stones could be discharged.[100] However, these weapons, on account of the difficulties of their manufacture, were rarely employed. That is why there is no reference to them in the civil war between Muḥammad Shāh and Fatḥ Shāh or in the war of resistance against Mīrzā Ḥaidar.[101] It was in the time of the later Shāh Mīrs or the Chaks that gunpowder came to be known in Kashmīr, but even then its use was on a restricted scale. It appears that Ghāzī Shāh was the first Sulṭān to possess a canon which he employed against Qarā Bahādur.[102] Subsequently in the war of succession between Yūsuf Shāh and Abdāl Chak muskets were used, for the latter is said to have been wounded by a shot.[103] Yūsuf Shāh's army, which was organised to resist the Mughal invasion under Rāja Bhagwān Dās, is said to have had 7,000 musketeers, but the number appears to be highly exaggerated.[104]

Mode of Fighting

From the very scanty information that is available regarding the military organisation under the Sulṭāns, it appears that army was divided into five corps: centre, two wings, vanguard and rearguard.[105] In the front were sometimes the elephants.[106] Unlike modern times, the commander of the army himself led the attack. If he was killed, the next in command took the field.[107] Sometimes there were single combats as a result of the challenge from one side to the other.[108] After this there was a general melée. The spirit of the soldiers was roused by the beating of kettle drums.[109] The troops did not wear any special dress, but bore some mark by which they could be distinguished from the enemy.[110] In addition to this they carried banners which were of blood-red colour.[111]

The most common method of warfare in which the Kashmīrīs excelled was the surprise attack usually delivered before dawn. It was employed both in the civil wars and against the foreign invaders. It was these surprise attacks which wore down Mīrzā Ḥaidar, and inflicted great loses on Qāsīm Khān, Akbar's general. They were, in fact, always employed whenever it was felt that, owing to the inferiority in numbers, a pitched battle would not be successful.

The guerilla type of warfare also found great favour with the Kashmīrīs. It was employed whenever the country was subjected to a foreign invasion. The Kashmīrī chiefs would then escape to the mountains and carry on resistance from there. They would cut off the supplies of the enemy, swoop down upon him from their mountain hideouts, and thus compel him to make peace and withdraw.

The forts which were situated at various strategic places, did not play any direct part either in the civil wars or at the time of foreign invasions. Wars were fought in the narrow mountain defiles and passes or on the plain, and the forts served only as stations from which the garrison could sally forth to attack the enemy. They were never employed to check the progress of the invading army which, in consequence, never stopped to besiege them. It is significant to remember that Srīnagar itself did not possess a fort. There were one fort in Naushahr (Srīnagar), but it was not strong. The battle for its capture was fought either in the neighbourhood or in the city itself. During the civil wars it was a common practice to destroy the bridges over the Jehlam in order to defend the city. But this method was rarely effective, for an enterprising commander was always able to force his way across the river.

Finance

The information existing in the chronicles about the fiscal affairs under the Sulṭāns is very meagre. It is, however, clear that the system of taxation did not always conform to the *Sharī'a*. The main heads of revenue were : (1) *Kharāj* (2) *Jizya*

(3) *Z̲akāt* and Customs Duty (4) other taxes (5) Assignments and Tribute.

Kharāj was realised both from Muslims and non-Muslims, for there is no evidence to suggest that the former were exempted from it and paid only an *'ushr* i.e. one-tenth.[112] When Shāh Mīr ascended the throne he fixed the revenue demand at one-sixth of the produce of land.[113] He fixed it at such a low rate partly in order to win the goodwill of the people, and partly because he realised that, since the material prosperity of the Valley had been declining for over two hundred years, the paying capacity of the peasant was very low. But under his successors the revenue demand was increased to one-third, and generally speaking this remained the rate of assessment throughout the Sultanate period.[114] In case there were famines or floods the government granted large remissions. Thus when a famine took place in the reign of Zainu'l-'Ābidīn, the Sulṭān reduced the rent to one-fourth, and in some places like Zainagīr to one-seventh.[115]

According to Mīzā Ḥaidar Dughlat land in Kashmīr was divided into four kinds: *Abī, Lalmī, Bāghī,* and meadow lands.[116] The first was the land which grew crops with the help of irrigation. Assessment on this was heavier than on other types. The second kind of land depended upon the natural rainfall. Since this could not be controlled, such lands were lightly taxed. The third kind on which fruit trees were planted were exempted from taxation under the Shāh Mīrs.[117] But although the early Chak rulers imposed a tax on gardens, it was abolished by Yūsuf Shāh.[118] The fourth kind, namely the meadow lands on the banks of rivers, were also not taxed, because they were swampy, and so were not fit for cultivation.[119]

Each village was assessed at so many *kharwārs* of rice, and the produce could not be removed from the threshing floor by the villagers until the state's share had been taken from it. The grain was stored by the government in the granaries built in the towns for the purpose, and then sold to the non-agricultural population at fixed prices. In this way prices were kept steady, and, in times of scarcity, cornering of grain was prevented, and people were enabled to buy it cheap.[120]

Jizya

No evidence exists in the chronicles to suggest that the *Jizya* was realized from the non-Muslims by the Shāh Mīr rulers before Sulṭān Sikandar. It was he who for the first time imposed it in order that his administration might conform to Islamic practices.[121] When Zainu'l-'Ābidīn came to the throne he reduced the *Jizya* from two *pals* of silver, collected under his father, to the nominal amount of one *māshā* of silver.[122] But even this was not collected, and the same was the practice under his successors.[123] When, however, Fatḥ Shāh became ruler for the second time his prime minister, Mūsā Raina, reimposed it under the influence of Shamsu'd-Dīn, and it continued to be collected during the regime of Daulat Chak, the prime minister of Sulṭān Ismā'īl Shāh II, and later under the Chak rulers.[124] But Yūsuf Shāh abolished it.[125] Ya'qūb Shāh, however, must have reimposed it, for when Akbar annexed Kashmīr, it was being realised from the Hindus and was finally abolished by him.[126]

Ẕakāt and Customs Duty

The *Ẕakāt* (Poor Tax) was collected from the Muslims according to the rates prescribed by the *Sharī'a.* The Ṣufīs and the *'Ulamā* of Kashmīr never ceased exhorting the people to pay the *Ẕakāt*.[127] This shows that it was not an obligatory but a voluntary tax. However, in the reigns of some Sulṭāns it was realised by the state just like other taxes. Thus under Sulṭān Sikandar every one paid the *Ẕakāt*.[128] Similarly Yūsuf Shah realised it from every person except the boatmen, who were regarded as too poor to pay it.[129] It is not known whether the *Ẕakāt* was deposited in a separate treasury or was lumped together with the secular taxes. Nor has it been recorded as to how it was spent. Probably most of the money which the Sulṭāns gave away to the poor, or spent in providing food and shelter to the travellers, the students, and the needy, came from the *Ẕakāt*. According to the *Sharī'a* the realisation of customs duty is forbidden, for the only legal taxes are *Ẕakāt*, *Kharāj* and *Jizya*.[130] But since the customs duty was collected at the frontiers, the jurists resolved this contradiction between theory and practice by bringing the customs duty under the heading of *Ẕakāt*.

Accordingly after the Muslim merchant had paid the *Ẕakāt* he was allowed to cross the frontier.[131] But in Kashmīr, in addition to this, he had also to pay a duty on articles of import and export at the customs-posts which were known as *Rāh-dārī*.[132] The Hindu merchants also had to pay duties on their goods. And, as we have seen, the guardians of the passes were there to see that there was no smuggling, and that duty was realised from every trader.[133]

Other Cesses

Under the Rājās all kinds of taxes had been realised from the people. The villagers who did not turn up to carry their allotted loads, were fined to the value of the latter. Only the priests of the temples were exempted from the corvée.[134] Fees were realised for such events as marriages, feasts and festivals,[135] and taxes were imposed on boatmen, artisans, cows, and even on night soil.[136] When Shāh Mīr seized power he cancelled many of the exactions of former times. Similarly Sulṭān Sikandar abolished *Bāj* and *Tamghā*,[137] while Sulṭān Zainu'l-'Ābidīn abolished other extra taxes, and prohibited his officers from imposing arbitrary fines upon the people. Later Yūsuf Shāh abolished the taxes on artisans, cows and gardens, and the *Ẕākat* on boatmen.[138] This means that either all the taxes had not been abolished at one stroke of the pen, or they were reimposed in the subsequent reigns, for we find the rulers abolishing them again and again. When the Mughals conquered the Valley they also claimed to have abolished many of the vexatious taxes like *Bāj* and *Tamghā*, the levy of two dams on fuel, poll-tax from the boatmen, and sheep from the villagers.[139]

Mines were another source of income. But no details of this are found in the chronicles. We only know that the people collected gold particles from the sandy banks of rivers. The share of the state was one-sixth in the time of Zainu'l-'Ābidīn, and probably the subsequent rulers also realised it at the same rate.[140]

Assignments and Tribute

The practice of giving jāgīrs to nobles and officials was common in Hindu times. When, however, Shāh Mīr established his rule, he refrained from giving assignments indiscriminately, for he thought that this made the nobles strong and encouraged rebellions. But his successors did not follow this policy, and liberally gave away jāgīrs. Under the later Shāh Mīrs the nobles, who were the *de facto* rulers of the country, compelled the Sulṭāns to assign them, with the exception of the crown lands, the whole Valley, which they divided among themselves. When the Chaks established their dynasty they expropriated these assignments and granted fresh ones to their courtiers and officials. These jāgīrs were hereditary and managed by their holders. But they could be confiscated in case of disloyalty on the part of the jāgīrdārs.[141]

The tribute realised from the neighbouring states, subject to Kashmīr, was uncertain, for it depended upon the ability of the central government to enforce the demand. The tribute was generally paid in kind. Thus from Ladākh and Baltistān the Sulṭāns received wool and leather,[142] and from Kishtwār they got saffron.[143]

NOTES

1. Jonar., p. 86.
2. See p. 137 *supra.*
3. See pp. 155-56, *supra*.
4. See Appendix B for the titles of the Sulṭāns.
5. Ṣiddīqī, *Caliphate and Kingship in Medieval Persia*, pp. 34, 39 sq.
6. Arnold, *The Caliphate*, chapt. viii.
7. H.M., ff. 171, 180a.
8. See pp. 129, 142, 161 *supra.*
9. H.M., f. 171b.
10. Temple, *The Word of Lallā*, p. 211; Śriv., p. 207.
11. B.S., ff. 132b, 140a.
12. H.M., f. 174a; B.S., f. 148b.
13. N.A., f. 76b; N.K., f. 36b.
14. Temple, *The Word of Lallā*, pp. 210–11; also Jonar., p. 76, and Śrīv., p. 267. For *Chatr* see also B.S. f. 148b.
15. The first Muslim ruler to have started the practice of giving away *khil'ats* was Hārūn ar-Rashīd. (Dozy, *Noms des Vetements chez les Arabs,* p. 14).

16. See p. 80, *supra*.
17. Śrīv., p. 173; Munich MS., f. 77a; H.M., f. 152b.
18. Jonar., p. 75; Śrīv., p. 107.
19. Temple, *The Word of Lallā*, p. 211.
20. Stein, BK. v, No. 214; BK. vi, No. 199 and n.
21. S.A., p. 40. But Śrīvara calls the chief minister as Saciva. (Śrīv., B.K. 3, No. 23).
22. B.S., f. 19a. Under Ḥasan Shāh, Malik Aḥmad was in charge of the civil administration, and Tāzī Baṭ was the commander-in-chief (Śrīv., p. 238).
23. H.M., f. 131b; B.S., ff. 81b-82a.
24. Munich MS., ff. 82b-83a; T.A., iii, 457-8.
25. Mu'īnu'd-Dīn Miskīn, *Ta'rīkh-i-Kabīr*, p. 289, says that Mullā Aḥmad 'Allāma, who came to Kashmīr from Turkistān with Bulbul Shāh, was the first person in Kashmīr to hold the office of *Shaikhu'l-Islām* under Shamsu'd-Dīn I. But this is not corroborated by any reliable authority. Besides, it seems unlikely for such an institution to have been introduced at such an early date.
26. See p. 127, *supra*.
27. B.S. f. 34b; H.M., f. 119b.
28. W.K., ff. 52a, 60a.
29. B.S., f. 31b.
30. T.A., iii, 495. On one occasion, under Ḥusain Shāh, Shāfi'ite law was also applied (See p. 156, *supra*). Muftīs were killed during Ḥusain Shāh's reign for giving a wrong *fatwa*.
31. For Mīr 'Adl see H.M., 159b, and compare him with *Shāḥīd* (Metz, *Renaissance of Islam*, pp. 227-29).
32. See p. 158 *supra*.
33. See p. 84, *supra*.
34. See p. 161 *supra*.
35. Śrīv., p. 173; Munich MS., f. 77a.
36. H.M., f. 152b.
37. Stein, BK., iv, Nos. 142-3.
38. Qureshī, *Administration of the Sultanate of Dehlī*, p. 71.
39. H.M., f. 189b.
40. Ibn Ḥasan, *Central Structure of the Mughal Empire*, p. 215.
41. Munich MS., f. 66a.
42. T.A., iii, 448, calls him *Ḥājib-i-Dar*.
43. Śrīv., p. 208. Kalhaṇa calls him *Mahāpratihārapīḍā*. (Stein, BK. iv, Nos. 142-43).
44. Compare him with *Amīr Ḥājib* or *Barbek* of the Delhi Court. See Qureshī, *Administration of the Sultanate of Dehlī*, pp. 61–2.

45. Śrīv., pp. 310, 313; Śuka, p. 405; A.N., iii, 764. Stein is wrong in saying that they were called Maliks, Malik was in reality a title conferred by the Sulṭāns upon their officials.
46. Other of its equivalents were *Dvārādhipa, Dvāreśa* etc., (Stein, BK. v, No. 214).
47. *Tuḥfatu'l-Aḥbāb,* p. 64; Jonar., p. 66; Srīv., p. 271.
48. Stein, ii, p. 392.
49. Jonar., p. 97.
50. See p. 96, *supra*.
51. Śrīv., p. 101.
52. H.M., f. 121b; Ḥasan, f. 122a.
53. Nasīb, ff. 205b sqq.
54. Jōnar., p. 43.
55. Śuka, p. 350.
56. H.M., f. 159b.
57. Stein, BK. v, No. 177 and n. Under Lalitāditya he was called *Mahābhāṇḍāgāra* (Stein, BK. iv, No. 143). Śrīv. (Bo. ed.), BK. 2, No. 24, calls him *Kośeśa.*
58. See p. 80, *supra.*
59. Śrīv., p. 184.
60. Jonar. (Cal. ed.), No. 886; In verse No. 945 he is called *Adhikārī.*
61. Śrīv., p. 279. In one instance he even supervised the construction of a bridge. (Jonar., p. 89).
62. Nasīb, f. 512a.
63. For further details of the duties of the *Muḥtasib,* see Qureshī, *Administration of the Sultanate of Dehlī,* pp. 164-7; also Von Kramer, *Orient under the Caliphs,* pp. 292 sqq. (Trans. Khudā Bakhsh).
64. Buhler, *Report of Tour* (J.A.S.B., xii 1876), pp. 29-30.
65. The documents continued to be written on *bhūrja* down to the 17th century. (Stein, BK. vii, No. 508).
66. Śrīv., pp. 155-6.
67. Stein, BK. v. No. 177.
68. Jonar. (Bo. ed.), Nos. 11, 1306.
69. See p. 88, *supra,* for the position of the Court Astrologer and Court Physician under Zainu'l-'Ābidīn. Compare Stein, BK. i, Nos. 118-19.
70. Under Ḥasan Shāh, Śrīvara was the head of the Music Department.
71. This change took place in the time of Sikandar.
72. A.A., ii, 367. In Hindu times the divisions were called Madavarājya and Kramarājya. (Stein, ii, 436).
73. Stein, ii, 436.

74. *Ibid.*, Śrīv., p. 156.
75. In Hindu times the governor was called *Maṇḍaleśa.* (Stein, BK. viii, No. 1117).
76. See p. 96, *supra*.
77. These were called *Viṣayas* in Hindu times. (Stein, ii, 437); also Śrīv. (Bo. ed.), BK. iv, No. 570.
78. Firishta, p. 657; T.H., ii, f 96a.
79. *Indische Studien*, xviii, p. 370; Stein, ii, 437 and n. 6.
80. Śrīv. (Bo. ed.), BK. iv, No. 570.
81. Nasīb, f. 513b.
82. A.A., ii, 367; *Haft Iqlīm*, f. 156a, gives the number of parganas as 32 and their income as 3 crore *tankas*.
83. Jonar. (Bo. ed.), No. 153.
84. Stein, BK. v., No. 175.
85. *Nūr-nāma*, f. 192b.
86. Ḥasan, f. 90a; H.M. (B.N.), f. 31a. Compare the Caṇḍalas with the Doms of Lawrence *valley*, p. 228. Under the Rājās also the Caṇḍalas acted as watchmen. (Stein, BK. viii, No. 309).
87. Śrīv., p. 303.
88. *Ibid.*, p. 304.
89. See p. 75, *supra*. In 1530 we find that Muḥammad Shāh, when he became Sulṭān for the fourth time, collecting taxes from Lohara. (Śuka, p. 368).
90. Śrīv., p. 123.
91. Śrīv., p. 284.
92. *Tuzuk-i-Jahāngīri,* ii, 148.
93. H.M., ff. 156a-b. For the employment of elephants under Harṣa of Kashmīr, see Stein, BK. vii, Nos. 1553-5.
94. Stein, BK. viii, No. 2010 and n.
95. Śrīv,. p. 105.
96. *Ibid.*, p. 112.
97. J.A.S.B., xlv, p. 36. Śrivara uses the word *vajra* which means weapon and not cannon. (Srīv., BK. I, chap. i, Nos. 72 sq.).
98. Śrīv. (Bo. ed.), BK. I, chap. iv, Nos. 19 sq. *Kṣara* means saltpetre. There is again a reference to *kṣara* in verse No. 28.
99. J.A.S.B., xiv, p. 36. It is important to note that Muslim writers confused *nafṭ (naphta*) with *bārūd* (gunpowder). See a discussion of this in David Ayalon, *Gunpowder and Firearms in the Mamlūk Kingdom,* pp. 9 sq.
100. J.A.S.B., xiv, pp. 40, 42. See W.K., f. 49b, for the stone which was thrown on the Khānqāh-i-Mu'allā and which damaged the roof. H.M., f. 151a is wrong in saying that it was a cannon ball.

101. According to B.S., f. 83b, there were 20 muskets used in Kashmīr during the civil war between Muḥammad Shāh and Fatḥ Shāh.
102. Śuka (Bo. ed.), No. 460. The word *topha* is used by Śrīvara which is a corrupt form of *top* meaning cannon.
103. A.A. (Blochmann), p. 535.
104. H.M., f. 189b.
105. *Ibid.,* f. 144a; A.N., iii, 770.
106. *Ibid.,* f. 156a. See Stein, BK. vii, Nos. 553-5, for the employment of elephants under the kings of Kashmīr.
107. B.S., f. 92b.
108. *Ibid.*
109. Śrīv., p. 288; Śuka., p. 386.
110. Śrīv., p. 293.
111. Jonar., p. 75; Śriv., p. 207.
112. In Kashmīr no *'ushrī* lands existed. Muslims and Hindus alike were subjected to the same rates of taxation. In the chronicles the word *kharāj* (land revenue) is constantly used.
113. Munich MS., f. 53b.
114. A.A., ii, 366.
115. Śrīv., p. 156.
116. T.R., (MS.), f. 15a; also A.A., ii, 352n. 3.
117. T.R., p. 425.
118. H.M., f. 182b.
119. T.R., p. 425.
120. Śrīv., p. 119; Munich MS., f. 75b. See also Stein, BK. viii, No. 61, for conditions under the Rājās; also BK. viii, Nos. 1245-7n.
121. H.M., f. 113b. According to Jonar., p. 60, Brahmans had to pay a fine for retaining their caste. This was, in fact, nothing else but the *Jizya*.
122. See p. 87, *supra.*
123. *Ibid.*
124. Śriv., pp. 388, 420.
125. H.M., f. 182; also H.M. (B.N.), f. 59a.
126. Suka, pp. 420-21.
127. Sayyid 'Alī, *Ẕakhīratu'l-Mulūk,* ff. 2b, 14b; Nasīb, f. 222a.
128. Munich MS., f. 64b, says that Sikandar exempted the merchants from the *Ẕakāt*, but this is apocryphal.
129. H.M., f. 182b.
130. Aghnides, *Muhammadan Theories of Finance,* p. 200.
131. *Ibid.,* pp. 261 sqq.
132. J.A.S.B., lxiv, pp. 385-6.
133. Jonar., p. 97. Hindu and Muslim merchants alike had to pay

customs duty.

134. Stein, BK. v, No. 174 and n.
135. *Ibid.*, BK. vii, No. 42; BK. viii, No. 1428.
136. *Ibid.*, BK. vii, No. 1107.
137. See p. 62, *supra,* for *Baj* and *Tamghā.*
138. H.M., f. 182b.
139. A.A., ii, 367. Moorcroft, *Travels,* pp. ii, 126-7, says that during his time bakers, butchers, boatmen, scavengers and even prostitutes were taxed.
140. See p. 83, *supra.*
141. Śrīv., p. 244.
142. Bernier, *Travels* in *the Mughal Empire,* p. 420. During the reign of Ibrāhīm Shāh, the Ladākhīs paid as revenue 500 horses, 1000 pieces of paṭṭu, 50 yaks and 200 tolas of gold. (T.A., iii, 481).
143. H.M., f. 167b.

Chapter 12

Social and Economic Conditions

The spread of Islām in Kashmīr from the latter half of the fourteenth century onwards brought about a great transformation in the life of the people. The cultural contacts that were established with Persia and Turkistān and the influx of a large number of Muslims from those countries also effected profound social changes. But despite this foreign impact, which was far-reaching, links with the past were not broken, for the Kashmīrīs refused to give up their beliefs and practices completely. That is why throughout the fourteenth and fifteenth centuries there was a constant conflict between those who wanted to cling to their traditional manners and customs, and those who were eager to introduce the Perso-Islamic way of life. In the end, however, the conflict was resolved by the fusion of the old and the new. This resulted in the emergence of a society in which the old ideas and institutions were mixed up with the new.

Society

Society in Kashmīr during the Hindu times was divided into four castes. But these divisions were not as rigid as in India. It was, for example, not uncommon for the rulers to take Ḍomba girls or prostitutes as their wives and make them their chief queens.[1] There were also instances of low-born persons rising to the highest positions in the state. Nevertheless, the Brahmans occupied a privileged position. Those who were in charge of temples were exempt from corvée and taxation.[2] The Brahman priests very often interfered in the affairs of the kingdom, and if they disapproved of anything, they fasted until the powers that be were coerced into surrender.[3]

With the spread of Islām, the status and influence of the Brahmans gradually declined, for their place was taken by Sayyids, *'Ulamā, Pīrs,* and other groups among the Muslims. Another important change that took place was that, with the exception of the Brahmans who resisted conversion, the members belonging to all other castes embraced Islām. As a result only one caste, namely, that of the Brahmans, survived, while the other three castes disappeared. However, many of the converts did not give up their surnames. Thus persons who bear the titles of Kauls, Baṭs, Aitūs, Mantūs, Ganā'īs, and Rainas (Razdan) are the descendants of Brahmans; while those who are called Māgres, Dārs (Hindu Dars or Dhars), Rainas (Rājpūts), Rāthōrs, Thākurs, Nāyaks, and Chaks have a Kṣatriya origin.[4] But there were some who after conversion gave up their caste names, and so began to be called by the profession which they adopted.[5] The Brahmans, who clung to their religion and caste, became divided in the course of time into two sub-castes; the Kārkuns who studied Persian and entered government service and Bhāṣā Bhaṭṭa who studied Sanskrit and looked after the religious affairs of the community.[6]

Although divisions in Kashmīr society based on caste disappeared for the most part, they were replaced by class distinctions which, in certain cases, retained the old rigidity. Islām no doubt provided a unifying and leavening force, and the Ṣūfīs tried to bridge the gulf between the different classes, but, owing to the economic disparities and functional differences, real social equality could not be achieved.

Nobility

At the head stood the Sulṭān and his family. Next came the nobles who were the heads of such families as Chaks, Māgres, Rainas, Dārs and Baṭs. They held big jāgīrs and the highest posts in the government. Their titles, privileges and jāgīrs, unlike those of the Mughal nobles, were hereditary, and could not be taken away from them except in case of disloyalty. Owing to their wealth and position the nobles employed a large number of retainers. They were generally men of culture, and patronized men of learning. They built religious edifices and gave endowments for educational purposes. Moreover, they supplied from their ranks the chief civil and military officers to the state, and protected it against foreign aggression. But they spent most of their energies in intriguing against one another to secure the king's favour; or, if the latter was weak, to usurp his functions and even to supplant him. It is in this way that the Chaks replaced the Shāh Mīrs, and founded their own dynasty. But the change did not put an end to the feudal rivalries and scramble for power. In fact the civil conflicts became so accentuated as to lead to foreign invasions, and to the eventual loss of Kashmīr's independence.

The families which played a distinguished part during the Muslim period were either of foreign origin or emerged into prominence under the Sulṭāns. The Chaks entered Kashmīr in the reign of Sūhadeva, while the Baihaqī Sayyids came in the time of Sikandar. The Rainas, Māgres, Dārs, and other families were of indigenous origin, but, with the exception of the first, the rest assumed importance only during the Muslim period. The princes were always called by the title of Khān, but sometimes the nobles had also 'Khān' attached to their names. Other titles that were conferred upon the nobles by the Sulṭāns were Malik, Amīru'l-Umarā', Khān-i-Zamān, Mīrzā,[7] and Shaukat Jung.

The Sulṭāns married within the families of Chaks, Māgres and the Baihaqī Sayyids, but they also entered into matrimonial alliances with the families of the Rājās of Jammu, Kishtwār, and Rajaurī and those of the rulers of Pakhlī and Sindh. The nobles generally married within their own families, but marriages between different families were not uncommon.[8] Although birth was an important factor in determining one's station in life, yet society was not a closed circle, for we find individuals of humble origin and families, unknown before, emerging into prominence by their ability and energy.

The Religious Class

After the nobles came the religious classes composed of the

'ulamā or theologians, the Sayyids, the Ṣūfīs and their descendants.

(a) *'Ulamā* : Islām as taught by the Prophet Muḥammad had no ordained clergy. However, with the rescension of the Qur'ān and the *Ḥadīs̤,* those learned in them assumed almost the position of ordained clergy as doctors and interpreters of law. And because of the latter function, combined with their profound learning and piety, the *'Ulamā* commanded great respect among the people. Moreover, Muḥammad was reputed to have said that the *'Ulamā* must be honoured for they are the successors of the prophets, and that he who honours them honours the Prophet of Islām and Allāh thereby.[9] Thus in Kashmīr, as in other Muslim countries, the *'Ulamā* were held in high respect. From among them were recruited the *Qaẓī, Muftīs,* and *Shaikhu'l-Islāms.* In theory the democratic principles were carried into effect in this class, but in practice there was a strong hereditary tendency. Many of the *'Ulamā* were of foreign origin, and were learned in Muslim theology, logic and *Ḥadīs̤*. The Kashmīrī *'Ulamā* after studying at the feet of some learned and pious man in Srīnagar proceeded to Samarqand, Herāt or Mecca, and returned after having undergone a course of training abroad. It was only then that they were regarded as full-fledged jurists. The *'Ulamā,* as a rule, led a simple and pious life. They held aloft the principles of the *Sharī'a,* and fought against any accretions and innovations in Islām. Their interest was, however, not confined merely to social and religious problems; they also sometimes took an active part in the politics of their day.

(b) *Sayyids :* In the fourteenth century a large number of Sayyids sought shelter in Kashmīr in order to escape from the wrath of first the Mongols and then of Tīmūr. They were attracted to the Valley owing to the peace that prevailed there compared to the social and political upheavals that were characteristic of Central Asia and Persia during this period. Moreover, they also came on account of the patronage that was extended to them by the Sulṭāns. And the process of immigration once begun continued down to the fall of the Sultanate.

Owing to their descent from Muḥammad, through his daughter Fāṭima, a special sanctity was attached to the Sayyids among the Muslims. They were treated with special respect, and the kings and nobles conferred upon them all kinds of privileges. Some of the Sayyids who came to Kashmīr were jurists and were appointed *Qāẓīs* and *Muftīs* by the Sulṭāns. Some took to the profession of teaching; others were men of piety and supplied recruits to the ranks of *Pīrs* and *Murshids* who acted as the spiritual preceptors of the ignorant masses. A few found their way into the villages and became agriculturists. There were still others, like the Baihaqī Sayyids, who turned to politics. They married in the family of the Sulṭāns and in this way entered the ranks of the Kashmīrī nobles. But because of their arrogance and ambition they aroused the jealousy of the Kashmīrī chiefs who formed a conspiracy to overthrow them. Gradually, however, the Baihaqī Sayyids, by pursuing a policy of moderation and patriotism, succeeded in removing from themselves the taint which they carried as foreigners and in establishing their confidence among the people. After this they played an important role in the social and political history of the Valley.

(c) Ṣūfīs : The *Pīrs* with their *Murīds* formed an important group in medieval Kashmīr, and exercised greater influence on the social, religious, and cultural life of the country than the *'Ulamā*. They were looked upon with great reverence by all classes of people because of their great learning and piety, but above all because they were supposed to possess miraculous powers. They led a life of simplicity, but they did not renounce the world or isolate themselves from the people and their problems. On the contrary, most of them led a normal life, had wives and children, and took an active interest in the affairs of the community.[10] Sayyid 'Alī Hamadānī held the opinion that Muslims should limit their desires according to the dictates of religion, but they should not annihilate them like the Hindu Sādhūs or Muslim Faqīrs.[11] He denounced the practice of crippling one's hands or feet, or unnecessarily inflicting bodily sufferings upon oneself. He believed in a balanced life, a golden mean.[12]

The *Pīr* lived in the *Khānqāh,*[13] built and endowed for him by the princes and nobles, with his family and his professional followers[14] who worshipped with him and were taught by him how to attain mystic experience. There was a simple initiation ceremony in which the disciple pledged devotion. After this he lived in close association with his *Pīr* until he reached the higher stages of initiation when he might go out to teach his master's way (*ṭarīqa*) and make new disciples.[15] When the *Pīr* died he was succeeded by a *Khalīfa* who stood high among the disciples for his moral, intellectual, and spiritual qualities. Sometimes hereditary principle was followed in making these appointments. The *Khānqāh* also had an Imām whose duty was to lead the prayers.[16]

There were six main Ṣūfī ordrs in medieval Kashmīr. These were Qādirīya, Suhrawardīya, Kubravīya, Naqshabandīya, Nūrbakhshīya, and Rishī. The first five were introduced from Persia and Turkistān, but the order of the Rishīs was of indigenous origin.[17] It was founded by Nūru'd-Dīn[18] who was born in the village of Kaimūh, two miles west of Bījbehāra, in 779/1377. His father was Shaikh Sālāru'd-Dīn, also a pious man, belonging to the family of the rulers of Kishtwār. Although an orthodox Muslim, Nūru'd-Dīn was much influenced in his ascetic outlook by the Hindu Sadhūs. Unlike Sayyid 'Alī Hamadānī and Shamsu'd-Dīn, he preferred a life of retirement, and was accustomed to withdraw to caves for mediation and prayer. He renounced the world and its pleasures, left his wife and children, and gave up taking meat. In his last days, he at first subsisted only on one cup of milk daily, but towards the end, he took nothing else except water, and died at the age of 63 in 842/1438.[19] He had a large number of disciples, the most prominent among whom were Bābā Naṣīru'd-Dīn, Bābā Bāmu'd-Dīn, Bābā Zainu'd-Dīn and Bābā Laṭīfu'd-Dīn. His tomb in Chrār, twenty miles south-west of Srīnagar, attracts thousands of people, both Hindus and Muslims, every year.

The tendency to asceticism became more and more pronounced among the Rishīs after the death of Nūru'd-Dīn, until from the sixteenth century onwards, disgusted by the greed and selfishness of the ruling class and the constant civil wars in the country, they completely cut themselves off from the world. They did not marry, abstained from meat, and subsisted on dry bread or wild fruits of the mountains. They lived away from human habitations, moving from place to place, and planting shady and fruit bearing trees for the benefit of the people.[20] Unlike Nūru'd-Dīn and his disciples, the Rishīs of the later period were for the most part illiterate, and did not possess any knowledge of their religion. Nevertheless, they led a life of piety, self-denial, simplicity, and virtue. In the time of Akbar and Jahāngīr there were about 2,000 Rishīs in the Valley.[21]

The Ṣūfīs played a very important role in spreading Islām in Kashmīr. Moreover, since in Ṣūfism there was a marked tendency towards social equality, the Ṣūfīs acted as a kind of bridge between the rich and the poor. The *Z̲ikr* ceremonies possessed not merely a devotional aspect, but also served a social purpose, for on these occasions different classes of people gathered together, and all differences of wealth and poverty were forgotten

The Ṣūfīs always raised their voice against oppression and injustice. Nūru'd-Dīn Rishī, for example, took an officer to task for oppressing the peasants of a village.[22] Similarly Sayyid 'Alī Hamadānī never ceased exhorting the rulers to rule with justice and mildness. The just ruler, according to him, would be nearest to God on the Day of Judgement, while the severest punishment would be inflicted on the tyrant.[23]

The Ṣūfīs also played the role of social reformers. Thus it was under the influence of Sayyid 'Muhammad Hamadānī that Sulṭān Sikandar banned all intoxicants, *sati,* and other evil practices. Makhdūm Ḥamzā called upon the people to lead a virtuous life, pay the religious taxes, and acquire knowledge.[24] He was once so angry with a drunkard that he hit him on the head with a stick which caused his death.[25]

In spite of these benefits conferred by Ṣūfism, it also played a reactionary role. Owing to its emphasis on other worldiness it popularised the philosophy of quietism and escapism which was best represented by the Rishīs of Kashmīr. Moreover, by the admission of alien practices and ideas, it became debased. The *Ziārats* and *khānqāhs,* with which the country was studded, became the centres of superstition and charlatanism. They began to be worshipped by the credulous masses who came there as pilgrims to beseech the aid of the saint. The saint worship still plays an important part in the life of a Kashmīrī, who is being constantly exploited by the *Pīrs* and their disciples.

Merchants, Shop-keepers, Petty officials and Artisans

Kashmīr's internal and external trade brought into existence a class of rich men who socially belonged to the same strata of society as the shopkeepers, and petty officials, but owing to their wealth they were able to associate with the kings and nobles, and sometimes took an active part in the affairs of the country. Thus Śrībhaṭṭa and Tuṭṭa were the two merchants who were much respected by Sulṭān Sikandar.[26] Khwāja Ḥājī, who acted as the agent of Mīrzā Ḥaidar Dughlat, was also a merchant, and played an important role in the politics of his period. Under Ḥusain Shāh Chak, Fatḥ Khwāja Baqqāl rose to become prime minister and was given the title of Khān-i-Zamān. His son, too, for a time enjoyed the confidence of the Sulṭān. The rich merchants lived in their fine houses situated on the Jehlam in Srīnagar and Bārāmūla.[27] The shop-keepers, petty officials, and artisans resided in the more congested areas of the towns.

The Masses

These included peasants[28] and artisans, boatmen, butchers, gardeners and other groups performing menial jobs. Originally Hindus, all of them had become Muslims by the time of Zainu'l-'Ābidīn. However, in spite of a change of religion, some of the features of the caste system clung to them. They retained their old caste rules and even their functions, and intermarriages between the different groups were exceptions rather than the rule. At the lowest rung of the ladder stood the caṇḏālas, ḏombas and camārs. The caṇḏālas acted as watchmen and performed menial jobs like handling the bodies of persons executed or killed in war.[29] They also carried on agriculture, but being poor, they sometimes took to thieving.[30] The ḏombas too were poor, and lived by stealing, and were morally lax. However, they were good soldiers and were enlisted in the army.[31] The camārs, who came to Kashmīr in the time of the Sulṭāns, performed the work of taking out the hides of dead animals.[32] The shepherds of the Valley were known as chaupāns and formed a distinct group.[33] But they intermarried with the galawāns.[34] Slavery, which played such an important part in the social and political life of medieval Islām, did not exist on any large scale in Kashmīr. It is true that some of the Sulṭāns employed slaves among whom a few rose to occupy high positions in the state; but there is no evidence in the chronicles to suggest that the merchants and the nobles also kept slaves. The institution of slavery was, in fact, looked upon with abhorrence by the Kashmīrīs.[35]

Position of Women

The position of women was the same as that of their sisters in Persia, Turkistān and India. The women of the upper classes lived in the seclusion of their houses. But those belonging to the lower classes, both in the towns and in the villages, could not afford the luxury of staying within the four walls of their houses, and moved about freely without a veil, doing out-door work, helping their husbands in the fields, in the gardens, or on the river.

As regards education it seems to have been widely spread among the well-to-do ladies, who were very cultured. They opened schools, built monasteries and mosques, and took an active interest in public affairs as is evident from the careers óf Sūra, Ḥayāt Khātūn, Gul Khātūn and Habbā Khātūn. The women of the lower classes, however, were illiterate, for they had neither the leisure to attend schools nor the means to employ private tutors. But as the life of Habbā Khātūn, the queen of Yūsuf Shāh, shows that opportunities were not wanting even for peasant girls who were keen to acquire knowledge.

Marriages were arranged, as at present, by parents. Polygamy was practised, but there is no evidence to suggest the existence of concubinage. Although prostitution was prevalent, yet with the exception of Ḥaidar Shāh and Ḥasan Shāh, who were fond of the society of women, the other Sulṭāns for the most part led a moral life and did not exceed the legally prescribed limit of four wives. The court life undr the Sulṭāns was free from those sexual perversities and orgies of debauchery which had been so prominent a feature of the later period of Hindu rule.

Dress

The dress of the upper classes was the same as that of the rich in Arabia, Persia, and Turkistān. It seems to have been introduced by Sayyid 'Alī Hamadānī in the reign of Sulṭān Quṭbu'd-Dīn,[36] and by the time of Sulṭān Sikandar even the Brahmans had begun to adopt it.[37] The lower portion of the body was covered with wide trousers (*sarāwīl*) of Persian origin. The upper portion had a chemise (*qamīṣ*) with full sleeves.[38] Over this was short vest (*Ṣadrī*). The outer robe was called *chōghā,* and descended to the ankles.[39] It had long, loose sleeves, and round the waist was a girdle.[40] The head-dress consisted of a small close-fitting cap covered with a cloth. This formed the turban.[41] The turbans worn by the *Qāẓīs* and *'Ulamā* were of black colour.[42] On festive occasions silk dresses were worn,[43] and silk robes were bestowed as *khil'ats* by the Sulṭāns on their courtiers.[44] The Sulṭāns and the nobles also wore ornaments.[45]

The dress of the lower classes, despite foreign influence, has not changed since the medieval times. Men put on a close fitting skull cap over their shaven heads. They did not wear drawers, but covered their bodies with a long, loose, large-sleeved woollen tunic, called *phairan* after the Persian *pīrahān,* open from the neck to the waist, and falling down to the ankles with a belt round the waist.[46] The foot-wear consisted of shoes made of grass.[47] The dress of the women was the same except that they had a fillet on the forehead, and above it was a black mantilla which fell from the head over the shoulders to the legs. The head dress of the Muslim women is called *kasābā,* while that of the Hindu women is known as *tarangā,* which is tied to a hanging bonnet falling to the heels from behind.[48] Owing to the cold climate of the Valley the Kashmīrīs took their bath at long intervals; and on account of poverty they did not possess more than one gown, which they used until it was worn out, and it was only then that they changed for a new one.[49]

Diet (Food and Drink)

Rice was, as it is today, the staple food of the Kashmīrīs, and that is why when the paddy crop failed, it led to famine. Rice was cooked in a variety of ways. Generally it was boiled and then eaten, and some of it was kept overnight to be taken in the morning.[50] Under Persian influence various kinds of *pilāvs,* like *zard-pilāv, trush-pilāv,* and *shulla-pilāv,* were introduced.[51] Very little wheat was consumed, because it was not much grown in the country.[52] Barley was regarded as a simple food, fit only for the poor, or for those who had renounced the world.[53] Meat, fish, eggs, and vegetables had since ancient times been the most important articles of Kashmīrī diet, and continued to be so under the Muslims.[54] Pork was eaten by a large section of the Hindus in the pre-Islamic period,[55] but it is not known if it was taken under the Sulṭāns as well. The flesh of fowl, ram, goat, and various birds was commonly eaten.[56] Horse's meat was also taken with relish.[57] Beef was introduced with the establishment of Muslim rule.[58] Still, until the time of Sulṭān Ḥasan Shāh, there were many Muslims who abstained from beef. But gradually beef dishes became popular, so that sometimes even Hindus partook of them.[59] There was a special market in Srīnagar where beef was sold.[60] Vegetables were dried up and preserved. A favourite dish of the Kashmīrīs was to cook fowl and bringals together.[61] A decoction of meat with vetches and soups of raisin and jujube were also prepared. Saffron and various kinds of spices formed important ingredients in the Kashmīrī cooking.[62]

Fruits were grown in such abundance that they were rarely bought or sold. The owner of a garden and the man who had no garden were all alike, for the gardens had no walls, and no one was prevented from picking the fruits.[63] Pears, cherries, plums, apricots, grapes, apples, and peaches were the principal fruits that were eaten. Mulberry was cultivated for its silk and so its fruit was not taken.[64] Some fruits like jujube, which had medicinal qualities, were likewise preserved.[65]

Drinking of wine was popular although it was frowned upon by the orthodox. As the Hindu religion specially recommended the use of wine on ceremonial occasions,[66] it was not an uncommon sight to see laymen and Brahman priests alike in a state of drunkenness during Hindu festivals.[67] The Muslims, who participated in these festivals, also freely partook of wine. Most of the Sulṭāns and their nobles too drank wine.[68] Zainu'l-'Ābidīn took it in moderation, but Ḥaidar Shāh was a confirmed drunkard, and as a result neglected his state duties. Ḥasan Shāh was in the habit of arranging drinking parties in his palace, or in the boats on the Jehlam, and used to get drunk on these occasions.[69] Besides alcohol, the use of other intoxicants like bhang and opium was also common.[70] In addition, butter-milk and various kinds of sherbets were taken. The use of betel-leaves, so common under the Rājās, does not find any mention in the chronicles of the Muslim period.

Pastimes

Among the indoor games dice and chess were popular.[71] Among the outdoor games polo (Persian, *chawgān*), which was probably introduced into Kashmīr from Ladākh, was much indulged in both by the Sulṭāns and by the nobles. Sulṭān 'Alī Shāh was very fond of the game, and it was while playing it that he was mortally wounded. Hunting was another favourite outdoor pastime of the upper classes.[72] Sulṭān Shihābu'd-Dīn enjoyed hunting lions, and on one occasion he nearly lost his life while trying to kill one with his sword.[73] Stags, patridges, deer, and leopards also offered sport.[74] Falconry and hawking were probably introduced from Persia.[75] The Kashmīrīs derived great pleasure, sitting in their skiffs and watching their hawks strike the wild-fowl or some other bird in mid-air, and fly back with the prey.[76] Besides these, other outdoor sports which were practised were archery, fencing, and javelin-throwing.

The game which the common people played was hockey.[77] Another form of their recreation was that on Fridays the youth of one section of the city of Srīnagar would challenge those of another section. After the place and hour had been fixed, both the sides would assemble with sticks and slings, and a free fight would ensue. This would lead to broken heads and limbs, and even deaths.[78]

The Kashmīrī acrobats and jugglers possessed great skill, and they amused the people by their performance.[79] From the time of Zainu'l-'Ābidīn the display of fireworks was a source of great enjoyment to the people. In spite of the ban by the *Sharī'a,* music was very popular with the Kashmīrīs, and offered both pleasure and diversion. Sulṭān Zainu'l-'Ābidīn initiated the practice of holding occasional concerts and musical events in the boats on the Jehlam. Some of his successors were fond of holding convivial parties with their boon companions in which wine flowed freely, and dancing girls and musicians sang and danced.

Houses

The houses were built in the same style as we see them today in the towns and the villages. Owing to the abundance of wood and the constant earthquakes, houses of stone and brick were not constructed.[80] They were two to four storeys high and sometimes even more.[81] They were built of planks of timber laid on each other to form a square, their interstices being filled with clay.[82] Near the forests the walls were formed of whole logs.[83] The roofs, which were pointed to throw off snow, were formed of small planks fastened together with cords, and were covered with a layer of earth on which white and violet lilies and tulips were grown.[84] This presented a lovely sight in spring. In the villages, near the lakes, the thatch in the dwellings of the poor was usually rice straw or of reeds.[85] The houses were ventilated with pretty, artistic, open-work instead of windows or glass.[86] The lower storey was used for keeping cattle. In the second storey lived the family. The other floors were used for keeping household chattels. In the loft, formed by the roof, wood and grass were stored.[87] Some of the houses had cellars.[88] The houses of the rich were situated on the banks of the Jehlam and had beautiful gardens attached to them.[89]

Social Intercourse between Hindus and Muslims

When Muslim saints and soldiers first set foot on the Kashmīr soil, they were received in a friendly manner. The soldiers were employed by the kings in their armies, while the saints were given complete freedom to preach their religion. It was only when Islām began to make rapid progress that it aroused the hostility of the Brahmans, who found their traditional values being upset, and some of the basic assumptions on which Hindu society was based being challenged.[90] However, in the course of time, realising the futility of opposition, they were compelled to adopt an attitude of tolerance and goodwill. These feelings were reciprocated by the Muslims. As a result, except for a communal clash which occurred in the reign of Ḥasan Shāh, the two communities live for the most part peacefully and amicably throughout the Sultanate period. Intermarriages between Hindus and Muslims were common; and when the latter took Hindu wives, they allowed them to retain not only their Hindu names but also their faith.[91] Hindus and Muslims visited each other's places of worship, and participated in each other's festivals. The Hindus respected Muslim saints, while the Muslims looked upon Hindu Sādhūs with reverence. Muslim mystics mixed freely with Hindu Yōgīs and held discussions with them.[92] The mystic songs of Lallā Ded and Nūru'd-Dīn Rishī stirred the souls of Hindus and Muslims alike to their deepest depths.

Spread of Islām

Buddhism flourished in Kashmīr from the reign of Aśoka to the end of the Kuṣana dynasty. But its decline began with the accession of the Gonanda dynasty, and when Hiuen Tsiang visited the Valley (circ. 631-33), he found that it had very considerably lost ground.[93] Despite this Buddhism continued to exist peacefully side by side with Hinduism, and Hindu rulers who endowed shrines of Śiva and Viṣṇu, with equal zeal made foundations of Buddhist Stūpas and Vihāras.[94] It is probably because of this that when Ou-k'ong visited Kashmīr in the middle of the eighth century (759-63), he got the impression that Buddhism was in a flourishing state,[95] though it was rapidly being replaced by Śaiva worship, which had always occupied the first place among the Hindu cults of the Valley.[96] Thus when Islām began to spread in Kashmīr, it had to encounter the resistance not so much of Buddhism as of Śaivism.

Muslim traders and soldiers of fortune began to enter Kashmīr from an early date. Kalhaṇa records that Lalitāditya's son and successor Vajrāditya "sold many men to the *melecchas,* and introduced into the country practices which befitted the *mlecchas*".[97] Later, Harṣa employed Turkish soldiers, and, under Muslim influence, adopted elaborate fashions in dress and ornaments.[98] During the reign of Bhikṣācara (1120-21) Muslim soldiers were again employed and sent to attack Sussala in Lohara.[99] From the accounts of Marco Polo, the Venetian traveller, it appears that already by the end of the thirteenth century there was a colony of Muslims in Kashmīr, for he says that the people of the Valley do not kill animals, but that, if they want to eat meat, they get the Saracens, who dwell among them, to play the butcher.[100] These "Saracens" must have been either emigrants from Turkistān or Hindus converted to Islām by the pietist missionaries from India and Central Asia.

The saint missionaries came in the wake of traders and adventurers, and it is they who were responsible for introducing Islām into the Valley. But unfortunately the chronicles do not throw any light on their activities. The first Ṣūfī of whom we have any record to have entered Kashmīr, was Balbul Shāh, who succeeded in converting Riñchana. The conversion of the ruler of the land was an important event, for it increased the prestige of Islām and led to the acceptance of the new faith by some of the nobles and, according to one tradition, by 10,000 inhabitants of the Valley. After Bulbul Shāh came other Ṣūfīs, but the most prominent among them was Sayyid 'Alī Hamadānī who, by his learning, piety and devotion, is said to have made 37,000 converts to Islām.[101] His work was continued by his disciples and his son Muḥammad Hamadānī, and by Nūru'd-Dīn Rishī and his disciples. Those who subsequently played an important role in the work of proselytisation were Shamsu'd-Dīn, Ḥamzā Makhdūm, Dā'ūd Khākī, and Sayyid Jamālu'd-Dīn Bukhārī. Stein says that the adoption of Islām by the great mass of the population of Kashmīr had become an accomplished fact during the latter half of the fourteenth century,[102] but a study of the chronicles shows that Muslims were still a minority in the time of Nūru'd-Dīn Rishī.[103] In reality, it was not until the end of the fifteenth century that a majority of the inhabitants of the Valley had embraced Islām.

So far as the rulers of Kashmīr were concerned, although they held the saints in great respect and built and endowed mosques and hospices for them, they kept aloof from their missionary activities. In fact, the saints themselves very seldom solicited state co-operation, and that is why in the accounts of their life and work rarely any reference is made to the Sulṭāns.[104]

The only Sulṭān who took keen interest in the work of proselytisation was Sikandar. However, much of his work was undone by Zainu'l-Abidīn, who permitted the temples destroyed by his father to be rebuilt, recalled the Brahmans who had fled to India, and allowed those who had changed their religion under compulsion to revert to their old faith. The successors of Zainu'l-'Ābidīn followed his liberal policy. The result was that Hinduism not only regained some of its lost position, but it even became militant. This provoked a reaction among a section of the Muslims, who resented the reconversion of their co-religionists to Hinduism and their adoption of non-Muslim practices.[105] The leader of the reaction was Shamsu'd-Dīn, the founder of the Nūrbakhshīya sect in the Valley. But his views were disliked by both Sulṭān Muḥammad Shāh and his minister Sayyid Muḥammad[106] who always protected the Hindus, whenever they were harassed by him or by his followers. It was because Shamsu'd-Dīn, was continuously opposed by Sayyid Muḥammad that he got disgusted and went away to Baltistān.[107] But after the fall of Sayyid Muḥammad, when Mūsā Raina became prime minister, Shamsu'd-Dīn returned to the Valley. But like Muḥammad Shāh, Fatḥ Shāh, who was now king, also did not approve of his ideals and methods. Once, while the Hindus were busy celebrating the Spring festival on the Kōh-i-Mārān, Shamsu'd-Dīn proceeded there with his followers and put a stop to the festivities on the ground that Muslims were participating in the religious ceremonies, while men and women in general were freely drinking wine and indulging in immoral practices. When next morning the Hindus complained to Fatḥ Shāh of Shamsu'd-Dīn's behaviour, he was so angry that he wanted to put him to death, but was dissuaded by his counsellors.[108] Despite Fatḥ Shāh's liberal policy Shamsu'd-Dīn, under the patronage of

Mūsā Raina, continued his activities, which occasionally hurt the religious susceptibilities of the non-Muslims. However, after the fall of Mūsā Raina until the end of the Sultanate, the Hindus lived in peace, enjoying complete freedom to practice their religion.

Thus the government under the Sulṭāns pursued, for the most part, a policy of non-interference in religious matters, and the success of Islām in the Valley was mainly due to the efforts of the Ṣūfīs. But it must be remembered that the Ṣūfīs alone would not have been able to achieve much if it had not been for certain objective conditions existing in the Valley. Kalhaṇa's account shows that social and political disintegration had started in Kashmīr from the beginning of the eleventh century. But at the same time anarchy seems to have prevailed in the religious sphere as well. There was a tendency in Hinduism during this period towards the growth of sectarianism. The priests were represented by uneducated temple minstrels, while Śaivism, to which a majority of the inhabitants of the Valley were attached, had degenerated into a mass of superstitions and rituals, and thus could no longer meet the spiritual demands of the people.[109] Nor could Buddhism, as practised in those days, offer any satisfaction.[110] On the other hand Islām, as introduced by the great Ṣūfī saints, was a simple monotheistic creed, free from ceremonials, caste, and priesthood. It thus appealed to the people, and won converts easily. The dissatisfaction of Riñchana with the Buddhist and Hindu beliefs and practices in typical of the spiritual unrest that had affected the minds of many in the country. Later, Lallā Ded raised her voice against idolatry, superstition, and lack of true spiritual values, but her efforts were wrecked on the rock of Brahman conservatism and dogmatism.

Another factor which helped the spread of Islām in the Valley, was the laxity of caste rules.[111] A rigid caste system acts as a strong cohesive force, and thus serves as a powerful defence mechanism against the infiltration of foreign ideas. But in Kashmīr, under Buddhist influence, there had been a relaxation of caste rules, and, as a result, the power of resistance of the Hindu society had been undermined. Islām, therefore, did not have to face the same degree of opposition there as it did in other parts of India, where the caste rules continued to be rigid, and the society was able to set up barriers against external influences. These facts go to explain why Islām's success in Kashmīr was much more rapid and complete than in any other part of this sub-continent.

Influence of Islām on Hindus

The influence of Islām began to be felt in Kashmīr from about the middle of the eighth century, long before the establishment of Muslim rule in the country. But with the foundation of the Sultanate and the influx of a large number of Persians and Turks, Hindu society began to be affected by greater and more profound changes. "As the wind destroys the trees and the locusts the *shālī* crop, so did the Yavanas destroy the usages of Kashmīra,"[112] and that " the kingdom of Kashmīra was polluted by the evil practices of the *mlecchas,*"[113] wrote Jonarāja. Similarly Śrīvara complained of the abolition of old practices and their substitution by new ones. He even went to the extent of saying that many of the misfortunes of the people of Kashmīr were due to the changes in manners and customs.[114] But despite these denunciations and protests, Hindu society could not be prevented from assimilating foreign ideas and practices. It was due to these influences that the Hindus began to adopt Muslim manners and dress, and some of them even began to take beef.[115] It was also the effect of Islāmic impact that caste rules began to weaken. Thus Śrīvara, writing in the time of Muḥammad Shāh, observed that men belonging to the four castes had lately adopted blameable practices, and had given up the performance of prescribed ceremonies.[116] In the course of time, with the exception of the Brahman caste, all the castes disappeared from Hindu society.

The influence of Islām can also be discerned on Advaita Śaivism, as represented by the teachings of Lallā Ded.[117] She was a famous Yōginī of Kashmīr who lived in the fourteenth century. She was greatly perturbed by the formalism of Śaivite beliefs and practices, by religious conflicts and the multiplication of sects.[118] It was at this time that she came into contact with

Sayyid 'Alī Hamadānī and Nūru'd-Dīn Rishī and learned of the doctrines of Islām and Ṣūfism.[119] It was under the influence of Islāmic ideas that she denounced the caste system, and criticised idolatry as a useless and even silly 'work'.[120] Although she regarded the world as an illusion, and longed for freedom from the desire for existence, yet there is evidence of Sayyid 'Alī Hamadānī's influence when she says that it is not necessary for a person to become a hermit in order to achieve the absorption of the Individual Self into the Supreme, but that even a householder can obtain ultimate Release provided he performed his religious and secular duties without any thought of gain or profit.[121] Furthermore, it was from the Ṣūfis that she learned to use words with a plain and esoteric meaning.[122] From them also she imbibed the doctrine of Divine Love, and, like them, she employed the word "Beloved" to denote the Godhead.[123] There also appears an echo of Ṣūfism in the mystic ecstasy that she experiences, and in her allegory of Awakening the Beloved. Thus she says[124] :

"When the moonlight ended with the dawn,
Mind of her Self with illusion mad
Lallā to the love of God had drawn,
Soothing the pain that had made him sad :
Cried to her Beloved : It is I,
Lallā, Lallā, that awakens Thee :
Buried in the crystal lake doth lie
All the defilement that darkened me."

Influence of Hinduism of Islām

While Islām brought about great changes in Hindu society in Kashmīr, it itself underwent a transformation in the course of time. This was because, although the people of Kashmīr changed their religion, they did not make a complete break with the past, but carried with them many of their old beliefs and practices to the new faith. Thus while they celebrated the Muslim festivals of 'Īdu'l-Fiṭr and 'Īdu'ẓ-Ẓuḥā they did not cease to participate in the Hindu festivals of Gaṇa-cakra, Caitra,[125] Vith-trawah[126] and Śrīpañcami.[127] They also continued to regard the Hindu places of worship as sacred, and instances were not wanting when they even indulged in idol worship.[128] Similarly, they retained the old superstitions that seeing of a comet, hearing of the barking of dogs, hooting of owls during the day, and crossing of the path by a serpent all foreboded disaster.[129] It is true that under the impact of Islām the rigours of the caste system were reduced, but, as has already been mentioned, the converts were reluctant to give up their customs, their caste rules regarding marriage, and sometimes even their caste functions.

The Sulṭāns of Kashmīr, though of foreign origin, were not far behind their Muslim subjects in assimilating Hindu beliefs and usages. This was, of course, inevitable, for they lived surrounded by a population a majority of which was Hindu at least for a hundred years after the establishment of the Sultanate. Moreover, most of the Sulṭāns had Hindu wives who, even after their conversion to Islām, clung to their customs and who could not fail to influence their royal consorts and their children.[130] Thus the Sulṭāns, like their Muslim subjects, participated in Hindu festivals, and some of them even visited temples to beseech the aid of the gods. They believed in witchcraft;[131] and, in order to avert famine and other calamities, they performed sacrifices and bestowed grants on the Brahmans, (Quṭbu'd-Dīn was convinced that the birth of a son to his queen was due to the blessings of a Brahman Yōgī)[132]; and, like the Hindu Kings of Kashmīr, they performed the *homa* ceremony at the time of the coronation at which the Shaikhu'l-Islām, instead of the Brahman priest, and the chief minister applied a *ṭīkā* (a mark on the forehead) to the ruler's forehead and made offerings of gold and flower.[133]

So far as Ṣūfism in Kashmīr, as introduced by the followers of the great orders, is concerned, it did not come under the influence of Advaita Śaivism in its doctrinal aspect. The evolution of Islamic mysticism into a well-developed system of thought and way of life had been achieved by the middle of the thirteenth century; and the ideas, if any, which it borrowed from Buddhist and Vedāntic philosophy, it did so in countries outside Kashmīr.[134] Moreover, the founders and chief exponents of the Qādirī, Kubravī, Suhrawardī, and Naqshbandī Orders in the Valley were in general orthodox in outlook, adhering to Islamic laws and practices and denouncing antinomianism and incarnationist tendencies.[135] They also frowned upon the extreme asceticism which sanctioned celibacy, the annihilation of all desires, self-torture, and an ivory-tower existence. But in spite of their attempts to maintain high Islamic ideals, Ṣūfīsm in Kashmir, as elsewhere, did in the end compromise with many of the traditional pactices which were openly polytheistic. Popular Islām in Kashmīr thus became diluted with foreign elements, and this character it has retained until to-day.

Nevertheless, it was not the Ṣūfīs but the Rishīs of Kashmīr who were the true spiritual heirs of the Hindu ascetics. Like the latter, the Rishīs practiced celibacy, inflicted bodily sufferings upon themselves, regarded this world as an illusion and withdrew from it. In their pantheistic beliefs also they were influenced by Advaita Śaivism. Moreover, unlike the Ṣūfīs, instead of participating in congregational prayers and *Ẕikr* ceremonies, they endeavoured to achieve the absorption of the Self into the Absolute by meditating alone in caves or jungles, away from human habitations.

Trade

Trade in medieval times played, as it does to-day, an important part in Kashmīr's economic life. It was a source of considerable revenue to the state; it stimulated manufactures; and it gave employment to a large number of people. Moreover, it brought wealth to the Kashmīrī merchants whose activities were not confined to the Valley alone, but extended as far afield as Bengal, the Coromandel Coast, Lhaṣa, Peking, Persia, and Central Asia.

Internal Trade

This consisted in articles boh imported and produced in the country. Among the first salt was very important, because Kashmīr did not produce any and depended entirely on supplies from outside. Then there were the luxury goods which would be described later. Among the articles produced in the Valley were shawls, silks, coarse woollen goods, and various other products of its handicrafts. Trade in all these articles was done by private merchants. But the trade in grain was carried on both by the state and the private traders. The state held large stocks of rice so that, whenever there was a rise in prices due to scarcity or speculation, it was brought into the market, thus bringing the prices down to their normal levels.[136] Besides, the state was opposed to the cornering of grain, and the private traders had to sell it at a small profit.[137] Because of these restrictions, merchants did not indulge in large scale transactions in grain. Control over the prices of other commodities was also regulated by monthly notifications.[138] This was done to check black-marketing. However, it appears that these controls did not materially hinder the growth of trade, for the Kashmīrī merchants in medieval times were quite prosperous.[139] The real obstacles to both internal and external trade were civil wars and foreign invasions.[140]

According to Mīrzā Ḥaidar the markets and streets of Srīnagar were all paved with hewn stones. In the markets only drapers and retail dealers were to be found. But tradesmen like the grocers, druggists, bear-sellers, and bakers did business in their own houses.[141] This was the practice in all the towns of Kashmīr until the coming of the Mughals, when the system gradually underwent some change, and all kinds of tradesmen began to transact business in the market, alhough, as Abū'l-Faẓl says, most of the selling and buying was still carried on by them in their own houses.[142]

Conveyance

The ordinary people moved about from place to place on foot, while the rich rode on horses, palanquins or litters.[143] But the most common form of conveyance was by boat, which was also the chief mode of transporting goods from one place to another. To places not situated on the rivers, goods were carried by men or on ponies along narrow tracks, for there were no roads fit for wheeled traffic. In fact, in ancient and medieval times carriages were things unknown to the people of the Valley.[144] The rivers were spanned by bridges, constructed of deodar wood, or by rope-bridges, generally formed of three cables made of twisted twigs. These rope-bridges were only meant for foot traffic, and animals had to be carried across them on men's backs.[145] Besides the rope-bridges, there were also bridges of timber, constructed according to the cantilever principle. These permanent bridges were introduced with the advent of Muslim rule, for under the Rājās only boat-bridges existed.[146] However, the use of the latter was not entirely given up by the Sulṭāns, because they could be easily broken up at the approach of the enemy. Sharafu'd-Dīn Yazdī in his *Ẓafar-nāma* notices the existence of such bridges across the Jehlam.[147]

External trade : Trade routes

Although Kashmīr was enclosed on all sides by huge mountains, she maintained close trade relations with the neighbouring countries. Her merchants were scattered over the different parts of Asia, and carried on an extensive trade, having establishments at Patna, Banāras, Lhasā, Kāthmāndu, Sining, Peking, and in the towns of Bengal, the Punjāb, Bhutān,[148] Khurāsān, Turkistān and on the Coromandel Coast.

Kashmīr's trade with the Punjāb was carried on through the passes in the Pīr Panjāl, while much of the trade of the Punjāb with Ladākh, Baltistān, and Eastern Turkistān passed through Kashmīr.[149] The town of Leh in Ladākh was the chief commercial depot of Kashmīr's import and export trade with Tibet, Turkistān, and China. Goods between Kashmīr and Leh were conducted through the Zōjī-Lā by horses in winter because of the pass being covered with snow, and by men in summer. From Srīnagar to Leh, if the conveyance was by men only, it took a month or a little more.[150]

Merchants who intended going to Yārqand stayed in Leh to make preparations for the journey by providing themselves with horses, provisions, and servants. From Ladākh their route lay through Sabu, Akhkan and Chou-jangal (great jungle), and thence to the pass of Karakōram. This was the road pursued by travellers in winter when there were no floods; but during summer, owing to the floods, they tavelled through the Nubra country.[151] After crossing the Karakōram the caravans arrived in Yārqand which was an important commercial centre and where routes from Ladākh, Tibet, China, Khotan, and India were joined by those leading to Kāshghar.[152] From Yārqand some of the caravans proceeded to Kāshghar and thence to Samarqand and Bukhārā,[153] while others set out towards China. The period taken by them to reach China from Kashmīr was three months.[154]

There was also another route which connected Kashmīr with Eastern Turkistān. This passed through Baltistān and across the high glacier-crowned Karākoram main range beyond it. This route was very difficult compared to that *via* Ladākh, because it led along precipices and across the great glaciers. It was only followed when the Ladākh route had to be abandoned owing to political troubles.[155]

Communication between Kashmīr and Transoxiana was also maintained through Gilgit. From Gilgit or Chitrāl the caravans crossed the Hindu Kush into Vakhān, and then after crossing the Pamir and the river Oxus, they reached Transoxiana.[156] Communication between Kashmīr and Persia existed through the Punjāb which had close trade relations with the latter.[157]

Kashmīrī merchants who desired to carry their goods to Tibet or Nepāl, proceeded from Leh to Kuti at the head of the pass. From Kuti some went to Tibet and thence to Sining and even to Peking, for much of Tibet's trade with China was conducted by the Kashmīrīs, who had their establishments at Lhasā and other principal towns of the country.[158] Others went to Kāthmāndu and thence by the Valley of Nepāl to Patna.[159] Kashmīrī merchants had their shops and offices in the town of Kāthmāndu, and they played an important part in the trade between Bengal, Nepāl, and Tibet.[160]

Imports

Salt and shawl-wool were the most important items of import. Most of the salt came from the Punjāb *via* the Pīr Panjāl route,[161] but some also was brought from Chan-thān *via* Ladākh. During the time of war, when the trade routes were not safe, the import of salt became difficult, and this caused great hardship to the people.[162]

Shawl-wool was imported from Rodok and Chan-thān,[163]

as well as from Ladākh and Yārqand.[164] According to an ancient agreement Tibet's shawl-wool was exported only to Ladākh, and similarly by ancient custom and engagements, its export from Ladākh was confined to Kashmīr alone. All attempts to convey it to other countries were punished by confiscation.[165] The shawl-wool was very important for Kashmīr, for upon it depended the livelihood of its weavers and the prosperity of its merchants.[166]

In addition to shawl-wool, Tibet exported to Kashmīr gold and musk,[167] while Ladākh exported woollen cloth which was brought and sold by the Ladākhī merchants.[168] The Punjāb supplied Kashmīr, besides salt, morocco leather, broad-cloth, embroidered cloth, and lac. Some of these articles were sent on the Ladākh and Yārqand through Kashmīr.[169] From Gilgit and Baltistān were brought silk-worm eggs.[170] From Khotan was imported *Yashab* (oriental jade) for which it had always been famous and the chief source of supply to the various countries of the East.[171] Khotan was also famous for its silks, carpets, paper, pottery, brass and copper vessels, and these were exported to Kashmīr.[172] Agate, opal, turquoise, and other kinds of precious stones were imported from Badakhshān, Bukhārā, and Yārqand.[173] The last also supplied Kashmīr, and through it to Northern India, cloth, felt of wool, and silks, well-known for their durability and their brilliant colours.[174] Kāshghar exported to Kashmīr musk and silk. From 'Irāq and Turkistān came horses, for the Kashmīrī breed was of a poor quality;[175] and from China the caravans brought musk, China-wood, rhubarb, swallow-wort, porcelain, silk, and tea.[176]

Exports

The most important article of Kashmīr's export trade was its shawls, which were sent to India, Central Asia, Tibet, and China, and, according to Abū'l-Faẓl, "to every clime".[177] Other articles which Kashmīr exported were musk, crystals, silks, woollen cloth, sugar, saffron, dried raisins, walnuts, paper, fresh fruits, timber, and horses.[178] Besides exporting those which Kashmīr herself produced, she also exported many articles which she obtained from other countries, for, as we have seen, she was a channel through which the Punjāb maintained trade relations with Ladākh, Baltistān, eastern Turkistān and Tibet. Srīnagar, the capital of Kashmīr, was a great entrepot where Turkish, Tibetan, Ladākhī, Baltī, Indian and Kashmīrī merchants brushed shoulders with each other. These traders had not only their rest houses in Kashmīr, but also their religious shrines.

Industries

Very scanty information exists in the Kashmīr chronicles regarding the manufactures in the Valley during the Sultanate period. We only know that Sulṭān Zainu'l-'Ābidīn encouraged the production of shawls, silks, paper, and glass, but no details about them are available. From the Mughal accounts it appears that shawls were manufactured on a large scale under the Sulṭāns, and were exported to various countries of the world.

Besides shawls, silk and paper, Kashmīr also produced woollen cloth which was then, as now, famous for its warmth and durability.[179] Other articles manufactured were carpets, copper and brass vessels, and glass-ware.

The silk industry was an ancient one in Kashmīr, but Zainu'l-'Ābidīn improved it by introducing better technique and better designs. Silk-worms were reared, and for their food the mulberry was cultivated and its fruit was not eaten by the people.[180] The paper industry was for the first time established in Kashmīr by Zainu'l-'Ābidīn. It was a state enterprise, and the Sulṭān took a special interest in it. The Kashmīrī paper was of silky texture and glossy appearance, and was in great demand in India where it was used for purposes of painting and writing. Under the Mughals also Kashmīr supplied the best quality of paper to India. George Forster, writing in 1783, says that "the Kashmirians fabricated the best writing paper of the East," and that it was formerly "an article of extensive traffic".[181] The Kashmīrī paper possessed the quality that once the ink had been washed off, it could again be used for writing.[182]

The number of factories and of the workers employed in them has not been mentioned in the chronicles. We only know about the shawl industry that in the time of Akbar there were 2,000 factories for making shawls.[183] And since under the

Mughals the industry did not suffer any decline, this must have been the nmber under the Sulṭāns also. But no estimate can be made at the present stage of our knowledge regarding the number of factories producing other articles.

Agriculture

Agriculture in Kashmīr had progressively declined during the last two centuries before the establishment of the Sultanate.[184] The invasion of Zuljū had further accentuated the process. As a result, villages had become depopulated and large tracts of land turned barren. The Shāh Mīr rulers did their best to check these tendencies and promote agriculture. They repopulated the villages, reduced the revenue demand, abolished many extra cesses, drained the marshes, and constructed new irrigation works. The result of their efforts was that the area under cultivation greatly increased, and the country became self-sufficient in foodstuffs. Under the Chaks also, except for a short period towards the end, agriculture remained in a flourishing state.[185]

The spring crops raised were wheat, barley, pea, bean, and mustard. The autumn crops consisted of rice, *mūng, māsh, moṭha,* and millet.[186] Rice, which has always been the staple food of the people, was grown extensively, but finer varieties were not much cultivated.[187] Wheat, which was small in grain and black in colour, was produced on a restricted scale.[188] Sugar-cane was grown around Mārtand.[189] Saffron was cultivated on the Pāmpūr Karēwa,[190] and some was also produced in the Paraspūr pargana.[191] The total amount grown in the Valley varied between 400 and 500 Hindustānī maunds.[192] The cost of one seer of saffron was ten rupees.[193]

It is generally held that the Mughal Emperors were the pioneers of gardening in Kashmīr. In reality, however, long before the Shālimār, Nishāṭ, and other Mughal gardens were constructed, the Shāh Mīr rulers had already laid out beautiful gardens in the Valley. Besides the Sulṭāns, the merchants and other well-to-do inhabitants also had a love for flowers and gardens, and their houses had gardens attached to them. Then there were the Rishīs, whose habit it was to plant shady and fruit-bearing trees wherever they stayed. In the gardens planted by the Sulṭāns, nobles, merchants and Rishīs, flourished different varieties of fruits such as apricots, apples, peaches, plums, grapes, almonds, and cherries. The flowers that grew wild and in the gardens, were narcissus, rose, jasmine, lily, iris, hyacinth, violet, and shamrock.[194]

The Condition of the Peasants

The lot of the peasants in the Valley under the Lohara dynasty had been an unhappy one. This was due to a number of causes. First, the throne was occupied during that period mostly by weak rulers who neglected the administration. Secondly, there were constant civil wars which brought great misery to the countryside. Thirdly, apart from the heavy revenue demand, the peasants had to pay all kinds of taxes and fines.[195] But, above all, the most oppressive measure to which they were subjected was the system of *begār* or corvée for transport purposes. The villagers had to present themselves to carry their allotted loads, and if they did not turn up, they were fined to the value of the latter at enhanced rates. Only the priests of the temple were exempted from the corvée. This measure was greatly resented by the peasants, because it kept them away too long from their paddy fields which required weeding or watering and constant supervision.[196]

With the establishment of the Shāh Mīr dynasty, the condition of the peasants distinctly improved. This was because they were protected from the exploitation of government officials, and measures were taken to develop agriculture. It is true that after the death of Ḥasan Shāh till the fall of the dynasty the peasants suffered a great deal due to civil wars and foreign invasions. But under the strong government of the Chaks prosperity returned to the countryside.[197] It was only in the reign of Ya'qūb Shāh that, owing to the Mughal invasion, cultivation declined and the peasants were impoverished.

However, although the peasant was definitely better off under the Sulṭāns than he had been under their predecessors, or was ever to be subsequently, the picture was not as rosy as has been painted by the chroniclers. In the first place, the peasant did not get complete relief from the burden of oppressive exactions which seemed to have continued in spite of the claims of successive rulers to have abolished them. Secondly, the Shāh Mīr rulers did not put an end to the corvée. In fact, from the time of Shihābu'd-Dīn, it was exacted even from the *hānjīs* who were required to serve the king seven days in every month.[198] Besides transport, compulsory labour was also taken for collecting saffron. Under the Shāh Mīrs men were forcibly employed to separate the saffron from the petals and the stamens, and for this they were given a certain quantity of salt as wages. But from the time of Ghāzī Shāh Chak they received eleven *taraks* of saffron flower, out of which one *tarak* was to be their wages, and for the remaining ten they had to supply a quarter *tarak* of saffron to the government. This custom was abolished by Akbar on his third visit to Kashmīr to the great relief of the peasants.[199]

Apart from the burden of corvée and taxes, the peasants also suffered at the hands of floods and famines. The floods in Kashmīr are caused by warm and continuous rains on the mountains which melt the snow and thus innundate the Valley. The area that is affected most is below Srīnagar where the depression of the land is slight.

The floods were usually followed by famines. But the latter were also caused by early snows and heavy rains, occurring at the time of the ripening of autumn harvest, thus damaging the crops and causing scarcity. During the famines the Sulṭāns did their best to alleviate the misery of the people by opening their grain stores and adopting various other relief measures. Nevertheless, the people suffered a great deal, and there was a considerable loss of life. The recurrent famines and floods marred the record of prosperity under the Sulṭāns.

Population

It is not possible to give a correct estimate of Kashmīr's population during the medieval period, for the chronicles do not throw any light on this point. They only state that the country's population was large. Thus the *Ẓafar-nāma* says that the land was thickly populated,[200] and similarly, Abūl-Faẓl speaks of the country's "numerous population".[201] Moreover, it appears from the existence of innumerable deserted village sies that the Valley possessed a larger population under the Sulṭāns than at present.[202]

The population was mainly concentrated in villages, and only a small portion of it lived in towns, the largest among them being Srīnagar called in the Persian chronicles Shahr-i-Kashmīr (City of Kashmīr). The number of villages has been variously estimated. Mas'ūdī (d.956) says that the number of villages in the Valley stood between 60,000 to 70,000.[203] According to Sharafu'd-Dīn Yazdī in the whole province—plains and mountains together—there were 100,000 villages.[204] The number of villages in the *Lokaprakāśa* is placed at 66,063.[205] This is also the oral tradition of the Brahmans throughout the Valley.[206] Jonarāja also gives the figure as 60,000.[207] Dimashqī (d. 1327) speaks of the Inner and Outer Kashmīr, the former containing 70,000 villages and the later more than 100,000. We can thus safely say that there were betwen 60,000 to 70,000 villages in Kashmīr during the Sultanate priod. The same was the number under early Mughal rule. The decline in the number of villages and consequently of the population itself began from the later Mughal or Afghān period.

NOTE

1. Stein, BK. v, Nos. 361 sqq; BK. vii, Nos. 1460-2.
2. *Ibid.*, BK. v, Nos. 174 and n. 174.
3. *Ibid.*, BK. vii, Nos. 13-4; BK. viii, No. 2076.
4. Lawrence, *Valley*, p. 306. Among the Rainas there are two groups: (1) Brahmans who call themselves Razdan. (2) Rājpūts who claim descent from the Rājās of Candra Baṅsi and who came to Kashmīr from Nagarkōt in the reign of Rājā Jayasimha. (T.H. i, ff 166a-b).
5. A practice common in Kashmīr (perhaps of older origin) is of giving a *krām*, a nickname, which is added to the original name by reason of the man's special calling, or because of some special circumstance which has occurred to him. (Knowles, *A Dictionary of Kashmīrī Proverbs and Sayings*, p. 115).
6. Kilam, *A History of Kashmīrī Pandits*, p. 53.
7. This title was given to the princes under the Chaks. (See H.M., f.

183b; and B.S., f. 169b).

8. Śrīv., pp. 223, 303; Śuka, p. 359.
9. Cited in Ashraf, *Life and conditions of the people of Hindustan,* p. 183.
10. The part which Bābā Ḥasan, Ḥamza Makhdūm and other Ṣūfīs played in the political events of their time has already been described in previous chapters.
11. 'Alī Hamadānī, *Ẕakhīratu'l-Mulūk,* f. 42a.
12. *Ibid.,* f. 41b.
13. The organisation of the *khānqāhs* in Kashmīr was the same as in India, Persia, and Turkistān.
14. In the *khānqāh* of Jadibal, the professional followers lived with their families, and were supported by the income of the endowment. (*Tuḥfatu'l-Aḥbāḇ,* p. 242 sqq.).
15. See Gibb, *Mohammedanism,* pp. 151-52, where the relations of the *Pirs* with their disciples is described. In Kashmīr also similar conditions existed. The disciple looked upon his *Pir* as the deputy of God and the Prophet, and regarded absolute submission to him as essential. (See Isḥāq, *Ḥilayatu'l-'Ārifin,* p. 12b, and also *Tuḥfatu'l-Aḥbāb,* pp. 99. 129 sq.).
16. Isḥāq, *Ḥilayatu'l-'Ārifin,* ff. 9a-b.
17. Rishī is a Sanskrit word meaning a saint, a sage, or an ascetic. According to local tradition of a legendary character, the founder of this order is supposed to be Khwāja Uways, Prophet Muḥammad's contemporary, who lived in Yemen. (Knowles, *A Dictionary of Kashmīrī Proverbs and Sayings,* p. 23).
18. Dā'ūd Mishkātī, *Asnāru'l-Abrār,* f. 63a.
19. For Nūru'd-Dīn's life see Nasīb, ff, 190b sqq.; F.K., ff. 215b sqq.; Miskīn, *Ta'rīkh-i-Kabīr,* pp. 92 sqq.; *Asnaru'l-Abrār,* ff. 62b sqq.
20. *Haft Iqlim,* f. 156a; Naṣīb, ff. 415a-17a; *Tuzuk-i-Jahāngīrī,* pp. 149-50.
21. *Tuzuk-i-Jahāngīrī,* ii, 149-50; Rāzī, *Haft Iqlim,* f. 156a. The Rishīs were Muslims, but J.N. Sarkar has not corrected the mistake of Jarrett (A.A., ii, 353) who called them Brahmans. (See *Tuzuk-i-Jahāngīrī,* ii, 149 and n.).
22. Nasību'd-Dīn, *Nūr-nāma,* f. 192b.
23. 'Alī Hamadānī, *Ẕakhīratu'l-Mulūk,* ff. 65b–7b.
24. Isḥāq. *Ḥilayatu'l-'Ārifin,* f. 12a.
25. Ibid., f. 2b.
26. Jonar. (Bo. ed.), No. 776.
27. *Tuzuk-i-Jahāngīrī,* ii, 134.
28. The Sayyid families which had taken to agriculture were

regarded as superior by the villagers.
29. Śrīv., pp. 192, 274.
30. *Ibid.*, p. 101.
31. Jonar., 95; Srīv. 284, 313.
32. Temple, *Word of Lallā*, pp. 207-8.
33. H.M., f. 153b.
34. Lawrence, *Valley*, p. 312.
35. H.M., f. 110a. For the dress under the Rājās, see Ray, *Early History and Culture of Kashmīr*, pp. 208-10.
36. See p. 56, *Supra.*
37. Jonar., p. 67.
38. Nasīb, f. 423a. There is also a reference on the same folio to a *kurta* of skin.
39. B.S., ff. 132b, 139b, refers to a *Qabā.*
40. Śrīv., p. 265.
41. *Ibid.*, pp. 214, 245, 265.
42. *Tuḥfatu'l-Aḥbāb*, p. 90.
43. Śrīv., p. 207.
44. Śrīv., p. 234.
45. *Ibid.*, pp. 207, 214, 330.
46. *Tuzuk-i-Jahāngīrī*, ii, 148. The *phairan* may have come from Khurāsān, and adapted from the *jubba* (See Dozy, *Dictionnaire de Noms des, Vetements chez les Arabes*, p. II), or it may have been adapted from the *qamīṣ* or chemise of the Persians which was open from the neck to the navel. (*Voyages du Chevalier Chardin en Perse*, iii, pp. 70, 111).
47. Nasīb, f. 423a.
48. See Pelsaert, *Remonstrantie*, p. 35, for the dress of Kashmīrī women.
49. *Tuzuk-i-Jahāngīrī*, ii, 148; Rāzī, *Ḥaft Iqlim*, f. 156a.
50. *Ibid.;* A.A., ii, 353.
51. *Tuḥfatu'l-Aḥbāb*, pp. 109, 130; Dā'ūd Mishka'tī, *Asrāru'l-Abrār*, f. 38b.
52. A.A., ii, 353; Śrīv., p. 274.
53. Śrīv., p. 276; also Stein, BK. viii, Nos. 1864 and n.
54. Yule, *Marco Polo*, i, 166; Stein, BK. viii, Nos. 1866-7; A.A., ii, 353. Abū Dulaf Mis'ar, who was attached to the court of the Sāmānids of Bukhārā and visited Kashmīr towards the end of the 10th century, says that Kashmīrīs ate wheat and fish, but no eggs, nor did they cut the neck of the animals. (G. Ferrand, *Relations de Voyages*, p. 89).
55. Stein, BK. vii, No. 1149.

56. These dishes were also popular in pre-Islamic Kashmīr. (See I.H.C. (1949), p. 134).
57. *Tazkira-i-Mullā 'Alī Raina,* f. 453a; Isḥāq, *Ḥilayatu'l-'Ārifin,* ff. 65b-6a.
58. *Tuḥfatu'l-Aḥbāb,* pp. 241, 246.
59. Śrīv., p. 235.
60. *Ibid.*
61. T.A., iii, 477.
62. Śrīv., p. 140.
63. T.R., p. 425; Firishta, ii, 641.
64. *Ibid.*
65. A.A., ii, 353.
66. *Nilamata,* Nos. 450-53, cited in Ray, *Early History and Culture of Kashmīr,* p. 208.
67. Śrīv., pp. 124, 126.
68. Once Mīr Shāh, a courtier of Zainu'l-'Ābidīn, got drunk and killed his wife. (Jonar., p. 80).
69. Śrīv., pp. 232, 245.
70. Isḥāq, *Ḥilayatu'l-'Ārifin,* f. 2b.
71. Śuka, p. 338.
72. Jonar., p. 45; Śrīv., p. 260.
73. Jonar., (Bo. ed.), Nos. 516 sqq. Jonar uses the word Siṁha which means a lion. But I have not been able to identify Kharga, the place where Shihābu'd-Dīn hunted. It must have been situated in the forests at the foot of the outer hills of Kashmīr.
74. A.A., ii, 354.
75. Compare Ashraf, *Life and Conditions of the people of Hindustān,* 289-91, for an account of the Chase under the *Sulṭāns* of Delhi.
76. A.A., ii, 354; Śrīv., p. 263.
77. Temple, *Word of Lallā,* p. 208.
78. Knowles, *A Dictionary of Kashmīrī Proverbs and Sayings,* p. 3.
79. Śrīv., p. 152; also Yule, *Marco Polo,* i, 177n. 2.
80. A.A., ii, 353.
81. *Ibid.,* 352.
82. Pelsaert, *Remonstrantie,* p. 34; also De Filippi, *Travels of Desideri,* p. 351.
83. Lawrence, pp. 249-50.
84. De Filippi, *Travels of Desideri,* p. 351. Compare this with Lawrence, pp. 249-50.
85. *Ibid.*
86. Palsaert, *Remonstrantie,* p. 34.
87. A.A., ii, 352.

88. B.S., f. 164a.
89. Bernier, *Travels*, pp. 397-8; *Tuzuk-i-Jahāngīri*, ii, 134.
90. See p. 238, *infra*.
91. The fact that some of the queens did not change their names on marriage to the Sulṭāns, shows that they retained their religious beliefs as well. Marriages between Hindus and Muslims were also common in Rajaurī, Ladākh and Baltistān. (See *Tuzuk-i-Jahāngīrī*, ii, 181; and I.A., xxxvii, p. 188).
92. The biographies of saints are full of references to such discussions.
93. Stein, i, Intro., p. 87.
94. *Ibid.*, p. 9.
95. *Ibid.*, ii, 358.
96. *Ibid.*, i, Intro., p. 8.
97 Stein, BK. iv, No. 397.
98. *Ibid.*, BK. vii, No. 1149; *Ibid.*, i, Intro., p. 112.
99. *Ibid.*, BK. viii, Nos. 885-6.
100. Yule, *Marco Polo*, i, 176-7.
101. Sa'ādat, *Bulbul Shāh*, pp. 7, 23.
102. Stein, i, Intro., 130.
103. Nasīb, f. 205a.
104. *Tuḥfatu'l-Aḥbāb*, pp. 156, 187. The accounts of saints are full of examples of Muslims adopting non-Muslim practices.
105. *Ibid.*, p. 63.
106. *Ibid.*, p. 63 sqq.
107. *Ibid.*, pp. 157-60.
108. Temple, *Word of Lallā*, p. 94.
109. Stein, i, Intro., p. 9.
110. Kalhaṇa's *Rājataraṅgiṇī* is full of examples of the laxity of caste system in Kashmīr.
111. Jonar., p. 57.
112. *Ibid.*, p. 59.
113. *Ibid.*, p. 67.
114. Śrīv., p. 235, 319.
115. *Ibid.*, p. 320.
116. For her life see Temple, *Word of Lallā*, pp. 2 sqq.; Barnett and Grierson, *Lallā-Vākyāni*, Intro.; I.A., L, pp. 302-12.
117. Temple, *Word of Lallā*, pp. 64-5.
118. *Ibid.*, pp. 2-3.
119. Barnett and Grierson, *Lallā-Vākyāni*, p. 39; also Temple, *Word of Lallā*, p. 166.
120. Temple, *Word of Lalla*, pp. 165, 191, 200-2. For the ideas of 'Alī Hamadānī on the same subject, see his *Ẕakhīratu'l-Mulūk* ff. 41a

sqq.

121. Temple, *Word of Lallā,* p. 216.
122. *Ibid.,* pp. 195-6.
123. Grierson and Barnett, *Lallā-Vākyāni,* Verse No. 105.
124. See pp. 87-8, *supra.*
125. *Tuzuk-i-Jahāngīrī,* ii, 167-8.
126. See p. 56, *supra.*
127. See p. 56, *supra.* Even in the time of Dā'ūd Khākī (1521-85) there were instances of Muslims worshipping idols. (See his *Asrāru'l-Abrār,* f. 276a).
128. Śrīv., pp. 153, 262.
129. Gul Khātūn, queen of Ḥaidar Shāh, favoured Hindu customs. (Śrīv., p. 229).
130. Jonar., p. 43.
131. *Ibid.,* p. 53.
132. Śrīv., p. 207. On the occasion of Ḥaidar Shāh's coronation the Treasurer, Ḥasan, performed these ceremonies.
133. Yūsuf Ḥusain, *l'Inde Mystique,* pp. 138 sqq.
134. Sayyid 'Alī Hamadānī believed in transcendental monotheism of Islam and rejected pantheism. This is quite clear from a study of his *Ẕakhīratu'l-Mulūk* and other works.
135. See p. 86, *supra.*
136. T.A., iii, 436.
137. *Ibid.*
138. *Tuzuk-i-Jahāngīrī,* ii, 147.
139. Śrīv., pp. 327, 334. In the civil war between Muḥammad Shāh and Fatḥ Shāh the merchants suffered a great deal.
140. T.R., p. 425; A.A., ii, 353.
141. Firishta, ii, 641; A.A., ii, 353.
142. Stein, BK. viii, No. 2298; Al-Bīrūnī, *Kitābu'l-Hind* (English trans.), p. 206.
143. Stein, BK. vii, 414.
144. Śrīv., pp. 155-6.
145. Stein, ii, 449.
146. *Ibid.;* Sharafu'd-Dīn, ii *Ẓafar-nāma,* p. 179.
147. Wessel, *Early Jesuit Travellers in Central Asia,* p. 150.
148. I.A., 1908, p. 192.
149. J.R.A.S., xii (1850), p. 373.
150. *Ibid.,* pp. 378-9; J.P.H.S., vi, No. 2, p. 148.
151. Stein Khotan, i, 88; Moorcroft, *Travels in Kashmir,* i, 346.
152. J.R.A.S., (1843), pp. 306 sqq.
153. Berner, *Travels,* pp. 425-6. See, also *Purchas His Pilgrimes* for the

trade of Yarqand and Kāshghar with Kashmīr and the neighbouring countries.

154. *Purchas His Pilgrimes* cited in J.P.H.S., vi, No. 2, p. 148; also vol. i, No. 2. p. 129.
155. *Ḥudūdu'l-'Ālam,* pp. 254, 363-4.
156. 20,000 camels passed yearly by Lāhore to Persia, (J.P.H.S., i, No. 2, p. 116).
157. Markham, *Mission of Bogle to Tibet,* pp. liv, 125.
158. *Ibid.*
159. *Ibid.,* pp. 127-8.
160. *Asrāru'l-Abrār,* ff. 122a, 123a; *Tuzuk-i-Jahāngīrī,* ii, 147; Lawrence, *Valley,* p. 393.
161. Śrīv., p. 327.
162. Two dependencies of Tibet lying to the east and south-east of Tibet.
163. J.R.A.S., vii (1843), pp. 283 sqq; *Ibid.,* xii (1850), p. 377; also *Kashmīr and its Shawls,* pp. 31-3.
164. Moorcroft, *Travels,* i, 347.
165. J.R.A.S., vii, p. 291. We do not know the quantity of shawl-wool imported during our period. But in the time of Moorcroft about 800 horse-loads were imported annually, each horse-load weighing about 28 *taraks.*
166. Markham, *Mission of Bogle to Tibet,* p. 121.
167. *Jonar.,* p. 18.
168. J.R.A.S., xii (1850), p. 377.
169. A.A., ii, 353.
170. Abel-Remusat, *Histoire de la Ville de Khotan,* pp. 119 sqq. describes in detail the qualities etc. of *Yashab.* Also Stein, *Khotan,* i, pp. 132-3.
171. *Ibid.* Commercial relations between Kashmīr and Khotan existed since ancient times. Coins of the Rājās and Sulṭāns of Kashmīr have been discovered in Khotan. (J.A.S.B., lxvii, pp. 28, 32).
172. Lawrence, *Valley,* p. 65.
173. Ujfalvy, *L'Art des Cuivres Anciens av Cachemere,* p. 22n.
174. *Tuzuk-i-Jahāngīrī,* ii, 148.
175. Bernier, *Travels,* pp. 425-6; *Purchas His Pilgrimes,* i, BK. iv, ch. 4, cited in J.P.H.S., vi, No. 2, 144, (Account of Finch). Use of tea in China can be traced to ancient times. Its use in the country in the middle of the ninth century is known from Arab sources. (Reinaud, *Voyages,* p. 40). It was introduced into Kashmīr from China. According to a tradition it was Mīrzā Ḥaidar who first brought it to the Valley.

176. A.A., ii, 353.
177. *Tuzuk-i-Jahāngīrī*, i, 92-3; A.A. (Blochmann), pp. 68-9, 140; also Pelsaert, *Remonstrantie*, pp. 35-6. The town of Pāmpūr was the centre of saffron trade.
178. Firdausī mentions in his *Shāh-nāma* that the dress of the army of Yezdigird, the last Sassanian ruler of Persia, was made out of the woollen cloth from Kashmīr. (J.R.A.S. (Bombay), xix, p. 241).
179. T.R., f. 16v; A.A. (Blochmann), p. 140.
180. Forester, *Journey from Bengal to England*, ii, p. 19.
181. M.T., iii, 2b.
182. Rāzī, *Haft Iqlim*, f. 156a.
183. Stein i, Intro., p. 130.
184. J.R.A.S., xxiii, p. 116.
185. A.N., iii, 81. For crops grown in modern times, see Lawrence, *Valley*, pp. 330 sqq. With a few exceptions the same crops were grown then as now.
186. A.A., iii, 353. Finer varieties were not cultivated because their yield was smaller compared to that of the common variety, and hence uneconomical to the peasants. Similar conditions were present until recent times. (See Lawrence, *Valley*, pp. 333, 335).
187. A.A., iii, 353.
188. Śrīv., p. 274; also p. 85, *supra*.
189. *Tuzuk-i-Jahāngīrī*, ii, 177-8.
190. A.A., (Blochmann), p. 90.
191. *Tuzuk-i-Jahāngīrī*, ii, 177-8; *Ibid.*, i, 92-3.
192. *Ibid.*, i, 92-3.
193. T.R., p. 425; Firishta, pp. 640-41; Sharafu'd-Dīn, *Ẓafar-nāma*, ii 179, says that all kinds of fruits were grown in plenty except oranges and lemons which could not be grown on account of the Valley's cold climate.
194. Stein, BK. vii, No. 42; BK. viii, No. 1428.
195. *Ibid.*, BK. v, No. 172 sqq. and nn.
196. J.R.A.S., xxiii, p. 116.
197. See p. 51, *supra*. This custom was abolished by 'Alī Shāh Chak. (B.S., f. 19a).
198. A.A. (Blochmann), p. 90.
199. Sharafu'd-Dīn Yazdī, *Ẓafar-nāma*, ii, 177-8.
200. A.A., ii, 353.
201. Stein, ii, 438.
202. Mas'ūdī, *Murūju'z-Ẓahab*, i, p. 373, ed. and trans. de Meynard.
203. Cited in T.R., p. 430. in the plains.
204. Stein, ii, p. 438.

205. *Ibid.*
206. Jonar. (Bo. ed.), No. 153.
207. *Ḥudūdu'l-'Ālam*, p. 254. Ibn al-Wardī and other Muslim writers place the number between 60,000 and 70,000.

Chapter 13

Cultural Activities

The standard of culture in Kashmīr during the Sultanate period was very high. The statement of Śrīvara[1] that everyone enjoyed poetry and attempted to compose verses is obviously an exaggeration, but there is ample evidence in the chronicles to suggest that there was a general appreciation of arts, letters, and music by the people of the Valley. The Kashmīrīs were extremely witty and intelligent, and were always ready with some appropriate saying.[2] They were very fond of music, and possessed great artistic sense.[3] They loved learning, and, as in olden days, they left their homes for distant places in India, Turkistān, and Persia to seek knowledge.[4] The Sulṭāns were not only patrons of art and culture, but some of them were themselves poets and musicians. Their courts were adorned with scholars, musicians, and painters, while their capital Srīnagar was embellished with magnificent palaces, mosques, monasteries, and gardens.

Persian Influence

The history of cultural relations between Kashmīr and Persia goes back to ancient times. This is evident from the tiles of the Hārvan Monastery near Srīnagar and from the ancient sculptures of Kashmīr which bear unmistakably Sasanian characteristics.[5] Similarly, Sasanian influence can be detected in the use of official designations like *dibir* or *divira* (after the Persian *dabīr*) and *ga ñjavara* (after the Persian *ganjwar*).[6] Nevertheless, until the fourteenth century, the dominant note in Kashmīr's culture had been Indian. It was only with the foundation of the Sultanate that more profound and endurable links were established with the centres of Persian culture,[7] and, as a result, the Indian influence was gradually replaced by the Perso-Islamic element, though it was never completely eliminated.

There were many reasons why cultural contacts between Kashmīr and Persia during the Sultanate period became much closer than they had ever been before. First, the progress of Islām in the Valley was intimately associated with the missionary activities of Ṣūfī saints from Persia and Central Asia like Bulbul Shāh, Sayyid 'Alī Hamadānī, his son Muḥammad Hamadānī, Mīr Shamsu'd-Dīn and many others. These Ṣūfīs played an important part in bringing about an Iranian orientation of Kashmīr's culture, for they were not only the missionaries of Islām, but were also zealous propagandists of the Persian language and culture. Secondly, with the spread of Islām in Kashmīr, it became natural for its Muslim inhabitants to look for their intellectual and spiritual inspiration to lands which had become centres of Islamic culture. Scholars, therefore, began to visit Herāt, Merv, Samarqand, and Bukhārā, which formed part of Persia's cultural empire, to learn at the feet of eminent jurists and devout Ṣūfīs, and drink deep from the fountain of Persian culture. Thirdly, from the reign of Shihābu'd-Dīn, Persians and Persianized Turks, attracted by the patronage extended to them by the Sulṭāns, began to enter Kashmīr in increasingly large numbers. These men exercised great influence on the social and cultural life of its people.[8] The Valley had also close cultural relations with Hindustān, but the latter's influence on her, during this period, appears to have been much less than that of Persia and Turkistān.

Persian Language

The result of the establishment of these religious and cultural ties with Persia and Central Asia was the spread of Persian in Kashmīr. Sanskrit had been the court language under the Hindu kings and under the early Shāh Mīrs, but from the reign of Shihābu'd-Dīn it began to be replaced by Persian which became the language of the educated classes, and even found its way into the villages. Ḥāfīz was not merely indulging in poetic imagination, but was stating a fact when he said[9]:

> The black-eyed beauties of Kashmīr and the Turks of Samarqand
> Sing and dance to the strains of Ḥāfīz of Shīrāz's verse.

The greatest contribution to the spread and development of Persian in Kashmīr ws made by Zainu'l-'Ābidīn who was himself a poet and the author of two prose works in Persian. He made it the state language, patronized poets and scholars, and encouraged the translation of historical and scientific works from Sanskrit into Persian.[10] The amount of literature produced during his reign was considerable, but as very little of it is extant, it is difficult to assess its quality. Stray verses of the Sulṭān and his court poets are found scattered in the chronicles, and if they can be any criteria, then Persian poetry must have achieved a high standard of development in Kashmīr under him. Zainu'l-'Ābidīn's son and successor, Ḥaidar Shāh, was also a poet and composed a book of songs. The next ruler Ḥasan Shāh, though not himself a poet, was a man of culture and patronized poets and learned men. The example set up by the Sulṭāns was followed by the nobles, who surrounded themselves with scholars and set up institutions of learning at their own cost. The queens and the ladies of the upper classes, too, were not far behind in their zeal to promote learning.

Under the later Shāh Mīrs, owing to constant civil wars and invasions, learning declined, but there was again a revival under the shortlived rule of Mīrzā Ḥaidar and the Chaks. Mīrzā Ḥaidar being himself a man of letters encouraged learning. Unfortunately, however, the names of scholars attached to his court, or of works produced under his patronage, are not known. Among the Chak rulers the most cultured man was Ḥusain Shāh. Himself a poet, he was fond of the society of poets and learned men. Mīr 'Alī, a poet and a calligraphist, came from Persia during his reign and wrote a long poem in praise of Kashmīr.[11] Mullā Bāqī, Mullā Nāmī I, and Mullā Nāmī II were the other poets attached to Ḥusain Shāh's court.[12] The most important poet who enjoyed 'Alī Shāh's patronage was Mullā

Mehrī. Muḥammad Amīn Mustaghnī, a Kashmīrī, was a courtier of Yūsuf Shāh and a good poet. Another poet connected with his court was Mīrzā 'Alī Khān, who was killed in the course of Ya'qūb Shāh's war with Rājā Bhagwān Dās.[13] Bābā Ṭālib Isfahānī arrived in Kashmīr during the time of Ghāzī Shāh. He was a good poet and enjoyed the respect of all the Chak rulers. When Akbar annexed Kashmīr, Bābā Ṭālib went to Agra and entered the Emperor's service.[14]

But the two most outstanding poets and scholars of the Chak period were Bābā Dā'ūd Khākī and Shaikh Ya'qūb Ṣarfī. Bābā Dā'ūd, the son of a noted scribe Shaikh Ḥasan Ganā'ī, was born in 1521. After completing his education, he served for a short period as tutor of Nāzuk Shāh's son. He then became a disciple of Shaikh Makhdūm Ḥamzā. During Ya'qūb Shāh's reign he proceeded with Ya'qūb Ṣarfi to the court of Akbar to seek his help against the Kashmīr ruler. On his return he fell ill and died at Anantnāg in 1585. He was a learned Ṣufī, and his poetry is permeated with religious and mystical ideas. He was the author of a number of books like *Dastūru's-Sālikīn, Virdu'l-Murīdīn, Qaṣīda-i-Jalāliyya* and others.[15]

Shaikh Ya'qūb Ṣarfī, the son of Shaikh Ḥasan Ganā'ī, was born in 1528 and died on July 25,1594. He memorized the Qur'ān when he was only seven, and began to compose verses in Persian at the same age. He studied in Lahore, Siālkōt, Samarqand, Mashhad, Mecca, and Madīnā under renowned teachers.[16] He was one of the most learned men of his age, and, according to Abū'l-Faẓl, "the greatest authority in religious matters".[17] He was the author in Arabic of an introduction to Faiẓī's *Tafsīr* entitled *Sawāṭi'ul-Ilhām*. He also wrote a commentary of *al-Ṣaḥīḥ* of *Bukhārī;* and, just before his death, he had nearly completed a commentary fo the Qur'ān.[18] Badā'ūnī regarded this work as "one of the most wonderful productions of his perfect genius".[19] Besides being a great prose writer, Ya'qūb Ṣarfī was also a good poet. He wrote many *ghazals* and *qaṣīdās,* and completed a *khamsa,* a series of five *maṣnavīs* in imitation of the *khamsa* of Niẓāmī.[20] "His genius," as Badā'ūnī observed, "was highly adapted to the composition of eloquent poetry".[21]

Sanskrit

Sanskrit learning in Kashmīr began to decline from about the middle of the twelfth century; but with the increasing employment of Persian as the language of administration and culture, this process was further accentuated. However, even after Sanskrit had ceased to be the official language, it continued to enjoy the patronage of many of the Sulṭāns, and Kashmīr could boast of a number of great Sanskrit scholars.[22] It was during the Sultanate period that Jonarāja, Śrīvara, Prājyabhaṭṭa, and Śuka wrote their chronicles. Besides writing a historical work, Śrīvara also translated Jāmī's *Yūsuf-u-Zulaikhā* into Sanskrit, and compiled *Subhāṣitāvalī* containing extracts from the works of more than 350 poets, both Kashmīrī and Indian.[23] Among other important works of the period, mention must be made of Jagaddhar Bhaṭ's *Stūti-Kusumāñjalī* written in 1450, and of Sita Kaṇṭha's *Bālabodhinī* written in 1475,[24] and of Varadarāja's *Śivasūtra-Vārttika* composed in the fifteenth century.[25] It must also be noted that, despite the growing popularity of Persian, the use of Sanskrit both for private and official purposes did not cease for a long time. In fact, very often, it was employed side by side with Persian. A number of Muslim graves of the fifteenth and sixteenth centuries are still in existence in Srīnagar and Bījbehāra which bear bi-lingual inscriptions : Sanskrit at the top, and Persian at the bottom. Stein refers to a deed of sale of as late a date as 1682, written in both Sanskrit and Persian.[26] Similarly, there is preserved in the Srīnagar Museum a bi-lingual will of Shaikh Makhdūm Ḥamza, a great Kashmīrī saint, dated 984/1576, and written on birch-bark. The Sanskrit version in the Śāradā characters on the right side cannot be deciphered, but the Persian text on the left is partly legible. In spite of these instances, however, it cannot be denied that Sanskrit fought a losing battle in the Valley, and by the end of the seventeenth century its use and study had become confined to a very small number of Brahman priests. Another effect of the spread of Persian was that it led to an influx of many foreign words into Sanskrit. As already mentioned, owing to Sasanian influence, some words like *dabīr* and *ganjwar* had come into official use in Kashmīr during the Hindu period. Now with the establishment of the Shāh Mīr dynasty, a much larger number of Persian words began to find their way into the Sanskrit language. Thus those parts of the *Lokaprakāśa* that were written during the Sultanate period contain many new words like *Shāhī, khawās, Suratrāṇa (Sulṭān)* and *Silah-dār*. These are not to be found either in those portions of the *Lokaprakāśa* whose authorship has been assigned to Kśemendra, or in Kalhaṇa's *Rājataraṅgiṇī*.[27] Similarly in the Sanskrit chronicles of Jonarāja, Śrivara, Prājyabhaṭṭa and Śuka, we find the use of a large number of Arabic, Persian and Turkish words like *khātonā (Khātūn)*[28] *khānagāha (khānqāh), Mallika (Malik), masjeda* or *masēdāha (masjid), madrasā,*[29] *ravāva (rabāb).*[30]

Kashmīrī Poetry

We have seen that while Sanskrit was the language of culture in the time of the Rājās, its place was taken by Persian during the Sultanate period. Kashmīrī, however, remained, as before, the mother tongue of a vast majority of the population. In fact, under the influence of Persian, it grew richer, and owing to the patronage it received at the hands of the Sulṭāns, it was able to develop a respectable poetic literature of its own.

The oldest author in Kashmīrī seems to be Lallā Ded,[31] for there is no reference in the chronicles of any earlier writer. She was a great poetess, and her poems are full of deep and philosophical meanings. But she expressed her thoughts in the simple language understood by the common people. That is why her verses are, even today, in every one's mouth in the Valley and quoted as sayings or maxims in the course of conversation. Her verses contain a large number of Sanskrit words,[32] but the later poets, particularly the Muslims, increasingly make use of Persian.[33] They model their poetry on Persian metre and employ Persian metaphors, similes and imagery. However, they do not remain indifferent to the indigenous legends and romances and to the appeal of their surroundings.[34]

Nūru'd-Dīn Rishī, Lallā Ded's contempoary and the patron saint of the Valley, was also like her a poet and enriched the Kashmīrī literature. His sayings, which are religious and didactic, are like those of Lallā Ded on the tip of every Kashmīrīs tongue.[35]

The first secular poem to have been written was *Bāṇāsuravadha* in the time of Sulṭān Zainu'l-'Ābidīn, who gave encouragement not only to Persian but also to the Kashmīrī language.[36] Another work of his reign as *Mahānayaprakāśa* by Sita Kaṇṭha. But some persons think that it was written before the fifteenth century. Two other works of Zainu'l-'Ābidīn's period, of which mention had already been made, were Nothosoma Pandit's *Jainacarita* and Yodhabhaṭṭa's *Jainaprakāśa*.[37]

In the Chak period the most outstanding poetic genius was Habbā Khātūn, the queen of Yūsuf Shāh. It was she who introduced '*Lols*'[38] or love lyrics in Kashmīrī poetry, and on the advice of Sayyid Mubārak, a Ṣūfī, she began to experiment with Persian metre. While the lyrics of Lallā Ded and Nūru'd-Dīn Rishī are mystical and didactic, Habbā Khātūn's lol-lyrics sing of human love, its disappointments, yearnings and fulfilment. They are full of emotion, music, rhythm and melody, and are sung even to this day by artisans, peasants and boatmen.

Education

Education was wide-spread in Kashmīr during the Sultanate period. Kings and nobles vied with each other in opening schools and endowing them with jāgīrs for their maintenance. As a result every village had a school. At the same time higher education was not neglected, and in Srīnagar there was a University. Monasteries were also centres of learning where education was imparted to students by able teachers.[39]

The system of education and the courses of study were the same as in the *madrasas* of India, Turkistān, and Persia. Generally at the age of five the child was put into the school where he was taught the Arabic alphabet and to read the Qur'ān.[40] He had then to learn the traditional sciences. Dogmatic Theology (*'Ilmu'l-Kalām*, *'Ilmu'l-Tawḥıd*), interpretation of the Qur'ān (*Tafsīr*), Tradition (*Ḥadīs̤*), Jurisprudence (*Fiqh*). But physical sciences were not neglected; and boys were trained in archery, swordsmanship, and horsemanship.[41]The heads of the institutions were eminent scholars, and students came from India, Herāt, and Turkistān to learn at their feet.[42]

The first Kashmīr Sulṭān to have established *madrasas* in different parts of the Valley was Shihābu'd-Dīn.[43] In addition he founded a college in Srīnagar called Madrasatu'l-Qur'ān for the study of the Qur'ān and *Ḥadīṣ*. When Quṭbu'd-Dīn came to the throne, he established a college in his new capital of Quṭbu'd-Dīnpūr and appointed Pīr Ḥājī Muḥammad Qārī as its Principal. It had a hostel attached to it where board and lodging was free for both teachers and pupils. The college existed till the establishment of the Sikh rule in Kashmīr when, owing to lack of patronage, it had to close down. Another educational institution of this period was called 'Urwatu'l-Wuṣqā which was founded by Sayyid Jamālu'd-Dīn Muḥaddiṣ who had come to Kashmīr with Sayyid 'Alī Hamadānī and had been persuaded by Quṭbu'd-Dīn to stay in the country. Quṭbu'd-Dīn's son and successor, Sikandar, opened many schools, and founded a college and a hostel attached to the Jāmi' Masjid which he had built. Mullā Afẓal Bukhārī taught in this college, and the village of Nāgām was assigned to him as jāgīr.[44]

But the Sulṭān who did most for the spread of education in the Valley was Zainu'l-'Ābidīn. He opened a school near his palace in Naushahr, and placed it in charge of Maulānā Kabīr. The Sulṭān himself occasionally went there to attend the Maulānā's lectures. For the maintenance of the school, and for the granting of scholarships to deserving candidates, he created an endowment with Maulānā Kabīr as its trustee. The institution survived until the middle of the seventeenth century. In addition to this school the Sulṭān also founded a college in Zainagīr, and a large *madrasa* at Sir in Dachhanpūr near Islāmabād with Mullā Ghāzī Khān as its principal. Another place where education was imparted was the hospice of Bābā Ismā'īl Kubravī, who later in the reign of Ḥasan Shāh became Shaikhu'-l-Islām. The fame of his learning was so wide-spread that students came to study under him from Herāt, India, and Transoxiana. It was the measure of Zainu'l-'Ābidīn's interest in education that he did not hesitate to give generous grants to institutions even outside the Valley. Thus to Madrasatu'l-'Ulūm at Siālkōt he contributed six lakhs of rupees, while his queen, Tāj Khātūn, gave away her valuable necklace. Besides the *madrasas,* the

Sulṭān also opened technical schools where people were taught paper-making, book-binding, and other arts which he had introduced into the country.

During the reign of Ḥasan Shāh also a number of *madrasas* were founded. Gul Khātūn, the mother of the Sulṭān, Ḥayāt Khātūn, his queen, Shāh Bēgum, the wife of his prime minister Malik Aḥmad, and nobles like Naurūz and Tāzī Bat took great interest in education and established schools at their own expense. Sulṭān Ḥasan Shāh himself founded Madrasa-i-Dāru'sh-Shifā at Pakhribal on the Dal Lake, and appointed Bābā Ismā'īl Kubravī as its head. The revenues of Bāghāt-i-Mālkhāna, lying between Nauhatta and the Dal, and of the village of Birhama in the Lār pargana were assigned to iṭ

The Chak rulers, too, like the Shāh Mīrs, were great patrons of education. Thus Ḥusain Shāh improved the Daru'sh-Shifā founded by Ḥasan Shāh, and, in addition, opened a college to which he assigned the revenues of Zainapūr. The college had a library and a hostel, which were also endowed. The principal of the college was Fatḥu'llāh Ḥaqqānī and his assistant was Akhūnd Mullā Darwīsh.

Minor Arts

One of the main achievements of the Sultanate period lies in the field of minor arts. But unfortunately it is not possible to trace the history of their development, as very few works of art of this period are extant. A flourishing textile art had existed in Kashmīr since ancient times. The Kashmīrī woollen cloth was famous for its warmth and durability, and is said to have been worn by the Sasānian army.[45] Kashmīr is believed to have learned sericulture from the Chinese during the time of the Rājās, but Zainu'l-'Ābidīn improved the manufacture of silk by introducing better methods of weaving, and by importing the decorative designs from Persia. As a result Kashmīr became famous for its silks.[46]

As regards the shawl industry, no conclusive evidence can be given of its origin. According to local tradition, recorded during the nineteenth century, the first Kashmīrī shawls were produced by Turkistān weavers who were invited by Zainu'l-

'Ābidīn to settle in the Valley.[47] It is also stated that the shawl industry was founded by Sayyid 'Alī Hamadānī in 1378.[48] However that may be, one thing is certain : that the shawl industry did not exist before the thirteenth century, for there is no reference to it either in Kalhaṇa's Rājataraṅgiṇī or any other source; and that it was developed under the patronage of the Sulṭāns with the help of weavers who came from Persia and Turkistān. These immigrants not only introduced new patterns but also a new technique—the twil-tapestry technique—which has a parallel in Persia and Central Asia but nowhere in India and Pākistān.[49] It is, however, impossible to trace the history of the development of this industry, because no shawl of a date earlier than the later half of the seventeenth century now survives. From Śrīvara we only learn that under Zainu'l-'Ābidīn Kashmīr had become famous for its shawls.[50] When the Mughals conquered the Valley the shawl industry was in a well-developed state. From this period onwards its development can be followed without much difficulty. But that is beyond the scope of this work.

The art of tinned metals used in northern India and Kashmīr was introduced from Persia.[51] The Muslims use copper cooking and eating vessels; and hence these have to be tinned before they can be employed with safety. The ewers of Kashmīr are mostly in red copper, embossed, enamelled, and tinned. Their handles are of brass, and represent the head and tail of a Chinese dragon,[52] while the floral decorations and forms are mainly Persian. But these decorations are scattered with such profusion as to show that the influence of the Hindu art has been retained. Thus from a study of the metal-works of Kashmīr it appears that the three ancient civilizations—Persian, Chinese, and Hindu—met in the Valley, but the influence of the first overshadowed that of the other two, although it was modified by the native mode of expression.[53] But this should not lead us to think that the Kashmīrīs were mere imitators. On the contrary, while they accepted foreign influence, they developed their own style. Thus some of their ewers are different from those of Persia; in fact some of their shapes are found nowhere in Asia. Moreover, Kashmīrīs excel in enamelling which did not find much favour with Muslim workers in Persia and elsewhere.[54] They also decorate their vases in a particular fashion which distinguishes their work from that of India and Persia. Thus the art of Kashmīr has also its original side. As Ujfalvy observes: "With Islām came Perso-Arab art in Kashmīr. The people, the most ingenious, perhaps in the entire world and certainly in Central Asia, found themselves in the presence of admirable models, and with their marvellous talent for imitation and execution they set themselves to work and create for their daily use a series of objects of art which soon surpassed the originals".[55]

In addition to the art of tinned metals, that of wood carving also flourished during the Sultanate period. There is evidence to show that this art existed in Kashmīr in ancient times; and since most of the edifices were built of wood during the medieval period, it continued to be cultivated. They only specimen of that period that has survived is the door of the mosque of Madanī bearing fine carvings and lattice-work. The existence of fine jali-screens in the Jāmi' Masjid and the mosque of Hamadānī show that these buildings must have possessed similar screens before, for when they were rebuilt during the Mughal period the original features were retained. As regards other minor arts, tradition credits Sulṭān Zainu'l-'Ābidīn with having introduced many of them. However, it is impossible to review them as not a single specimen of that period has survived.

Painting

It is impossible to enter into a detailed discussion of Kashmīr painting since not a single work of the Sultanate period has survived the devastating cataclysms of civil strife and foreign invasion.[56] However, there is evidence to show that Kashmīr had maintained a high artistic tradition for centuries and had its own style. Mullā Jamīl was a famous painter in the service of Zainu'l-'Ābidīn.[57] Akbar had a group of five painters from Kashmīr, but we cannot assess the influence, if any, which the Kashmīr style of painting exercised on the Mughal school.[58] However, as Brown says: "Very delicate effect is said to have been obtained by the Kashmīrī painters. They allowed water to stand until it had completely evaporated, leaving a slight sediment, which they used as a background tint to the profile of a portrait, as it left a faint but charming contrast of tone between the flesh colour and the ground".[59]

Calligraphy

The Sulṭāns of Kashmīr were great patrons of the art of calligraphy. But unfortunately not a single manuscript of calligraphic significance has survived. However, some mosques and tombs still bear Persian and Arabic inscriptions in elegant *naskh* and *nasta'līq*, which show that the art of calligraphy had been carried to a high degree of perfection in Kashmīr. From the inscriptions of the reigns of Zainu'l-'Ābidīn and Ḥasan Shāh it appears that only the *naskh* style was cultivated during that period; but under the later Shāh Mīrs and the Chak Sulṭāns it was the *nasta'līq* style that came into vogue. During the time of Zainu'l-'Ābidīn a number of calligraphists came to the Valley from Persia and Turkistān and were given jāgīrs. The Sulṭān had a number of copies made of Zamakhsharī's commentary of the Qur'ān.[60] The greatest calligraphist of the Chak period was Muḥammad Ḥusain who, when Kashmīr was annexed by the Mughals, entered the service of Akbar. The Emperor was so much impressed by the grace, beauty, and symmetry of his compositions that he conferred upon him the title of *Zarrīn-Qalam* (Gold-pen).[61] Another noted calligraphist of the Chak period was 'Alī Chaman Kashmīrī. He, too, was patronised by Akbar.[62] Under Jahāngīr and Shāhjahān also some of the most prominent calligraphists were of Kashmīrī origin.

Sculpture

The relief,[63] illustrated elsewhere in this book, was found in Ushkur, near Bārāmūla, by Father de Ruyter of the Church Mission School at Bārāmūla, and is the only piece of sculpture belonging to the Sultanate period that is extant. It bears the equestrian portrait of a warrior on horseback. The man is shown wearing two garments: a tight inside tunic with a high collar joined with a hook; an upper coat with short sleeves, heavily embroidered, fastened by a girdle in four folds around his waist. The legs are unfortunately broken, but a portion of the lower garment, probably a *sirwāl,* which comes down in angular folds, can be discerned. The man is armed with a bow, a quiver full of arrows, a big sword, two daggers, a battle-axe, a mace and a shield. The horse is shown caparisoned with a richly embroidered cloth, tied to the body with belts. The relief is reminiscent of a Central Asian horseman both from the point of view of costume and the treatment of the figure. It also throws light on contemporary military equipment. The inscription on the slab is in the Śārada script, and bears the date of Friday the ninth of the dark fortnight of *Magha* in the year 82 of the *Laukika* era which corresponds to A.D. 1506.

Architecture

The Sulṭāns of Kashmīr, like the Great Mughals, were great builders. But unfortunately, with the exception of a few tombs and mosques, all their buildings have perished. The architecture of their period can be divided under two heads: (1) The masonry style (2) The wooden style. One of the buildings belonging to the first category, which still exists, is the tomb of Zainu'l-'Ābidīn's mother in Srīnagar. Although it is constructed on the plinth of an ancient temple, the brick structure above the plinth is built in the style of a Muslim tomb. With the exception of the niches of either side of the gateway, which are like those found at Mārtand, the pointed arches in each wall-face and the brick arch over the gateway are all Islamic. The outer walls are studded at inervals with glazed blue bricks, while the whole structure is surmounted by four small cupolas and a large central dome. But all the domes possess more or less the same features. The central dome is placed on a lofty drum, the wall of which is pierced by arched openings. The walls underneath the accessory domes are decorated with blind arcades. Below the arcades is a moulding and a dentil decoration. This feature—the cupolas at the four corners with a dome in the centre—appears for the first time in this building in the history of Indo-Muslim architecture. The next appearance, with slight modifications, is in Shēr Shāh's tomb at Sasarām.

Horseman in low relief
Dated 1506 A.D. University Museum, Philadelphia, U.S.A.

Another building in Srīnagar representing the masonry style is the tomb of Sayyid Muḥammad Madanī, who came as an envoy to Kashmīr from Madīnā in the reign of Sikandar. Constructed in 848/1444, it is now in a dilapidated condition; but until recently it possessed two interesting features. The first was its coloured tile-work which was introduced from Persia and was different from the tile-work of the Mughals.[64] The tile-work of this tomb is in square units with various brilliant colours, such as blue, red, brown, green and yellow, on the same piece; whereas the tile-work of the Mughals, being almost invariably cut in small irregular shapes to fit the different forms and colours of the design, has the appearance of mosaic.

But the most significant feature of the building was the representation of a beast in polychrome tiles in the southern half of the spandrel of the archway in the east facade. The body of the beast is of a leopard, and the trunk is that of a human being whose head, chest, and shoulders are missing, but who appears to be shooting with a bow and arrow at its own tail which ends in a kind of dragon's head, while nearby a fox is quietly looking on from among flowers and cloud-forms. The background of the representation is blue, the leopard's body is yellow with green spots, the trunk of the man is red, the dragon's head and the fox are reddish brown, and the flowers are of various colours. The use of cloud-forms and dragon's head are suggestive of Chinese and Persian influence.[65]

It was, however, not the masonry style but the wooden style of architecture that was more common in the Valley. Although building in wood was not unknown in Hindu times, it became more popular under the Sulṭāns. This is perhaps due fo the fact that buildings constructed of wooden framework are less liable to fall in earthquakes than an edifice of brick or stone. Moreover, the change of religion required "the hasty erection of buildings for public worship on a much larger scale than had been required by Hindu ritual; wood was abundant and easily worked; hence its substitution for stone, and the fashion, having once set in, continued to spread after the occasion for it had ceased".[66]

The mosques and tombs are all built in a similar style. They are all square in plan. But while the mosques of Madanī and Hamadānī are self-contained square buildings, the Jāmī' Masjid at Srīnagar consists of a group of square buildings, enclosing a spacious courtyard and connected together by a colonnade. The walls are constructed sometimes of masonry and sometimes of logs laid across each other horizontally, the spaces between the logs being in some cases filled with brick work. Since the Kashmīrīs were ignorant of the art of joinery, the logs were generally fastened to one another by a stout wooden pin. Nor did they adopt any other means like struts, trusses or diagonal members to secure lateral rigidity. The roofs of these buildings are covered with turf laid on birch-bark which is impervious to both rain and snow. The birch-bark is placed on boards which are supported on rafters. The ceilings of the chambers are supported by high posts, all of single deodar trees, which enhance the beauty and grace of the buildings. The pyramidal roof is surmounted by a steeple; and the final, which is covered with metal, is in the shape of an outspread umbrella. The steeples have sloping gables projecting from the sides. Window openings and balustrades possess fine jali screens. The angles of the eaves are ornamented with wooden pendants suspended from the corners, and almost immediately beneath the eaves project heavy cornices corbelled out from the wall-face on logs laid crosswise forming a dental crown. This form of Kashmīrī architecture is very similar to the wooden buildings of other mountainous countries like Nepāl, Norway and the Austrian Tyrol. But this does not mean a common origin. The fact is that the characteristics, such as the methods of laying logs, stepped roofs, and the employment of brich-bark and turf as roof covering, and many other features, were independently evolved in Kashmīr because of its special climatic conditions and the easy availabiliy and abundance of timber. It would also be wrong to suggest that the architectural style and method of constructing these buildings were borrowed from Buddhist pagodas. For, in the first place, by the time of the Sulṭāns not a single pagoda was in existence in the Valley; and in the second, the architecture of the pagodas is quite different from that of the wooden buildings of Kashmīr.

Section of the doorway of Khanqah-i-Mu'alla

Section of the celling of Khanqah-i-Mu'alla

The mosque of Hamadānī in Srīnagar, better known as Khānqāh-i-Mu'allā, which stands on the right bank of the Jehlam on an irregular masonry foundation, is a typical example of the wooden architecture of the Valley. Exclusive of its verandahs and extensions, it is in plan a square, of seventy feet side and is two storeys in height, which up to the eaves is nearly fifty feet from the ground. The pyramidal roof projecting over the whole structure is built in three tiers, and is surmounted by an open pavilion for the *mu'azzin*, over which rises the steeple with its finial 125 ft. from the ground. Around the building are higher structures such as arcades, verandahs and porticos, their openings being filled with lattice work. On the ground floor is the hall which is rectangular in plan measuring 63 feet by 43 feet, the original square having been reduced by the construction of small chambers on its north and south sides. The interior hall has no great significance from the point of construction, but is tapering eight-sided ornamented posts, the arched and recessed *miḥrāb*, its panelled walls and ceilings painted in multicoloured designs, and the valuable prayer carpets of different colours on the floor give it an air of elegance and dignity.

The Jāmi' Masjid of Srīnagar, built by Sikandar in 1400, contains all the typical features of the Kashmīrī wooden style already described, while preserving the conception of the orthodox mosque plan. It was many times destroyed by fire, but was each time restored. The final reconstruction was effected by Aurangzēb who seems to have retained the original plan. The building consists of a courtyard some 240 feet square, surrounded on all four sides with wide colonnades. The outer wall is of masonry, having projecting entrances on all three sides except the west. The main entrance is on the south side and consists of a recessed portico leading across the colonnade into the interior courtyard. A series of arched arcades with a clerestory goes round the courtyard, but in the centre of each side there is a square frontage containing an archway, while above it is the usual pyramidal roof and steeple already described. Of these four structures the one on the west, which is the largest, denotes the position of the nave of the sanctuary.

Tomb of Sainu'l'Abidin's mother

Gate of the Mosque of Madani

This is entered through the great archway, and is contained within a double range of tall wooden posts, with an arched *miḥrāb* occupying the interior wall, thus giving an air of spaciousness and breadth to this portion of the building. But the real greatness of the conception lies in the lofty colonnades extending around the entire building. They are composed of ranges of high and graceful posts, each made out of a single deodar trunk, varying from 25 feet to 50 feet in height, all amounting to 378 in number. The whole structure, owing to its breadth and spaciousness, its stately proportions and its graceful columns, is most impressive.

The mosque of Madanī is another edifice constructed of wood and adjoins the tomb of Madanī which has already been described. Its heavy corbelled cornice is very much like that of the mosque of Hamadānī. This mosque is in a very bad state of preservation. An inscription on the doorway suggests that both buildings were erected at the same time in 848/1444. The mosque was also, like the tomb, built on the site of an old Hindu temple, and just as two carved stone columns have been used in the inner chambers of the tomb, so some similar columns have been used in the porch of the mosque.

The bridges in Kashmīr were constructed according to the cantilever principle. The main supports or piers are formed of layers of deodar logs resting on a foundation of uncemented stones enclosed in a triangular wooden frame. The layers are laid alternately lengthwise and across, each projecting slightly beyond the one immediately beneath it. This contrivance gives the piers the shape of an inverted pyramid, and, by reducing the span, permits the logs to be laid across one pier to the other, thus forming the roadway. Until 1952 two bridges built on the old pattern existed in Srīnagar. But the floods of that year washed away one of them called Fatḥ Kadal, the third bridge, and a new one was constructed in its place. The sixth bridge, known as Nau Kadal, was rebuilt towards the end of 1954.[67]

Music

The medieval period saw a great development of music in Kashmīr. The Sulṭāns were great patrons of music and their courts were thronged with musicians from various parts of

India, Central Asia, and Persia. Sulṭān Zainu'l-'Ābīdīn was a great lover of music and occasionally held musical concerts. His son and successor Ḥaidar could play excellently on musical instruments, while his grandson, Ḥasan Shāh, who was a musician, invited great artists from the Deccan so that they might introduce new elements in Kashmīrī music and thus enrich it. Ḥasan Shāh had even a music department of which Śrīvara was the head.[68] Mīrzā Ḥaidar Dughlat also did a great deal for the development of music in the Valley. But perhaps the greatest patron and connoisseur of music among the medieval rulers of Kashmīr was Yūsuf Shāh. His queen Habbā Khātūn was a great musician and introduced the melody of *Rāst Kashmīrī*. With downfall of the Chaks, owing to the absence of royal patronage, Kashmīrī music did not achieve any further development.

Kashmīrī music is the product of diverse elements, which have blended with one another. But the chief contribution to its development was made by Persia and Turkistān.[69] In fact, the main schools of music in the Valley were founded by the Īrānī and Tūrānī musicians in the time of Sulṭān Zainu'l-'Ābidīn.[70]

The classical music of Kashmīr is known as *Sūfiāna Kalām,* which borrowed its style from Persian music.[71] It has about fifty-four *maqāmāt* (modes), out of which some are like the Indian *rāgas,* and bear Indian names like *Bhairavīn, Lalit* and *Kalyān,* while others have Persian names, as for example, *Isfahānī, Dūgāh, Panjgāh, 'Irāq, Rāst-i-Fārsī* and *Sehgāh.*[72] The most prevalent *tāls* are *Sehtāls, Nīmdūr, Dūr-i-Khafīf* and *Turkī Ẓarb.* These *tāls* are different from those of India. The *bōls* too are different. Moreover, unlike the Indian classical music, the *Ṣūfiāna Kalām* is always sung in chorus.[73] In this respect Kashmīrī music is unique. Formerly singing was done to the accompaniment of *Ḥāfiẓ Naghma,* a dance which expressed the meaning of songs by physical movements. The accompanying instruments are *Dhukrā Santūr, Sāz* and *Sitār.*[74] Other musical instruments common were *Mizmār* (a kind of flute) and *Taṁbūr* (lute or guitar).[75] The most popular instrument used in folk music is the *Rabāb* which was borrowed from Persia. 'Ūd, which was introduced in the time of Zainu'l-'Ābidīn,[76] is also common.

The most popular types of folk music are the *Chhakkrī, Taṁbūr Naghma* and *Bcha Naghma,* all of which are sung in chorus with often a little dancing. Among these the most common is the first which is sung in spring to the accompaniment of the *Rabāb.*[77]

NOTES

1. Śrīv., p. 144.
2. Bernier, *Travels,* pp. 402, 415; Grierson and Barnett, *Lallā-Vākyāni,* Intro. p. 1.
3. *Rāzī, Haft Iqlim,* f. 156a.
4. Compare this with Hiuen Tsiang's statement in *Si-Y-Ki,* i, p. 148 (Trans. Beale).
5. Kāk, *Handbook of Partāb Singh Museum, Srīnagar,* pp. 4, 65.
6. Stein, BK. v, No. 177.
7. These were not confined to the narrow geographical limits of modern Persia, but extended to Central Asia and Northern India and even as far as Asia Minor.
8. Jonar., pp. 57-8.
9. Browne, *Literary History of Persia,* iii, 283.
10. See p. 90, *supra.* For more details, see my article in *Indo-Iranica,* vii, No. 3.
11. W.K., f. 61a; T.H., iv, f. 278b.
12. H.M., f. 160a; T.H., iv, ff. 278b-9a.
13. H.M., f. 180a; T.H., iv, ff. 279a-b.
14. A.A. (Blochmann), p. 676 and n.
15. W.K., f. 63b; Ṣūfī, ii, 457.
16. A.A. (Blochmann), p. 651 and n. 2; also Miskīn, *Ta'rīkh-i-Kabīr,* pp. 170-71.
17. A.A. (Blochmann), p. 191; also M.T., ii 266.
18. M.T., iii, 200-1; Ṣūfī, ii, 360.
19. *Ibid.,* iii, 201.
20. *Ibid.,* p. 200 and n. 1.
21. *Ibid.,* iii, 360.
22. Śāstrī, *Laugākṣi-Gṛhya-Sūtras,* Intro. p. 3, (*Kashmīr Series of Texts and studies,* No. XLix).
23. Buhler, *Report on Tour,* p. 61.
24. This information was supplied to me by the Research and Publication Dept. Srīnagar.
25. *Kashmīr Series of Texts and Studies,* No. XLiii.
26. J.R.A.S., 1900, pp. 187 sqq.
27. *Indische Studiene,* xviii, pp. 294, 347, 350.

28. Śrīv., p. 157.
29. *Ibid.*, pp. 225-7.
30. *Ibid.*, p. 136.
31. Grierson, *Linguistic Survey of India*, viii, part ii, p. 237.
32. She sometimes used Persian words like *Shikār*. (Verse 15).
33. Nūru'd-Dīn uses words like *āshakh* (Persian, *āshiq*) and *lāmakān*. (Kaul, *Kashmīrī Lyrics*, verse, 10). Habbā Khātūn uses words like *pyāla, Shīsha, sumbul, gul, bulbul, dil, dīdar* etc. (*Ibid.*, Verses, 43-45, 58, 68).
34. Kaul, *Kashmīrī Lyrics*, Intro., p. xv.
35. See Kaul, *Kashmīrī Lyrics*, for some specimens of his songs; also *Tazkira-i-Mashā'ikh-i-Kashmīr* by Nasīb.
36. Grierson, *Linguistic Survey of India*, viii, part ii, p. 237.
37. See p. 89, *supra*.
38. It is a Kashmīrī word meaning "a complex of love, longing, and a tugging at the heart." (Kaul, *Kashmīrī Lyrics, Intro.* xi).
39. *Khawāriqu's-Sālikīn*, f. 155b; W.K., f. 41a.
40. *Tazkira-i-Mullā Raina*, ff. 511a-b.
41. *Ibid.*, f. 513a.
42. H.M., f. 118b; W.K., f. 41a.
43. N.A., f. 29b; G.A., f. 110b; also S.A., p. 10.
44. Miskīn, *Ta'rīkh-i-Kabīr*, p. 290.
45. J.R.A.S. (Bombay), xix, p. 241.
46. Śrīv., p. 151. T.A., iii, 457, says that very fine silk threads were produced in Kashmīr during this period.
47. Hugel, *Travels in Kashmīr*, pp. 116-19; also *Journal of the Royal Society of Arts*, lxxx, p. 309.
48. *Jammu and Kashmīr State Handbook*, p. 309.
49. See for more details, the excellent article by John Irwin, *The Kashmīr Shawls (The Marg*, vi, No. I, pp. 43-50).
50. Śrīv., p. 151.
51. George Watt, *Indian Art Exhibition* (1903), p. 16.
52. Ujfalvy, *L'Art des Cuivres Anciens au Cachemere*, p. 10. But Duhousset, *Les Arts Decoratifs au Petit-Thibet an Cachemere*, p. 386 (*Revue d'Ethnographie*, Spt.-Oct., 1882) says that these handles represent a dauphin and not a dragon.
53. Ujfalvy, *L'Art des Cuivres Anciens an Cachemere*, p. 26.
54. *Ibid.*, p. 29; *The Legacy of Islam*, p. 122.
55. Ujfalvy, p. 28.
56. Ṣūfī, ii, 555, says that in the Victoria and Albert Museum there is a remarkable set of twenty-four paintings which were produced in Kashmīr before the Mughal conquest. But according to Mr. John Irwin, Assistant Keeper, Indian Section, "the Museum

possesses nothing of Kashmīrī origin (except a few shawl pieces) earlier than the 19th century."

57. T.A., iii, 439.
58. Brown, *Indian Painting under the Mughals*, p. 121.
59. *Ibid.*, p. 189.
60. Ṣūfī, ii, 558.
61. A.A. (Blochmann), p. 109.
62. *Ibid.*
63. My attention was directed by Dr. Suniti Kumar Chatterjee to the existence of the relief in the Museum of the University of Pennsylvania. The Curator of the Museum very kindly sent me a reproduction of it as well as a copy of the University Museum Bulletin in which the relief has been described in detail. I am obliged to Dr. K.K. Ganguli of Calcutta University for helping me to write the description of the relief.
64. Now only half a dozen tiles are left on the building. A few are in the Srīnagar Museum, but the rest have been taken away by the people as sacred relics. The tiles in the Patna Museum belonging to this building appear to be of the Mughal period.
65. *Archaeological Survey of India Report*, (1906-7), pp. 163-4.
66. *Calcutta Review*, 1872, p. 30.
67. There are still some small bridges over the canals built according to the old pattern.
68. Śrīv., p. 231.
69. *Kashmir*, iv, No. 6, p. 135.
70. A.A. (Blochmann), p. 680n.
71. *Kashmīr*, iv, No. 6, pp. 135-7.
72. *Mīrzā Naṣir, Buḥūru'l-alḥān*, p. 15. All these *maqāms* are included in the *maqāmāt* of Persian music. See *Tuzuk-i-Jahāngīrī*, ii, p. 148, where reference has been made to the use of Indian Musical modes. Also see *Zamāna*, vol. 27, No. 164, pp. 194-95.
73. *Kashmīr*, iv, No. 6: *Tuzuk-i-Jahāngīrī*, ii, p. 148.
74. *Kashmīr*, iv, No. 6; *Ibid.*, i, No. 14.
75. B.S., f. 26a; *Tuzuk-i-Jahāngīrī*, ii, p. 148.
76. Śrīv., p. 136 *'Ūd* was probably an Iranian instrument. In Ḥijāz it was borrowed from Ḥīra which was predominantly under Persian influence.
77. *Kashmīr* i, No. 14 and iv, No. 4. Rabāb was specially favoured in Khurāsān, and it must have been introduced into Kashmīr from there in the time of Zainu'l-'Ābidīn. It was, however, a national instrument of the Arabs. (See Farmer, *History of the Arabian Music*, p. 210).

Chaper 14

Conclusion

We have seen that the Sultanate was founded in Kashmīr not as a result of foreign invasion, but by a *coup d'état* from within the country. Hindu rule in the Valley had been in a decadent state for nearly two centuries before the rise of the Shāh Mīr dynasty. The kings who occupied the throne were weak and their ministers corrupt; the Brahmans were dissatisfied with the ruling class; civil strife was almost continuous; trade languished, and agriculture was at a standstill. It was on account of these factors that Shāh Mīr, though a foreigner whose religion and culture were quite different from those of the inhabitants of Kashmīr, was able to seize power and lay the foundation of his dynasty. Tired of civil war and anarchy, the people not only did not resist him, but they greeted him as a saviour, and willingly submitted to him, hoping that he would give them peace and good government. For the same reason his successors also continued to enjoy popular support, and no attempt was made to overthrow their power.

The Kashmīrīs were not, on the whole, disillusioned in their new rulers, for under the able rule of Shāh Mīr and his successors trade revived, agriculture flourished, the burden of taxation was lightened, and life and property were rendered secure. Moreover, Kashmīr under them once again opened its doors to foreign influences from Persia and Turkistān. This led to a clash of cultures, which resulted in a fresh renaissance in the country. Owing to the fusion of the old and new elements a new type of architecture and music came into existence; Kashmīrī language was enriched; but, above all, great progress was made in painting and the minor arts.

The impact of this foreign culture was so profound and far-reaching that even today the people of Kashmīr bear its impress. Diet and dress, marriage and morals, manners and customs, art and literature were all affected by influences which radiated from Persia and Turkistān. But in many respects the changes brought about were only superficial: they were more in form rather than in spirit. There was change but no violent break. Customs, language, beliefs and practices were too deeply embedded in the people to be uprooted and replaced. The Kashmīrīs assimilated the new values, but the past was not eliminated; it was allowed to blend with the new. The result was the emergence of a society which, though differing from the old, as rooted in Indo-Kashmīrī traditions. This is evident from a study of the Kashmīrī language and literature, art and architecture, religious beliefs and social life.

The government in medieval Kashmīr was an enlightened secular despotism. The rulers for the most part ignored the advice of the *'Ulamā,* flouted the *Sharī'a,* and pursued policies which were dictated not by religious but by practical and political considerations. From the contemporary accounts it is clear that the Sulṭāns drew their inspiration not from the Islamic ideals but from the monarchical traditions of India, Kashmīr, and Persia.

The society in this period was feudal[1] and based on class distinctions; but, unlike contemporary societies, slavery did not exist. The king and the nobles led a very cultured life. They were interested in literature, played chess and polo, and cultivated music and the arts. However, in matters of sex, their outlook was on the whole puritanical. They showed no special inclination for the delights of the harem; they kept no concubines; and they hardly ever degraded themselves by indulging in licentious revelries. The influence of the *'Ulamā* and Ṣūfīs was great, but it was generally confined to social and religious matters. Artizans and merchants, though forming a respectable section of the society, were politically unimportant. The peasantry, which formed the bulk of the population, being exposed to the hazards of floods and famines and exploitation by government officials, did not enjoy that well-being to which they were entitled by their labour. The period was characterised by great religious toleration. With the exception of Sikandar who persecuted the Hindus, Mīrzā Ḥaidar who tyrannised the Nūrbakhshīyas and Shī'ites, and Ya'qūb Shāh who was intolerant towards the Sunnis, the Kashmīr rulers adopted an extremely liberal policy. The Kashmīrīs were superstitious, and were exploited both by the Mullā and the Pandit. Witty and intelligent, they were then, as now, very active and industrious. They were also very charitable; and they were so hospitable that they would not touch food without a guest. However, not only were they suspicious but also hostile towards foreigners, and it took a long time before their suspicion and hostility gave place to confidence and friendliness. The Kashmīrīs were brave and good fighters, and the lack of martial spirit which foreigners have attributed to them in modern times, is not due to any innate deficiency of courage, but is the result of a long period of political servitude.

Extent of the Kingdom

The Sulṭāns of Kashmīr, like most kings, desired self-aggrandisement. But there were two factors owing to which they could not fully realize their ambition. First, Northern India ws during this period ruled by the Sulṭāns of Delhi and later on by the Mughals who were more powerful than the rulers of Kashmīr. Under the circumstance, the latter never embarked on a career of conquest. It was only Shihābu'd-Dīn who tried to extend his kingdom beyond the Sutlej, but he met with such resistance that he had to withdraw. No Kashmīrī ruler ever again made an attemp to follow his example. The other factor which set a limit to the policy of expansion of the Sulṭāns, was the geographical situation of Kashmīr. Since the Valley was surrounded by layers upon layers of huge mountain walls, the invasion of the countries beyond them was a difficult task. Even if an invasion was undertaken, as was done by Shihābu'd-Dīn, it could not effect any permanent occupation, for it was impossible to control distant countries across high mountain ranges from the Kashmīr Valley. The area of operation of the

Sulṭāns was, therefore, confined to the sub-montane regions adjoining Kashmīr on the west and the south.

The extent of the kingdom over which the Sulṭāns exercised authority varied from time to time. Shāh Mīr and his son 'Alā'u'd-Dīn ruled only the Kashmīr Valley. Since they were pre-occupied with internal problems of law and oder, they never attempted to extend their kingdom. It was Shihābu'd-Dīn's son, who, after consolidating his position at home, embarked on a career of conquest. The kingdom which he brought under his rule was retained by his successors and the Chaks with occasional changes of boundaries. Thus their kingdom comprised the following territories : (1) The Valley of Kashmīr which was the heart and centre of the whole kingdom. (2) The region of the Outer Hills which extended from the Rāvī in the east to the Jehlam in the west and comprised Jammu, Rajaurī and Pūnch. (3) Bhadrawāh, the Valley of the Chināb, and Kishtwār which lay between the Outer Hills and the high ranges around the Valley of Kashmīr. (4) Ladākh and Baltistān. (5) The Kishangangā Valley and the Pakhlī region which lay between the upper courses of the Jehlam and the Indus.

Of this kingdom only the Kashmīr Valley, and later on Lohara (Pūnch), were directly administered from Srīnagar, while the rest of the territory was governed by its own Rājās who, however, paid tribute to the Sulṭān. It is important to remember that it was the policy of the kings of Kashmīr to exercise some kind of control over the territories surrounding the Valley because of their economic and strategic importance. Thus Ladākh was necessary for Kashmīr because it supplied wool required for the Kashmīrī shawls, and was the centre of Kashmīr's trade with Tibet, China, and Turkistān.[2] The control of Pūnch, Rajaurī, and Jammu was necessary, for these places served as a spring board for an invasion of Kashmīr. Moreover, the occupation of Pūnch and the hilly areas around Kashmīr was also required as they were inhabited by turbulent tribes, who were accustomed to swoop on the Valley, plunder its inhabitants, and carry off owmen and children.[3] But despite all this, the hold of the Sulṭāns over these territories, on account of the difficulties of communication across the high mountain barriers, was always weak and loose; and it ceased to exist during periods when the Valley was torn by civil strife and ruled by feeble kings.

CAUSES OF THE FALL OF THE SULTANATE

The Shāh Mīr dynasty produced from Shamsu'd-Dīn to Zainu'l-'Ābidīn a succession of able rulers who, by reducing the crushing burden of taxation and by maintaining a fairly regular system of administration, guaranteed to the population a period of relative tranquillity after the chaos and misrule of the Lohara period. But under the successors of Zainu'l-'Ābidīn, who were weak and incompetent, the state of the country reverted, with short interludes of stability, to that which had existed before the establishment of the Sultanate. Ḥaidar Shāh, his son, and Ḥasan Shāh, his grandson, spent most of their time over the wine cup or listening to music, and neglected the administration which was left into the hands of their unscrupulous courtiers who robbed the people to enrich themselves. Muḥammad Shāh, Fatḥ Shāh, and the subsequent rulers, though not dissolute, proved incapable of controlling those elements which were leading the kingdom to its fall. The result was that the Shāh Mīr dynasty was overthrown. The Chaks, who succeeded, at first ruled with wisdom and firmness, but the fourth ruler, Yūsuf Shāh, passed his time in ease and luxury and neglected public affairs. His son and successor Ya'qūb, though possessed of great energy and courage, was self-willed and intolerant, and was, therefore, unable to counter the dangers, both internal and external, which threatened the country.

One of the causes of the downfall of Hindu rule in the Valley had been the failure of the kings to crush the Ḍāmaras. Lilitāditya had laid down that the villagers should not be left with a greater food supply than was required for one year's consumption, nor more oxen than were wanted for the tillage of their fields.[4] This he had done in order to prevent the growth of a landed aristocracy which might cause him trouble. But unfortunately his successors did not act on his principles; nor did they adopt any other measures to check the power of the

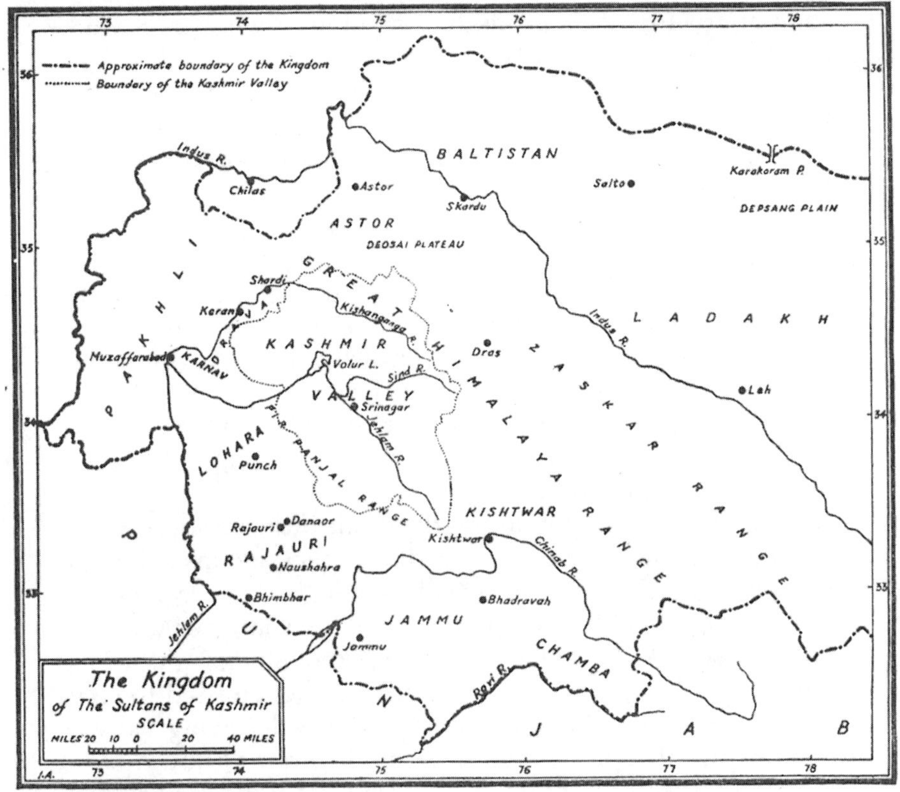

feudal lords. Shāh Mīr and his successors also made no attempt to strike at the basis of the system. The only thing which they did was to crush the turbulent chiefs and grant jāgīrs to those families who were prepared to serve them faithfully. They also tried to keep them weak and dependent by a policy of divide and rule. This system worked well so long as the rulers were strong, but after the death of Zainu'l-'Ābidīn, when the throne was occupied by weak kings, it broke down, for the internal feuds revived, and the country was distracted between the warring houses struggling for the possession of the Sulṭān. In the end, through this welter of confusion, the Chaks emerged victorious by defeating their rivals, the Māgres and the Rainas. They at first ruled in the name of the Shāh Mīr Sulṭāns, but soon afterwards they themselves assumed sovereign powers and founded their dynasty.

The Chak rule, it must be remembered, was based on the hegemony of the Chak tribe. The Chaks, as a rule, unlike the Shāh Mīrs, did not raise to prominence any other family other than their own. In this way they endeavoured to make their rule strong and stable. But unfortunately this system, too, did not last long, because internecine dissensions and rivalries started, and the members of the ruling house did not hesitate to make common cause with the rival families against their own kinsmen. This led to constant conflicts, and as a result the country was once more plunged into chaos and anarchy. It was left to the Mughal Emperor Akbar to establish law and order by destroying the feudal system and substituting in its place rule by the Mughal officers.

The lack of any definite and fixed rule of succession caused no small measure of social and political chaos and instability in the kingdom. Shamsu'd-Dīn had established a precedent by nominating his eldest son Jamshēd as his successor. But his younger son 'Alā'u'd-Dīn refused to acknowledge Jamshēd as Sulṭān, and himself laid claim to the throne. This led to civil war Shihābu'd-Dīn made a new departure by depriving his own sons of the throne in favour of his brother Quṭbu'd-Dīn. Similarly Zainu'l-'Ābidīn designated his younger brother Maḥmūd as his heir apparent. But when the latter died, he declared his second son Ḥājī Khān his successor to the exclusion of the eldest, Adham Khān. And soon afterwards, since Ḥājī revolted, he proclaimed Adham his heir apparent. However, in the end, disgusted with all his sons he refused to nominate any one, leaving the title to the throne to be decided by force of arms. On the other hand, Zainu'l-'Ābidīn's grandson, Ḥasan Shāh, left it to his queen to choose a ruler after his death, although his own preference was for Fatḥ Khān, son of Adham Khān, since his own sons were minors. When he died, Sayyid Ḥasan, the Wazīr and brother of the Queen Mother, set up Ḥasan Shāh's son, Muḥammad Shāh, as ruler. But this did not prevent Fatḥ Khān from claiming the throne. The result was that for thirty years the country was plunged into almost continuous internecine wars.

Under the Chaks also there was no fixed rule of succession. Ghāzī Shāh, the founder of the dynasty, appointed his brother Ḥusain Shāh as his successor. When Ḥusain Shāh became Sulṭān, he tried to divert the succession to his own son, but failed because his brother 'Alī Shāh rose in rebellion against him and seized the throne. Before he died, 'Alī Shāh had his son Yūsuf crowned as king. But Abdāl, his brother, put forth his own claim to the throne on the ground that it was the practice in the family that when a ruler died his brother suceeded him. This led to an armed conflict with Yūsuf. Although he was killed and Yūsuf was victorious, other members of the lateral branch of the Chaks were not wanting in advancing their titles to the throne. Yūsuf Shāh's son and successor Ya'qūb had to contend with the rival claimants, and this was one of the reasons why he failed to mobilise all the forces for the defence of the Valley against the Mughals.

The sectarian discord between the Sunnīs and the Shī'ites also contributed to the downfall of the Sultanate. Until the end of the fifteenth century the Muslim population of Kashmīr consisted mainly of Sunnīs, the Shī'ites being numerically and politically unimportant. But with the arrival of Mīr Shamsu'd-Dīn in 1502, the number of Shī'ites gradually increased and they became politically influential. This roused the hostility of the Sunnī chiefs who, incited by the orthodox *'Ulamā,* came into conflict with the Shī'ite nobles. However, we must be careful not to overemphasize the importance of the religious factor, for, though religious differences added to the confusion in Kashmīr, the main causes responsible for the civil wars were the personal jealousies and ambitions of the feudal chiefs. That is why we find that very often the alignment of forces cut across religious differences. Thus, at first, in the reign of Mīrzā Ḥaidar, the Sunnī and Shī'ite chiefs were pitted against one another, but later on, realising that Mīrzā Ḥaidar was exploiting their differences in order to consolidate his position, they joined together and overthrew him.

Under the Chak rulers also, owing to the liberal policy pursued by them until the time of Yūsuf Shāh,[5] the internecine conflicts were not in the least influenced by religious considerations. It is true that the affairs of Yūsuf Aindar and Qāẓī Ḥabīb embittered the relations between the two communities.[6] When Yūsuf was executed, the Shī'ites were filled with great resentment against the Sunnīs; and similarly, when later on, Qāẓī Almās and Qāẓī Ganā'ī were executed for having sentenced Yūsuf to death, it created great bitterness among the Sunnīs. However, it did not lead to any armed conflict. In fact, the ill feelings engendered by these events would have been forgotten had it not been for Ya'qūb Shāh who began to pursue an intolerant policy towards the Sunnīs. He first of all tried to compel Qāẓī Mūsā to recite the name of 'Alī in the public prayers, and when this was refused, he reopened the question of the death sentence pronounced on Yūsuf, and had Mūsā put to death. This turned the Sunnī 'Ulamā and nobles against Ya'qūb. As a result, some of them proceeded to the court of Akbar and requested him to annex Kashmīr, and when the Emperor sent an army for its invasion, they acted as guides.

The continuous discord and civil war weakened the administration, adversely affected trade and agriculture, and caused a decline in the general prosperity of the Valley. Another serious consequence of this internal strife was that it led to foreign invasions and to the eventual conquest of the Valley. On Ḥasan Shāh's death one group of nobles set up his son Muḥammad Shāh on the throne. But shortly afterwards the latter was replaced by Fatḥ Shāh who was supported by another party. Thrice Muḥammad Shāh became ruler, and thrice he was deposed. Finally, early in 1517, he proceeded to the court of Sikandar Lodī (1489-1517) and sought his help. After this it became a common practice with the Kashmīrī princes and nobles to proceed, on being defeated by their rivals, to the courts of the Delhi Emperors and invoke their help. In 1540, while Abdāl Māgre brought a Mughal army from the Punjāb under Mīrzā Ḥaidar, his rival Kājī Chak secured the aid of Shēr Shāh. This invitation of foreign troops proved disastrous to the independence of Kashmīr, for although Mīrzā Ḥaidar came as a deliverer, he made himself master of the country. After the fall of Mīrzā Ḥaidar, when the Chaks came to power, Kashmīr was again subjected to foreign invasions through the invitations of its discontented nobles and princes. But these were repelled by the courage and resourcefulness of 'Īdī Raina, Daulat Chak and Ghāzī Chak. In January 1580, Yūsuf Shāh, driven from his country, proceeded to Fatḥpūr Sīkrī and sought the help of Akbar. This was readily given, and although it was not employed, it provided the Emperor with a *casus belli* for the invasion of Kashmīr. Yūsuf's successor, Ya'qūb, carried on a valiant resistance against the Mughal armies, but owing to the internal disunity, he failed to drive out the invaders. The result was that Kashmīr lost her independence. "People say", wrote Du Jarric, "that this kingdom was one of the most formidable in these parts, and that the Great Mogor would never have been able to subdue it but for the factions which existed among the inhabitants".[7]

For centuries Kashmīr, protected by its mountain ramparts, had lived an isolated life, little affected by the outside happenings. The invasions of the Arabs, Maḥmūd of Ghaznī, and Tīmūr had passed her by, while the rise and fall of dynasties in the plains of Hindustān had failed to disturb the course of her history. But with the Mughal conquest her isolation was ended, and henceforth she came within the orbit of Indian politics. Kashmīr lost her separate identity and became like any other province of the Mughal Empire, while Srīnagar sank to the status of a provincial town.

Another effect of the fall of the Sultanate was that the Kashmīrī ruling families of Chaks, Māgres, Rainas, and Dārs were replaced by a hierarchy of Mughal officers who became responsible for the administration of the country. Besides, the defence of the Valley, too, was undertaken by the Mughals. The result of this was that the Kashmīrīs gradually lost their martial spirit and fighting qualities of which they had given proof on many occasions in their struggles against the invaders. Furthermore, Kashmīr during the Sultanate period had achieved a high standard of culture, but with the disappearance of her independence, her culture gradually declined. Srīnagar was denuded of poets, painters, and scholars, who had once adorned the courts of the Sulṭāns, because, owing to the absence of local patronage, they were compelled to leave the Valley and seek their livelihood elsewhere. They entered the service of the Mughal Emperors, and added to the brilliance of the imperial court, thereby precipitating the cultural impoverishment of Kashmīr.

NOTES

1. I have used feudalism here in the sense that power in Kashmīr was mainly derived from land, and the conferring of jāgīrs was a very important social and political institution. But this feudalism should not be confused with the feudalism of Western Europe which had quite a different basis.
2. See the section on Trade under Chapter XII.
3. Sein, BK. i No. 317n.; Śriv., pp. 278, 334-35.
4. Stein, BK. iv, Nos. 347-52.
5. A.N., iii, 763.
6. *Ibid.,* Śuka, p. 304, also notes the Sh-'ite and Sunnī differences during the reign of Ya'qūb Shāh.
7. Du Jarric, *Akbar and the Jesuits,* p. 76.

APPENDIX A

The Nūrbakhshīya Sect of Kashmīr

The founder of the Nūrbakhshīya sect was Sayyid Muḥammad b. Muḥammad b. 'Abdu'llāh who was born in Qā'in in Kohistān in 795 A.H./1393 A.D. After finishing his education he became a disciple of Khwja Isḥāq of Khatlān, who was himself a disciple of Sayyid 'Alī Hamadānī.[1] Khwāja Isḥāq gave him the title of "Nūr Bakhsh" and conferred upon him the mantle of Sayyid 'Alī Hamadānī, and then acclaimed him as the *Mahdī*, the Lord of his time, and Imām. But this brought Sayyid Muḥammad Nūr Bakhsh to the notice of Shāh Rukh, Timūr's son and successor, who had him thrown into prison. As he did not completely renounce his pretensions, he had to undergo thrice long terms of imprisonment; and it was only at Shāh Rukh's death in 850 A.H./1447 A.D. that he finally secured his freedom. He then settled in Ray where he died in 869 A.H./1464 A.D. at the age of seventy-three. He was succeeded by his son Shāh Qāsim as his Khalifa (d. 981 A.H./1573 A.D.).[2]

The Nūrbakhshīya movement was of a mystical character. Sayyid Muḥammad Nūr Bakhsh claimed to have seen the divine light and to have received the esoteric teachings of 'Alī through the Imām Ja'far-i-Ṣādiq. He believed in Ṣūfī pantheism and in the renunciation of this world's vanities. To achieve *"fanā"* the merging of the Self into the Divine, it was necessary to submit completely to the will of the Master, and then to undergo a long course "of service, solitude, meditation, and companionship." The organisation of the Nūrbakhshīya *khānqāhs* was similar to that of the *khānqāhs* belonging to the other Ṣūfī orders; and the *Ẕikr* ceremonies of the Nūrbakhshīya also resembled those performed by the Ṣūfīs belonging to the Qādīrī, Kubravī and Naqshbandī Orders. But their most important ceremonies were performed during the *Araba'īn,* when new members initiated into the Nūrbakhshīya mysteries, whole night vigils were maintained, prayers offered, and lectures delivered with quotations from Ghazzālī, Bistāmī, and Junaid. *Ghazals* too were recited during these days, and they had such an effect that the Ṣūfīs went into ecstasies and started dancing.[3]

In his teachings, Sayyid Muḥammad Nūr Bakhsh was also influenced by Shī'ism. Like the Shī'ites he believed that the Imām should be immaculate, just, brave, the knower of all things, and a descendant of 'Alī and Fāṭima. He enjoined love for the *Ahl-i-Bait* (the family of the Prophet), and both he and his followers never ceased emphasizing that their object was to spread the religion of Muḥammad and the Twelve Imāms.[4] The Nūrbakhshīyas celebrated Muḥarram, and some of them even wore black dress as an expression of grief for the martyrdom of Ḥusain.[5] They practised *Mut'ah,* reviled 'Āisha, the wife of the Prophet, and the first three Caliphs. However, like the Sunnis, they accepted the *Ijmā'* or the consensus of opinion, though they rejected the practices forced upon by the rulers and represented as the result of *Ijmā'*. Their claim was to revive the teachings of Muḥammad, enforce the *Shari'a,* and root out innovations and accretions that had crept into Islām.[6] Their ideas are contained in the work known as *Fiqh-i-Aḥwaṭ*.[7]

The Nūrbakhshīya sect in Kashmīr was introduced by Shamsu'd-Dīn who was born in the village of Kund near Solghan. His father was a Mūsavī Sayyid, and his mother came from a Sayyid family of Qazvīn.[8] No details are available of his early life, and how he was converted to the Nūrbakhshīya beliefs. However, it appears from his subsequent career that he must have received good education, for we know that he was eloquent of speech and a man of learning. These qualities brought him to the notice of Sulṭān Ḥusain Mīrzā Bāiqarā (1469-1506) of Herāt, who took him into his service and sent him as his envoy in 1481 to the court of Sulṭān Ḥasan Shāh of Kashmīr.[9] He stayed in the Valley for eight years. Being an envoy he could not carry on his missionary activities openly. He therefore preached secretly, and converted Bābā Ismā'īl Kubravī and Bābā 'Alī Najjār to his faith. He was however found out, and owing to the hostility of the orthodox *'Ulamā,* he was compelled to leave Kashmīr.[10] On his return to Herāt he aroused the suspicions of Sulṭān Ḥusain Mīrzā on account of his religious views. Alarmed at this, Shamsu'd-Dīn left the Sulṭān's service, and went to live with Shāh Qāsim, the son of Sayyid Muḥammad Nūr Bakhsh, at Ray. Meanwhile, news came from Kashmīr that Bābā Ismā'īl, whom he had appointed as his representative, had renounced the Nūrbakhshīya beliefs and had relapsed into orthodoxy.[11] As Shamsu'd-Dīn possessed first-hand knowledge of the Valley, Shāh Qāsim directed him to proceed there and revive and spread the Nūrbakhshīya ideas.[12] Shamsu'd-Dīn was however anxious to go to Baghdād and take the place of Maulānā Burhānu'd-Dīn who had died. But on Shāh Qasim's advice and insistence, he agreed to proceed to Kashmīr.[13]

Shamsu'd-Dīn left Ray about the end of September, 1501, accompanied by a number of ṣufīs and their families.[14] On the way he paid a visit to the tomb of Imām Raẓā at Mashhad. He then travelled to Qandahār, and from there proceeded to Multān. Thence he set out towards the Salt Range, and after spending his winter there, he entered Kashmīr early in the spring of 1502 by the Pūnch-Bārāmūla route.[15]

On reaching Srīnagar he won the confidence of Bābā 'Alī Najjār who handed over to him all his disciples.[16] But the most important convert that he made at this time was Mūsā Raina, a powerful noble of Kashmīr, who gave him money to carry on his work,[17] and land at Jaddi Bal to build a *khānqāh*. The foundation of the hospice was laid in 1503-04, and it was built the next year.[18] But in spite of the initial success, Shamsu'd-Dīn had to face great obstacles later on. He was opposed by Sayyid Muḥammad Baihaqī.[19] Muḥammad Shāh's prime minister, and by the orthodox *'Ulamā* who were hostile to the new creed. Sayyid Muḥammad had, on the advice of the *'Ulamā,* opposed the construction of the Khānqāh-i-Nūrbakhshīya by Shamsu'd-Dīn, and had only given him permission on account of Mūsā

Rainā's influence.[20] However, he raised all kinds of difficulties in the way of Shamsu'd-Dīn's activities, and even began to persecute his followers. Shamsu'd-Dīn therefore left Kashmīr with fifty of his followers, and went to Baltistān where he continued his missionary activities, and succeeded in converting many of its Buddhist inhabitants to his creed.[21] He remained there for two months until the defeat and death of Sayyid Muḥammad[22] in 1505, when at the invitation of Mūsā Rainā he returned to Srīnagar. Shamsu'd-Dīn's great opportunity came when Mūsā Rainā became prime minister after the fall of Shams Chak. During the period he remained in power, he gave full support to Shamsu'd-Dīn in his activities. A further source of strength to the latter was the conversion of Tājī Chak and other Chak nobles. Thus by the time Shamsu'd-Dīn Died[23] the Nūrbakhshīya had gained a strong footing in the Valley. After his death his work was carried on by his son Dāniyāl and other of his Khalīfās.

But the Nūrbakhshīyas suffered a great setback in the time of Mīrzā Ḥaidar Dughlāt, who persecuted them thinking that if there was uniformity of religion in Kashmīr there would be peace in the country.[24] After the fall and death of Mīrzā Ḥaidar in 1551 the Chaks began to play a dominant role in the politics of the Valley, and, as a result, the Nūrbakhshīyas were once again permitted to preach and practice their religion freely. But, meanwhile, a great change had come over the Nūrbakhshīya beliefs. Under the influence of Persia where Shāh Ismā'īl, the founder of the Safavid dynasty (1502-1736), had declared Shī'ism or the doctrines of the *Twelvers* as the state religion, the Nūrbakhshīya took on increasingly the character of a Shī'ite movement. It gradually shed those of its doctrines which were in conflict with Shī'ism, until there was nothing left to distinguish it from the latter. Thus the Chaks, who enjoyed a brief spell of power in Kashmīr and who had been converted to the Nūrbakhshīya by the efforts of Shamsu'd-Dīn, called themselves Shī'ites.[25] When Akbar conquered the Valley in 1586, there were still some Nūrbakhshīyas[26] left, but in the course of time they disappeared, some becoming Sunnīs, while others embracing Shī'ism. In remote areas, however, where external influences had some difficulty in penetrating, the Nūrbakhshīyas survived, but their beliefs and practices were greatly diluted by the influence of the local Sunnī communities.[27]

NOTES

1. See for his life A.A. Hikmet, *Les Voyages d'un Mystique Persan de Hamadān aū Kashmīr (La journal Asiatique,* cexi, pp. 54 ff; also *Yaghma,* iv, No. 8, pp. 337 ff).
2. For a detailed account of the life of Sayyid Muḥammad Nūr Bakhsh, see Mīrzā Ma'ṣūm, *Ṭarā'iqu'l-Ḥaqā'iq,* pp. 143-44; and Nūru'llāh Shūshtarī, *Majālisu'l-Mu'minīn,* pp. 313 ff. See also Muḥammad Shafī, *The Nūrbakhshīya Sect (Oriental College Magazine,* Feb. 1925). The article in the *Encycl. of Islam,* vol. iii, is mainly based on the *Majālisu'l-Mu'minīn.*
3. *Tuḥfatu'l Aḥbāb,* pp. 120-24. The MS. is not folioed but paged, and therefore I have referred to page numbers.
4. Nūru'llāh Shūshtarī, *Majālisu'lMu'minīn,* p. 315; *Tuḥfatu'l-Aḥbāb,* pp. 20, 23. Nūru'llāh Shūshtarī regards Sayyid Muḥammad as a Shī'ite, but this is incorrect, because the latter's pantheistic ideas and his claim to be an Imām and a Mahdī were completely opposed to the Shī'ite doctrines
5. *Majālisu'l-Mu'minīn,* p. 317.
6. *Ibid.,* 315; *Tuḥfatu'l-Aḥbāb,* p. 20. See also *Ta'rīkh-i-Rashīdī,* but Mīrzā Ḥaidar is not always just to the Nūrbakhshīya.
7. Chaks maintained that the book was not written by Shamsu'd-Dīn. But this is incorrect. See Firishta, p. 647 (Bombay Edition).
8. B.S., f. 60a.
9. *Tuḥfatu'l-Aḥbāb,* p. 13; also W.K., f. 36b; and B.S., ff. 60a-b.
10. *Tuḥfatu'l-Aḥbāb,* p. 4.
11. *Ibid.,* p. 6.
12. *Ibid.,* p. 8.
13. *Ibid.,* pp. 14-16.
14. *Tuḥfatu'l-Aḥbāb,* p. 3.
15. *Tuḥfatu'l-Aḥbāb,* pp. 24-25.
16. During the absence of Shamsu'd-Dīn, Bābā 'Alī had remained, unlike Bābā Ismā'īl Kubravī, attached to the new creed. (See *Majālisu'l-Mu'minīn* (MS.) f. 67b.).
17. *Tuḥfatu'l-Aḥbāb,* p. 29.
18. *Ibid.,* p. 64.
19. The Baihaqi Sayyids came to Kashmīr during the reign of Sulṭān

Sikandar (1389-1413). They married in the royal family, and played an important part in the political affairs of the Valley.

20. *Tuḥfatu'l-Aḥbāb,* 54-55.
21. *Ibid.*, pp. 63-64.
22. When this news was communicated to Shamsu'd-Dīn, he was so angry with the messenger that he belaboured him for bringing such a bad news. Shamsu'd-Dīn, unlike common expectations, felt sad and prayed for the long life of the sons of Sayyid Muḥammad who had survived the civil war. (B.S.), ff. 76b-77a; *Tuḥfatu'l-Aḥbāb*, p. 70.
23. *Tuḥfatu'l-Aḥbāb* does not record the date of Shamsu'd-Dīn's death. But from a study of the work it appears that he must have died just before the first invasion of Kashmīr by Mīrzā Ḥaidar in 1533. (See also N.A., f. 69b).
24. B.S., f. 111b. See pp. 137 sqq. *supra,* for details of this persecution.
25. *Firishta* says that during his time most of the soldiers were Shī'ites. The Chaks, who were Shī'ites, maintained that Shamsu'd-Dīn was a Shī'ite.
26. A.A., ii, 354.
27. For the Nūrbakhshīyas in modern times, see Census of India, 1911, Vol. XX, Kashmīr, part 1, p. 105; and Biddulph, *Tribes of the Hindu Kush,* p. 125.

APPENDIX B

Currency, Coinage, Weights and Measures

Currency

Persian annals of Kashmīr hardly throw any light on the monetary system under the Shāh Mīrs and the Chaks. The little information that we get is from Abūl Faẓl's *Ā'īn* and from the four Sanskrit chronicles.

The monetary system of Kashmīr did not undergo any basic change under the Sulṭāns, but remained more or less the same as it had been under the Rājās.[1] The coinage under the Sulṭāns consisted almost entirely of copper, the copper coins being called Kasiras or Pūnchhus.[2] But the unit of the Kashmīr monetary system was the cowrie, which was used for fractional payments or minor purchases.[3] Zainu'l-'Ābidīn is said to have struck coins in lead and brass. Silver coins were uncommon, while gold coins were rare. In fact, it should be noted that gold and silver did not form an important part of the actual coined currency of Kashmīr. However, it appears that under the Chaks silver and gold coins were more in use than under the Shāh Mīrs. This is probably due to the close relation with the Mughal Empire.[4]

The Kashmīr currency under the Sulṭāns consisted of *dīnār*, *bāhagani*, *pūnchhu*, *hath*, *sāsun*, *lakh*, and *crore*. The following were their values:

12 *Dīnārs*	=	1 *Bāhagani*
2 *Bāhagani*	=	1 *Pūnchhu*

4 *Pūnchhu* = 1 *Hath*
10 *Hath* = 1 *Sāsun*
100 *Sāsun* = 1 *Lakh*
100 *Lakh* = 10,000,000 *Dīnārs* or 1 *Koṭi* (Crore)

In addition to these coins other types of coins were also used. Thus, copper pieces of Toramāṇa were current under the Sulṭāns before the time of Ḥasan Shāh. But the latter, finding that they were no longer circulating, struck a new coin called *dvidīnārī* made of lead.[5] There is also reference in the chronicles to *ashrafis* and *tankas* which Muḥammad Shāh's queen spent to erect a *khānqāh* for Mīr Shamsu'd-Dīn.[6] Sometimes bullion took the place of gold and silver coins. Thus under Sikandar and Zainu'l-'Ābidīn the *Jizya* was paid in silver. Under the Chaks it was paid in *paṇas*. But what coin is meant by the *paṇa* is not clear.[7] Rice was also employed in payments of rents, fines, and interest. All wages and salaries were paid in *kharwārs* of rice. Thus the monetary system of Kashmīr, though based on the cowrie unit, was represented in its main bulk by a copper coinage and was supplemented in all important transactions of public business and private life by *kharwārs* of rice.[8]

Coinage

On the basis of the coins of the Kashmīr Sulṭāns, hitherto obtainable, the conclusions arrived at by Rogers, Lane-Poole, Wright, and others still remain unchallenged. It is therefore difficult to say anything beyond summarising the views of these writers. Fresh light can only be thrown in case some new and varied specimens are unearthed.

No coins of the Kashmīr Sulṭāns are known to exist earlier than those of Sulṭān Sikandar. The silver coins bearing the name of Shams Shāh should be regarded as belonging to Shamsu'd-Dīn II and not to Shamsu'd-Dīn I, the founder of the Sultanate in Kashmīr.[9] The Kashmīr coins possess certain characteristics which distinguish them from the coins of the Sulṭāns of Delhi. In the first place they are extremely inartistic. As Rogers observes: "Kashmīrīs were the worst die-sinkers of the world".[10] Moreover, the coins vary very little, and there is a certain monotony about them. Secondly, they are not very helpful in fixing the dates of accession and regnal periods of the rulers. This is due partly to the fact that the dates on a large number of coins are not legible, and partly because the same date is employed by successive rulers. No consideration was paid to chronology when the Sulṭāns struck coins in honour of their predecessors.[11]

Copper Coins

The copper coins are very common. However, as they are not obtainable in a legible form, they are not useful in fixing the chronology of Kashmīr. They are round in shape with an average diameter of 8" and weight varying from 71 to 100 grams. The obverse has a bar (a line across the middle of the coin) with a central knot of arabesque design. The knot is in some cases elaborate; in others it consists of a carelessly formed circle. The name of the king is written below the bar, but above come the word *Sulṭānu'l-A'ẓam*. In every case, except that of Zainu'l-'Ābidīn, the word *Shāh* is added to the name. But Zainu'l-'Ābidīn is the only Sulṭān who calls himself *Nā'ib-i-Amīru'l-Mū'minīn*. The reverse is occupied completely with "*Ẓarb-i-Kashmīr*" and the year is added in Arabic words. The coins of Ḥusain Shāh, 'Alī Shāh, and Yūsuf Shāh mention the year in Persian instead of Arabic.[12]

Although some of the coins of Zainu'l-'Ābidin conform to the bar and knot form, he was the only ruler to have introduced a new type. He not only struck coins in copper, but also in brass. His coins have the word *ẓarb* crossed by the word *Kashmīr,* and around these words is a quarterfoil lozenge with elaborate knots in the outer corners.[13] In some of his coins on the obverse the names and titles are in double-circle, surrounded by a circle of dots.[14] Unlike Zainu'l-'Ābidīn's silver coins, which have the date 842 A.H., his copper coins bear 841 and 851.[15] What is the significance of these dates, it is impossible to say. A copper coin of Muḥammad Shāh and Fatḥ bears the date 874/1470.[16] This must have been coined in honour of Ḥaidar Shāh who reigned from 1470 to 1472. One coin of Ḥusain Shāh bears the date 977/1569-70, which must have been struck towards the end of his reign. The coin of Yūsuf Shāh bearing 986/1578-9 must have been struck immediately after his accession early in 1579.[17]

Silver Coins

The silver coins are square-shaped, and their weight varies from 91 to 96 grains, and breadth from 6" to .65". The lightest coin is of Shamsu'd-Dīn II, and the heaviest is that of Yūsuf Shāh.[18] There is a certain monotony about the silver coins: they are all square-shaped and have some kind of lozenge on the reverse.[19] The silver coins are not as common as the copper ones.

As has already been pointed out, the coins of the Kashmīr Sulṭāns are not much useful from the point of view of determining chronology. Thus though Zainu'l-'Ābidīn reigned for fifty years, all his silver coins have the date of 842 both in figures and words: the figures appearing on the obverse, and the words in Arabic on the margin of the reverse. This date is in fact borne on the coins of rulers who reigned long after 842, so they do not help in determining the chronology of the period, but only add to the confusion.[20] Thus the silver coins of Ibrāhīm Shāh (i) and Ibrāhīm Shāh (ii) are dated 842 in Arabic words.[21] Similarly the silver coins of Muḥammad Shāh, which are rare, also bear 842.[22] However, one of his coins bears the date 895/1490 and that of Fatḥ Shāh the date 896.[23] These coins are very important. Muḥammad Shāh's coin bearing the date 895 must have been coined towards the close of his first reign, while Fatḥ Shāh must have struck his coin at his accession after November 14, 1490, when the year 896 began. Ḥaidar Shāh's coins bear the date 874/1470 which was the year of his accession. But it must have been struck after May 12, 1470, when Zainu'l-'Ābidīn died, and before the beginning of 875 which began on June 30, 1470. Although Ḥasan Shāh's coins have the year 842 in Arabic words, on the obverse they have the date 876/1472, the year of his accession.[24] The coins of Ḥusain Shāh Chak bear the date 970/1562-63, which signifies the year of his accession. Another of his coin bears 972. The coins bearing the name of 'Alī Shāh Chak must have been minted by his son Yūsuf Shāh because of the dates ranging from 987 to 990 which they bear. These must have been coined by Yūsuf Shāh in honour of his father. However, one coin bearing the date 980 was coined by 'Alī Shāh himself. Another coin of his bearing the date 986/1578-79 must have been minted by him towards the end of his reign. One of Yūsuf Shāh's coins, which must have been struck shortly after his accession, is dated 987. Like the copper coins, the silver coins of Ḥusain Shāh. 'Alī Shāh, and Yūsuf Shāh bear the dates in Persian.

On the obverse the silver coins have the inscription *Ẓarb-i-Kashmīr*, enclosed within a lozenge-shaped border of wavy lines, and the date is inscribed in the segments outside the lozenge. The reverse contains the name of the king with his title. All the Shāh Mīr Sulṭāns have the title of *Sulṭānu'l-A'ẓam* and *Shāh* with the exception of Zainu'l-'Ābidīn who has only the first title. The Chak rulers call themselves *Pādshāh* and *Ghāzī*, but, in addition, each ruler adopts a separate title.

In the time of Nāzuk Shāh, while Ḥaidar Shah was the *de facto* ruler of Kashmīr, coins were struck in the name of Humāyūn. These coins are of the same type as those of the preceding kings. One of the coins bears Ḥ, which is a letter of Mīrzā Ḥaidar's name. The dates of these coins fall within the period during which Mīrzā Ḥaidar ruled.[25] One silver coin, however, bears the name of Nādir Shāh with the date 957/1550. No king of such a name ruled Kashmīr. It must have been, therefore, the title or second name of Nāzuk Shāh II, and must have been struck towards the close of Mīrzā Ḥaidar's rule. There are also other coins of Nādīr Shāh, but they are not legible.[26] A few silver coins bearing the name of Islām Shāh and the date 957 have also been found. Since he never ruled Kashmīr, the nobles of the country must have struck them as a compliment to him and in order to get his support against Mīrzā Ḥaidar.[27]

The number of gold coins so far discovered is very small. Each of them weighs about 175 grains. The obverse presents the *kalima* in a circle. The mint name is represented in Arabic by the epithet *Dāru's-Sulṭānat* (Seat of the Sultanate and by a motto "May it be preserved from destruction". The reverse contains the name of the Sulṭān and his titles. But there is a great diversity of reverse legend. Zainu'l-'Ābidīn is called *Nā'ib-i-Amīru'l-Mū'minīn Quṭbu'd-Dīn Abū'l-Mujāhidu'l'Ādilu's-Sulṭān.* Ḥaidar Shāh's gold coin also bears on the reverse *Nā'ib-i-*

Khalīfatu'r-Raḥmānu's-Sulṭān. Zainu'l-'Ābidīn and Ḥaidar Shāh are the only Sulṭāns of Kashmīr who regard themselves as deputies of the reigning Caliph. A gold coin of Ḥasan Shāh is called *Nagīn-i-Mulk khātim-i-Sulaimān* (Signet of the kingdom, Solomon's seal). The coins of Humāyūn, Ibrāhīm Shāh, and Mubārak Shāh bear different legends.[28]

Weights and Measures

16 *Māshas*	=	1 *Tola*
80 *Tolas*	=	1 *Seer*
$7\frac{1}{2}$ *Pals*	=	1 *Seer*
4 *Seers* or 1 *Maund*	=	*Tarak* (5 *Seers* of present day)
16 *Taraks*	=	1 *Kharwār*
1. *Kharwār*	=	lbs. or 83 *Seers* of present day.
1 *Gira*	=	$2\frac{1}{4}$ *Inches*
16 *Giras*	=	1 *Gaz*
20 *Giras*	=	1 *Gaz* (employed in measuring pashmina cloth).

In India land was divided into plots each of which was called *bigha.* But in Kashmīr each plot was called *patta.* This was equal to 1 *bigha* and 1 *biswa* according to the *Ilāhī Gaz* which is equal to 33 inches of the present day. The Kashmīrīs, however, reckoned $2\frac{1}{2}$ *pattas* as equal to 1 *bigha* (Kashmirī).[29] Under Zainu'l-'Ābidīn the length of the *jarib* was increased,[30] but the details are not known.

NOTES

1. See Stein, ii, 308-28, for more details about the monetary system of Kashmīr.
2. *Ibid.,* 312, 315.
3. Śrīv., p. 101; see also Stein, ii, 324.
4. *Ibid.,* 318.
5. Śrīv., p. 228.

6. S.A., p. 48.
7. Stein, ii, 318, and n. 48.
8. *Ibid.*, 328.
9. J.R.N.S., xiii (vth series), p. 261.
10. J.A.S.B., lxv (1896), p. 223.
11. *Ibid.*, liv (1885), pp. 95-7.
12. *Ibid.*, xiviii (1879), p. 282.
13. *Ibid.*
14. *Ibid.*, p. 284.
15. Lane-Poole, *Coins of the Muhammadan States of Indian*, pp. 71-2.
16. J.A.S.B., liv (1885), p. 96.
17. *Ibid.*, xlviii (1879), p. 285.
18. *Catalogue of Coins in the Indian Museum*, Calcutta, p. 190; also J.A.S.B., liv (1885), p. 97.
19. *Ibid.*
20. J.R.N.S., xiii (vth series), p. 257.
21. J.A.S.B., liv (1885), p. 125.
22. *Ibid.*, p. 110.
23. Lane-Poole, *Coins of the Muhammadan States of India*, pp. 76-8.
24. J.A.S.B., liv (1885), pp. 96-7.
25. J.A.S.B., liv (1885), p. 116.
26. *Ibid.*, p. 97.
27. *Ibid.*, p. 119.
28. J.R.N.S., xiii (vth series), pp. 261 sqq.
29. A.N., iii, 830-31.
30. T.A., iii, 436.

APPENDIX C

The Chronology and Genealogy of the Sulṭāns of Kashmīr

There are two main reasons why the chronology of the Sulṭāns of Kashmīr is so obscure. In the first place, the chronicles do not agree with each other in regard to the dates of accession of the rulers and their regnal periods. In the second, the coins are not much helpful in fixing the chronology.

Sir Wolseley Haig was the first to make a serious attempt to fix the chronology of the Kashmīr rulers; but the mistake which he made was that he mainly utilised the *Tabaqāṭ-i-Akbarī*, the *Ta'rīkh-i-Firishta,* and *the A'īn-i Akbarī,* and completely ignored the Sanskrit chronicles.[1] Recently Dr. A.K. Majumdar has made a study of the subject; but, while he has made use of the Sanskrit chronicles and the Mughal accounts, he has not consulted the Persian chronicles of Kashmīr.[2] Only when all the important authorities have been carefully studied, can the chronology and the genealogy of the Medieval rulers of Kashmīr be correctly constructed.

The most reliable authority for the early history of the Shāh Mīr dynasty upto the 19th year of Zainu'l-'Ābidīn's reign is Jonarāja. Śrīvara, his pupil, is a contemporary authority for the period from about 1459 to 1486, the year of Muḥammad Shāh's first reign. There should, therefore, be no difficulty in regarding the dates given by Jonarāja and Śrīvara as correct. Ḥaidar Malik, the author of the *Bahāristān-i-Shāhī*, Abū'l-Fazl, and Niẓāmu'd-Dīn have all derived their chronology from the Sanskrit accounts. That in spite of this their dates differ not only from each other but also with those assigned by Jonarāja and Śrīvara, is due to the fact that they made mistakes in converting the *Laukika* era, which is a solar era, into the *Hijra,* which is a lunar era.

Some of the dates assigned by Jonarāja and Śrīvara can be checked by the coins of the Sulṭāns and by the contemporary Persian accounts. Thus the date of the accession of Zinu'l-'Ābidīn given by Jonarāja as 1420 is supported by the *Ta'rīkh-i-Mubārak Shāhī,* a contemporary authority.[3] The year assigned for the death of the Sulṭān by Śrīvara is 1470. This date agrees with the date of Ḥaidar Shāh's accession as determined by legends on coins.[4] The date of Ḥaidar Shāh's death in 1472 is corroborated by legends on the coins of his son and successor Ḥasan Shāh.[5] The date of the latter's death and the dates in connection with the first reign of his son, Muḥammad Shāh, have been given by Śrīvara. And since the latter was connected with the court of Ḥasan Shāh we must accept his chronology.

The main difficulty that arises is in connection with the dates of the first period of Fatḥ Shāh's reign. This is because there is a gap in Prājyabhaṭṭa's account from 1486 to 1514. When Śrīvara left off writing his narrative, the throne was occupied by Fatḥ Shāh. At the time Śuka began his work, we find Fatḥ Shāh again on the throne. Now, as is evident from the Persian chronicles of Kashmīr, Fatḥ Shāh did not rule all the time during this period. Actually the period was divided between him and Muḥammad Shāh, the former ruling for seven years (1486-1493)[6] and latter for twelve years (1493-1505). In 1505, Fatḥ Shāh for the second time captured the throne and ruled for nine years (1505-14).[7] It is to this period of Fatḥ Shāh's reign that Śuka refers and not to his first. Moreover, the events which Śuka describes took place not in Fatḥ Shāh's first reign, but in his second reign. This is evident from a study of the Persian chronicles of Kashmīr. Niẓāmu'd-Dīn and Abū'l-Faẓl, however, make the mistake of regarding the second reign of Fatḥ Shāh as his first reign. That is why Fatḥ Shāh, according to them, ruled twice and Muḥammad Shāh four times, although in reality they ruled thrice and five times respectively.

Muḥammad Shāh captured power for the third time in 1514.

he had ruled only nine months when Fatḥ Shāh invaded the Valley and seized the throne for the third time.[8] Driven from the Valley, Muḥammad Shāh proceeded to Sikandar Lodī and secured his help. Now Sikandar Lodī died on November 21, 1517, and so Muḥammad Shāh must have received help about the middle of that year. With the aid of the Afghān troops Muḥammad Shāh succeeded in defeating Fatḥ Shāh and occupying the throne. He ruled for about twelve years (1517-28) for the fourth time. He was dethroned by his Wazīr, Kājī Chak, who raised his son, Ibrāhīm, to the throne. Meanwhile, Kaji's rival, Abdāl Māgre, proceeded to Delhi, and having obtained the aid of Bābur, conquered the Valley. He dethroned Ibrāhīm Shāh, and in his place set up Nāzuk Shah, the son of Fatḥ Shāh, on the throne (1529). But Nāzuk Shāh ruled only for a year, for Muḥammad Shāh was released from prison and enthroned in 1530. This date of Muḥammad Shāh's fifth restoration must be regarded as correct, because, according to the *Tabaqāṭ-i-Akbarī*, Bābur's death took place shortly after this event.[9] Muḥammad Shāh ruled until his death in 1537.[10] He was succeeded by his son Shamsu'd-Dīn;[11] and on the latter's death in 1540, Kājī set up his own son-in-law, Ismā'īl, another son of Muḥammad Shāh, on the throne.[12] When Mīrzā Ḥaidar occupied Kashmīr, Ismā'īl fled the country, and Nāzuk Shāh was proclaimed king. He remained on the throne until 1552, when he was deposed by Daulat Chak in favour of Ibrāhīm, who had ruled before.[13] But Ghāzī, on seizing power, enthroned Ismā'īl; and on the latter's death in 1557 his son Ḥabīb was made Sulṭān. But in 1561, Ghāzī himself assumed the crown, and thus founded the Chak dynasty.[14]

The chronology of the subsequent rulers of Kashmīr does not present any difficulty, and can easily be fixed with the help of contemporary accounts.

NOTES

1. Haig, *The Chronology and Genealogy of the Muhammadan Kings of Kashmīr*, (J.R.A.S., 1918), pp. 451-68).
2. Majumdar, *A Note on the Chronology of the Sulṭāns of Kashmīr in*

Chronology of the Shāh Mīr Dynasty

		A.D.			A.D.
1.	Shamsu'd-Dīn I	1339	11.	Muḥammad Shāh (iii)	1514
2.	Jamshēd	1342	12.	Fatḥ Shāh (iii)	1515
3.	'Alā'u'd-Dīn	1343	11.	Muḥammad Shāh (iv)	1517
4.	Shihābu'd-Dīn	1354	13.	Ibrāhīm Shāh (i)	1528
5.	Quṭbu'd-Dīn	1373	14.	Nāzuk Shāh (i)	1529
6.	Sikandar	1389	11.	Muḥammad Shāh (v)	1530
7.	'Alī Shāh	1413	15.	Shamsu'd-Dīn II	1537
8.	Zainu'l-'Ābidīn	1420	16.	Ismā'īl Shāh (i)	1540
9.	Ḥaidar Shāh	1470	14.	Nāzuk Shāh (ii)	1540
10.	Ḥasan Shāh	1472	13.	Ibrāhīm Shāh (ii)	1552
11.	Muḥammad Shāh (i)	1484	16.	Ismā'īl Shāh (ii)	1555
12.	Fatḥ Shāh (i)	1486	17.	Habīb Shāh	1557
11.	Muḥammad Shāh (iii)	1493			–1561
12.	Fatḥ Shāh (ii)	1505			

Chronology of the Chak Dynasty

1.	Ghāzī Shāh	1561	4.	Yūsuf Shāh (ii)	1580
2.	Ḥusain Shāh	1563	6.	Ya'qūb Shāh (i)	1586
3.	'Alī Shāh	1570	7.	Ḥusain Shāh	1586
4.	Yūsuf Shāh (i)	1578-79	6.	Ya'qūb Shāh (ii)	1586
5.	Lohar Shāh	1579			–88

the A'īn-i-Akbari (J.A.S.B., xxii, pp. 86-97).

3. See p. 69 and n. 8.
4. J.A.S.B., lxv, (1896), p. 225, cited in J.R.A.S., 1918, p. 456.
5. If J.R.A.S., 1918, p. 457.
6. B.S., f. 77b. B.S. gives the date in *Laukika* era as 81/1505. The *Ḥijra* date of 907/1501 is incorrect.
7. Śuka, p. 34 f.
8. Śuka, p. 347.
9. T.A., iii, 463.
10. B.S., ff. 102a-b; Śuka, p. 375.
11. B.S., 102b; Śuka, 375.
12. See p. 146 and n. 7, *supra*.
13. B.S., 106a; H.M., 144b.
14. See p. 151 and notes 3-5, *supra*.

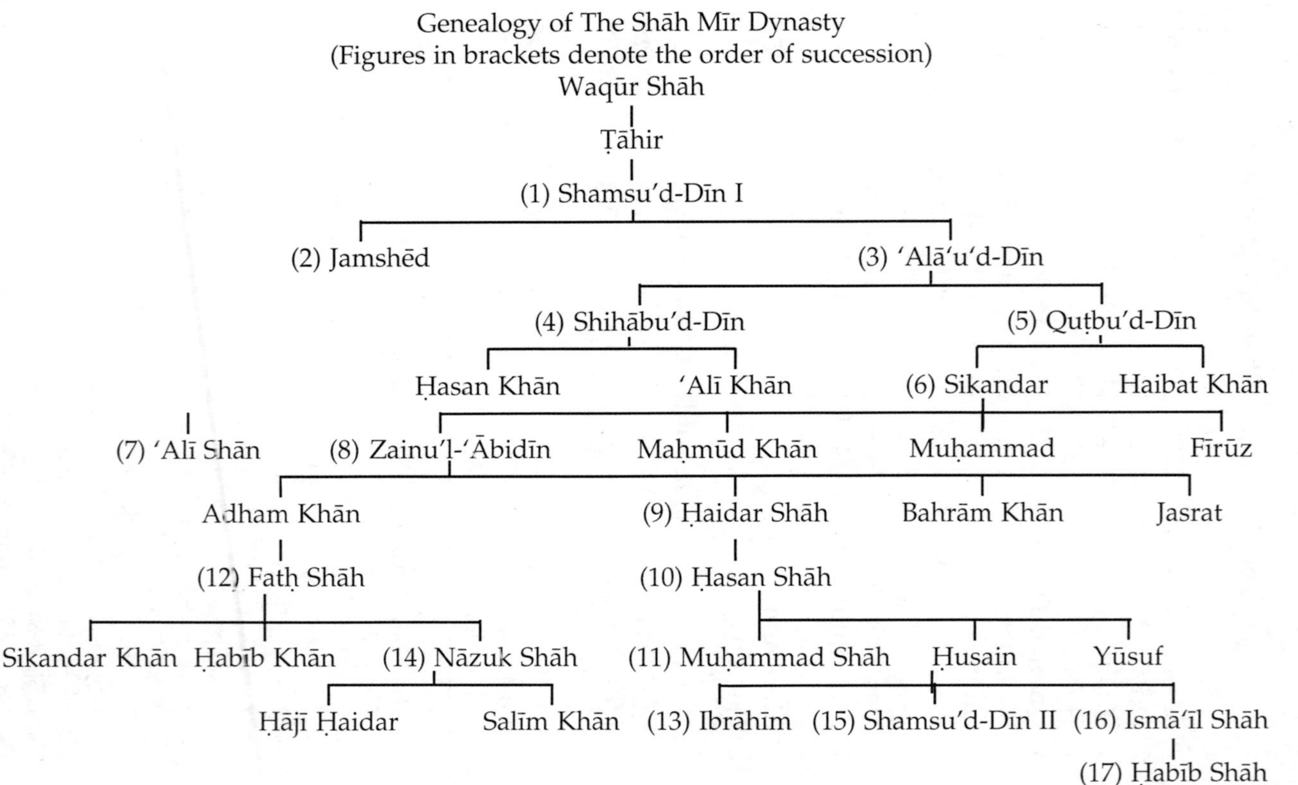
Genealogy of The Shāh Mīr Dynasty
(Figures in brackets denote the order of succession)
Waqūr Shāh
Ṭāhir
(1) Shamsu'd-Dīn I
(2) Jamshēd
(3) 'Alā'u'd-Dīn
(4) Shihābu'd-Dīn
(5) Quṭbu'd-Dīn
Ḥasan Khān
'Alī Khān
(6) Sikandar
Haibat Khān
(7) 'Alī Shān
(8) Zainu'l-'Ābidīn
Maḥmūd Khān
Muḥammad
Fīrūz
Adham Khān
(9) Ḥaidar Shāh
Bahrām Khān
Jasrat
(12) Fatḥ Shāh
(10) Ḥasan Shāh
Sikandar Khān
Ḥabīb Khān
(14) Nāzuk Shāh
(11) Muḥammad Shāh
Ḥusain
Yūsuf
Ḥājī Ḥaidar
Salīm Khān
(13) Ibrāhīm
(15) Shamsu'd-Dīn II
(16) Ismā'īl Shāh
(17) Ḥabīb Shāh

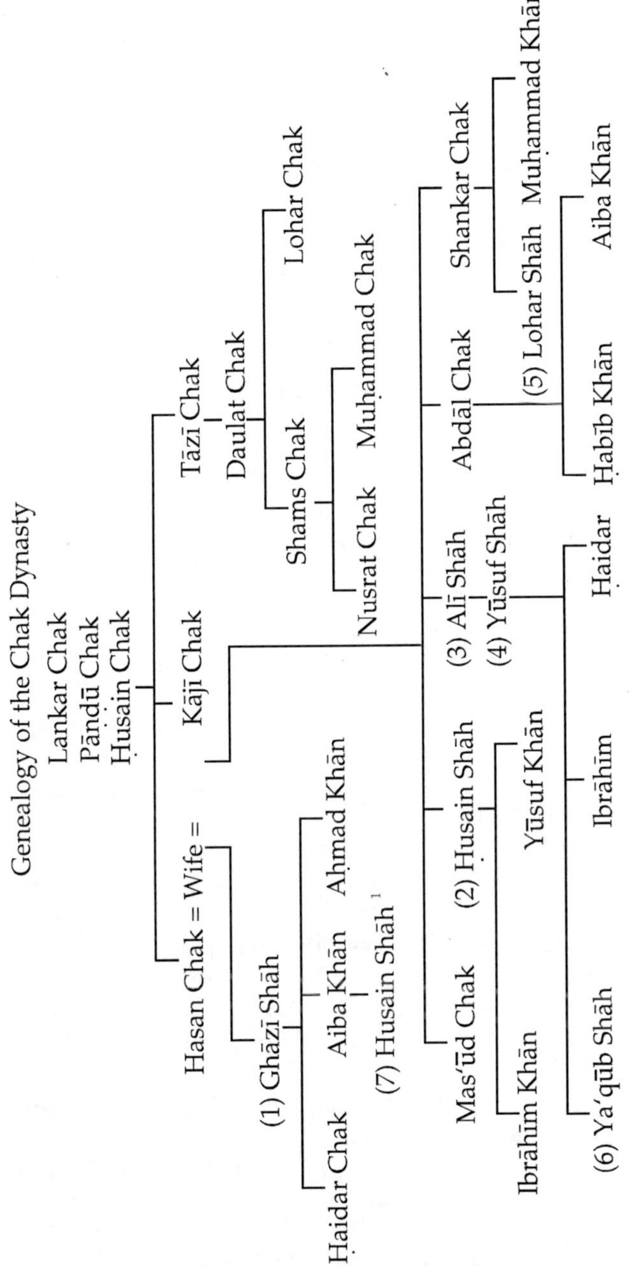
Genealogy of the Chak Dynasty
Lankar Chak
Pāndū Chak
Ḥusain Chak
Hasan Chak = Wife =
Kājī Chak
Tāzī Chak
Daulat Chak
Lohar Chak
Shams Chak
Nusrat Chak
Muḥammad Chak
(1) Ghāzī Shāh
Ḥaidar Chak
Aiba Khān
Aḥmad Khān
(7) Husain Shāh [1]
Mas'ūd Chak
(2) Ḥusain Shāh
(3) Alī Shāh
(4) Yūsuf Shāh
Abdāl Chak
Shankar Chak
Ibrāhīm Khān
Yūsuf Khān
(5) Lohar Shāh
Muḥammad Khān
(6) Ya'qūb Shāh
Ibrāhīm
Ḥaidar
Ḥabīb Khān
Aiba Khān

Appendix D

Bibliography

Of the chief works to which reference has been made

I. *Persian Manuscript Sources*

Abā Rafī'u-Dīn Aḥmad, *Nawādiru'l-Akhbār*, B.M. Add. 24029.
'Abdu'llāh, *Ta'rīkh-i-Dā'ūdī*, I.O. 224.
'Abdu'l-Qādir Khān, *Ḥashmat-i-Kashmīr*, A.S.B. 42.
Amīn Aḥmad Rāzī, *Haft Iqlīm*, A.S.B. 282.
Bābā Nasīb, *Taẕkira-i-Mashā'ikh-i-Kashmīr*, A.S.B. 260.
Badī'u'd-Dīn Abū'lQāsim, *Gauhar-i-'Ālam*, A.S.B. 189.
Bahāristān-i-Shāhī, Anonymous. (a) I.O.509. (b) B.M. Add. 16, 706.
Dā'ūd Mishkātī, *Asrāru'l-Abrār*, R.P.D., Srīnagar.
Ganēsh Dās *Ta'rīkh-i-Rājgān-i-Jammu* or *Rājdarshanī*.
(a) I.O. 507. (b) B.M. Or. 1634.
Ḥaidar Malik, *Ta'rīkh-i-Kashmīr*, (a) I.O. 510.
(b) Bib. Nationale, Blochet, i, 626.
(c) R.P.D. Srīnagar.
Ḥasan b. 'Alī Kashmīrī, *Ta'rīkh-i-Kashmīr*, Bodleian 315.
Khwāja Isḥāq Qārī, *Hilyatu'l-'Ārifīn*, B.M. Or. 1868.
Khwāja Ni'matu'llāh Harawī, *Ta'rīkh-i-Khān-Jahānī*, A.S.B. 101.
Majmū'a dar Ansāb Mashā'ikh-i-Kashmīr, Anonymous, A.S.B. 79.
Malfuẓāt-i-Tīmūrī, A.S.B. 85.
Mīrzā Ḥaidar Dughlat, *Ta'rīkh-i-Rashīdī*, A.S.B. 210.
Muḥammad A'ẓam, *Wāqi'āt-i-Kashmīr*, A.S.B. 41.
Muḥammad Sharīf an-Najafī, *Majālisu'l-Salāṭīn*, B.M. Add. 30, 779.
Mullā Aḥmad b. Ṣubūr Kashmīrī, *Khawāriqu'l-Sālikīn*, R.P.D. Srīnagar.
Mullā 'Alī Raina, *Taẕkiratu'l-'Ārifīn*, R.P.D. Srīnagar.

Nārāyan Kaul "'Ājiz," *Ta'rīkh-i-Kashmīr*, Buhār 80.
Nasību'd-Dīn Ghāzī, *Nūr-nāma,* R.P.D. Srīnagar.
Nūru'd-Dīn Ja'far Badakhshī, *Khulāṣatu'l-Manāqib,* Tubingen University Library, W.Germany.
—*Manqabatu'l-Jawāhir,* R.P.D. Srīnagar.
Nūru'llāh Shushtarī, *Majālisu'l-Mu'minīn,* A.S.B. 276.
Pandit Śivājī Dar, *Aḥwāl-i-Mulk-i-Kishtwār,* R.P.D. Srīnagar.
Pīr Ḥasan Shāh, *Ta'rīkh-i-Ḥasan,* 4 vols. R.P.D. Srīnagar.
Sayyid 'Alī, *Ta'rīkh-i-Kashmir,* R.P.D. Srīnagar.
Sayyid 'Alī, Hamadānī, *Ẕakhīratu'l-Mulūk, A.S.B.* 1380.
Shaikh 'Abdu'l-Wahhāb, *Futūḥāt-i-Kubravīya,* R.P.D. Srīnagar.
Ta'rīkh-i-Kashmīr, Anonymous. K. Hof-Und Staatsbibiliothek, Muenchen. Aumer 267.
Tuḥfatu'l-Aḥbāb, Anonymous. Collection of Āghā Sayyid Muḥammad Yūsuf of Badgām, Kashmīr.

II. *Persian, Sanskrit and Arabic Printed Sources and Translations*

'Abdu'r-Raḥmān b. Aḥmad Jāmī, *Nafaḥātu'l-Uns.* Calcutta 1858–59.
Abū'l-Faẕl, *Akbar-nāma,* tr. H. Beveridge. 3 vols. Bib. Ind. Calcutta 1897-1939.
—*Ā'in-Akbarī.* vol. i, tr. Blochmann. Bib. Ind. Calcutta 1927.
vols. ii & iii, tr. Jarrett. Second ed. J.N. Sarkar, Bib, Ind. Calcutta 1948-49.
'Afīf, Shams Sirāj, *Ta'rīkh-i-Fīrūz Shāhī,* ed. Vilāyat Ḥusain. Bib. Ind. Calcutta 1891.
Bābur, Emperor, *Bābur-nāma,* Eng. tr. A.S. Beveridge, 2 vols. London 1921.
Badā'ūnī, 'Abdu'l-Qādir, *Muntakhabu't-Tawārīkh,* Eng. tr. by Ranking, Lowe, and Haig. 3 vols. Bib. Ind. Calcutta 1884-1925.
Balāẕurī, *Futūḥu'l-Buldān,* ed. Rizwān Muḥammad Rizwān, Cairo 1932.
Baranī, Ẕiyāu'd-Dīn, *Ta'rīkh-i-Fīrūz Shāhī,* Bib. Ind. Calcutta 1862.
Al-Bīrūnī, *Kitābu'l-Hind,* tr. into English as *Al-Biruni's India* by E.C. Sachau. 2 vols. London 1888.
Briggs, J., *History of the rise of the Mahomedan power in India, till the year* 1612, being an Eng. tr. of the *Ta'rīkh-i-Firishta.* 4 vols. Calcutta 1808-10.

Al-Dimashqī, *Nukhbat al-Dahr fi 'Ajā'ib al-Barr wa'lBaḥr,* tr. into French as *Manuel de la Cosmographie du Moyen Age* by M.A. Mehren. Copenhagen 1874.

Dutt. J.C., *Kings of Kashmira,* being a translation of the Sanskrit works of Kalhaṇa, Jonarāja, Śrīvara, Prājyabhaṭṭa and Śuka. 3 vols. Calcutta 1879-98.

Elliot, H.M. & Dawson, J., *History of India as told by its own historians.* 8 vols. London 1866-77.

Firishta, Muḥammad Qāsim, *Ta'rīkh-i-Firishta.* Bo. ed. 1832.

Ḥājī Mu'īnu'd-Dīn Miskīn, *Ta'rīkh-i-Kabīr,* Amritsar A.H. 1322.

Ḥudūdu'l-'Ālam, Anonymous, ed. and tr. V. Minorsky. E.J.W. Gibb Memorial Series, Oxford 1937.

Ibn Hauqal, *Kitāb Ṣūrat al-Arẓ.* Opus Geographicum. 2 parts. ed. J.H. Kramers. Leiden 1938.

Al-Idrīsī, *Nuzhat al-Mushtāq fi Ikhtirāq al-Āfāq,* Portion relating to India edited by S.Maqbūl Aḥmad as *India and the Neighbouring Territories.* Aligarh 1954.

Jahāngīr, Emperor, *Tuzuk-i-Jahāngīrī,* Eng. tr. A. Rogers, ed. H. Beveridge. 2 vols. London 1909-14.

Jonarāja, *Rājataraṅgiṇī.* (a) Calcutta 1835. See Dutt for Eng. tr. —(b) ed. P. Peterson. Bombay 1896.

Kalhaṇa, *Rājataraṅgiṇī,* Eng. tr. M.S. Stein. 2 vols. London 1900. Also Eng. tr. R.S. Pandit. Allahabad 1935.

Kashmīr Series of Texts and Studies. Nos. xlix, xliii.

Khwāja 'Abdu'l-Bāqī Nihāwandī, *Ma'āṣir-i-Raḥīmī,* ed. Hidāyat Ḥusain. 3 vols. Bib. Ind. Calcutta 1910-31.

Khwāndamīr, Ghiyāṣu'd-Dīn, *Ḥabību's-Siyar.* 3 vols. Bombay 1857.

Lokaprakāśa, tr. into German by A. Weber, *Indische Studien,* xviii, 289-412.

Mas'ūdi, *Murūju'z-Ẕahab (Les Prairies d'or),* text and French tr. by C. Barbier de Meynard and Pavet de Courteille, 9 vols. Paris 1861-77.

Minhāj b. Sirāj Juzjānī, *Ṭabaqāt-i-Nāṣirī,* tr. H.G. Raverty. Bib. Ind. Calcutta 1881.

Mīrzā Ḥaidar Dughlat, *Ta'rīkh-i-Rashīdī,* tr. E.D. Ross and N. Elias. London 1895.

Mīrzā Ma'ṣūm, *Ṭa'rīqu'l-Ḥaqā'iq.* Tehrān 1316/1898-99.

Niẓāmu'd-Dīn, Bakhshī, *Ṭabaqāt-i-Akbarī,* ed. B. Dey and Hidāyat Ḥusain. 3 vols. Calcutta 1927-35. Eng. tr. B. Dey. 3 vols. Bib. Ind. Calcutta 1927-39.

Nūru'llāh Shushtarī, *Majālisu'l-Mu'minīn*. Tehrān 1299/1882.

Ouseley. W., *The Oriental Geography of Ibn-Haucal* (tr. from Persian). London 1800.

Prājyabhaṭṭa *Rājāvalipatākā*. (a) Calcutta 1835. See Dutt for English tr. —(b) ed. P. Peterson. Bombay 1896.

Rāzī, A.A., *Haft Iqlīm*, ed. E.D. Ross etc. vol. i Bib. Ind. Calcutta 1939.

Riẓā Qulī Khān "Hidāyat", *Riyāẓū'l-'Ārifīn*. Tehrān 1305/1887-88.

Ṣamṣāmu'd-Daula Shāh Nawāz Khān, *Ma'āṣiru'l-Umarā*, tr. H. Beveridge, revised and completed by Baini Prashad. Calcutta 1911-41.

Ṣayf b. Muḥammad b. Ya'qūb al-Harawī, *Ta'rīkh-Nāma-i-Harāt*, ed. M.Z. Ṣiddiqī. Calcutta 1943.

Sharafu'd-Dīn 'Alī Yazdī, *Zafar-nāma*, ed. Maulavī M. Ilāhdād. 2 vols. Bib. Ind. Calcutta 1885-88.

Śrīvara, *Jaina-Rajataraṅgiṇī*. (a) Calcutta 1835. See Dutt for Eng tr. —(b) ed. P. Peterson. Bombay 1896.

Stein, M.A., Kalhaṇa's *Rājataraṅgiṇī, A Chronicle of the Kings of Kashmīr*, see Kalhaṇa.

Śuka, *Rājataraṅgiṇī*. (a) Calcutta 1835, See Dutt for Eng. tr. —(b) ed. P. Peterson. Bombay 1896.

Yaḥya b. Aḥmad Sirhindī, *Ta'rīkh-i-Mubārak Shāhī*. Bib. Ind. Calcutta 1931.

III. *Travellers' Accounts*

Aḥmad Shāh Naqshbandī, Route from Kashmīr, *via* Ladākh, to Yārkand, J.R.A.S., 1850, xii, pp. 372-85.

Bernier, F., *Travels in the Mughal Empire* 1556-68, ed. A. Constable and V.A. Smith. Oxford 1914.

Chardin, J., *Voyages du Chevalier Chardin, en Perse, et autres Lieux de l'Orient* ... L. Langles. 10 vols. Paris 1811.

Du Jarric, P. *An Account of the Jesuit Missions to the Court of Akbar*, tr. by *C.H. Payne as Akbar and the Jesuits.* Broadway Series, London 1926.

Fillipo, De Filippi, *The Travels of Ippolito Desideri of Pistoia* 1712-27. London 1937.

Forster, G., *A Journey from Bengal to England, through the northern part of India, Kashmire, etc...* 2 vols. London 1808.

Hoyland, J.S., *The Empire of the Great Mogol.* A translation of *De Laet's Description of India and Fragments of Indian History.* Bombay 1928.

Hügel, B.C., *Travels in Kashmere and the Panjāb*. London 1845.

'Izzatu'llāh, Mīr, Travels beyond the Himalayas in 1812, *J.R.A.S.*, 1843, vii, 283-342.

Laet, De, see Hoyland.

Markham, R., (ed.) *Narratives of the Missions of George Bogle to Tibet and of the Journey of Thomas Manning to Lhasa.* London 1879.

Moorcroft, W., & Trebeck, G., *Travels in the Himalayan Provinces of Hindustān, and the Punjāb; in Ladākh and Kashmīr...* ed. by H.H. Wilson. 2 vols. London 1841.

Pelsaert, F., *Remonstrantie,* tr. by W.H. Moreland and P. Geyl as *Jahāngīr*'s India. Cambridge 1925.

Purchas, S., *Hakluytus Posthumus or Purchas his Pilgrimes.* London 1905-07.

Torrens, H.D., *Travels in Ladakh, Tartary and Kashmir*. London 1863.

Trebeck, G., see Moorcroft.

Vigne, G.T., *Travels in Kashmīr, Ladak, Iskardo,.* etc., 2 vols. London 1842.

Wessel, C., *Early Jesuit Travellers in Central Asia* 1603-1721. The Hague 1924.

Yule, H., *The Book of Ser Morco Polo,* ed. and tr. by Sir H. Yule. 2 vols. London 1903.

IV. *Secondary Works.*

Abel-Rémusat, M., *Nouveaux Mélanges Asiatiques* ... 2 vols. Paris 1829.

—*Histoire de la Ville de Khotan, tirée des Annales de la Chine et traduite du Chinois.* Paris 1820.

Aghnides, N.P., *Muhammadan Theories of Finance.* New York 1916.

Aḥmet-Zekī Valīdī, Ein türkisches Werk von Ḥaydar-Mirza Dughlat. *Bulletin of S.O.S.*, 1935-37, viii, 985-89.

Archaeological Survey of India Report 1906-7. See Nicholls, W.H.

Arnold. T.W., *The Caliphate.* Oxford 1924.

—*The Preaching of Islam.* London 1913.

—ed. *The Legacy of Islam.* Oxford 1931.

Ashraf, K.M., *Life and Conditions of the People of Hindustān* (1200-1550). *J.A.S.B.*, 1935, i, No. 2. pp. 103-359.

Ayalon. D., *Gunpowder and Firearms in the Mamlūk Kingdom.* London 1956.

Ayrout, H.H., *Moeurs et Coutumes des Fellahs.* Paris 1938.

Banerjee, S.K., *Humāyūn Pādshāh,* vol. i. Oxford 1938. vol. ii, Lucknow 1941.

Bates, C.E., *A Gazetteer of Kashmīr and the Adjascent Districts of Kishtwār etc ...* Calcutta 1873.

Benī Prasād, *History of Jahāngīr.* Allahabad 1940.

Beveridge, H., Father Jerome Xavier. *J.A.S.B.,* 1888, lvii, part I, 33-9.

Biddulph, J., *Tribes of the Hindoo Koosh.* Calcutta 1880.

Birdwood George C.M., *The Industrial Arts of India.* London 1880.

Bretscheneider, E., *Medieval Researches from Eastern Asiatic Sources.* 2 vols. London 1888.

Brown, P., *Indian Architecture (Islamic Period).* London 1942.

—*Indian Painting under the Mughals.* Oxford 1924.

Browne, E.G., *A Literary History of Persia.* 4 vols. London and Cambridge 1902-24.

Bühler, G., Report of a Tour in search of Sanskrit Manuscripts made in Kashmīr, Rājputāna and Central India. *J.R.A.S.* (Bombay). 1877, xii (Extra number).

Cambridge History of India, vol. iii, Cambridge 1927. vol. iv, Cambridge 1937.

Chatterjī J.C., *Kashmīr Śaivaism.* Srīnagar 1914.

Coomaraswamy, A.K., A Relief and Inscription from Kashmīr, *The University of Pennsylvania Museum Bulletin,* ii, No. 6, 202-6.

Cunningham, A., *The Ancient Geography of India, the Buddhist Period.* London 1871. Re-edited S.M. Sastri. Calcutta 1924.

De Bourbel, F., *Routes in Jammu and Kashmīr.* Calcutta 1897.

Delmerick, J.C., Coins of the Kings of Delhi ... and Kashmīr. *J.A.S.B.,* 1876, xlv, 291-97.

Dey, N.L., *The Geographical Dictionary of Ancient and Medieval India.* London 1927.

Dozy, R.P.H., *Dictionnaire détaillé des noms de Vêtements chez les Arabes.* Amsterdam 1845.

Drew, Frederick, *The jummoo and Kashmīr Territories.* London 1875.

Duhousset, E., Les Arts décoratifs au Petit-Thibet au Cachemere. *Revue d'Ethnographie,* Sept.-Oct. 1882.

Elliot, H.M., *Memoirs on the History ... Races of the North-Western Provinces of India,* ed. J.Beames. London 1869.

Encyclopaedia of Islam. Leyden 1913—
Farmer, H.G., *A History of the Arabian Music to the 13th Century.* London 1929.
Fauq, Muḥammad Dīn, *Mukammal Ta'rīkh-i-Kashmīr* (Urdu). Lahore 1910.
—*Ta'rīkh-i-Bud Shāh* (Urdu). London 1944.
Fergusson, J., *History of the Indian and Eastern Architecture.* 2 vols. London 1910.
Ferrand, G., *Relations de Voyages et Textes geographique arabes, persans et turcs relatifs à l'Extreme—Orient.* 2 vols. Paris 1913, 1914.
Francke, A.H., *Antiquities of Indian Tibet.* 2 vols. Calcutta 1914-26. —*History of the Western Tibetan Regions.* London 1907. See also Sāhnī.
Gervis, Pearce. *This is Kashmīr.* London 1954.
Ghoshal, U.N., The Dynastic Chronicles of Kashmīr. *I.H.Q.*, xviii, 195-207; xix, 156-72.
Gibb, H.A.R., *The Arab Conquests in Central Asia.* R.A.S. London 1923.
—*Mohammedanism.* London 1949.
Grierson, G., *Linguistic Survey of India,* vol. viii.
—and Barnett, L.D., (ed. and tr.) *The Wise Sayings of Lallā-Vākyānī.* R.A.S. Monograph, vol. xvii. London 1920.
Growse, F.S., Architecture of Kashmīr. *Calcutta Review,* 1872, liv, 15-34.
Ḥabīb, M., *Sulṭān Maḥmūd of Ghaznīn.* Aligarh 1927.
Ḥabību'llāh, A.B.M., *The Foundation of Muslim Rule in India.* Lahore 1945.
Haig, W., The Chronology and Genealogy of the Muhammadan Kings of Kashmīr *J.R.A.S.*, 1918, 451-68.
Ḥekmat, A.A., *Az Hamadān tā Kashmīr, Yaghmā,* iv, No. 8, 337-43.
—Les Voyages d'un Mystique Persan de Hamadān au Kashmīr. *Journal Asiatique,* 1952, ccxl, 53-66.
Hiuen Tsiang, *Si-yu-ki. Buddhist Records of the Western World,* tr. from the Chinese by S. Beal. 2 vols. London 1883.
Howorth, H.H., *History of the Mongols.* 4 vols. London 1876-1927.
Hutchinson, J., & Vogel, J.P.H., History of the Kishtwār State *J.P.H.S.*, iv, 30-8.
—History of the Jammu State. *J.P.H.S.*, viii, 103-51.
—History of the Pūnch State. *J.P.H.S.*, ix, 106-27.
—History of the Rajaurī State. *J.P.H.S.*, ix, 131-49.

Ibn Ḥasan, *The Central Structure of the Mughal Empire*, Oxford 1936.
Irwin, J., The Kashmīr Shawl. *The Marg*, 1952, vi, No. I, 43-50.
Jarrett, H.S., Note on an Inscription Found in Kashmīr. *J.A.S.B.*, 1880, xlix, 16-20.
Kāk, R.C., *Ancient Monuments of Kashmīr*. London 1933.
—*Handbook of the Archaeological and Numismatic Section of the Sri Partāp Museum*. Srīnagar 1923.
—An Outline of the History Kashmīr, *J.I.H.*, 1926, iv. part 3, 29-42; 1927 v, part I, 1-19.
Kaul, A., History of Kashmīr. *J.A.S.B.*, 1913, ix, No. 5, 195-203.
—Life Sketch of Laleshwarī, *I.A.*, 1921, L, 302-12.
—A life of Nand Rishī. *I.A.*, 1930, lix, 28-30.
Kilam, J.L., *A History of Kashmīrī Pandits*. Srīnagar 1955.
Knight, E.F., *Where Three Empires meet*. London 1893.
Knowles, J.H., *A Dictionary of Kashmīrī Proverbs and Sayings*. London 1885.
—*Folk-tales of Kashmīr*. London 1893.
Lane-poole, S., *The Coins of the Muhammadan States of India*. London 1883.
—*The Muhammadan Dynasties, Chronological and Genealogical Tables. Westminister* 1894.
Lawrence, W.R., *The Valley of Kashmīr*. London 1895.
Loewenthal, I., Some Persian Inscriptions found in Srīnagar *J.A.S.B.*, 1864, xxxiii, No. 3, 278-90.
Maclagen, R., On Early Asiatic Weapons, *J.A.S.B.*, 1876, xlv, 30-71.
Majumdar, A.K., A Note on the Chronology of the Sulṭāns of Kashmīr in the *Ā'īn-i-Ākbarī*. *J.A.S.B.*, 1956, xxii, 85-97.
Majumdar, R.C., *The Classical Age*, Bombay 1954.
Majumdar, S.N., *Cunningham's Ancient Geography of India*. Calcutta 1924.
Mez, A., *Die Renaissance des Islams*. tr. Khudā Bakhsh and Margoliouth. Patna 1937.
Mīrzā Furṣatu't-Daula, *Buḥūru'l-al-Hān*. Bombay 1132/1719-20.
Mīrzā Ẕafaru'llāh Khān, *Taẕkira-i-Rājgān-i-Rajaur* (Urdu). Julundhar 1907.
Modi, J.J., Cashmere and the Ancient Persians. *J.R.A.S.* (Bombay), 1895, xix, 237-49.
Mohan Lāl Aima, The Music of Kashmīr, *Kashmīr*, iv, No. 6, 135–37.
Nāẕim, M., *The Life and Times of Sulṭān Mahmūd of Ghazna*.

Cambridge 1931.
Newall, D.J.F., A Sketch of the Mahomedan History of Cashmere. *J.A.S.B.*, 1854, xxiii, 409-60.
—Some Account of the Rishīs or Hermits of Kashmīr. *J.A.S.B.*, 1870, xxxix, 265-70.
Nicholls, W.H., Muhammadan Architecture in Kashmīr. *Archaeological Survey of India Report* 1906-7. Calcutta 1909.
Prawdin, M., *The Mongol Empire,* tr. by Eden and Cedar Paul. London 1940.
Qureshī, I.H., *The Administration of the Sultanate of Dehlī,* Lahore 1944.
Ray, H.C., *The Dynastic History of Northern India,* 2 vols. Calcutta 1931-36.
Ray, S.C., *Early History and Culture of Kashmīr.* Calcutta 1957.
Reinaud, M, *Mémoire géograprique, historique et scientifique sur l'Inde* ... Tome xviii. Paris 1849.
—*Relations des Voyages faits par lès Arabes et les Perses dans i'Inde et la Chine.* Paris 1845.
Rieu, C., *Catalogue of Persian MSS. in the British Museum.* 3. vols. London 1879-83. (Supplement, 1895).
Rogers, C.J., The Square Silver Coins of the Sulṭāns of Kashmīr. *J.A.S.B.*, 1885, liv, 92-139.
—Rare Kashmīr Coins, *J.A.S.B.*, 1896, lxv, 223-25.
—The Copper Coins of the Sulṭāns of Kashmīr, *J.A.S.B.*, 1879, xlviii, 277-85.
Rose, H.A., *Glossary of Punjāb Tribes and Castes.* 2 vols. Lahore 1942.
Sa'ādat, Muftī Muḥammad Shāh, *Bulbul Shāh Ṣāheb* (Urdū), Lahore 1360/1941.
Sāhnī, D.R., & Francke, A.H., References to the Bhauṭṭas in the Rajataraṅgiṇī. *I.A.*, 1908, vol. 37, 181-92.
Shafī', M., The Nūrbakhshīya Sect. *Oriental College Magazine* (Urdū), i, No. 1, Feb. 1925, 3-15; May 1925, 49-68; August 1929, 1-15.
—The Nūrbakhshīya Sect., *Proc. of the Third Oriental Conference,* 1924, 683-705.
Ṣiddiqī, A.H., *Caliphate and Kingship in Medieval Persia.* Lahore 1942.
Śiva Nārāyan, Kashmīr Music. *Ẕamāna*, (Urdū) 1916, vol. 27, No. 164, 193-97.
Smith, V.A., *Akbar the Great Mogul* 1542-1605. Oxford 1919.
Stein, M.A., *Ancient Khotan.* 2 vols. Oxford 1907.
—Notes on the Ancient Topography of the Pīr Panjāl Route, *J.A.S.B.*,

1895, lxiv, 376-86.
—Memoir on Maps Illustrating the Ancient Geography of Kashmīr. *J.A.S.B.*, lxviii, 1899 (extra No. 2), 1-232. This article is also included in Kalhaṇa's *Rajataraṅgiṇī* tr. by Stein as Memoir of the Ancient Geography of Kashmīr, ii, 345-494.
—A Sanskrit Deed of Sale Concerning a Kashmirian *Mahābhārata* MS. *J.R.A.S.*, 1900, 187-94.
Storey, C.A., *Persian Literature, A Bio-Bibliographical Survey* Section II. Fasc. 2 and 3. London 1936-49.
Sūfī, G.M.D., *Kashīr.* 2 vols. Lahore 1948-49.
Temple, R.C., *The Word of Lallā, the Prophetess.* Cambridge 1924.
—*Journals kept in Hindustān, Kashmīr, Sikkim and Nepāl* ... 2 vols. London 1887.
Ujfalvy, CH.-E.De, *L'Art des Cuivres anciens au Cachemere et au Petit Thibet.* Paris 1883.
Vambéry, A., *History of Bokhara from the Earliest Period down to the present.* London 1873.
Vogel, see Hutchinson.
Walter, H.A., Islam in Kashmīr. *The Moslem World,* 1914, iv, 340-52.
Weber, A., see *Lokaprakāś.*
Whitehead, R.B., The Gold Coins of Kashmīr. *The Numismatic Chronicle and Journal of the Royal Numismatic Society* (London), 5th series, vol. 13, 257-67.
Wilson, H.H., *Glossary of Judicial and Revenue Terms and Useful Words,* London 1855.
Winternitz, M., *Geschichte der indischen Litteratur,* vol. iii, Leipzig 1920.
Wright, H.N., *Catalogue of the Coins in the Indian Museum, Calcutta.* Vol. ii, Oxford 1907.
Yūsuf Ḥusain, *L'Inde mystique au Moyen Age,* Paris 1929.

Index